PRINCIPLE-BASED PARSING

Studies in Linguistics and Philosophy

Volume 44

The titles published in this series are listed at the end of this volume.

PRINCIPLE-BASED PARSING:

Computation and Psycholinguistics

Edited by

ROBERT C. BERWICK

Artificial Intelligence Laboratory, MIT

STEVEN P. ABNEY

Bell Communications Research

and

CAROL TENNY

Department of Linguistics, University of Pittsburgh

KLUWER ACADEMIC PUBLISHERS

DORDRECHT / BOSTON / LONDON

Library of Congress Cataloging-in-Publication Data

```
Principle-based Parsing : computation and psycholinguistics / edited
  by Robert C. Berwick, Steven P. Abney, Carol Tenny.
      p.    cm. -- (Studies in linguistics and philosophy ; v. 44)
  Includes indexes.
  ISBN 0-7923-1173-6 (HB : acid-free paper)
  1. Parsing (Computer grammar)  2. Computational linguistics.
3. Psycholinguistics.   I. Berwick, Robert C.   II. Abney, Steven P.
III. Tenny, Carol.   IV. Series.
P98.5.P38P75  1991
006.3'5--dc20                                                    91-2587
```

ISBN 0-7923-1173-6

Published by Kluwer Academic Publishers,
P.O. Box 17, 3300 AA Dordrecht, The Netherlands.

Kluwer Academic Publishers incorporates
the publishing programmes of
D. Reidel, Martinus Nijhoff, Dr W. Junk and MTP Press.

Sold and distributed in the U.S.A. and Canada
by Kluwer Academic Publishers,
101 Philip Drive, Norwell, MA 02061, U.S.A.

In all other countries, sold and distributed
by Kluwer Academic Publishers Group,
P.O. Box 322, 3300 AH Dordrecht, The Netherlands.

Printed on acid-free paper

Printed in the Netherlands

TABLE OF CONTENTS

EDITORIAL PREFACE

Aside from the first chapter, the contents of this volume represent papers presented at the MIT Parsing Project Lecture Series during the years 1987–1989. Steven P. Abney and Carol Tenny served as coordinators for these first two years of the lecture series, and assembled and edited the initial papers. Thanks are due to the Kapor Family Foundation for its generous support that has made this lecture series possible. Jay Keyser cheerfully lent his not inconsiderable weight to the enterprise. The John Simon Guggenheim Foundation and the National Science Foundation under a Presidential Investigator Award (grant DCR-85552543) greatly assisted in preparation of the first chapter and the volume as a whole. We would also like to thank the American Association for Artificial Intelligence, for permission to reprint Samuel S. Epstein, 'Principle-Based Interpretation of Natural Language Quantifiers', from *Proceedings of the AAAI-88*, pp. 718–723. Finally, we would like to express our gratitude to Martin Scrivener, our editor, for enthusiasm, encouragement, and for all those other things that editors do so well.

ROBERT C. BERWICK

PRINCIPLES OF PRINCIPLE-BASED PARSING

1. INTRODUCTION: PRINCIPLES AND PARSING

This book chronicles the first stirrings of a revolution in the study of natural language processing, language variation, and psycholinguistics— what some have called *principle-based parsing*.

To begin, perhaps it is simplest to say what principle-based parsing is *not*. A traditional view of grammar description, and so parsing, relies on many thousands of individual, language-particular, and construction-specific rules. This is true whether the rules are used by a context-free parser, an augmented transition network, a deterministic LR-type parser like the Marcus parser, or a logic grammar of almost any stripe.

Whatever the parsing method used, the key point is that rule-based systems attempt to spell out surface word order phrase patterns such as passive or dative, pattern by pattern and language by language. For example, a typical rule-based system will encode the format of a passive sentence such as *Mary was kissed by John* in a particular *if-then* format that includes the details of English-particular morphology (the *be* form followed by a verb with an *en* ending) plus the absence of a logical object in its expected position, along with a particular left-to-right ordering of phrases. Note that this is as true of the context-free rule that might be written as S→NP *be* V *ed+passive* as it is of the *if-then* grammar rules of Marcus' (1980) system, or the augmented transition network rules handling passive as described in Bates (1978) that use register assignments and arc ordering. Each encodes the same construction-based information in roughly the same way. Further, the same view pervades language acquisition systems grounded on rules, like that of Berwick (1985): acquiring a grammar amounts to the piecemeal acquisition of many construction-specific rules.

Principle-based language analysis replaces this standard paradigm with another world view: rules are covered by a much smaller set of *principles* that reconstitute the vocabulary of grammatical theory in such a way that constructions like passive *follow* from the deductive in-

1

R. C. Berwick et al. (eds.),
Principle-Based Parsing: Computation and Psycholinguistics, 1–37.
© 1991 *Kluwer Academic Publishers. Printed in the Netherlands.*

teractions of a relatively small set of primitives. On this view there is
no 'passive rule'. Passive constructions result from the interactions of
deeper morphological and syntactic operations that 'bubble to the surface' as the sentences we happen to describe as active or passive. The
goal of the rest of this book is to show how this principle-based approach
leads to exciting new models for parsing and language translation, different psycholinguistic avenues, and changes in our view of language
acquisition.

Figure 1 illustrates the fundamental difference between rule- and
principle-based approaches. The top half of the figure shows a conventional rule-based approach. Each sentence type is described by a
different rule. The bottom half of the figure shows a principle-based
approach. Intuitively, note that one can get the multiplicative effect of
$n_1 \times n_2 \times \ldots$ rules by the interaction of $n_1 + n_2 + \ldots$ principles. A
dozen principles, each with 2 or 3 degrees of freedom or *parameters* can
thus encode many thousands of rules. This approach has therefore been
dubbed *principles-and-parameters* theory.[1]

Let us see how principles can replace rules in our passive example.
One general principle says that verb phrases in sentences must either
begin with a verb in some languages, or *end* with a verb in others (those
are the degrees of freedom or parameterization in this particular principle). This basic description of the tree shapes in a language, dubbed
$\overline{X}$ *theory*, gives us part of the variation between languages like English
and Spanish on the one hand, and languages like German and Japanese
on the other. In English, the verb must come first, with the object after; in Japanese, the reverse. A second principle, called the *Case filter*,
says that all pronounced or *lexical* noun phrases like *ice-cream* must
receive Case, where Case, roughly speaking, is an abstract version of
the Latinate system that gives objective Case to objects, oblique Case
to objects of prepositions, nominative Case to sentence subjects, and so
forth. Case is assigned either from an active verb like *ate* or an auxiliary verb like *was*; the adjectival verb *eaten* does not assign case. A
third principle, called the *Theta-criterion* or θ-criterion, insists that every verb must discharge its *Thematic arguments* and every noun phrase
must receive a thematic role, completing a description or *thematic structure* representation of 'who did what to whom'. So for example, *eat* can
mean to eat *something* (the 'Affected Object' in earlier parlance) and
discharges a thematic role of a noun phrase, while *persuade* could have
either a noun phrase or a noun phrase and a proposition as its thematic

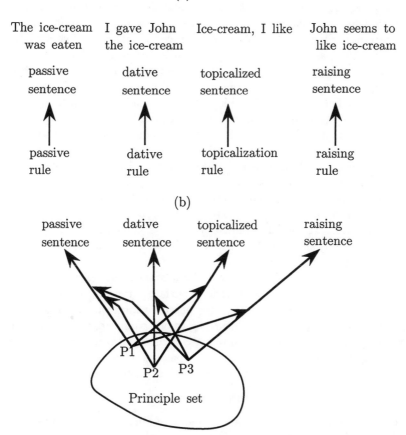

Figure 1: The difference between rule-based and principle-based systems is shown schematically in this figure. The top half (a) illustrates a rule-based system, with one rule per construction like passive or dative. The bottom half of the figure (b) illustrates a principle-based system. Sentence types are derived from a much smaller basis set of more fundamental principles that deductively interact to yield the effect of constructions like passive.

roles (*persuade John* or *persuade John that Bill is a fool*. A fourth principle, *Movement* (or *Move-α*), lets one move any phrase α to any available 'landing site'. A fifth general principle is *Trace theory*: any moved phrase leaves behind a phonologically empty category, a *trace*, coindexed with the original phrase, and bearing a certain configurational relationship with the moved phrase. A sixth constraint, *Binding theory*, determines when one noun phrase (a trace or not) can be coidentified with another, as in *John thinks that he likes ice-cream* where *John* and *he* can refer to the same person. And so on; we will see details of these principles in the chapters to come. A useful taxonomy for principles developed by Fong in this volume is to brand them either as *filters*, ruling out possible structures fed into them, or *generators*, admitting possible new structures. Thus the Case filter and Theta-criterion behave like filters because they are gates permitting only certain structures to pass, while $\overline{\text{X}}$ theory and movement act as generators, because they output at least as many structures as they receive.

Seeing how these principles operate in concert gives us a chance to understand how the passive conspiracy works and at the same time review the standard model of phrase structure assumed by all the authors of this book, as shown in figure 2. Conceptually (but not computationally!) the principles fit together on a four-fold scaffolding tied together in an inverted 'Y': a representation of a sentence's underlying thematic structure or *D-structure*; a sentence's surface structure or *S-structure*, roughly, an augmented parse tree; a phonetic form or *PF*; and a sentence's *Logical form*, or *LF*. Returning to our passive example sentence, we begin with a representation of its D-structure. Our goal is to show how this D-structure can surface as a 'passive' form *the ice-cream was eaten* without ever making reference to an explicit 'passive rule'.

$$[_S [_{NP} \triangledown] [_{VP} \text{ was eaten } [_{NP} \text{ the ice-cream}]]]$$

Here $\triangledown$ is an empty position, a legitimate landing site for a noun phrase (NP), and the basic tree shape, indicated by the usual bracketing, is set by $\overline{\text{X}}$ constraints. Note that Thematic structure makes explicit reference to the properties of lexical items, in this case that *eat* requires a thing that gets eaten.

As figure 2 shows, D-structure is related to S-structure by the Move-α relation plus some of the other constraints mentioned earlier. S-structure then serves as a springboard for two 'interface systems': on the left it maps via phonological rules to an interface with the outside world,

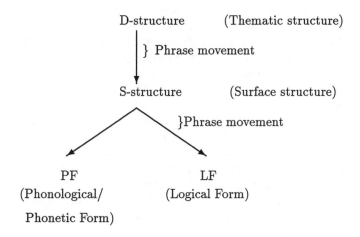

Figure 2: The conventional inverted 'Y' model of phrase structure used in the principle-and-parameters theories described in this book. It includes four levels of representation: (1) D-structure, or the level of *Thematic structure*, essentially 'who did what to whom'; (2) S-structure, or *Surface structure*, related to D-structure by the displacement of NPs from their D-structure positions; (3) PF, the interface to speech, related to S-structure by a phonological mapping; and (4) LF, *Logical form*, an interface to other cognitive systems such as inferential processes, representing quantifier and NP-NP relations and related to S-structure again by the displacement of certain phrases (so-called *LF movement*). The lexicon, not shown, is a source of thematic and phonological information.

namely, a spoken or phonetic form (PF)—this is the sentence that we actually see (more properly hear). On the right S-structure maps to an interface for other cognitive systems of an inside mental world, a representation of quantificational and noun phrase–noun phrase relationships, or Logical form; this relation is also mediated by a general relation of phrase movement, suitably constrained. (*Warning*: though this sketches a *logical* picture of the principle-based components, it does *not* say *how* these representations are to be computed, piece-by-piece or even if at all, or in what order. It is not even clear that we need all these representations, computationally speaking. *That* is a serious topic that all the authors must tackle.)

How then does the passive cabal get off the ground? *Ice-cream* cannot receive Case from an adjectival form like *eaten*. (We know that *eaten* is adjectival by the way that it mimics the analogous *John was sad.*) So *ice-cream* must move, and can move, to the available empty landing site at the front. Now *ice-cream* receives nominative Case from *was*, meeting the Case filter. Further, *eat* can now discharge its thematic role of Affected Object, and all visible noun phrases in the sentence receive a distinct thematic role, because the trace left behind by movement gets the discharged thematic role just as if it were the object of *eat*, and the trace's link with *ice-cream* ensures that *ice-cream* receives that thematic role as well. Taken together, there is no explicit passive rule. It is implicit in the inference from the principles. Importantly, the deductive chain from principles to surface form is very much longer than the link from the usual if-then rules to surface form. It is very much like reasoning from first principles, and it gives us the first hint of the computational thickets we must cut through to gain from a principle-based approach, as we shall see below.

If you concluded this was a lot of pain for little gain, then you were right. In just the same way, making *one* chemical compound out of a vast stock of molecules and bonding principles seems like overkill. Still, we can learn much from this small example, namely what the principle-based enterprise is all about.

The first lesson is that the *same* small set of principles can be recombined, over and over in different ways, yielding the entire array of surface sentences, and, by varying the parameters, different dialects and languages.

Second, note that the principles themselves are highly *abstract* and *heterogeneous*, often stated as a set of *declarative constraints*, unlike a more uniform representation like a set of context-free rules in a derivational framework. That is, we can imagine the set of well-formed sentences as those that dodge their way through a gauntlet of quite different representational constraints, rather than as the generative derivation from some S starting symbol. To this extent, the principle-and-parameters approach casts off the old garb of formal language theory with its emphasis on strings and languages. To take but one example, the notion of a *language* with its *grammatical* and *ungrammatical* strings becomes nearly meaningless: instead, there are simply structures that pass more or less of the way through the gauntlet. (To be sure, as note 1 points out, many recent linguistic theories have adopted a similar declarative framework. Even so, the declarative character of the principles-and-parameters approach itself is hotly debated, as noted in the chapters by Correa and Johnson.) In addition, the principles themselves *apply at different places*. For instance, movement of phrases and constraints on movement apply at the D-structure and S-structure interfaces, while the Case filter applies at S-structure itself (on some accounts).

Third, the principles-and-parameters approach stresses the importance of the *lexicon* (for example, as the source of thematic role constraints and possibly all language-particular variation), leading quite naturally to a focus on cross-linguistic variation, universal constraints, and language acquisition. On this view, there is one basic 'chassis' for all human grammars, with parametric variations setting the range of possible variations. For instance, Japanese differs from English in part because Japanese $\overline{X}$ constraints place phrasal heads—verbs in verb phrases, prepositions in prepositional phrases—*last* rather than *first*. Learning Japanese rather than English, then, is partly a matter of setting this $\overline{X}$ parameter to *head final* rather than *head first* (see Kazman's chapter for more on this). Finally, the highly modular and abstract character of principles leads directly to a heterogeneous view of language use, and an emphasis on how linguistic principles actually enter into human cognition.

Each of the chapters focuses on one or more of these major issues. Abney, Correa, Epstein, Fong, Johnson, and Stabler stress the major architectural and computational design features of principle-based parsers, including the issues of computational efficiency and program control flow in parsing. Dorr, Kashket, and Kazman treat the topic of cross-linguistic variation and the lexicon as it bears on machine translation; the parsing of languages as diverse as English and its near opposite, the Australian aboriginal language Warlpiri; and language acquisition. Thankfully, these parsers are not just speculative fancies; each author has a computer-implemented parsing model to show and tell. Finally, completing the circle, Abney, Gorrell, Kurtzman, Crawford, Nychis-Florence, Pritchett, and, to some extent, Stabler, take up specific psycholinguistic issues that connect facts about human sentence processing to the architectural modularity of principle-based systems. (A fourth area, language change, deserves a place as well but regrettably there are few computational studies of diachronic syntax—particularly ironic given Chomsky's original inspiration—1955, 1975—from language change.)

2. THE PRINCIPAL PROBLEM WITH PRINCIPLES

So far, all this discussion has been mere advertisement. The principle-based approach asks as many questions as it answers. Can it really work at all? To see that principle-based parsing *can* work, we shall first sketch in broadbrush the chief problems with principle-based parsing. We then review how the authors have solved these problems, showing how their solution fit under two unifying umbrellas: the division of parsing algorithms into control plus data structures (section 3); and parsing as search (section 4).

To begin, note that the picture in figure 2 merely sets out *what* is to be computed, in the sense of Marr (1982), not *how* the computation should proceed. Yet the gap between simply stating constraints and solving them can be huge; as noted by Abelson and Sussman (1985), it's one thing to define square-root(x) as the set of all y's such that $y^2 = x$, and quite another matter to write a square root algorithm. So it is by no means clear that principle-based parsing is possible at all—perhaps it is just as difficult as with earlier transformational theories.

Second, two related computational difficulties lie at the heart of principle-based parsing: *overgeneration* and *slow parsing*. The first problem plagues such systems precisely because the constraints of a principle-based system are heterogeneous and parceled out to many different components that we run into a computational brick wall at the start. By design, any single principle will not constrain the ultimate sentence structures very much. Thus we already know before we begin that a key problem faced in principle-based analysis is overgeneration: too many illicit structures will be produced that never mate with the input sentence. For instance, even a *simple* $\overline{\text{X}}$ theory, without recursion, can generate thousands of possible structures—just imagine three layers of tree structure with left- and righthand sides, each filled with any one of, say, 10 possibly different lexical categories. Then, each of these several thousand structures branches out a half-dozen or more new possible S-structures each, via Move-α. This is not just idle speculation, but hard-won computational and psycholinguistic experience. For instance, Fong has confirmed that there are tens of thousands of $\overline{\text{X}}$ possibilities for even a simple sentence, a result seconded by Kolb and Thiersch (1988) for German. Coping with overgeneration is therefore an important theme that runs throughout the parsing analyses in this book.

Slow parsing is the natural heir of overgeneration. But there is more to poor performance than that. As the bottom half of figure 1.1 shows, the other reason is that the deductive chains from principles to surface forms are now much longer than before. Modularity, then, is both a blessing and a curse. Simply enumerating possibilities will be slow because there are too many of them and a long way between sentence and structure. If one has to figure out from first principles how to open the front door, then getting around can become very slow indeed.

This raises yet another immediate question. Why then use principles at all? Why not simply 'compile out' small *lemmas* that store the repeated deductive chains, like the piece of reasoning about passive that we carried out earlier? But wouldn't this lemma then be a rule? Would we lose what little we've gained? One can see then that every *architectural* question about the relation between linguistic theory and the data structures of an implemented theory looms behind the overgeneration and parsing time problems. We won't answer these vital questions completely here—that's what the rest of the book is about—but we can at least see right away the centrality of overgeneration and slow parsing to the whole enterprise.

The general outline of what to do seems clear enough: starting from an input sentence, an orthographic representation of PF, we must 'invert the Y diagram' and recover at least the S-structure and the information in D-structure and LF, if not those structures themselves. Since all the filters and generators are grounded in phrase structure definitions—the Case filter must look at a particular *configuration* of tree structure, such as a verb next to an NP—we must somehow bootstrap ourselves from the input sentence and start building phrases. This is by no means easy. One cannot just reverse the arrows in the figure because the mappings are not obviously one-to-one and the constraints one needs aren't always immediately at hand (but see below on this point).

For instance, given the orthographic PF form *the ice-cream was eaten*, in order to build an S-structure it makes sense to bring thematic constraints from the lexicon into play, namely that *eat* might demand something eaten, because after all S-structure is in part a product of thematic constraint. But this information is hidden from PF's direct view back in D-structure. At the same time we have the problem of guessing that there is a phonologically null *trace* after *was eaten* that does not even show up in the input sentence. Similarly, consider the $\overline{\text{X}}$ component. Typical English structures would include forms for *John ate*, *John ate the ice-cream*, *John thought ice-cream was wonderful*, and so on. But the bare $\overline{X}$ component says simply that $\overline{X} \rightarrow X \{Complements\}$, where *Complements* can be nothing, or an NP; or a PP; or a CP (a propositional complement); or NP CP, and so on. However, some of these will be impossible depending on the verb. We can't have an NP as a complement of *think* as in *John thought ice-cream* (of course there is an elliptical construction that looks like this but is simply a truncation of a full propositional complement). If this is so, then expanding the skeletal $\overline{X}$ template out to a full set of complements will waste time and computer money because all expansions will be tested even though we know in advance that some are not possible. For instance, if the sentence were *John ate*, then an overzealous system might just invent an empty element after *ate*, to satisfy the NP complement possibility. But it is far better to consult the lexical entry for the allowable complements. We need to factor in information from the lexicon into the system at the PF–S-structure interface—even though this is not the logical arrangement of the 'Y' diagram where the lexicon hooks into the D-structure alone.

Thus as it stands the inverted 'Y' model does not seem well suited for parsing. Historians of transformational grammar may recall that this is precisely the same paradox that faced a much earlier generation of transformational grammar parsing pioneers (early systems at MIT and IBM, described in Petrick, 1965; and those at MITRE, reviewed by Zwicky *et al.*, 1965): transformations only apply to some structure, so we must first conjure up some structure from the sentence to start with, perhaps by employing a distinct *covering grammar*—a modified S-structure that can be used to start the jigsaw puzzle—and by carefully building inverse transformations that can be coupled with their forward generative counterparts. As we shall see, some of their solutions can be used in modern dress, but in addition we can do better now because we know more about control structures and computation, in particular trade-offs in search techniques that can model the covering grammar idea and much more besides. What is more, the theory has changed: there are no ordered, language-particular rules; traces and moved NPs can appear only in certain positions, not anywhere, so deletion is restricted. All this helps.

Let us then turn to our two umbrella views of the authors' solutions to overgeneration and slow parsing, beginning with algorithms viewed as control plus data structures.

3. MAKING PRINCIPLE-BASED PARSING WORK:
CONTROL AND DATA STRUCTURES

Figure 3 summarizes where all the authors stand on these matters. In what follows we shall refer to that figure and table I for a bird's eye view of the entire book. We shall now explore each branch of this taxonomy.

For those who have implemented parsers—Abney, Correa, Dorr, Epstein, Fong, Johnson, Kashket, Kazman, and, at the borderline with psycholinguistics, Stabler—there are two chief clamps to place on overgeneration, following the familiar division of computer algorithms into *control structures* (*how* something is computed) plus *data structures* (*what* is computed). Half of these parsers cut down on overgeneration by adopting both flexible control structures and data structures, while the other half do their work with flexible data structures alone, leaving the control structure fixed. Those who work at principle-based psycholinguistics—Gorrell, Kurtzman *et al.*, and Pritchett—carve up their hypotheses in the same way, only their game is complementary to the computer investigations. They aim at confirming or disconfirming 'the facts of the matter' about the use of principles. Do human sentence processors *actually* interweave principles and constraints—Do people actually use the Case filter or access lexical or thematic information when parsing? If so, when?

3.1. *Flexible Control Structures*

Of those using flexible control structures—Epstein, Fong, Johnson, and Stabler—Epstein alone commits to Lisp-based, hand-built exploration of six different control regimes, based on well-known heuristics that attempt to do as much filtering as early as possible, or as cheaply as possible, or by building as little structure as possible. (We shall take a closer look at these control regimes in section 4 on search below.) His domain is that of quantifier scope interpretation, and the tradeoff between the modularity of four simple principles for fixing scope and computational efficiency, as in *Every professor expects several students to read many books*, which has 70 possible candidate LFs, but just a few viable ones. By carefully attending to principle ordering, and banking on the local and compositional nature of scope, Epstein achieves remarkably good parsing time, often reducing many thousands of possible LFs to just a handful.

The remaining flexible control structure devotees—Fong, Johnson,

Table I

A summary of what each author has proposed computationally for their parser, in terms of flexible and fixed control structures.

Flexible Control Structure	
Epstein	Heuristic ordering strategies & others for computing logical form
Fong	Manual & automatic ordering of principle modules for optimal speed
	Covering grammar for S-structure
Johnson	5 different control structures, incl. coroutining, ordering, & combining principles
Stabler	Clause selection ordering for online semantic interpretation
Fixed Control Structure	
Correa	Attribute grammar to enforce local and long-distance constraints; Covering S-structure grammar that includes moved phrases
Dorr	Coroutined Earley parser and principle-based constraints
	Covering S-structure grammar
Kashket	Bottom-up multi-pass parser projecting words into $\overline{X}$ structures separating linear order & hierarchical structure for free word order languages
Abney	Bottom-up multi-pass parser separating prosodic structure; small phrase 'chunks'
	(projected bottom-up from $\overline{X}$ structures); and full S-structure
Kazman	Coroutined bottom-up $\overline{X}$ parser plus principle-based constraints; parameterized for language acquisition
Psycholinguistics: Fixed Control Structure	
Gorrell	Verb subcategory constraints applied as soon as possible
Pritchett	Thematic (theta) theory applied as soon as possible
Kurtzman	Verb constraints applied as soon as possible

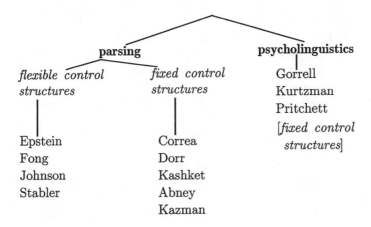

Figure 3: A tree diagram showing the computational territory the authors cover. The basic breakdown is into parsing and psycholinguistics. The implemented parsers fall into two camps: those with fixed control structures, and those separating control structure from data structure. The psycholinguistic studies all implicitly adopt fixed control structures.

and Stabler—have explicitly chosen an implementation language that allows one to make a clean separation of the parsing algorithm into control plus data structures—Prolog or some variant of first-order logic. This is a big advantage, because it allows one to separately abstract away from control structure issues. For example, Johnson's chapter amounts to a skillful set of finger exercises that explore an entire range of possible control structures, embodied in a series of five parsers, including some that order principles automatically, some that coroutine structure building and principle application, and some that avoid explicit construction of D-structure or S-structure entirely, building only Logical form. The beauty of using logic here is that the new parsers are *provably* equivalent to Johnson's original. It is very difficult to do this by hand, as Correa's attempt shows. We sketch these parsers further in section 4 below on search.

Fong and Stabler drive home the flexibility point, demonstrating how data and control structure partitioning yields tremendous power: Fong shows that one can reorder principles to construct many *hundreds* of different parsers within a single theory, even parsers that dynamically adapt their structure (the order in which principles are applied) according to what sentence types have been parsed before. This is an intriguing result for psycholinguistics, since it allows for individual variation in parsers from person to person, within a certain parametric envelope. Stabler establishes that ordering principles lets semantic interpretation proceed online, because one can start interpretation before an entire S-structure is built, thanks to a control regime that differentially queues at the front those statements that deal with semantic interpretation. In *the ice-cream was eaten* we can get an interpretation for *the ice-cream* before we arrive at *eaten*.

Logic also admits relatively transparent renderings of the English that linguists use in theories. There is a problem here—the usual one of getting from English to logic—but that's a problem for everybody. Logic still has all the virtues of directness: readability; easy modification in the face of theories in flux; verifiability of faithfulness to the original text. It is even the *historical* wellspring of generative grammar: after all, Chomsky's original *Morphophonemics of Modern Hebrew* (1953) that started the modern generative enterprise in motion consciously borrowed the notion of an axiom system because that was the only machinery then *au courant* in which to run a recursive syntax. As Johnson's paper argues, deductive inference is still perhaps the clearest way to to think about how to 'use' knowledge of language. In a certain sense, it even seems straightforward. The terms in the definitions like the one above have a suggestive logical ring to them, and even include informal quantifiers like *every*; terms like *lexical NP* can be predicates, and so forth. In this way one is led to first-order logic or Horn clause logic implementation (Prolog) as a natural first choice for implementation, and there have been several such principle-based parsers written besides those described by the authors of this volume who have built Prolog implementations of principle-based theories. (see Sharp, 1985; Kolb and Thiersch, 1988). Parsing amounts to using a theorem prover to search through the space of possible satisfying representations to find a parse, a metaphor that we'll explore in detail just below.

How then can a theory written in English be mapped into logic? Here for example, following Fong (1991 forthcoming) is a typical statement of the Case filter: "At S-structure, every lexical NP needs Case" (Lasnik and Uriagereka, 1988, p. 20). How are we to implement this statement as part of a parsing program? Those who live by the Horn clause must also die by it: We must actually translate the English connectives such as *needs* or *every* and the required feature checking (the property of being *lexical* on NPs), into logical formulas. But in fact this can readily be done. Fong's system (surveyed in his chapter but fully detailed in Fong, 1991 forthcoming) states principles purely declaratively, as in his version of the Case filter:

```
:- caseFilter in_all_configurations CF where
        lexicalNP(CF) then assignedCase(CF).

lexicalNP(NP) :- cat(NP,np), \+ ec(NP).
assignedCase(X) :- X has_feature case(Case), assigned(Case).
```

This says, close in spirit to the original English, that the Case filter is met if, in all configurations (CF) where there is a lexical NP, then make sure that Case has been assigned to that NP configuration. The Prolog has been augmented a bit with more abstract macros such as in_all_configurations that render the code closer to the English. (Following Fong we read the second clause lexicalNP(NP) as stating that a lexical NP is one that has the category feature *np* and is *not* an empty category. As is conventional, \+ means negation-as-failure—if we can't prove something to be an *ec* or empty category then it is not one. Finally, the comma is a conjunction.)

The point is that the person who writes the Case filter statement need not be concerned whether this statement is implemented by a tree-walking procedure that climbs over all the nodes one by one, or by some other method that combines nodes together first (for more on this, see section 4).

It is interesting to compare Fong's encoding of the Case filter with Johnson's and Correa's. They are very much alike. Johnson, for instance, says, "The Case filter as formulated in PAD [his parser] applies recursively throughout the S-structure, associating each node with one of the three atomic values *assigner*, *receiver*, or *null*" (p. 49). He also observes (p. 62) that "this association of constituents with 'properties' described here is reminiscent of the way a tree automaton associates tree nodes with automaton 'states' ". Further, it's the locality of the constraint that makes this possible—it applies only to a restricted configuration of a verb and verb phrase adjacent to a noun phrase, for example.

Correa has done precisely the same thing in other garb: he uses *attribute grammars* where the grammar has built into it an augmented S-structure that includes the effects of the lexicon plus local movement. An attribute grammar is an ordinary context-free grammar plus attribute information, which we can think of as separate memory registers attached to the different parse tree nodes. The attributes are 'typed'— that is, each has a certain *domain* defined in advance that can hold only certain values (*e.g.,* the *Case* type might hold possible Case assignment values like nominative or Accusative) We assign values to the attributes by means of rules attached to the context-free expansions; this information can be passed either from mother and sisters to daughter (an *inherited* attribute) or from daughter to mother (a *synthesized* attribute). Thus attributes can pass information down and from tree substructures below so that local constraints like the Case filter can be applied, as Correa notes: "the attribute *Case* is associated with NP, the categories of potential Case assigners, such as V[erb] and P[reposition]... The domain of the attribute is [nominative, accusative, dative, ... nil], which includes the special value *nil*" (p. 96). Here, the Case *assigner* and *assignee* are determined by the attribute rules themselves, where the attribute values are in brackets.

S→ NP VP

attribution:
NP[*Case*] ← if VP[*tensed*] then *Nominative*, else VP[*Case*]

Case filter:
if ¬NP[*empty*] (an empty category) then NP[*Case*]≠ *nil*

Not only is this almost exactly Fong's definition, but Correa even implicitly hints at Johnson's suspicions: as is known, *unrestricted* attribute grammars are more powerful than tree automata, but if one restricts the attribute grammar so that it can be evaluated in one depth-first left-to-right pass over the derivation tree, as seems to hold in Correa's system, then such a grammar's language is equal to the yield (fringe) of the languages recognizable by deterministic tree automata (Engelfriet and Filè, 1979). Thus there seems to be a connection between tree automata and restricted attribute grammars of the kind needed for natural grammars, unifying all three accounts. All structurally *local* constraints, including X̄ theory and Thematic theory, can be formulated in this way, it appears. It would be a useful probe this connection in more detail to *prove* it to be so.

Besides these local conditions, there remain 'long-distance' principles: movement of NPs and *Wh*-phrases in sentences like *What did you think John ate*, where there is a *chain* of traces or empty categories linking *what* to a position before *John* and then to a position after *ate*. The same things happens with LF where quantifier phrases like *several students* are moved about so that they can take wide scope in a sentence like Epstein's above. How can these be modeled? Here again, the authors are in basic agreement: instead of explicitly computing these chains via a derivation from D-structure to S-structure or S-structure to LF, they have all opted to formulate chains as a set of constraints *on* S-structure itself. Astonishingly enough, this *works*. For instance, Fong's parser can actually parse basically all of the several hundred example sentences in Lasnik and Uriagereka's textbook (1988), just the way the theory intends. *Astonishingly* is the right word because it hardly seems believable at first that one could actually translate all of several linguists' often incompatible written ideas into a logical formulation that zooms in on *just* the correct analysis of many hundreds of sentence types. It is by no means clear that this translation can even be done into Prolog (as Stabler, 1991 forthcoming, argues), and that powerful first-order theorem provers will be required. But it has been done; it works; and it works quickly (in just a few seconds on an older model Lisp machine).

For whatever reason, this declarative formulation seems much more computationally tractable. Again a full proof waits in the wings, but historically at least, under close scrutiny generative conditions have slowly given way to declarative admissibility constraints (for example, compare the discovery by Peters and Ritchie, 1973, that context-sensitive rewrite rules have been used for local tree *analysis*, and under this interpretation they admit only context-free languages. See section 4 for more discussion). This is also a viable linguistic option, advanced by Koster (1978) and others. Thus it is no surprise that Correa, Dorr, Epstein, Fong, and Johnson all use constraints on S-structure representations to encode long-distance phenomena. This choice also has a linguistic effect: D-structures are not actually computed by any of these parsers, as Johnson demonstrates in detail, even though D-structure information is factored into the parsers (again see section 4 for how this is done). The psycholinguists paint the same picture: D-structure information is tapped, but nowhere need one compute D-structures explicitly.

3.2. *Fixed Control Structures, Flexible Data Structures*

Turning now from those who have advocated the separation of control and data structures, those authors who have chosen Lisp or a close cousin for their implementation language—Abney, Correa, Dorr, Kashket, and Kazman (and, more casually, psycholinguists like Gorrell and Pritchett)—have bound their fates to a fixed parsing control structure.

Of those embracing fixed control structures, most, like Abney, Correa, Dorr, Kashket, and Kazman, have opted for a basically bottom-up implementation using the two-decade old idea of a *covering grammar*— a phrase structure grammar that augments S-structure, tapping into the lexicon, movement, and other constraints to come up with a different grammar than S-structure, yet one that incorporates all these D-structure effects at once. D-structure is no longer directly computed; the modularity of the theory is partially destroyed in order to salvage computational efficiency. The psycholinguists Gorrell, Kurtzman *et al.*, and Pritchett also find this nonexplicit D-structure approach attractive.

The key point to attend to, though, is *why* covering grammars can be successfully revived at all, after more than two decades. The answer is that a theory built on principles rather than rules has two advantages: first, a natural and simple covering grammar—as mentioned, the one formed by augmenting $\overline{\text{X}}$ structure with movement and some thematic and Case constraints; and second, a much simpler notion of transformation. In the older approach, each transformational rule had to be spelled out by means of a complex structural description (an *if* condition) that dictated when it applied, followed by a structural change (the *then* part), as in this subject formation example from Petrick (1973, p. 33) that attaches a *Wh*-NP to the Auxiliary position, to convert *e.g.*, *will who eat ice-cream* into *who will eat ice-cream*, checking that the sentence has not already been turned into a question. Each subtree component is marked with a number (1 through 6, 6= the Sentence; 1= boundary marker #, 2= the Auxiliary tree; 3= NP; 4= any subtree X; and 5= a boundary marker #). The transformation adjoins component 3, the *Wh*-NP, to subtree 2, leaving behind nothing:

RULE SUBJFRMA (subject formation)
structural

description:	S1	#	AUX	NP	X	#
	1	2	3	4	5	

constraints: ∨ *not* S1 marked +*Ques*
                NP is marked +*Wh*

structural

change:		1	(3 2)	0	4	5

Note that on top of these detailed surface-patterned conditions, rules were marked as obligatory or optional, cyclic or postcyclic, and so forth. *None* of this is required in the principle-based framework. The movement of the *Wh*-NP is allowed because there is a 'landing site' (the Complementizer position at the front of a clause, not known in the earlier formulation), and because the resulting move passes all the other modular conditions. Nothing more has to be stated beyond what is already needed for other general properties of the system; there isn't any specific rule of subject formation. Because each principle-based constraint contributes just a bit to the overall constraint that fixes possible surface sentence forms, we have a fighting chance. For example, one can show that an S-structure covering grammar can be small enough to succumb to LR-parsing techniques, with a parsing table of only a few hundred entries (smaller than what's needed for a typical computer programming language; see Fong, 1991 forthcoming). This is possible only because each component does not try to do too much at once; the allowable $\overline{X}$ structures are really quite simple.

We have already briefly outlined Correa's technique in this computational war: using attribute grammars, he can handle the local constraints like Thematic theory that are obvious candidates for local tree attribute assignments. What about long-distance constraints? Again, a chain is composed from strictly local tree attribute assignments: in the *What did you think John ate* example, we can build the chain link by link in both directions. From the top down, we can propagate a chain value ever downwards, step by step; from the bottom up, we can propagate the proper value upwards: first a link is made between the empty category NP position after *ate* and the complement position before *John*, by 'passing up' the attribute via attributed assignment from the NP position to the complement position; then this attribute value is passed up once more to the front of the sentence to link up with the value passed down from *what*. No D-structure is used; instead, Correa assumes, following Koster (1978), that empty categories can be *base generated* in S-structure itself.

Because there are two types of chains in the theory—movement to so-called argument or *A* positions, like the Subject of a sentence in passive constructions, and movement to nonargument or $\overline{A}$ positions like the complement position at the head of a sentence in *Wh*-questions, Correa uses two attributes, *A* and *AB* ('A-bar' or $\overline{A}$). However, as he notes, this chain composition algorithm has its own gaps. There can be only one *A* or $\overline{A}$ chain formed per phrase. Since only two attributes are used, one can only move out one NP to an argument position. This is a problem, since Scandanavian languages evidently admit many more than one *Wh* word at the head of a sentence, and even problematic in English, where so-called *parasitic gap* sentences such as *Which book did I buy without reading*, where there are *two* empty categories, one after *buy* and one after *reading*, that are both linked to *which book*. One can show that these empty categories are both $\overline{A}$—roughly, they are both variables, linked to the logical operator *which book* (see Lasnik and Uriagereka, 1988, p. 78 for discussion). But this cannot work with only one *AB* attribute. This problem underscores the difficulty of hand-crafting an algorithm that combines many different linguistic principles: one can never be quite sure that it is logically correct. The reader is invited to check whether Correa's account of 'structural' determination of empty categories is in fact correct, and then judge whether a logic programming approach would have been better.

Dorr adopts a *coroutined*, hand-built covering grammar to get parsers for Spanish, German, and English translation. To do this, Dorr interleaves a conventional Earley parser with principles by applying constraints when phrases are started or completed. The system also assumes an augmented covering grammar that incorporates phrase movement and thematic constraints, thus leaving aside D-structure at run-time. To cover several languages, like Fong and Johnson, Dorr implements a specification language as a buffer between the parametric vocabulary of linguistic theory and the algorithmic guts beneath: at the top level, different languages apply the Case filter or not, and have their phrasal Heads first or final; this information is then compiled behind the scenes into a covering grammar that includes some details about possible phrase movement and Thematic constraints. Note that many constraints remain untested, so this grammar will overgenerate. It is this covering grammar that the Earley parser actually works with. The system starts work by projecting from an input word the maximal covering $\overline{\text{X}}$ augmented structure possible, *e.g.*, the Spanish *vio* (*ver*, *to see*) is projected to a VP. When a phrase is completed, then, much like Correa's system, one can stop structure building and propagate certain features and carry out certain tests like Case assignment and Thematic role assignment; these are done procedurally rather than via the formal machinery of attribute grammar. For example, Dorr shows how the projection of the V to a VP then institutes a search for an NP clitic (*la*, *he*) as a thematic role of *ver* to the left of the verb, given information in the lexicon. Despite these procedural differences, the bottom-up algorithm and its subtree by subtree construction remain close to Correa's model.

Kashket's parser for the free-word order language Warlpiri also uses a bottom-up parser that *starts* with the lexicon to project phrases, which are then tied to each other by other, thematic principles. This makes a great deal of sense given the word order freedom of Warlpiri. All the possible permutations of phrases are permitted, and noun phrases can even be interwoven with other noun phrases. There are 24 possible ways of saying the following sentence, where we have listed just one other possible permutation:

Karli   *ka-rna-rla*   *punta-rni*   *ngajulu-rlu kurdu-ku*
boomerang *imperf*-1s-3d take-*nonpast* I-*erg*   child-*dat*
'It is the boomerang I am taking from the child'

Kurdu-ku ka-rna-rla   *ngajulu-rlu karli*   *punta-rni*
child-*dat* *imperf*-1s-3d I-*erg*   boomerang take-*nonpast*
'From the child I am taking the boomerang'

To make order out of this apparent word salad, Kashket again turns to the bottom-up and lexical projection style parsing used by Correa and Dorr. Each lexical item is first projected bottom-up into its $\overline{\text{X}}$ counterpart. For instance, *kurdu-ku* (child-dative) is projected to form an NP subtree, bottom-up. A second pass then applies the principles of Thematic theory and Case to sweep subtrees into larger structures, according to the Case markers, like the dative *ku*, attached to the ends of words. It is by using the Case markers and an S-structure that contains no left-to-right precedence information at all that absolutely free order can be handled. Importantly, Kashket shows that Case marking is also operative in languages like English, but here, since marking is carried out by the inflection in second position and the verb marking to its right, English winds up with a basically fixed Subject-Verb-Object order. Thus, on this view, there are no 'fixed' or 'free' word order languages. As with passive constructions, this is an artifact of a superficial analysis. Languages can vary according to a parameterization of Case marking, from free to fixed order, even within the same language (adjunct prepositional phrases are relatively free in English because their Case is inherently fixed, like the Warlpiri NPs, rather than assigned).

Abney's work is closely allied to Kashket's. Abney too uses a bottom-up parser (but a parallel bottom-up parser) for phrase *chunks*. His twist is to add a three-stage bridge between (1) prosody (intonational patterns); (2) phrase chunks as a mediating between prosodic phrases and syntactic phrases; and (3) full syntactic phrase construction via thematic role determination. The prosodic level aims to capture some of the constraint in spoken input. 'Chunks' are extracted from a sentence including prosodic salience peaks, like *the bald man was sitting on his suitcase*—namely, [the bald man], [was sitting], and [on his suitcase]. These are quite close to the projections that Kashket defines. Given the prominence of prosodic cues in Warlpiri, perhaps this is not so surprising. The grammar of chunks is again a covering grammar for $\overline{X}$ structure plus some movement factored in. Next, a second-stage pass, like Kashket's, pastes some of these phrases together, following the constraints of Case theory and Thematic theory—for example, it attaches *on his suitcase* to *was sitting*.

Kazman is the only author to explicitly address the problem of language acquisition in a principle-based system. His parsing design mirrors Kashket's and Abney's: for each word in the sentence, the parser first constructs NPs, VPs, etc., according to $\overline{X}$ theory. A second stage then attempts to attach the phrases to one another, subject to Case theory, Thematic theory, and so forth. Next, by parametrically varying the parameters—*e.g.*, by turning off the Case filter—Kazman strives to reproduce the patterns of child language, tested by using the altered parser to process actual examples of child speech. Using four sets of 50 sentences each from two children, he shows that this parameterization works: the lobotomized parser adequately describes child speech from about age 2, and, by changing the parameters, arrives at an 'adult' parsing competence.

The psycholinguistic studies also all (implicitly) adopt fixed control structures—bottom-up parsers, some (like Gorrell's) parallel and close in design to Kazman's or Abney's, some not. Regardless of the parsing design, the basic point that each one of them drives home is that principle application and interpretation takes place as *soon* as possible. In particular, Gorrell, Kurtzman *et al.*, and Pritchett show that information from subcategorization frames or thematic theory—roughly, what phrase subtypes/thematic roles can be associated with each verb, as whether a verb is transitive or not—seems to be used early on in parsing, and, more generally, principles and constraints are applied as soon as possible. This supports Stabler's point; not so surprising perhaps, but the authors do more. They go on to show that this early-as-possible constraint accounts for the human sentence processor's abilities in processing locally ambiguous sentences (*after the child had visited the doctor prescribed a course of injections/after the child has sneezed the doctor prescribed a course of injections*); garden path sentences, as in *after Steve ate the soup proved to be poisoned*; and the difficulty of finding the 'gaps' associated with *Wh*-phrases, as in *what did John escape from*, where *what* is associated with the position after *from*.

4. SEARCH AND PRINCIPLE-BASED PARSING

As we have seen, overgeneration and how to avoid it is *the* key theme of principle-based parsing and psycholinguistics. To better understand the overgeneration issue as the tie that binds all the chapters together, we now turn to our second unifying umbrella, the metaphor of *parsing as search*. Our parsing task is a classic search problem. We must enumerate a space of possibilities, shown conventionally as a branching tree (*not* a phrase structure tree!) of possible paths, and apply tests to rule out some, perhaps all of these paths; those surviving are the valid parses. Overgeneration is one symptom that our searching algorithm fares poorly. For each author the key to reducing overgeneration is some way to exploit the modularity of a principle-based system, recasting the principle modules to avoid exhaustive search. Let us see how.

Figure 4 sketches the main possibilities as a kind of graphical taxonomy of what the authors do. Each figure 4(a) to 4(d) shows a portion of a search tree for discovering the possible parses. Each circle standing for some *enumerator* or *next path generator* plus a (partial) structure already built; the result will be either a single new branch (if no constraints are applied); a single new branch or perhaps a dead end (if the enumerator is applying a constraint like the Case filter); or many new branches (if the enumerator is applying a generator like Move-α). Each possibility leads to further enumerations, possibly casting some structures out as we go, until we arrive at the fringe of the tree where entire parses are found, and either ruled OK or out. Note that in order not to miss any parses, the *entire* space of logical possibilities must be exhaustively explored, but we can limit the exhaustion by cutting down the number of nodes and branches generated (we want the *branching factor* or number of new paths generated at any step to be as small as possible) and reducing the cost of enumeration at each node. The graphical sketches lay out the basic methods for doing this. We shall now consider them, one by one.

Parts (a) and (b) of the figure illustrate the most direct and costly ways of coping with overgeneration: ignore it. In (a), given a sentence, we build *all* possible structures, without applying any constraints, not even looking at the input sentence, and *then* apply all constraints to each candidate structure in turn. This simple and well-known strategy, dubbed *analysis by synthesis*, was proposed in the the earliest discussions of parsing with transformational grammars (see Petrick, 1965 for additional historical discussion).[2] Alternatively, as in (b), we could generate each candidate structure in turn, and as each is completed, *test* it against the constraints, then generate the next structure, and so on. This is the familiar *generate-and-test* paradigm of artificial intelligence.

Left unconstrained, methods (a) and (b) suffer from serious, even fatal, overgeneration. This was was well known from earlier work in search and is demonstrated again Johnson's chapter via his first parsing model (PAD1) that adopts generate-and-test search method (b)—it might not even terminate, as Johnson indicates, because one could generate an infinite number of D-structures first, as would be true of any reasonable recursive syntax, and one might not ever get to the next enumeration stage). To take another example, Correa's chapter notes that Barss' (1983) and Chomsky's (1981) specifications of the conditions on chain formation are just that: *specifications* of algorithms, not algorithms themselves. Strictly interpreted as algorithms, they generate *all possible* movements in S-structure first, and then test each one in turn. Correa shows that this blind generate-and-test approach takes exponential time in the length of the input string, but that his attribution grammar that builds up chains by evaluating substructures piece by piece is evidently linear time—a vast improvement, if correct.

Somehow then we must mix the constraints from the lexicon and $\overline{\text{X}}$ theory together with the constraints like the Case filter that apply at other levels, and do so piecemeal *without* losing the advantages of

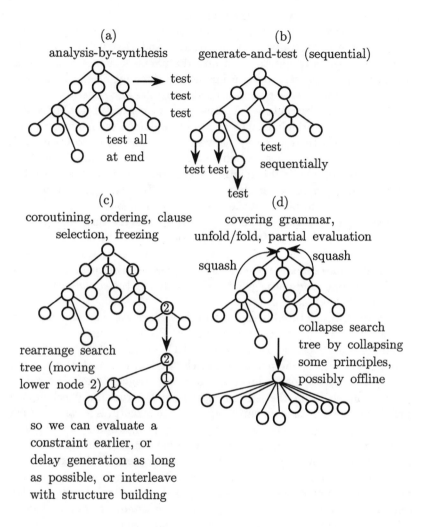

(a)
analysis-by-synthesis

test
test
test

test all
at end

(b)
generate-and-test (sequential)

test
sequentially

test test

test

(c)
coroutining, ordering, clause
selection, freezing

rearrange search
tree (moving
lower node 2)

so we can evaluate a
constraint earlier, or
delay generation as long
as possible, or interleave
with structure building

(d)
covering grammar,
unfold/fold, partial evaluation

squash   squash

collapse search
tree by collapsing
some principles,
possibly offline

Figure 4: All the different strategies for speeding up principle-based parsing can be viewed as techniques for better enumerating or searching a space of possibilities. Parts (a) and (b) of the figure illustrate exhaustive enumeration methods that are too computationally intensive. The authors use the methods sketched in parts (c) and (d) of the figure to reduce the search space itself.

principles that we sought in the first place.

In fact, in one way or another all the authors have adopted ways to weave the constraints from the lexicon and D-structure back into S-structure, so as to get one foot into the phrase structure door as required to apply the remaining principles. Ultimately, all these methods are based on the observation that most principles and constraints apply locally to parse substructures. Therefore, if some structural subpart fails to make it past a principle, such as *I am proud John* (which violates the Case filter since there is no *of* between *proud* and *John* to Case mark *John*) then a larger structure built out of this, such as *I think that I am proud John* will inherit this failure. Therefore, there is no need to apply *all* constraints on the *entire* parse structure. It is enough to apply the right constraints to pieces of the parse tree as it is built.

Techniques (c) and (d) in the figure do exactly this, and *all* the authors have tried to cure the overgeneration problem by adopting one or more of these methods. Their approaches follow directly from the logical possibilities for reducing the enumerated space—either cutting down the number of nodes and paths generated, or reducing the enumeration cost. Let's run through each in turn.

The method pictured in figure 4(c) shows how the related techniques dubbed *freezing* (Johnson's second parser, PAD2), *principle reordering* (used by Fong), *clause selection* (Stabler), or *parse table coroutining* (used by Dorr) can help reduce search. These are control structure strategies. As the parse proceeds, different principles may be called on, now drawn from the lexicon, now from D-structure, checking the well-formedness of the currently hypothesized structures as we go. Such *coroutining* is quite common in compilers for programming languages as a way to interleave phrase building with other kinds of constraint checking, and that's obviously just the ticket we need here. If the experiences of the authors are any guide, these methods can quite effective (for example, Fong's parser just takes a few second on even relatively complex sentences such as *This is the book that I filed without reading*, which is difficult to accommodate at all in an ATN approach).

Though each of these authors use distinct tools, they amount graphically to the same thing as shown in figure 4 part (c) and in another form in figure 5(c). On the left, we have some search tree with the generators and constraints arranged in a particular order, resulting in a bushy tree with many enumeration circles. On the right, we have rearranged the search tree by moving one of the enumeration nodes, marked *2* higher up in the tree. How can this help? If the newly promoted node winnows out many structures, then subsequent generators like Move-α will have fewer structures to expand on. The new search tree on the right illustrates.

How are each of these part (c) methods implemented? Johnson and Fong examine automatic means of determining the dataflow dependencies among principles and ordering the parsing system offline so that it does not compute unwanted constraints. For example, as we saw earlier, it makes little sense to apply the Case filter constraint if there is no assignment of Case (which in turn depends on establishing certain structural relationships between verbs, prepositions, and nouns).

Johnson concentrates on semi-automatic logic programming techniques for handling D-structure, S-structure, PF, and LF dependencies, including the so-called *freeze* technique drawn from Prolog research that suspends the computation of one conjunct, say, Move-α, while the parser works on another that the conjunct depends on, like S-structure. Thus we say that Move-α is *delayed* on S-structure.[3] Because no S-structure is initially available, this immediately delays, or freezes, any computations involving Move-α, until the first node of S-structure is built. See figure 5(b). Then Move-α is applied while the further recovery of S-structure is frozen; and so on. (Note also that this parser recovers D-structure by using a declarative description of Move-α and then running the system backwards, as can be done in Prolog.) In this way principles can be *automatically* and systematically coroutined with structure building.

Fong also focuses on principle ordering effects but *without* coroutining, and uses a finer grain size than Johnson, arranging a proposed twenty-odd principle bundles or modules like a deck of cards as in figure 5(a). By rearranging the deck, subject to the logical dependencies of the theory (as we have seen, some things *must* be computed before others: we can't apply the Case filter until Case is assigned) we can explore all the logically possible conjunct orderings, assess their effect on parsing efficiency—evidently there can be an order of magnitude difference in parsing times for the same sentence depending on the arrangement of the deck—and even add a means to learn the best way to juggle the deck for a particular type of input sentence.

Fong's method does assume a modified generate-and-test approach: an entire S-structure is built before any other constraints are applied. From a different angle, (see part (b) of the figure) but akin to John-

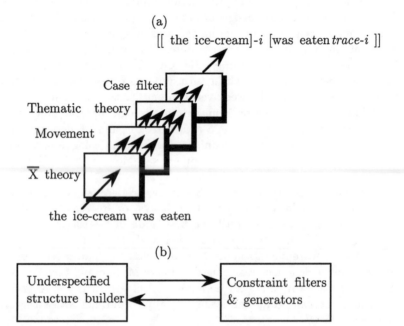

Figure 5: The principles-and-parameters theory can be organized for processing in two distinct ways, as shown in parts (a) and (b) of this figure. First, it can be pictured as set of 20 or so modules or groups of principles, arranged like a deck of cards as in the top half of the figure, (a). An orthographic representation of a sentence like *the ice-cream was eaten* is input at one end, and, if the sentence is completely well-formed, one or more valid parse structures emerges unscathed at the other end. The arrows emerging out of each box show that some modules act like filters that can cut down the number of structures that pass through them, while other principles act like generators that expand the space of possibly valid structures. The bottom half of the figure, (b), illustrates a coroutined processing model where structure building and constraint application are interleaved.

son, Stabler shows that the generate-and-test method is not forced upon us. The parsing algorithm need not produce an *entire* S-structure before beginning to incrementally compute an associated Logical form or calculating its truth-conditional interpretation, even assuming conventional branching for English phrase structure (contrary to what some researchers have assumed).[4]

Dorr develops a coroutining strategy that interleaves the phrase construction carried out by a standard context-free parser (swinging into action when phrase like an NP is started or completed) with additional constraint checking (does the NP meet the Case filter). As Fong, Stabler, and Johnson demonstrate, this can be done automatically in a logic-based approach, based on the widely explored notion of *selection rules* or *ordering strategies*. Citing Johnson and following Fong and Stabler, suppose we regard a well-formed (sentence, LF structure) pair (what Johnson dubs the *parse relation*) as the first-order logic *conjunction* of the various PF, S-structure, D-structure, and LF constraints:

$\forall d\text{-}struc, s\text{-}struc, lf, pf, \overline{X}(d\text{-}struc) \wedge \text{CaseFilter}(s\text{-}struc) \wedge \text{LF}$
$PF(pf, s\text{-}struc) \wedge LF(lf) \Rightarrow Parse(pf, lf)$
(Johnson, this volume, p. 49)

The details don't matter here. What does matter is that we can decide to work on *any* one of the conjuncts at any time—and then, as we dive down into those conjuncts themselves, we can stop and build a part of D-structure, or apply the Case filter, or whatever. Naturally, it makes the most sense to work on a conjunct whose 'internals' will be partly grounded on what we already know, and this in turn depends on the input sentence and the 'dataflow dependencies' of the theory itself—what principles are wired to what other principles. For instance, as we have seen, it's unwise to start out enumerating all possible D-structures before checking what's in the input sentence. It makes more sense to first build a piece of the S-structure by projecting it from the input sentence. For example, in our *ice-cream* sentence, we can use conventional techniques and $\overline{X}$ theory to deduce that *the ice-cream* is a noun phrase, and *was eaten* a verb phrase. Now we have a skeleton S-structure on which to hang the other inferences about Case and Trace theory. Better still, as Johnson and Stabler's chapters observe, by interleaving the construction of structures and the applications of constraints, we need not trap ourselves in the hopeless task of first enumerating an endless sequence of D-structures.

Plainly then the order in which one works on conjuncts can make a vast difference in parsing efficiency, as is well known from work by Smith and Genesereth (1985) and others on *search tree rearrangement*. To see this in more detail, consider the following simple example definition from their work: to check if x has an aunt, $aunt(x)$, see if x has a mother y and that person y has a sister z:

$$aunt(x) = mother(x, y) \land sister(y, z)$$

Now to compute, say, $aunt(elissa)$ it matters a great deal whether we start in on the first conjunct or on the second. If we start on the first, we will compute $mother(elissa, y)$, bind y to some value, say, $marilyn$, and then check $sister(marilyn, z)$, which will then succeed or fail accordingly. But if we started on the second conjunct, we would initially compute $sister(y, z)$, for all possible values of y and z—that is, we would first find *all* the sister pairs in the universe, and *then* check each one to see if one of them was the mother of Elissa. This would clearly be much more expensive! Smith and Genesereth show, sensibly enough, that the optimal conjunct ordering essentially depends on applying the best-winnowing constraints as early as possible delaying hypothesis-expanding modules as long as possible. The connection to principle-based parsing ought to be clear: computing all the sisters first before looking at Elissa is very much like enumerating all the D-structures before looking at the constraining input sentence.

The search speedup methods just described in part (c) of figure 4 are all geared to different control strategies that coroutine. Most of the remaining search improvements work as in figure 4 part (d): by squashing the enumeration tree, accordion-wise. As the figure shows, this attempts to collapse two (or more) search nodes into one larger one that meets *both* sets of constraints or generators covered by the individual nodes. The general idea is to apply constraints sooner, rather than later, and so avoid exploring structures that cannot possibly participate in a solution. As we shall see, there are many ways to collapse the search tree, but for now it is enough to see that collapsing reduces the size of the search space. It simply squashes together the constraints/enumerators in such a way that one larger predicate is applied rather than the sequential conjunction of several.

This helps, because the number of branches generated is cut down immensely. To take a concrete example, the number of bare $\overline{X}$ structures possible might number in the many thousands (roughly 80,000 according to Fong's experiments, 1991 forthcoming); but the number of $\overline{X}$ structures plus following NPs that meet the Case filter and thematic constraints are only about 100. Thus if we tested this system sequentially we would first generate 80,000 possibilities, then run each of these by the Case filter, reducing the number to about 2000, and then through the Thematic constraints to yield 100 outputs—82,100 tests. In contrast, if we carry out all the tests jointly, as one giant enumerator, we generate only about 100 branches.

Note that collapsing search tree nodes is not *necessarily* cheaper. Squashing the search tree can go too far and make the enumerator's job harder. If the enumerator is computationally expensive, then the savings from fewer branches explored can be swept under by the extra computation. Again consider one concrete example, *Mary likes her mother*, where there are two Logical forms, one where *her* is *Mary* and one where *her* is some other person, not named in the sentence; this is conventionally indicated by indexing, or linking of *Mary* and *her*. If we squash all constraints together, then we must in effect build *two* separate structures, checking all the constraints (in concert) twice. But we could squash everything *except* the computation of the indexing. Then we just have to apply our giant combined predicate, *sans* LF, yielding *one* structure, and from there use indexing to generate the two output possibilities. It turns out that this last approach takes less time because the enumerator does not have to go through the construction of another entire tree structure that is easily derived from a single common form. More generally, if computing the proper structural configurations required to apply a constraint or principle is expensive, then the benefits of collapsing search nodes can outweigh the costs. This is where a smart offline computation can help, by figuring out in advance in what configurations certain principles and constraints will never apply.

In general though there are big savings to be had in squashing the search space, so big that almost all the authors—Abney, Correa, Dorr, Epstein, Fong, Gorrell, Johnson, Kashket, Kazman, Kurtzman *et al.*, Pritchett, and Stabler—adopt it in one form or another. How then is this accordion move played out?

The first compression technique, covering grammars, simply collapses several constraints together—for example, $\overline{X}$ tree structures, plus Move-α plus thematic constraints—to create a new phrase structure grammar that has more detail than just $\overline{X}$ theory alone. The collapsed search space is smaller because it has additional constraints built in, but still covers the same sentence territory as before. We illustrated above how much this can reduce the search space: we look just at possible $\overline{X}$ plus movement configurations, instead of first generating all possible $\overline{X}$ configurations.

Most of the authors who have built parsers—Abney, Correa, Dorr, Fong, Epstein, Kashket, and Johnson—take this tack. In effect, they propose to recover not simply S-structure, but rather a closely related representation described by a covering grammar. As described earlier, this is simply a new grammar that has lexical (thematic) constraints and Move-α factored into it. The new representation is called a covering grammar simply because it does not include *all* the constraints of the original principle-based system—if it did, we would just have rules again—so it must of necessity *cover more* possible structures than the original principles. Once again this technique should be familiar to historians of the field: early transformational parsers used covering grammars in just this way to bootstrap an initial, but overgenerating, tree structure on which to decamp the structural descriptions of (inverse) transformations.

Such an approach is possible because of a number of changes in the theory of grammar advanced by the authors, of which the most important is perhaps the view promoted by Koster (1978), namely, the so-called *base-generation hypothesis*: if as standardly assumed the $\overline{X}$ structures are describable by a context-free grammar, and if S-structure is derived from D-structure by moving phrases into positions where they *could* have been generated originally by the $\overline{X}$ grammar, then the S-structure can plainly be generated by a context-free grammar straight out, without appealing to D-structure at all.[5]

To be concrete, recall our passive example again: *the ice-cream was eaten*. To say that the noun phrase Subject 'landing site' in this sentence is base generated is to say simply that there is an $\overline{X}$ template in the form S→NP VP, which of course there must be for ordinary sentences anyway. To take another example, we could write a covering grammar to accommodate *Wh*-questions like *what did John eat* by changing the the $\overline{X}$ module to include the templates $\overline{S}$→ *what* S and VP→V NP_e, where NP_e is a trace or lexically null noun phrase. The new grammar is *not* pure $\overline{X}$ theory—it actually looks more like a conventional context-free rule-based system, or even something akin to the original conception of Generalized Phrase Structure Grammar with its system of displaced 'fillers' like *what* and gaps like NP_e. Despite appearances though, the new system is *not* really rule-based, since the principles like the Case filter or Binding theory still apply as before.

We might think of the new covering grammar as a run-time version of a principle-based system where certain of the principles have been 'compiled' together. The covering grammar computation is done off-line, much as a compiler would work. If such a compiler is smart enough, it can detect principle combinations that never arise, and so eliminate predicate tests that would be wasteful. For example, consider $\overline{X}$ theory, phrase movement, and Thematic theory again, in particular the assignment of thematic roles. Assignment occurs only under certain structural configurations. While we could apply the Thematic theory constraints to *all* configurations (as in fact is done by Johnson), in fact this may be computationally inefficient, since assignment patently does not occur in all configurations. We can compute *offline* that thematic role assignment occurs only if the structures involved include the phrasal categories NP, S, and the intermediate phrasal $\overline{X}$ categories $\overline{N}$, $\overline{V}$, $\overline{P}$, and $\overline{A}$(intermediate adjective phrases). We do *not* have to apply the Thematic constraints if the structural configuration happens to include other phrases, like PP, AP, etc. Thus, a clever compiler can save us from much useless work.

Of course, compared to programming languages, we don't know as much yet about natural language grammar 'compiling'. The authors in this book have taken two approaches to this compile-time/run-time trade-off: some, like Dorr, Epstein, Fong, and Kashket, have done it by hand; others, like Johnson in his PAD parsers 3–5, have taken a more formal, automatic route and used the notions of *partial interpretation* and the related notion of *unfold/fold* transformations possible in logic programs (Tamaki and Sato, 1984). The unfold/fold idea, which is a close cousin of the notion of *partial evaluation*, is to run deductive interaction of selected principles for a bounded number of steps, offline and without an input sentence—the principles are 'folded' together to derive new predicates that are a combination of the old. This is a provably valid reaxiomatization of the original system.

To take a simple example in another domain, if we had the combination $\sin(x) \cdot \sin(x) + \cos(x) \cdot \cos(x)$, then we can evaluate this expression offline to $\sin^2(x) + \cos^2(c)$ and then with a second step to 1. Here we have replaced a runtime computation with a constant—some computational work for zero runtime work. Note that this indeed exactly what a programming language compiler tries to do. It is also what the covering grammar method attempts by hand. The great advantage of the fold/unfold method is that the reaxiomatized system is provably equivalent to the original: we are guaranteed that the same parse relation can be deduced in the modified system as before. Ensuring this by hand can be a much more tedious task. Even so, the automatic partial evaluation methods are not completely understood. (For one thing, figuring out where and how deeply to partially evaluate can be difficult, and the resulting system *still* applies the predicates it has folded together to some structures where it cannot possibly succeed. Refer to Correa's efforts at reformulating chain algorithms.) Thus hand-coding covering grammars still has a place in the sun, until we have a better understanding of the trade-offs in offline compilation vs. runtime constraint application.

More importantly for computation, using such a covering grammar gets at the root of one of the problems in recovering the inverse mapping from S- to D-structure—by eliminating D-structure. We can ditch D-structure and incorporate the Theta-criterion and Move-α constraints as well-formedness conditions on representations S-structures—as filters that either let certain S-structures pass or not, rather than as conditions on the derivation of one representation from another. As mentioned earlier, this shift from generative to declarative constraints on representations is another hallmark of the principle-based approach. We have seen that this *seems* to make computation easier, and have given some reasons why, though this has never been formally proved. Correa, Johnson, and Fong all take the line, with Johnson establishing that D-structure surgical removal is logically correct (the same parsing relation can be 'inferred' as before). Historically this line of reasoning extends back to McCawley's 1968 paper viewing context-sensitive rewrite rules as declarative constraints on trees, essentially template filters, *e.g.*, the rules S→NP VP; VP→ Verb+*animate*; NP→noun___V+*animate* is interpreted as admitting a set of trees dominated by an S(entence) node with an NP dominating a noun on the left *if* there is a verb marked +*animate* to the immediate right of the noun. The work of Peters and Ritchie (1973) proved that this declarative formulation was computationally simpler than the generative one, since it admitted only context-free languages despite tapping context-sensitive admissibility conditions like the template above. Modern principle-based theory awaits something like this demonstration as a precise comparison of generative vs. declarative representations of grammars.

5. CONCLUSION

Still, the central achievement of principle-based parsing stands: two decades past the 1960s we now *can* build efficient principle-based parsers. The reason? Our computational armamentarium is stronger. We know more about principle interleaving, freezing, and clause selection. The theory is more constrained: there is no extrinsic ordering or complicated rule conditionals; landing sites are limited by structure preservation, and empty categories are restricted in their distribution.

The moral should be clear. There are more things on a principle-based heaven and earth than dreamed of in a simple philosophy of parsing. Thinking about principles liberates us from the homogeneous rule-based format to open before us much wider logical possibilities for parsing control structures, hence a much wider range of design strategies and psycholinguistic outcomes than before. The working systems and results described in this volume form the beachhead of a much broader wave of principle-based research to come.

ACKNOWLEDGEMENTS

This chapter has benefited from discussion with Steve Abney, Bonnie Dorr, Ed Stabler, and, especially, Sandiway Fong. This work has been supported by NSF Grant DCR-85552543 under a Presidential Young Investigator Award, by the Kapor Family Foundation, and by a John Simon Guggenheim Memorial Fellowship. All remaining errors are of course the responsibility of the author.

NOTES

[1] This shift is certainly not unique to principles-and-parameters theory. Many other current linguistic theories, among them Generalized Phrase Structure Grammar (GPSG) and Head-driven Phrase Structure Grammar), have gradually shifted to declarative constraints that are not construction-specific. For instance, modern GPSG theory is full of principles that fix the well-formedness of surface strings without spelling out explicitly their detailed phrase structure: the Foot Feature Principle, the Head Feature Convention, and the Control Agreement Principle replace explicit phrase structure rules with constraint sets. These theories too no longer contain large numbers of particular rules, but declarative schemas constrained according to syntactic and morphological principles.

[2] As defined here, generate-and-test subsumes the more particular strategy of analysis by synthesis, because in classic analysis-by-synthesis we would enumerate all possible D-structure, S-structure, PFs (and LF) quadruples first, and only then test them against the input sentence PF; generate-and-test subsumes this particular enumeration strategy by admitting any possible sequence of interleaved quadruple generation

and testing against the input.

[3] 'Freezing' is not the sole province of Prolog; it amounts roughly to the delayed binding technique of many other computer programming languages, as described for example for Scheme in Abelson and Sussman (1985).

[4] Indeed, in later work, Fong (1991 forthcoming) adopts just such an approach, *interleaving* structure-building and principle filtering or generating Again, instead of waiting for an entire S-structure to be built before applying any constraints, and then 'tree walking' to jog through the entire structure, checking each constraint, one can combine two or more constraints—say, the Case filter and restrictions on Move-α—into one larger predicate, and use that super-predicate to guarantee that any tree nodes produced incrementally satisfy the constraints to begin with. This method saves the parser's feet from tree walking, and is generally faster; it is a close cousin of partial evaluation or the reaxiomatization 'unfold–fold' technique used by Johnson, described later on.

[5] Emonds' (1976) *Structure Preserving Hypothesis*—that landing sites for moved phrases are also base generated—is of course central to the base generation approach. On the base generation view, it is impossible for there to be a derivational history that records the mapping from D-structure to S-structure and so any approach that relies on intermediate steps between the two in a crucial way—such as first moving a phrase to an intermediate position and then deleting a trace—is not replicable in the base-generation model. The empirical examples that distinguish between the two approaches are quite subtle, however, as has been noted in the literature (see, *e.g.*, Chomsky, 1981, for discussion and the references cited in Correa's chapter). The sheer empirical fact that a context-free base plus movement can be replaced by a structurally equivalent 'covering grammar' that is exactly or close to context-free underscores the connection between the base-generation approach and efforts like GPSG that also strive to eliminate the D-structure to S-structure mapping.

REFERENCES

Abelson, H. and G. Sussman: 1985, *Structure and Interpretation of Computer Programs*, MIT Press, Cambridge, Massachusetts.

Bates, L.: 1978, 'The Theory and Practice of Augmented Transition Network Grammars', in L. Bolc (ed.), *Natural Language Communication with Computers*, Lecture Notes in Computer Science no. 63, Springer-Verlag, New York, pp. 191–260.

Berwick, R.: 1985, *The Acquisition of Syntactic Knowledge*, MIT Press, Cambridge, Massachusetts.

Chomsky, N.: 1953, *Morphophonemics of Modern Hebrew*, Garland Press, New York (republication of M.S. dissertation, University of Pennsylvania).

Chomsky, N.: 1955, 1975, *The Logical Structure of Linguistic Theory*, University of Chicago Press, Chicago, Illinois.

Chomsky, N.: 1981, *Lectures on Government and Binding: The Pisa Lectures*, Foris, Dordrecht, Holland.

Engelfriet, J. and Filè, G., 1979: 'The Formal Power of One-visit Attribute Grammars', Memorandum 217, Twente University of Technology, Twente, Netherlands.

Emonds, J.: 1976, *A Transformational Approach to Syntax*, Academic Press, New York.

Fong, S.: 1991 forthcoming, *Computational Properties of Principle-Based Grammatical Theories*, Ph.D. dissertation, MIT Department of Electrical Engineering and Computer Science, Cambridge, Massachusetts.

Kolb, H. and C. Thiersch: 1988, 'Levels and Empty Categories in a Principles and Parameters Approach to Parsing', unpublished manuscript, Tilburg University, Tilburg, The Netherlands.

Koster, J.: 1978, 'Conditions, Empty Nodes, and Markedness', *Linguistic Inquiry* 9, 551–593.

Lasnik, H. and J. Uriagereka: 1988, *A Course in GB Syntax: Lectures on Binding and Empty Categories*, MIT Press, Cambridge, Mass.

Marcus, M.: 1980, *A Theory of Syntactic Recognition for Natural Language*, MIT Press, Cambridge, Massachusetts.

Marr, D.: 1982, *Vision*, W.H. Freeman, San Francisco, California.

McCawley, J.: 1968, 'Concerning the Base Component of Transformational Grammar', *Foundations of Language* 4, 55–81.

Peters, S. and R. Ritchie: 1973, 'Context-Sensitive Immediate Constituent Analysis: Context-Free Languages Revisited', *Mathematical Systems Theory* 6, 324–333.

Petrick, S.: 1965, *A Recognition Procedure for Transformational Grammars*, Ph.D. dissertation, Department of Linguistics, Massachusetts Institute of Technology, Cambridge, Massachusetts.

Petrick, S.: 1973, 'Transformational Analysis', in R. Rustin (ed.), *Natural Language Processing*, Algorithmics Press, New York, pp. 27–41.

Sharp, R.: 1985, *A Model of Grammar Based on Principles of Government and Binding*, M.S. dissertation, Department of Computer Science, University of British Columbia, Vancouver, British Columbia.

Smith, D. and M. Genesereth: 1985, 'Ordering Conjunctive Queries', *Artificial Intelligence* 26, 171–215.

Stabler, E.: 1991 forthcoming, *The Logical Approach to Syntax: Foundations, Specifications and Implementations of Theories of Government and Binding*, MIT Press, Cambridge, Massachusetts.

Tamaki, H. and T. Sato: 1984, 'Unfold/Fold Transformation of Logic Programs', *Proceedings of The Second International Logic Programming Conference*, Uppsala University, Uppsala, Sweden, pp. 127–138.

Zwicky, A., J. Friedman, B. Hall, and D. Walker: 1965, 'The MITRE Syntactic Analysis Procedure for Transformational Grammars', *Proceedings of the 1965 Fall Joint Computer Conference* 27, Spartan Books, Washington, D.C., pp. 317–326.

MIT Artificial Intelligence Laboratory, Rm. 838,
545 Technology Square,
Cambridge, MA   02139, U.S.A.

MARK JOHNSON

DEDUCTIVE PARSING: THE USE OF KNOWLEDGE
OF LANGUAGE

1. INTRODUCTION

Current linguistic theory distinguishes a competent speaker's knowledge of a language from the way in which that knowledge is used. This chapter describes a framework for modeling the relationship between knowledge of language and its use. The 'Parsing as Deduction' framework[1] models knowledge of a language as an axiom system, and knowledge about the utterances of that language as logical consequences of these axioms. The use of knowledge of a language to generate knowledge about some particular utterance can then be regarded as the deduction of the relevant consequences in the theory defined by the axioms.

This chapter introduces the Parsing as Deduction (PAD) approach and shows that it can provide an explanation of how it is that knowledge of a language of the form attributed to human language users by modern Government-Binding (GB) theory (Chomsky, 1981; van Riemsdijk and Williams, 1986) can generate knowledge of the utterances of that language.[2] This demonstration introduces a sequence of simple deductive parsers for GB theory which are explicitly constructed to incorporate some of the features of that theory that distinguish it from other current linguistic theories. The parsers take Phonetic form (PF) representations as their input and produce Logical form (LF) representations as their output, and unlike many GB parsers, make explicit use of the four levels of representation that GB attributes to an utterance, viz. D-structure, S-structure, PF, and LF. A 'grammar' for these parsers consists entirely of a set of parameter values for the principles of GB theory, and the parsers' top-level internal structure transparently reflects some of the principles of that theory; thus $\overline{X}$ and thematic or theta (θ) theories apply at D-structure, Case theory applies at S-structure, Move-α is stated as a relation between D- and S-structure, and LF-movement relates S-structure and LF.[3]

Viewing parsers as highly specialized inference procedures naturally distinguishes the knowledge of language used by the parser (embodied as

39

R. C. Berwick et al. (eds.),
Principle-Based Parsing: Computation and Psycholinguistics, 39–64.
© 1991 *Kluwer Academic Publishers. Printed in the Netherlands.*

axioms and inference rules) from the manner in which this knowledge is put to use (the inference control strategy that directs the application of the inference rules). All of the parsers discussed in this chapter use the same 'knowledge of language'; they differ only in how they put it to use. The choice of inference control strategy is a major determinant of the computational efficiency of the parser. I describe an inference control strategy in which the parser 'coroutines' between the principles of grammar, ensuring that all existing nodes are well-formed before constructing any new nodes.

Finally, I discuss a conceptual shift embodied in the deductive language processing. Most parsing models are *representation-oriented*, in that the processor's task is taken to be the construction of a representation or representations of the utterance to be parsed. In contrast, the deductive model of processing is knowledge-oriented; the emphasis is on the knowledge of a language used by the processor to infer knowledge of an utterance of that language (the one being parsed or generated), and the control strategy that specifies how this knowledge will be used. Use of knowledge about a level of representation does not entail the explicit construction of that representation, as I demonstrate by exhibiting a parser that uses knowledge of D-structures in the parsing process, yet avoids the explicit construction of this level of representation.

In the remainder of this section I sketch the aspects of GB theory relevant to the discussion below; for more detail the reader should consult one of the standard texts (*e.g.*, van Riemsdijk and Williams, 1986).

Chomsky (1986, p. 3) identifies the following three basic questions in the study of language.

(1) (a) What constitutes knowledge of language?

     (b) How is knowledge of language acquired?

     (c) How is knowledge of language put to use?

Chomsky's GB theory directly addresses questions (1a) and (1b), and the Parsing as Deduction hypothesis provides a possible answer to question (1c). GB theory posits four distinct representations of an utterance, D-structure, S- structure, PF and LF. To a first approximation, D-structure configurationally represents the thematic or predicate-argument structure of the utterance, S-structure represents the utterance's surface grammatical structure, PF represents its phonetic form, and LF represents the scopal relationships between the quantificational

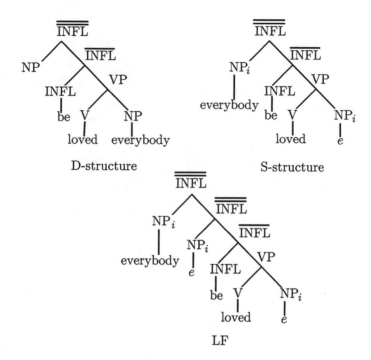

Figure 1: Levels of representation of GB theory.

elements present in the utterance. The PF and LF representations constitute the interface between language and other cognitive systems external to the language module (Chomsky, 1986, p. 68). For example,
the PF representation *Everybody is loved* together with the D-structure,
S-structure and LF representations shown in figure 1 might constitute a
well-formed quadruple for English.

In order for such a quadruple to be well-formed it must satisfy all of
the principles of grammar; *e.g.*, the D-structure and S-structure must be
related by Move-a, the D-structure must satisfy $\overline{X}$ theory and θ theory,
and so forth. This is shown schematically in figure 2, where the shaded
rounded boxes indicate the four levels of representation, the boxes indicate relations that must hold simultaneously between pairs of structures,
and the ellipses designate properties that must hold of a single structure. This diagram is based on the organization of GB theory sketched

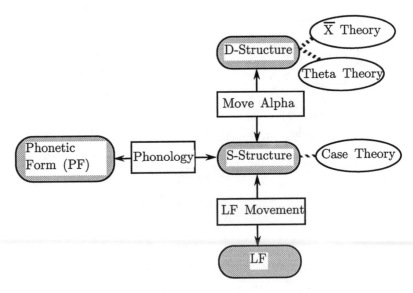

Figure 2: The organization of (some of) the principles of GB theory.

by van Riemsdijk and Williams (1986, p. 310), and represents the organization of principles and structures incorporated in the parsers discussed below.

The principles of grammar are parameterized, so that the structures they admit depends on the value of these parameters. These principles are hypothesized to be innate (and hence universally true of all human languages, thus they are often called *Universal Grammar*), so the extra knowledge that a human requires in order to know a language consists entirely of the values (or settings) of the parameters plus the lexicon for the language concerned. The syntax of the English fragment accepted by the parsers discussed below is completely specified by the following list of parameters. The first two parameters determine the $\overline{\text{X}}$ component, the third parameter determines the Move-α relation, and the fourth parameter identifies the direction of Case assignment.

(2) headFirst.
    specFirst.
    movesInSyntax(np).
    rightwardCaseAssignment.

2. THE PARSING AS DEDUCTION HYPOTHESIS

As just outlined, GB theory decomposes a competent user's knowledge of a language possessed into two components: (i) the universal component (Universal Grammar), which is the knowledge of language possessed by every human language user, and (ii) a set of parameter values and a lexicon, which together constitute the knowledge of that particular language above and beyond the universal component. Universal Grammar is presumably part of the human genetic endowment, whereas the specific knowledge of a particular language over and above UG must be learned by each language user.

The relationship between these two components of a human's knowledge of a language and the knowledge of the utterances of that language that they induce can be formally described as follows: we regard Universal Grammar as a theory in the formal logic sense, *i.e.*, a deductively closed set of statements expressed in a specialized (formal) language,[4] and the lexicon and parameter values that constitute the specific knowledge of a human language beyond Universal Grammar as a set of formulae in that logical language. In the context of the theory of of Universal Grammar, these formulae imply statements describing the linguistic properties of utterances of that human language; these statements constitute knowledge of utterances that the parser has obtained from its knowledge of language.

In its weakest form the Parsing as Deduction hypothesis merely claims that there is calculus capable of deriving linguistic knowledge of utterances (*e.g.*, their well-formedness, and so forth) from (an axiomatization of) knowledge of a language (*e.g.*, its grammar), which is equivalent to the claim that knowledge of utterances can be effectively enumerated from knowledge of language (assuming that the Church-Turing thesis is correct). Although even this weak formulation may be incorrect, I am primarily interested in a stronger interpretation of the hypothesis: that the computational processes underlying language use can be profitably viewed as a sequence of deductive operations applied to expressions that are interpreted as denoting linguistic entities. Under this interpretation the hypothesis could 'fail' in an additional way: it may not be possible to provide a consistent semantics for the expressions used in the computation in such a way that the computational steps can be interpreted as (validity-preserving) deductive steps.[5]

The nature of the logical language used by the parser and the linguistic properties attributed by the parser to utterances are matters for empirical investigation. The parsers presented below use the Horn-clause subset of first-order logic as their logical language, and the linguistic properties of utterances they compute are instances of the 'parse' relation. This relation is true of a PF-LF pair if and only if there is a D-structure and an S-structure such that the D-structure, S-structure, PF, LF quadruple is well-formed with respect to all of the (parameterized) principles of grammar. That is, I am assuming for simplicity that the language processor can be viewed as computing specific instances of the 'parse' relation, *i.e.*, the input to the language processor are PF representations and that the processor produces the corresponding LF representations as output.[6]

The relationship between the parameter settings and lexicon to the 'parse' relation is sketched in figure 3.[7]

The Horn clause subset of first-order logic used here to express knowledge of language and utterances was chosen purely on the basis of its familiarity and simplicity, and no theoretical significance should be attached to it. There are three distinct components to a deductive parser:

(3) (a) the language(s) in which inferences are expressed;

    (b) the inference rules, which specify the allowable manipulations of the statements of that logical language; and

    (c) the control strategy, which directs the application of these inference rules.

The inference rules constitute the basic operations of the inference procedure. The control strategy specifies the manner in which a inference procedure uses the inference rules to determine the consequences of its axioms. It corresponds directly to the control strategy of a parser; just as there are top-down, bottom-up, deterministic and nondeterministic parsing strategies there are top-down, bottom-up, deterministic and nondeterministic inference control strategies (Kowalski, 1980). Indeed,

Knowledge of the Language

Parameter Settings   headFirst.
                          specFirst.
                          movesInSyntax(np).
                          rightwardCaseAssignment.

Lexicon   thetaAssigner(love).
                          thetaAssigner(loved).
                          nonThetaAssigner(love).
                          . . .

.........⇓ imply in the theory of Universal Grammar.........
Knowledge of Utterances of the Language.

parse([everybody,-s,love,somebody],
    [everybody$_i$ [somebody$_j$ [$_{\bar{I}}$ [$_{NP}$ e_i]
    [$_{\bar{I}}$ [$_I$ -s] [[$_{\bar{V}}$ [$_V$ love] [$_{NP}$ e_j]]]]]]])

parse([everybody,-s,love,somebody],
    [everybody$_j$ [somebody$_i$ [$_{\bar{I}}$ [$_{NP}$ e_i]
    [$_{\bar{I}}$ [$_I$ -s] [[$_{\bar{V}}$ [$_V$ love] [$_{NP}$ e_j]]]]]]])

Figure 3: Knowledge of a language and its utterances.

many parsing algorithms naturally generalize to inference control strategies (Pereira and Warren, 1983; Pereira and Shieber, 1987). While
simple-minded control strategies perform inferences in a 'blind' fashion by simply enumerating all possible consequences of their axioms,
there are goal-directed control strategies that direct the application of
inference rules such that the inference process takes place relatively efficiently.

Finally, while inference procedures for general purpose theorem provers are usually required to be sound and complete (*i.e.*, the procedure is
capable of deducing exactly all of the logical consequences of the axioms),
it seems likely that the inference procedure employed by the human
language processor is logically incomplete; *i.e.*, there are properties of
utterances that follow logically from the grammar, but the processor
is unable to find them. Following Marcus (1980) we might attempt
to explain garden path effects in this fashion, perhaps in terms of the
interaction between a deterministic control strategy and a restriction on
the architecture of the working memory available to the processor.

The Parsing as Deduction hypothesis is theoretically attractive for
a number of reasons. First, one of the key assumptions in GB theory
is that the parameter settings and the lexicon of a language constitute
the knowledge of a language (over and above the principles of Universal
Grammar) that a language learner acquires. But merely acquiring the
parameter settings for a language is only half the story. We must show
how these settings can be put to use in order for the account of acquisition to be complete. That is, we must show how a language learner
can use the parameter settings that determine a language to obtain a
parser for that language. But this presupposes a systematic connection
between parameter settings and parsers that can be exploited to generate a parser of exactly the kind provided by the Parsing as Deduction
hypothesis.[8]

Second, the Parsing as Deduction hypothesis cleanly separates the
knowledge of language used by the processor from the use to which that
knowledge is put. For example, the same knowledge of language can be
used by both the parser and the generator, thus explaining why it is
that the language that we speak is by and large the language that we
hear.[9] Propositional knowledge is often more flexible than procedural
knowledge, in that it can often be applied in a variety of different ways
to different tasks. To the extent that knowledge of language is in fact
applied to a variety of different tasks, this is an argument for a propo-

sitional encoding of that knowledge, and thus the Parsing as Deduction hypothesis.

Third, modern GB theory incorporates a substantial deductive structure. Rather than describing a construction such as Passive in terms of a single rule that produces such a construction, the properties of passive and other constructions follows from a complex interaction of the principles of Universal Grammar, in this case, θ theory, Case theory, and Move-α. Parsers guided by procedural rules, such as the parser described by Marcus (1980), can only indirectly exploit the deductive structure of the theory of grammar, whereas deductive parsers can exploit it directly. Thus if it is in fact the case that the correct theory of grammar has a rich deductive structure, we might expect that the processor to be deductively based in order to exploit this structure.

However, I consider the major reason for pursuing the Parsing as Deduction hypothesis to be that it enables a number of interesting questions about language processing to be formulated with respect to a model firmly connected to specific assumptions about linguistic theory and grammar. The clean separation of the declarative specification of the knowledge used in the parsing process from the procedural specification of the inference control strategy provides a foundation on which many interesting ideas about language processing can be developed and empirically tested with respect to specific assumptions about the knowledge of language employed.

3. THE LOGICAL STRUCTURE OF THE PAD PARSERS

In this section I begin describing a sequence of model deductive parsers for GB called the PAD parsers. The primary purpose of the PAD parsers is to demonstrate that deductive parsers for GB can actually be constructed. These implementations demonstrate that GB deductive parsers are physically realizable. All of the PAD parsers use the same knowledge of language (but see the caveat on PAD1 below); they differ only as to how they put it to use. The following summarizes the parsers discussed below.

(4)

Parser	Important Features
PAD1	Generate-and-test control strategy
PAD2	Coroutine control strategy
PAD3	Reaxiomatization of UG with same effect as coroutining in PAD2
PAD4	Reaxiomatization of UG that avoids D-structure construction
PAD5	Reaxiomatization that avoids D- and S-structure construction

The PAD parsers incorporate several of the features that distinguish GB from other theories of grammar. These parsers differ from many other extant GB parsers in that they make crucial use of all four levels of representation of GB theory. In particular, the constraints on S-structures that result from the interaction of Move-α with principles constraining D-structure (*i.e.*, $\overline{X}$ and θ theories) are used constructively throughout the parsing process. For example, PAD has no direct specification of a 'rule' of passive, but it does possess the relevant knowledge of $\overline{X}$ theory and θ theory, both applying at D-structure, Case theory applying at S-structure, and the Move-α relation to deduce the properties of the passive construction. None of the parsers employ ad hoc (and often computationally inefficient) devices such as 'covering S-structure grammars' to generate candidate S-structures that are then filtered by the principles of grammar.

The PAD parsers are only 'model' parsers. The fragment of English they accept could only be called 'restricted'. They have no account of *Wh*-movement, for example, and incorporate none of the principles of Bounding theory. The Move-α component is also simplified, in that at most one node can be moved over any other node. Because PAD1 uses a 'generate-and-test' control strategy, it only terminates if its $\overline{X}$ component generates only a finite number of D-structures: the other parsers have no such restriction. For simplicity all of the parsers employ a top-down control strategy inherited from the underlying Prolog implementation and thus may fail to terminate if left-recursive structures are admitted, but it is straightforward to extend the left-corner techniques described by Pereira and Shieber (1987) to avoid this problem.

According to the Parsing as Deduction hypothesis, the parser is effectively a special-purpose inference procedure computing over the theory of Universal Grammar. To construct a deductive parser for GB one builds a specialized theorem-prover for GB theory, provides it with parameter settings and a lexicon as axioms, and uses it to derive the consequences of these axioms that describe the utterance of interest.

The inference procedure for Universal Grammar utilized by the PAD parsers is constructed using a Horn-clause theorem-prover (a Prolog interpreter). The Horn-clause theorem-prover is provided with an axiomatization U of the theory of Universal Grammar as well as the hypotheses H that represent the parameter settings and lexicon. Since a set of hypotheses H imply a consequence F in the theory of Universal Grammar if and only if $H \cup U$ implies F in first-order logic, a Horn-clause theorem-prover using axiomatization U is capable of deriving the consequences that follow from H in the theory of Universal Grammar. In effect, the PAD parsers use a first-order logic theorem-prover and the axiomatization U together to 'simulate' a special-purpose inference procedure for the theory of Universal Grammar.[10] Thus the PAD parsers have the logical structure diagrammed in figure 4 on the next page.

The clause given in figure 4 as part of the axiomatization of GB theory is the actual Prolog code used in the PAD1 and PAD2 parsers to represent the top-level structure of the 'parse' relation. This clause can be represented in standard first-order logic as:

(5) $\forall ds,\, ss,\, lf,\, pf, \overline{X}(ds) \,\wedge\, \theta(ds) \,\wedge\, \text{Move-}\alpha(ds, ss)$
$\quad\quad \text{Case}(ss) \,\wedge\, \text{Phonology}(pf, ss) \,\wedge\, \text{LfMovement}(ss, lf) \Rightarrow$
$\quad\quad \text{Parse}(pf, lf).$

Thus the top level structure of the knowledge of language employed by these parsers mirrors the top level structure of GB theory.

Ideally the internal structure of the various principles of grammar should reflect the internal organization of the principles of GB (*e.g.*, Case assignment should be defined in terms of Government), but for reasons of simplicity and ease of presentation the principles are axiomatized directly here. For reasons of space a complete description of the all of the principles is not given here; however a sketch of one of the principles, the Case filter, is given in the remainder of this section. The other principles are implemented in a similar fashion.

The Case filter as formulated in PAD applies recursively throughout the S-structure, associating each node with one of the three atomic values *assigner*, *receiver*, or *null*. These values represent the Case properties of the node they are associated with; a node associated with the property *assigner* must be a Case assigner, a node associated with the property

Knowledge of Language

Axiomatization of Universal Grammar

parse(String, LF) :—
xBar(infl2,DS),
theta(infl2,0,DS),
moveAlpha(DS,[],SS,[]),
caseFilter(infl2,0,SS),
phonology(String/[],SS),
lfMovement(SS,LF).

Parameter Settings

headFirst.
specFirst.
movesInSyntax(np).
rightwardCaseAssignment.

Lexicon

thetaAssigner(love).
thetaAssigner(loved).
nonThetaAssigner(love).
. . .

. . . . $\Downarrow$ imply in First-order Logic . . . .
Knowledge of Utterances of the Language.

parse([everybody,-s,love,somebody],
  [everybody$_i$ [somebody$_j$ [$_{\bar{I}}$ [$_{NP}$ e_i]
   [$_{\bar{I}}$ [$_I$ -s] [[$_{\bar{V}}$ [$_V$ love] [$_{NP}$ e_j]]]]]]])

parse([everybody,-s,love,somebody],
  [everybody$_j$ [somebody$_i$ [$_{\bar{I}}$ [$_{NP}$ e_i]
   [$_{\bar{I}}$ [$_I$ -s] [[$_{\bar{V}}$ [$_V$ love] [$_{NP}$ e_j]]]]]]])

Figure 4: The structure of the PAD parsers.

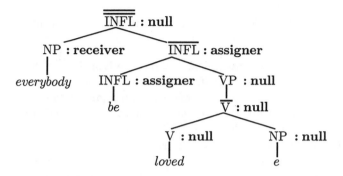

Figure 5: The Case properties associated with nodes.

receiver must be capable of being assigned Case, and a node associated with the property *null* must be neutral with respect to Case. The Case Filter determines if there is an assignment of these values to nodes in the tree consistent with the principles of Case assignment. A typical assignment of Case properties to the nodes of an S-structure in English is shown in figure 5, where the Case properties of a node are depicted by the boldface annotations on that node.[11,12]

The Case filter is parameterized with respect to the predicates 'rightwardCaseAssignment' and 'leftwardCaseAssignment'; if these are specified as parameter settings of the language concerned, the Case filter permits Case assigners and receivers to appear in the relevant linear order. The lexicon contains definitions of the one-place predicates 'noCase', 'assignsCase' and 'needsCase' which hold of lexical items with the relevant property; these predicates are used by the Case filter to ensure the associations of Case properties with lexical items are valid.

Specifically, the Case filter licenses the following structures:

(6) (a) a constituent with no Case properties may have a Case assigner and a Case receiver as daughters iff they are in an appropriate order for the language concerned;

(b) a constituent with no Case properties may have any number of daughters with no Case properties;

(c) a constituent with Case property C may be realized as a lexical item W if W is permitted by the lexicon to have Case property C; and

(d) Infl(ection) (Ī) assigns Case to its left if its I(nfl) daughter is a Case assigner.

This last statement appears to be a 'glitch' in the formulation of the Case filter, but in fact it reflects a 'glitch' in the version of GB on which PAD is based. In this version Case assignment to subject position does not follow from the general principles of Case assignment, rather 'something extra' needs to be stated; this 'extra statement' appears as the last statement of the Case filter.

This axiomatization of Universal Grammar together with the parameter values and lexicon for English is used as the axiom set of a Prolog interpreter to produce the parser called PAD1. Its typical behavior is shown below.[13]

:parse([everybody, − s, love, somebody], LF)
LF = everybody::iˆ somebody::jˆ infl2:
              [np:i, infl1:[infl: # (− s), vp:[v1:[v: # love, np:j]]]]
LF = somebody::jˆ everybody::iˆ infl2:
              [np:i, infl1:[infl: # (− s), vp:[v1:[v: # love, np:j]]]]
No (more) solutions

:parse([sally, − s, sleep], LF)
LF = infl2:[np: # sally, infl1:[infl: # (− s), vp:[v1:[v: # sleep]]]]
No (more) solutions

:parse([harry, be, loved], LF)
LF = infl2:[np: # harry, infl1:[infl: # be, vp:[v1:[v # loved, np:[]]]]]
No (more) solutions

4. AN ALTERNATIVE CONTROL STRUCTURE FOR PAD

Because it uses the SLD inference control strategy of Prolog with the axiomatization of Universal Grammar shown above, PAD1 functions as a 'generate-and-test' parser. Specifically, it enumerates all D-structures that satisfy $\overline{X}$ theory, filters those that fail to satisfy θ theory, computes the corresponding S-structures using Move-α, removes all S-structures that fail to satisfy the Case filter, and only then determines if the terminal string of the S-structure is the string it was given to parse. If the

$\overline{\mathrm{X}}$ principle admits infinitely many D-structures the resulting procedure is only a semi-decision procedure, *i.e.*, the parser is not guaranteed to terminate on ungrammatical input.

Clearly the PAD1 parser does not use its knowledge of language in an efficient manner. It would be more efficient to coroutine between the principles of grammar, checking each existing node for well-formedness with respect to these principles and ensuring that the terminal string of the partially constructed S-structure matches the string to be parsed before creating any additional nodes. Because the Parsing as Deduction framework conceptually separates the knowledge used by the processor from the manner in which that knowledge is used, it is straightforward to specify an inference control strategy that applies the principles of grammar in the manner just described. The PAD2 parser incorporates the same knowledge of language as PAD1 (in fact textually identical), but it uses an inference control strategy inspired by the 'freeze' predicate of Prolog-II (Cohen, 1985; Giannesini *et al.*, 1986) to achieve this goal. Because PAD2 uses this control strategy it is not necessary to require that the $\overline{\mathrm{X}}$ principles generate only finitely many D-structures.

The control strategy used in PAD2 allows inferences using specified predicates to be delayed until certain arguments of these predicates are at least partially instantiated. When some other application of an inference rule instantiates such an argument the current sequence of inferences is suspended and the delayed inference performed immediately. Below we list the predicates that are delayed in this manner, and the argument that they require to be at least partially instantiated before inferences using them will proceed.

(7)

Predicate	Delayed on
$\overline{\mathrm{X}}$	D-structure
θ theory	D-structure
Move-α	S-structure
Case filter	S-structure
Phonology	not delayed
LF-Movement	S-structure

With this control strategy the parsing process proceeds as follows. Inferences using the $\overline{\mathrm{X}}$, θ, Case, Move-α and LF-movement principles are immediately delayed since the relevant structures are uninstantiated. The 'phonology' principle (a simple recursive tree-walking predicate that collects terminal items) is not delayed, so the parser begins

performing inferences associated with it. These instantiate the top node
of the S-structure, so the delayed inferences resulting from the Case
filter, Move-α and LF-movement are performed. The inferences associated with Move-α result in the instantiation of the top node(s) of the
D-structure, and hence the delayed inferences associated with the $\overline{X}$ and
θ principles are also performed. Only after all of the principles have applied to the S-structure node instantiated by the 'phonology' relation and
the corresponding D-structure node(s) instantiated by Move-α are any
further inferences associated with the 'phonology' relation performed,
causing the instantiation of further S-structure nodes and repetition of
the cycle of activation and delaying.

Thus the PAD2 parser simultaneously constructs D-structure, S-
structure and LF representations in a top-down left-to-right fashion,
functioning in effect as a recursive descent parser. This top-down behavior is not an essential property of a parser such as PAD2; using
techniques based on those described by Pereira and Shieber (1987) and
Cohen and Hickey (1987) it is possible to construct parsers that use the
same knowledge of language in a bottom-up fashion.

One of the interesting aspects of the Parsing as Deduction framework is that it permits the investigation of different control strategies
with respect to a fixed body of knowledge of language.[14] By using an
inference control strategy that is sensitive to the instantiation of the
partially constructed representations of the utterances it is possible to
use the knowledge of language incorporated into the PAD parsers in an
efficient manner. An interesting (and potentially difficult) research topic
would be to investigate the relationship between parser performance and
control strategy over a variety of different inputs, and compare this with
actual psycholinguistic performance data, thus perhaps providing psychological evidence that the human parser uses some particular control
strategy.

5. USING KNOWLEDGE VS. CONSTRUCTING REPRESENTATIONS

Most work in computational linguistics and psycholinguistics tacitly assumes that the task of a parser for a particular theory of grammar is
the construction of at least some of the syntactic representations posited
by that theory, and the claim that a processor uses a particular level of
representation is often viewed as entailing that it constructs that level

of representation. However, in this section I show that the Parsing as Deduction framework allows us to separate the use of knowledge of a syntactic representation from its explicit construction, and demonstrate the former does not imply the later. I do this by exhibiting two deductive parsers that make crucial use of knowledge of D-structures, yet do not construct any such structures.

In fact this should be an uncontroversial point, since many standard parsing algorithms avoid the explicit construction any syntactic representation. For example, even though there are context-free grammar in which some strings of length n are $O(c \cdot n)$ ways ambiguous (and thus any parser which enumerated all tree structures dominating such strings would require exponential time) the Earley algorithm is capable of recognizing any string of length n generated by such a grammar in at most n^3 time. This is possible precisely because the Earley algorithm does not enumerate all trees dominating the input string. The PAD4 parser avoids explicit construction of D-structures, and the PAD5 parser avoids explicit construction of both D-structures and S-structures. The PAD3 parser serves as an introduction to the PAD4 and PAD5 parsers; it constructs both D-structures and S-structures. (The PAD parsers produce LF representations as output, hence all of the PAD parsers explicitly construct LF representations). These parsers use the same parameter settings and lexicon as PAD1 and PAD2, and they provably compute the same PF-LF relationship as PAD2 does. The particular techniques used to construct PAD3–5 parsers depend on the internal details of the formulation of the principles of grammar adopted here and are not of intrinsic interest, and I do not claim that they will generalize to other formulations of these principles. Nevertheless, their existence demonstrates that the fact that a language processor makes explicit use of knowledge of D-structure and S-structure does not imply that that processor actually constructs these representations. It may be the case that the human language processor does in fact construct both the D-structures and S-structures of the utterances it processes, but this would then be a contingent rather than a necessary fact.[15]

Recall that the knowledge of a language incorporated in PAD1 and PAD2 consists of two separate components, (i) parameter values and a lexicon, and (ii) an axiomatization U of the theory of Universal Grammar. The axiomatization U specifies the deductively closed set of statements that constitute the theory of Universal Grammar, and clearly any axiomatization U' equivalent to U (i.e., one that axiomatizes the same set of statements) defines exactly the same theory of Universal Grammar. Thus the original axiomatization U of Universal Grammar used in the PAD parsers can be replaced with any equivalent axiomatization U' and the resulting system will entail exactly the same knowledge of the utterances of the language.[16]

A deductive parser using U' in place of U may perform a different sequence of inference steps[17] but ultimately it will infer an identical set of consequences.[18] Usually the reaxiomatization U' is chosen so that the resulting parser possesses certain desirable properties; for example, it may perform more efficiently, or, as in the case described here, it may perform its computation in a special way. There are standard techniques for replacing an axiomatization with an equivalent reaxiomatization that is often more efficiently computationally when used with a fixed inference control strategy, such as the SLD control strategy of Prolog (see *e.g.*, Pereira and Shieber, 1987). The PAD3 parser uses the same parameter values and lexicon as PAD1 and PAD2, but it uses a reaxiomatization of Universal Grammar obtained by applying the unfold/fold transformation described and proved correct by Tamaki and Sato (1984). Essentially, the unfold/fold transformation is used here to replace a sequence of predicates each of that recursively traverses the same structure by a single predicate recursive on that structure that requires every node in that structure to meet all of the constraints imposed by the original sequence of predicates. In the PAD3 parser the $\overline{\mathrm{X}}$, θ (theta), Move-α, Case, and Phonology principles are folded and replaced by the single predicate p that holds of exactly the D-structure, S-structure PF triples admitted by the conjunction of the original principles, effectively 'compiling' the coroutining strategy of PAD2 into the single predicate p. The structure of PAD3 is shown in figure 6.

Because the reaxiomatization technique used here replaces the original axiomatization with a provably equivalent one, the PAD3 parser provably infers exactly the same knowledge of language as PAD1 and PAD2. Because PAD3's knowledge of the principles of grammar that relate D-structure, S-structure and PF is now represented by the single recursive predicate p that checks the well-formedness of a node with respect to all of the relevant principles, PAD3 exhibits the coroutining behavior of PAD2 rather than the 'generate-and-test' behavior of PAD1, even when used with the standard SLD inference control strategy of Prolog.[19] PAD3 constructs D-structures, just as PAD1 and PAD2 do. However, a simple analysis of the data dependencies in PAD3 (now

Knowledge of Language

Reaxiomatization of Universal Grammar
parse(PF,LF) :—
(PF/[],DS,SS,infl2,0,[],[],0),
lfMovement(SS,LF).

....

Parameter Settings
headFirst.
specFirst.
movesInSyntax(np).
rightwardCaseAssignment.

Lexicon   thetaAssigner(love).

thetaAssigner(loved).
nonThetaAssigner(love).

...

.... ⇓ imply in First-order Logic ....
Knowledge of Utterances of the Language.

parse([everybody,-s,love,somebody],
    [everybody$_i$ [somebody$_j$ [$_{\bar{I}}$ [$_{NP}$ e_i]
    [$_{\bar{I}}$ [$_I$ -s] [[$_{\bar{V}}$ [$_V$ love] [$_{NP}$ e_j]]]]]]])

parse([everybody,-s,love,somebody],
    [everybody$_j$ [somebody$_i$ [$_{\bar{I}}$ [$_{NP}$ e_i]
    [$_{\bar{I}}$ [$_I$ -s] [[$_{\bar{V}}$ [$_V$ love] [$_{NP}$ e_j]]]]]]])

Figure 6: The structure of the PAD3 parser.

viewed as a computer program) shows that in this particular case no predicate uses the D-structure value returned by a call to predicate p; even when p calls itself recursively, the D-structure value it returns is ignored). Therefore replacing the predicate p with a predicate p' exactly equivalent to p except that it avoids construction of any D-structures does not affect the set of conclusions computed by this program.[20] The PAD4 parser is exactly the same as the PAD3 parser, except that it uses the predicate p' instead of p, so it therefore computes exactly the same PF-LF relationship as all of the other PAD parsers, but it avoids the construction of any D-structure nodes. That is, the PAD4 parser makes use of exactly the same parameter settings and lexicon as the other PAD parsers, and it uses this knowledge to compute exactly the same knowledge of utterances. It differs from the other PAD parsers in that it does not use this knowledge to explicitly construct a D-structure representation of the utterance it is parsing.

This same combination of the unfold/fold transformation followed by a data dependency analysis can also be performed on all of the principles of grammar simultaneously. The unfold/fold transformation produces a predicate in which a data-dependency analysis identifies both D-structure and S-structure values as ignored and hence deletable. The PAD5 parser uses the resulting predicate as its axiomatization of Universal Grammar, thus PAD5 is a parser which uses exactly the same parameter values and lexicon as the earlier parsers to compute exactly the same PF-LF relationship as these parsers, but it does so without explicitly constructing either D-structures or S-structures.

To summarize, this section describes three parsers. The first, PAD3, utilized a reaxiomatization of Universal Grammar, which when coupled with the SLD inference control strategy of Prolog resulted in a parser that constructs D-structures and S-structures 'in parallel', much like PAD2. A data dependency analysis of the PAD3 program revealed that the D-structures computed were never used, and PAD4 exploits this fact to avoid the construction of D-structures entirely. The techniques used to generate PAD4 were also used to generate PAD5, which avoids the explicit construction of both D-structures and S-structures. All these parsers make use of knowledge of D-structure: the parameter values and lexical information relevant to $\overline{\text{X}}$ and θ theory specify constraints on the D-structure representations of utterances of the language. PAD1–3 ensure that the D-structures satisfy these constraints by explicitly constructing and testing them. PAD4 and PAD5 avoid the explicit construction of D-structure by enforcing other constraints that ensure that such a D-structure could in fact be constructed if desired. PAD4 and PAD5 use knowledge of the constraints that apply to D-structure to do this; thus they show that use of knowledge of a representation of GB theory does not imply its explicit construction.

6. CONCLUSION

This chapter describes several deductive parsers for GB theory. The knowledge of language that they use incorporates the top-level structure of GB theory, thus demonstrating that parsers can actually be built that directly reflect the structure of this theory. I argued that the definite connection between the theory of grammar and a parser for that grammar of the kind posited by the Parsing as Deduction hypothesis has several theoretical advantages with respect to language acquisition, the nature of knowledge of language and the multiple uses to which that knowledge can be put.

This work might be extended in several ways. First, the fragment of English covered by the parser could be extended to include a wider range of linguistic phenomena. It would be interesting to determine if the techniques described here to axiomatize the principles of grammar and to reaxiomatize Universal Grammar to avoid the construction of D-structures could be used on this enlarged fragment. Johnson (1989) describes a slightly more complex axiomatization of Move-α than the one employed in the PAD parsers, and shows that while the coroutining techniques of PAD2 and the unfold/fold transformation of PAD3–5 yield only semi-decision procedures with this axiomatization, there is an axiom transformation that yields an equivalent top-down parser.

Second, the axiomatization of the principles of Universal Grammar could be reformulated to incorporate the 'internal' deductive structure of the components of GB theory. For example, one might define c-command or government as primitives, and define the principles in terms of these. It would be interesting to determine if a deductive parser can take advantage of this internal deductive structure in the same way that the PAD parsers utilized the deductive relationships between the various principles of grammar. Exactly how this could be done is still unknown, and one of the most complex (and interesting) aspects of deductive parsing is determining the relationship between the precise form of the axiomatization of knowledge of language and the inference control strategies that most successfully put it to use.

Third, it would be interesting to investigate the performance of parsers using various inference control strategies. The coroutining strategy employed by PAD2 is of obvious interest, as are its deterministic and nondeterministic bottom-up and left-corner variants. In fact, variants of the PAD parser and its descendants currently exist that use Earley deduction and left-corner control strategies (Pereira and Warren 1983; Pereira and Shieber, 1987). These only scratch the surface of possibilities, since the Parsing as Deduction framework allows one to straightforwardly formulate control strategies sensitive to the various principles of grammar. For example, it is easy to specify inference control strategies that delay all computations concerning particular principles (e.g., binding theory) until the end of the parsing process.

Fourth, one might attempt to develop specialized logical languages that are capable of expressing knowledge of languages and knowledge of utterances in a more succinct and computationally useful fashion than the first-order languages. Currently it is not clear exactly what such languages might be, or even what properties of linguistic structures they should be able to express. Two possibilities seem particularly interesting here. The 'D-theory' approach of Marcus et al. (1983), in which the parser maintains a description of the utterance being parsed, seems especially amenable to formulation as a logical system. Alternatively, it may be possible to develop a formalism which exploits the closure properties of tree automata (Gécseg and Steinby, 1984); such a system might be especially useful for formalizing theories of grammar in which the well-formed linguistic structures are intersection of the structures that satisfy a set of principles of grammar.

ACKNOWLEDGEMENTS

Steven Abney, Robert Berwick, Nelson Correa, Tim Hickey, Elizabeth Highleyman, Ewan Klein, Peter Ludlow, Martin Kay, Fernando Pereira, and Whitman Richards all made helpful suggestions regarding this work, but all responsibility for errors remains my own. The research reported here was supported by a grant from the Systems Development Foundation to the Center for the Study of Language and Information at Stanford University and by a Postdoctoral Fellowship awarded by the Fairchild Foundation through the Brain and Cognitive Sciences Department at MIT.

NOTES

[1] This term is the title of the seminal paper of the same name by Pereira and Warren (1983), which in turn has its roots in work on logic programming initiated by Colmerauer and Kowalski in the 1970s. The connection between logic and generative grammar goes back still further; the rewriting rules used in the formalization of the notion of 'proof' were one of the sources of inspiration for transformations of early generative linguistics.

[2] This goal thus differs from that of work in computational linguistics that seeks merely to discover an algorithm capable of mapping between the parser's input to its output representations, and hence does not directly address the problem of how a language processor can use of knowledge of language of the kind posited by GB theory.

[3] The parsers described here can therefore be regarded as 'principle-based', using Berwick's (1987, 1991 forthcoming) terminology, and are strongly related to other 'principle-based' parsers. In this chapter I use the term 'principle' to refer to a component of the knowledge of language (i.e., the theory of grammar) employed by the parser, rather than properties of the parser itself. Although the Parsing as Deduction hypothesis is itself agnostic as to whether the knowledge of language used by the language processor is principle-based, principle-based theories can be naturally implemented using deductive processing models.

[4] I use the term 'logical language' here to avoid confusion with 'human language'.

[5] It is also possible that the Parsing as Deduction hypothesis is formally correct, but that it provides no additional insight into the use of knowledge of language.

[6] As Berwick and Weinberg (1984) point out, humans are capable of interpreting ill-formed inputs, yet the 'parse' relation specified here would not hold between any such PF and any LF. Further, the fact that humans are consciously aware of the meaning of the beginning of an utterance before that utterance has ended suggests that the parser's output is not a single monolithic structural description of its input, but consists rather of a sequence of partial descriptions of the linguistic properties of the utterance being processed. Although it is not yet clear what linguistic properties of an utterance the parser does compute, there is no reason to suspect that they could not be formulated in the Parsing as Deduction framework.

[7] For simplicity I approximate the phonology relation in this and following examples with the 'yield' or 'terminal string' function.

[8] Note that any principle based parser should exhibit this property.

[9] The parsers described below can all be run 'in reverse', i.e., given an LF as input, they produce the corresponding PF as their output. It seems likely that in a practical implementation of a larger fragment one could use the same knowledge of language (in this case, the parameter settings, lexicon and axiomatization of GB theory) for parsing and production, but that differing control strategies would be used in each case. Miller and Nadathur (1986) describe a logic programming system in which the same specification can be used efficiently as both a parser and generator.

[10] Thus in the PAD parsers the knowledge of language of Universal Grammar is accorded propositional status. This is not implied by the Parsing as Deduction hypothesis. See Chomsky (1986, pp. 266–268) for discussion of this issue.

[11] These annotations are reminiscent of the complex feature bundles associated with

categories in GPSG (Gazdar *et al.*, 1986). The formulation here differs from the complex feature bundle approach in that the values associated with nodes by the Case filter are not components of that node's category label, and hence are invisible to other principles of grammar. Thus this formulation imposes an informational encapsulation of the principles of grammar that the complex feature approach does not.

[12] The association of constituents with 'properties' described here is reminiscent of the way a tree automaton associates tree nodes nodes with automaton 'states'. It seems likely that the $\overline{X}$, θ, and Case filter principles can be modeled as tree automata, since the relevant relationships that these principles require are all strictly local.

[13] For the reasons explained below, the $\overline{X}$ principle used in this run of parser was restricted to allow only finitely many D-structures.

[14] The Parsing as Deduction framework shares this property with the 'logic programming' approach from which it is derived. Thus Kowalski's (1979) maxim 'Algorithm = Logic + Control' is equally applicable in the parsing context. Kowalski (1979) discusses several different control strategies that might be used by deductive parsers.

[15] The absence of D-structure 'garden path' phenomena suggests that the human parser does not deterministically construct D-structure representations. If it were the case that D-structures were deterministically constructed we would expect the human parser to 'garden path' on sentences with a local D-structure ambiguity. One of the pair of examples shown below should cause a D-structure garden path because their common prefix is consistent with two D-structures, one of which has a pleonastic it filling the matrix subject position, the other with an empty matrix subject position:

(i) It seems very likely that the computer has been stolen

(ii) It seems very likely to have been stolen

[16] Allowing reaxiomatization here seems reasonable since Universal Grammar is an abstract specification of the innate structure of the language faculty, and it seems unlikely that the human language processor consists of a general-purpose inference engine that uses a purely propositional representation of Universal Grammar (*i.e.*, it is a device similar in structure to PAD1 or PAD2). Thus I claim that the important property of the axiomatization of Universal Grammar is its deductive closure rather than its textual form. On the other hand, it seems more plausible that the parameter values and the lexicon constitute propositionally represented knowledge of a language, since they must be learned explicitly by the language user. Importantly, the reaxiomatizations of Universal Grammar described here use the parameter values and the lexicon explicitly during the parsing process, thus respecting their (potential) propositional status.

[17] A Horn-clause theorem-prover that uses a reaxiomatization U equivalent to U simulates another theorem-prover for Universal Grammar; the knowledge of language is provably the same in both cases, but that knowledge of language may be used in a different fashion. Thus a parser using a reaxiomatization can be viewed as simulating a Universal Grammar theorem-prover with a different abstract control structure.

[18] This ignores the possibility that one of the inference procedures will fail to terminate.

[19] Although in terms of control strategy PAD3 is very similar to PAD2, it is computationally much more efficient than PAD2, because it is executed directly by Prolog, whereas PAD2 is interpreted by a metainterpreter incorporating the 'delay' control structure itself implemented in Prolog.

[20] The generation of the predicate p' from the predicate p can be regarded an example of compile-time static garbage-collection (I thank T. Hickey for this observation). Clearly, a corresponding run-time garbage collection operation could be performed on the nodes of the partially constructed D-structures in a parser like PAD2 that applies all constraints to a node simultaneously, thus if PAD2 were executed by a system with sufficiently powerful garbage collection facilities, explicit construction of complete D-structures could be avoided here also.

REFERENCES

Berwick, R.: 1991 forthcoming, 'Principle-Based Parsing', in T. Sells, S. Shieber, and T. Wasow (eds.), *Foundational Issues in Natural Language Processing*, MIT Press, Cambridge, Massachusetts.

Berwick, R. and A. Weinberg: 1984, *The Grammatical Basis of Linguistic Performance*, MIT Press, Cambridge, Massachusetts.

Chomsky, N.: 1981, *Lectures on Government and Binding: The Pisa Lectures*, Foris, Dordrecht, Holland.

Chomsky, N.: 1986, *Knowledge of Language: Its Nature, Origin and Use*, Praeger Publishers, New York.

Cohen, J.: 1985, 'Describing Prolog by its Interpretation and Compilation', *Communications of the Association for Computing Machinery* **28**, 1311–1324.

Cohen, J. and T. Hickey: 1987, 'Parsing and Compiling Using Prolog', *ACM Transactions on Programming Languages and Systems* **9**, 125–163.

Gazdar, G., E. Klein, G. Pullum, and I. Sag: 1985, *Generalized Phrase Structure Grammar*, Basil Blackwell, Oxford.

Gècseg, F. and M. Steinby: 1984, *Tree Automata*, Akadémiai Kiadó, Budapest, Hungary.

Genesereth, M. and N. Nilsson: 1987, *Logical Foundations for Artificial Intelligence*, Morgan Kaufmann, Los Altos, California.

Giannesini, F., H. Kanoui, R. Pasero, and M. Caneghem: 1986, *Prolog*, Addison-Wesley, Reading, Massachusetts.

Johnson, M.: 1989, 'Move-α and the Unfold-Fold Transform', unpublished manuscript, Brown University Department of Cognitive and Linguistic Sciences, Providence, Rhode Island.

Kowalski, R.: 1979, *Logic for Problem Solving*, North Holland, New York.

Marcus, M.: 1980, *A Theory of Syntactic Recognition for Natural Language*, MIT Press, Cambridge, Massachusetts.

Marcus, M., D. Hindle, and M. Fleck: 1983, 'D-Theory: Talking about Talking about Trees', *Proceedings of the 21st Annual Meeting of the Association for Computational Linguistics*, Cambridge, Massachusetts, pp. 129–136.

Miller, D. and G. Nadathur: 1986, 'Some Uses of Higher-Order Logic in Computational Linguistics', *Proceedings of the 24th Annual Meeting of the Association for
Computational Linguistics*, Columbia, New York, pp. 247–256.

Pereira, F. and S. Shieber: 1987, *Prolog and Natural Language Processing*, University
of Chicago Press, Chicago, Illinois.

Pereira, F. and D. Warren: 1983, 'Parsing as Deduction', *Proceedings of the 21st
Annual Meeting of the Association for Computational Linguistics*, Cambridge,
Massachusetts, pp. 137–144.

Tamaki, H. and T. Sato: 1984, 'Unfold/Fold Transformation of Logic Programs',
Proceedings of the Second International Logic Programming Conference, Uppsala
University, Uppsala, Sweden, pp. 127–138.

Van Riemsdijk, H. and E. Williams: 1986, *Introduction to the Theory of Grammar*,
MIT Press, Cambridge, Massachusetts.

Cognitive and Linguistic Sciences,
Brown University,
Providence, Rhode Island 02192, U.S.A.

SANDIWAY FONG

THE COMPUTATIONAL IMPLEMENTATION OF PRINCIPLE-BASED PARSERS

1. INTRODUCTION

Recently, there has been some interest in the implementation of grammatical theories based on the principles and parameters approach (Correa, this volume; Johnson, this volume; Kolb and Thiersch, 1988; and Stabler, 1991 forthcoming). In this framework, a fixed set of universal principles parameterized according to particular languages interact deductively to account for diverse linguistic phenomena. Much of the work to date has focused on the not inconsiderable task of formalizing such theories. The primary goal of this chapter is to explore the computationally relevant properties of this framework. In particular, we address the hitherto largely unexplored issue of how to organize linguistic principles for efficient processing. More specifically, this chapter examines if, and how, a parser can reorder principles to avoid doing unnecessary work. Many important questions exist. For example: (1) What effect, if any, does principle-ordering have on the amount of work needed to parse a given sentence? (2) If the effect of principle-ordering is significant, then are some orderings much better than others? (3) If so, is it possible to predict (and explain) which ones these are?

By characterizing principles in terms of the purely computational notions of 'filters' and 'generators', we show how how principle-ordering can be utilized to minimize the amount of work performed in the course of parsing. Basically, some principles, like Move-α (a principle relating 'gaps' and 'fillers') and Free Indexing (a principle relating referential items) are 'generators' in the sense that they build more hypothesized output structures than their inputs. Other principles, like the Theta-criterion (θ-criterion) that places restrictions on the assignment of thematic relations, the Case filter that requires certain noun phrases to be marked with abstract Case, and Binding theory constraints, act as filters and weed-out ill-formed structures.

A novel, logic based parser, the Principle Ordering Parser (called the PO-PARSER), was built to investigate and demonstrate the effects

R. C. Berwick et al. (eds.),
Principle-Based Parsing: Computation and Psycholinguistics, 65–82.
© 1991 *Kluwer Academic Publishers. Printed in the Netherlands.*

of principle-ordering. The PO-PARSER was deliberately constructed in a highly modular fashion to allow for maximum flexibility in exploring alternative orderings of principles. For instance, each principle is represented separately as an atomic parser operation. A structure is deemed to be well-formed only if it passes all parser operations. The scheduling of parser operations is controlled by a dynamic ordering mechanism that attempts to eliminate unnecessary work by eliminating ill-formed structures as quickly as possible. (For comparison purposes, the PO-PARSER also allows the user to turn off the dynamic ordering mechanism and to parse with a user-specified (fixed) sequence of operations; see the appendix for examples.)

Although we are primarily interested in exploiting the (abstract) computational properties of principles to build more efficient parsers, the PO-PARSER is also designed to be capable of handling a reasonably wide variety of linguistic phenomena. The system faithfully implements most of the principles contained in Lasnik and Uriagereka's (1988) textbook. That is, the parser makes the same grammaticality judgments and reports the same violations for ill-formed structures as the reference text. Some additional theory is also drawn from Chomsky (1981) and (1986). Parser operations implement principles from Theta theory, Case theory, Binding theory, subjacency, the Empty Category Principle (ECP), movement at the level of Logical form as well in overt syntax, and some Control theory. This enables it to handle diverse phenomena including parasitic gap constructions, strong crossover violations, passive, raising, and super-raising examples.

2. THE PRINCIPLE ORDERING PROBLEM

This section addresses the issue of how to organize linguistic principles in the PO-PARSER framework for efficient processing. More precisely, we discuss the problem of how to order the application of principles to minimize the amount of 'work' that the parser has to perform. We will explain why certain orderings may be better in this sense than others. We will also describe heuristics that the PO-PARSER employs in order to optimize the the ordering of its operations.

But first, is there a significant performance difference between various orderings? Alternatively, how important an issue is the principle ordering problem in parsing? An informal experiment was conducted using the PO-PARSER described in the previous section to provide some indication on the magnitude of the problem. Although we were unable to examine all the possible orderings, it turns out that order-of-magnitude variations in parsing times could be achieved merely by picking a few sample orderings.[1]

2.1. *Explaining the Variation in Principle Ordering*

The variation in parsing times for various principle orderings that we observed can be explained by assuming that overgeneration is the main problem, or bottleneck, for parsers such as the PO-PARSER. That is, in the course of parsing a single sentence, a parser will hypothesize many different structures. Most of these structures, the ill-formed ones in particular, will be accounted for by one or more linguistic filters. A sentence will be deemed acceptable if there exists one or more structures that satisfy every applicable filter. Note that even when parsing grammatical sentences, overgeneration will produce ill-formed structures that need to be ruled out. Given that our goal is to minimize the amount of work performed during the parsing process, we would expect a parse using an ordering that requires the parser to perform extra work compared with another ordering to be slower.

Overgeneration implies that we should order the linguistic filters to eliminate ill-formed structures as quickly as possible. For these structures, applying any parser operation other than one that rules it out may be considered as doing extra, or unnecessary, work (modulo any logical dependencies between principles).[2] However, in the case of a well-formed structure, principle ordering cannot improve parser performance. By definition, a well-formed structure is one that passes all relevant parser operations. Unlike the case of an ill-formed structure, applying one operation cannot possibly preclude having to apply another.

2.2. *Optimal Orderings*

Since some orderings perform better than others, a natural question to ask is: Does there exist a 'globally' optimal ordering? The existence of such an ordering would have important implications for the design of the control structure of any principle-based parser. The PO-PARSER has a novel 'dynamic' control structure in the sense that it tries to determine an ordering-efficient strategy for every structure generated. If such a globally optimal ordering could be found, then we can do away with the run-time overhead and parser machinery associated with calculating individual orderings. That is, we can build an ordering-efficient parser simply by 'hardwiring' the optimal ordering into its control structure. Unfortunately, no such ordering can exist.

The impossibility of the globally optimal ordering follows directly from the 'eliminate unnecessary work' ethic. Computationally speaking, an optimal ordering is one that rules out ill-formed structures at the earliest possible opportunity. A *globally* optimal ordering would be one that always ruled out every possible ill-formed structure without doing any unnecessary work. Consider the following three structures (taken from Lasnik's book), where t is a a *trace* or *empty category*, bound to its antecedent as shown by subscripting.

(1) (a)*John$_1$ is crucial [$_{CP}$[$_{IP}$ t_1 to see this]]

    (b)*[$_{NP}$John$_1$'s mother][$_{VP}$ likes himself$_1$]

    (c)*John$_1$ seems that he$_1$ likes t_1

Example (1a) violates the Empty Category Principle (ECP). Hence the optimal ordering must invoke the ECP operation before any other operation that it is not dependent on. On the other hand, example (1b) violates a Binding theory principle, 'Condition A'. Hence, the optimal ordering must also invoke Condition A as early as possible. In particular, given that the two operations are independent, the optimal ordering must order Condition A before the ECP and vice-versa. Similarly, example (1c) demands that the 'Case Condition on Traces' operation must precede the other two operations. Hence a globally optimal ordering is impossible.

2.3. *Heuristics for Principle Ordering*

The principle-ordering problem can be viewed as a limited instance of the well-known conjunct ordering problem (Smith and Genesereth, 1985). Given a set of conjuncts, we are interested in finding all solutions that satisfy all the conjuncts simultaneously. The parsing problem is then to find well-formed structures (*i.e.*, solutions) that satisfy all the parser operations (*i.e.*, conjuncts) simultaneously. Moreover, we are particularly interested in minimizing the cost of finding these structures by reordering the set of parser operations.

This section outlines some of the heuristics used by the PO-PARSER to determine the minimum cost ordering for a given structure. The PO-PARSER contains a dynamic ordering mechanism that attempts to compute a minimum cost ordering for every phrase structure generated during the parsing process.[3] The mechanism can be subdivided into two distinct phases. First, we will describe how the dynamic ordering mechanism decides which principle is the most likely candidate for eliminating a given structure. Then, we will explain how it makes use of this information to reorder parser operation sequences to minimize the total work performed by the parser.

2.3.1. *Predicting Failing Filters*

Given any structure, the dynamic ordering mechanism attempts to satisfy the 'eliminate unnecessary work' ethic by predicting a 'failing' filter for that structure. More precisely, it will try to predict the principle that a given structure violates on the basis of the simple structure cues. Since the ordering mechanism cannot know whether a structure is well-formed or not, it assumes that all structures are ill-formed and attempts to predict a failing filter for every structure. In order to minimize the amount of work involved, the types of cues that the dynamic ordering mechanism can test for are deliberately limited. Only inexpensive tests such as whether a category contains certain features (*e.g.*, ±anaphoric, ±infinitival, or whether it is a trace or a nonargument) may be used. Any cues that may require significant computation, such as searching for an antecedent, are considered to be too expensive. Each structure cue is then associated with a list of possible failing filters. (Some examples of the mapping between cues and filters are shown below.) The system then chooses one of the possible failing filters based on this mapping.[4]

(2)

Structure cue	Possible failing filters
trace	Empty Category Principle, and Case Condition on traces
intransitive	Case filter
passive	Theta-criterion Case filter
nonargument	Theta-criterion
+anaphoric	Binding theory Condition A
+pronominal	Binding theory Condition B

The correspondence between each cue and the set of candidate filters may be systematically derived from the definitions of the relevant principles. For example, *Condition A* of the Binding theory deals with the conditions under which antecedents for anaphoric items, such as *each other* and *himself*, must appear. Hence, Condition A can only be a candidate failing filter for structures that contain an item with the +anaphoric feature. Other correspondences may be somewhat less direct: for example, the Case filter merely states that all overt noun phrase must have abstract Case. Now, in the PO-PARSER the conditions under which a noun phrase may receive abstract Case are defined by two separate operations, namely, Inherent Case Assignment and Structural Case Assignment. It turns out that an instance where Structural Case Assignment will not assign Case is when a verb that normally assigns Case has passive morphology. Hence, the presence of a passive verb in a given structure may cause an overt noun phrase to fail to receive Case during Structural Case Assignment, which in turn may cause the Case filter to fail.[5]

The failing filter mechanism can been seen as an approximation to the cheapest-first heuristic in conjunct ordering problems. It turns out that if the cheapest conjunct at any given point will reduce the search space rather than expand it, then it can be shown that the optimal ordering must contain that conjunct at that point. Obviously, a failing filter is a 'cheapest' operation in the sense that it immediately eliminates one structure from the set of possible structures under consideration.

Although the dynamic ordering mechanism performs well in many of the test cases drawn from the reference text, it is by no means foolproof (see the appendix for an example). There are also many cases where the prediction mechanism triggers an unprofitable reordering of the default order of operations. (We will present one example of this in the next section.) A more sophisticated prediction scheme, perhaps one based on more complex cues, could increase the accuracy of the ordering mechanism. However, we will argue that it is not cost-effective to do so. The basic reason is that, in general, there is no *simple* way to determine whether a given structure will violate a certain principle.[6] That is, as far as one can tell, it is difficult to produce a cheap (relative to the cost of the actual operation itself), but effective approximation to a filter operation. For example, in Binding theory, it is difficult to determine if an anaphor and its antecedent satisfies the complex locality restrictions imposed by Condition A without actually doing some searching for a binder. Simplifying the locality restrictions is one way of reducing the cost of approximation, but the very absence of search is the main reason why the overhead of the present ordering mechanism is relatively small.[7] Hence, having more sophisticated cues may provide better approximations, but the tradeoff is that the prediction methods may be almost as expensive as performing the real operations themselves.

2.3.2. *Logical Dependencies and Reordering*

Given a candidate failing filter, the dynamic ordering mechanism has to schedule the sequence of parser operations so that the failing filter is performed as early as possible. Simply moving the failing filter to the front of the operations queue is not a workable approach for two reasons.

Firstly, simply fronting the failing filter may violate logical dependencies between various parser operations. For example, suppose the Case filter was chosen to be the failing filter. To create the conditions under which the Case filter can apply, both Case assignment operations, namely, Inherent Case Assignment and Structural Case Assignment, must be applied first. Hence, fronting the Case filter will also be accompanied by the subsequent fronting of both assignment operations, unless of course they have already been applied to the structure in question.

Secondly, the failing filter approach does not take into account the behavior of 'generator' operations. A generator may be defined as any parser operation that always produces one output, and possibly more than one output, for each input. For example, the operations corresponding to $\overline{\text{X}}$ rules, Move-α, Free Indexing, and LF Movement are the generators in the PO-PARSER. (Similarly, the operations that we have previously referred to as 'filters' may be characterized as parser operations that, when given n structures as input, pass n and possibly fewer than n structures.) Due to logical dependencies, it may be necessary in some situations to invoke a generator operation before a failure filter can be applied. For example, the filter Condition A of the Binding theory is logically dependent on the generator Free Indexing to generate the possible antecedents for the anaphors in a structure. Consider the possible binders for the anaphor *himself* in *John thought that Bill saw himself* as shown below:

(3) (a)*John$_i$ thought that Bill$_j$ saw himself$_i$

     (b) John$_i$ thought that Bill$_j$ saw himself$_j$

     (c)*John$_i$ thought that Bill$_j$ saw himself$_k$

Only in example (3a) is the antecedent close enough to satisfy the locality restrictions imposed by Condition A. Note that Condition A had to be applied a total of three times in the above example in order to show that there is only one possible antecedent for *himself*. This situation arises because of the general tendency of generators to overgenerate. But this characteristic behavior of generators can greatly magnify the extra work that the parser does when the dynamic ordering mechanism picks the wrong failing filter. Consider the ill-formed structure **John seems that he likes t* (a violation of the principle that traces of a noun phrase cannot receive Case.) If however, Condition B of the Binding theory is predicted to be the failure filter (on the basis of the structure cue *he*), then Condition B will be applied repeatedly to the indexings generated by the Free Indexing operation. On the other hand, if the Case Condition on Traces operation was correctly predicted to be the failing filter, then Free Indexing need not be applied at all. The dynamic ordering mechanism of the PO-PARSER is designed to be sensitive to the potential problems caused by selecting a candidate failing filter that is logically dependent on many generators.[8]

2.4. *Linguistic Filters and Determinism*

In this section we describe how the characterization of parser operations in terms of filters and generators may be exploited further to improve the performance of the PO-PARSER for some operations. More precisely, we make use of certain computational properties of linguistic filters to improve the backtracking behavior of the PO-PARSER. The behavior of this optimization will turn out to complement that of the ordering selection procedure quite nicely. That is, the optimization is most effective in exactly those cases where the selection procedure is least effective.

We hypothesize that linguistic filters, such as the Case filter, Binding Conditions, ECP, and so on, may be characterized as follows:

(4) **Hypothesis**: Linguistic filters are side-effect free conditions on configurations

In terms of parser operations, this means that filters should never cause structure to be built or attempt to fill in feature slots.[9] Moreover, computationally speaking, the parser operations corresponding to linguistic filters should be deterministic. That is, any given structure should either fail a filter or just pass. A filter operation should never need to succeed more than once, simply because it is side-effect free.[10] By contrast, operations that we have characterized as generators, such as Move-α and Free Indexing, are not deterministic in this sense. That is, given a structure as input, they may produce one or more structures as output.

Given the above hypothesis, we can cut down on the amount of work done by the PO-PARSER by modifying its behavior for filter operations. Currently, the parser employs a backtracking model of computation. If a particular parser operation fails, then the default behavior is to attempt to resatisfy the operation that was called immediately before the failing operation. In this situation, the PO-PARSER will only attempt to resatisfy the preceding operation if it happens to be a generator. When the preceding operation is a filter, then the parser will skip the filter and, instead, attempt to resatisfy the next most recent operation and so on.[11] For example, consider the following calling sequence:

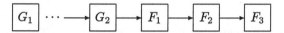

Suppose that a structure generated by generator G_2 passes filters F_1 and F_2, but fails on filter F_3. None of the three filters could have been the cause of the failure by the side-effect free hypothesis. Hence, we can skip trying to resatisfy any of them and backtrack straight to G_2.

Note that this optimization is just a limited form of dependency-directed backtracking. Failures are traced directly to the last generator invoked, thereby skipping over any intervening filters as possible causes of failure. However, the backtracking behavior is limited in the sense that the most recent generator may not be the cause of a failure. Consider the above example again. The failure of F_3 need not have been caused by G_2. Instead, it could have been caused by structure-building in another generator further back in the calling sequence, say G_1. But the parser will still try out all the other possibilities in G_2 first.

Consider a situation in which the principle selection procedure performs poorly. That is, for a particular ill-formed structure, the selection procedure will fail to immediately identify a filter that will rule out the structure. The advantages of the modified mechanism over the default backtrack scheme will be more pronounced in such situations, especially if the parser has to try several filters before finding a 'failing' filter. By contrast, the behavior of the modified mechanism will resemble that of

the strict chronological scheme in situations where the selection procedure performs relatively well (*i.e.*, when a true failing filter is fronted).
In such cases, the advantages, if significant, will be small. (In an informal
comparison between the two schemes using about eighty sentences from
the reference text, only about half the test cases exhibited a noticeable
decrease in parsing time.)

3. CONCLUSIONS: THE UTILITY OF PRINCIPLE-ORDERING

In the framework of the PO-PARSER, dynamic principle-ordering can
provide a significant improvement over any fixed ordering. Speed-ups
varying from three- or four-fold to order-of-magnitude improvements
have been observed in many cases.[12]

The control structure of the PO-PARSER forces linguistic principles
to be applied one at a time. Many other machine architectures are
certainly possible. For example, we could take advantage of the independence of many principles and apply principles in parallel whenever
possible. However, any improvement in parsing performance would come
at the expense of violating the minimum (unnecessary) work ethic. Lazy
evaluation of principles is yet another alternative. However, principle-
ordering would still be an important consideration for efficient processing
in this case. Finally, we should also consider principle-ordering from the
viewpoint of scalability. The experience from building prototypes of the
PO-PARSER suggests that as the level of sophistication of the parser increases (both in terms of the number and complexity of individual principles), the effect of principle-ordering also becomes more pronounced.

APPENDIX

Examples of Parsing Using the PO-PARSER

This section contains some examples of parsing using the implemented
system. The 'core' portion of the PO-PARSER, consisting of a lexicon,
various principle definitions, and a bottom-up $\overline{X}$-parsing machine, is
written entirely in Prolog. The principle-ordering mechanism and user-
interface portions are independently written in Lisp. The complete system runs on a Symbolics 3650 workstation.

The following snapshot shows the result of parsing the ambiguous
sentence *John believes that Mary likes him.* Since the parser recovers all

possible parses, it returns two parses, one for the case where *John* and *him* are interpreted as being coreferential, and the other when *him* is coreferential with a third person, not named in this sentence.

```
                        Principle-Ordering Parser
 Examples      Tracing       Toolkit      Options     Failures    Orderings    Refresh        Quit
Output                                                                               Filters
Example: John believes that mary likes him               [3,pg30]      1
                                                                               1      Theta Criterion
Structure passes all operations:                                              2
[  [ ][ [  John] [ [] [  [ believes][ [  that][ [  mary] [ [] [  [  likes][  hin] ]]]]]]]   2     Case Filter
 C2 C  I2 NP    a  I1 I 0 VP V    C2 C    I2 NP   I  I1 I VP V       NP  2     2
                                                                               2      Case Condition
NP: (index _0) apos (case non) (theta agent) (a -) (p -) (rc +) (agr ((t)) ((sg)) ((n)))    2
I: (index _0) (past -) (agr ((t)) ((sg n)) ((n f n))) (hop (past -)) (hop (agr ((t)) ((sg n)) ((n f n))))   2
V: (past -) (agr ((t)) ((sg n)) ((n f n))) (norph believe s) (grid agent (proposition)) (ecn oblig)   2      Condition A
NP: (index _1) apos (case non) (theta agent) (a -) (p -) (rc +) (agr ((t)) ((sg)) ((f)))   2
I: (index _1) (past -) (agr ((t)) ((sg n)) ((n f n))) (hop (past -)) (hop (agr ((t)) ((sg n)) ((n f n))))   2
V: (past -) (agr ((t)) ((sg n)) ((n f n))) (norph like s) (grid agent (patient))   2      Condition B
NP: (index _2) apos compl (case acc) (theta patient) (norphc acc) (a -) (p +) (rc +) (agr ((t)) ((sg)) ((n)))   2
                                                                               2      Condition C
Structure passes all operations:                                              2
[  [ ][ [  John] [ [] [  [ believes][ [  that][ [  mary] [ [] [  [  likes][  hin] ]]]]]]]   12
 C2 C  I2 NP    0  I1 I 0 VP V    C2 C    I2 NP   I  I1 I VP V       NP  0     1      Realize PF
NP: (index _0) apos (case non) (theta agent) (a -) (p -) (rc +) (agr ((t)) ((sg)) ((n)))    2
I: (index _0) (past -) (agr ((t)) ((sg n)) ((n f n))) (hop (past -)) (hop (agr ((t)) ((sg n)) ((n f n))))   2      ECP
V: (past -) (agr ((t)) ((sg n)) ((n f n))) (norph believe s) (grid agent (proposition)) (ecn oblig)
NP: (index _1) apos (case non) (theta agent) (a -) (p -) (rc +) (agr ((t)) ((sg)) ((f)))         Generators
I: (index _1) (past -) (agr ((t)) ((sg n)) ((n f n))) (hop (past -)) (hop (agr ((t)) ((sg n)) ((n f n))))   1
V: (past -) (agr ((t)) ((sg n)) ((n f n))) (norph like s) (grid agent (patient))   1      Parse PF
NP: (index _0) apos compl (case acc) (theta patient) (norphc acc) (a -) (p +) (rc +) (agr ((t)) ((sg)) ((n)))   1
                                                                               12     Parse X-Bar
No (nore) parses                                                              1
                                                                               1      Theta Role Assignment
                                                                               2
                                                                               2      Inherent Case Assignment
                                                                               12
                                                                               12     Move Alpha
                                                                               2
                                                                               2      Structural Case Assignment
                                                                               1
                                                                               1      Free Indexing
                                                                               2
                                                                               2      Coindex Subject & INFL
```

(In the second structure, the pronoun *him* has the same index, 0, as *John*. For the first parse, the pronoun is given a separate index, 2.) The list of parser operations on the right-hand-side of the screen provides useful statistics on the execution of the parse. (The panel is also used to provide an 'animated' display of the behavior of the system during parsing. The box surrounding each principle briefly 'flashes' each time the principle is invoked.) There are two numbers associated with each parser operation. The top number records how many times that operation was invoked during parsing. The bottom number indicates how many times the operation succeeded. For example, we can immediately trace the source of the referential ambiguity to the free indexation operation, because it is the only generator that produced two structures from one input. (As we will show later, the numbers will also serve to identify the failing principle in cases of ungrammatical input.)

The PO-PARSER allows the user to experiment with various orderings. The following snapshot shows three distinct orderings:

Static Orderings

Column 1	Column 2	Column 3
Parse PF	Parse PF	Parse PF
Parse X-Bar	Parse X-Bar	Parse X-Bar
Move Alpha	Move Alpha	Move Al
Realize PF	Inherent Case Assignment	Free Ind
Theta Role Assignment	Structural Case Assignment	Coindex Subje
Theta Criterion	Case Filter	Conditi
Free Indexing	Free Indexing	Conditi
Coindex Subject & INFL	Coindex Subject & INFL	Conditi
Condition A	Condition A	Conditi
Inherent Case Assignment	Condition B	ECP
Structural Case Assignment	Condition C	Inherent Case
Case Filter	ECP	Structural Case
Condition B	Case Condition	Case Fi
Condition C	Theta Role Assignment	Case Cond
ECP	Theta Criterion	Theta Role A
Case Condition	Realize PF	Theta Criterion
		Realize PF

Reorder Operations

Parse PF
Parse X-Bar
Move Alpha
Free Indexing
Coindex Subject & INFL
Condition A
Condition B
Condition C
ECP
Theta Role Assignment
Theta Criterion
Realize PF
Inherent Case Assignment
Structural Case Assignment
Case Condition
Case Filter

Abort   Done

Each list of parser operations is just a permutation of the panel of operations shown in the previous snapshot. Each list should read in a 'top-down' fashion, that is, the topmost operation will be executed first, the operation immediately below the topmost will be executed next, and so on, down to the bottom operation. The leftmost list is the default ordering used in the previous example. In this session, we have created two alternative permutations as test orderings.

The pop-up menu shown above, allows the user to arbitrarily reorder parser operations, simply by 'moving' each operation around. (The system also keeps track of logical dependencies between the various operations, hence, it will prevent the construction of ill-formed orderings, for example, Inherent Case Assignment is never allowed to 'follow' the Case filter.) For the purposes of the next example, the position of the Case filter in the list will be the salient difference between the middle and the rightmost orderings. That is, the Case filter appears as 'early' as possible in the middle, and as 'late' as possible in the rightmost ordering (as shown in the pop-up menu).

The following snapshot shows the result of running the parser using the rightmost ordering on the ungrammatical example *It was arrested John:

```
                    Principle-Ordering Parser
 Examples    Tracing      Toolkit    Options    Failures   Orderings      Refresh       Quit
 Output                                                                        Filters
 Example: *It was arrested John                     [45,pg17]          Ca   2
 No (nore) parses                                                                Theta Criterion
                                                                            1
                                                                            1   Case Filter

                                                                            1   Case Condition
                                                                            1
                                                                            2   Condition A
                                                                            2
                                                                            2   Condition B
                                                                            2
                                                                            2   Condition C
                                                                            2
                                                                            1   Realize PF
                                                                            1
                                                                            2   ECP
                                                                            2
                                                                               Generators
                                                                            1   Parse PF
                                                                            2
                                                                            2   Parse X-Bar
                                                                            2
                                                                            2   Theta Role Assignment
                                                                            2
                                                                            1   Inherent Case Assignment
                                                                            1
                                                                            2   Move Alpha
                                                                            2
                                                                            1  Structural Case Assignment
                                                                            1
                                                                            2   Free Indexing
                                                                            2
                                                                            2   Coindex Subject & INFL
                                                                            2
```

Of course, the system returns no parses for this ungrammatical sentence. Note that the statistics collected for the Case filter indicates that it was the failing filter in this case. (Every other operation succeeded at least once, only the Case filter failed to pass a single structure.) The important to note about this diagram, is that every operation listed was 'exercised' at least once. The next snapshot shows the result of parsing the same sentence, but using the middle ordering instead:

```
                      Principle-Ordering Parser
  Examples      Tracing      Toolkit      Options     Failures     Orderings    Refresh         Quit
  Output                                                                            Filters
 □Example: *It was arrested John                        [45,pg17]        Ca
  No (nore) parses                                                                Theta Criterion

                                                                         2
                                                                               Case Filter

                                                                               Case Condition

                                                                               Condition A

                                                                               Condition B

                                                                               Condition C

                                                                               Realize PF

                                                                                  ECP

                                                                                Generators
                                                                         1
                                                                               Parse PF
                                                                         2
                                                                         2
                                                                               Parse X-Bar
                                                                         2
                                                                               Theta Role Assignment
                                                                         2
                                                                               Inherent Case Assignment
                                                                         2
                                                                         2
                                                                               Move Alpha
                                                                         2
                                                                         2
                                                                               Structural Case Assignment
                                                                         2
                                                                               Free Indexing

                                                                               Coindex Subject & INFL
```

As before, the system returns no parses. (Of course, variations in ordering cannot affect the logic of the parser. That is, the parses produced in each case must be the same.) However, in this case the parser achieves the same result, but with much less work. That is, the ungrammatical sentence has been ruled out as early as possible. Observe that the statistics indicate that many fewer parser operations were invoked in this case.

Finally, the user can also allow the system to pick its own ordering via the dynamic ordering mechanism. The following snapshot shows the result of parsing the same example using dynamic ordering:

The snapshot also contains information about any choices that the ordering mechanism made during execution. In this situation, the relevant structure cues are NONARG (from the nonargument *it*) and PASSIVE (from *was arrested*). Since a nonargument cannot be assigned a theta-role, this suggests that the Theta-criterion may be the failing filter. Similarly, the presence of the passive element prevents *arrested* from assigning Case to its complement (*John*), which suggests the Case filter as the failing filter. The passive element also prevents the external theta-role of *arrested* from being assigned to the noun phrase in subject position (*it*). Hence, there will be a total of two 'votes' for the Theta-criterion and one for the Case filter. Thus, the ordering mechanism will pick the Theta-criterion as the most likely failing filter, and reorder the operations accordingly. Actually, it turns out, for the structure under consideration, that the Theta-criterion was not the optimal choice. The ordering mechanism then reevaluates its choice, and collects votes in the same fashion as before. The outcome of the voting is unchanged, but the Theta-criterion has already been applied. Hence, the system picks the Case filter as the most likely failing filter (the correct choice) on the second attempt.

ACKNOWLEDGEMENTS

The author is deeply indebted to Robert C. Berwick for his support and guidance. This work is supported by an IBM Graduate Fellowship.

NOTES

[1] The PO-PARSER has about twelve to sixteen parser operations. Given a set of one dozen operations, there are about 500 million different ways to order these operations. Fortunately, only about half a million of these are actually valid, due to logical dependencies between the various operations. However, this is still far too many to test exhaustively. Instead, only a few well-chosen orderings were tested on a number of sentences from the reference. The procedure involved choosing a default sequence of operations and 'scrambling' the sequence by moving operations as far as possible from their original positions (modulo any logical dependencies between operations).

[2] In the PO-PARSER for example, the Case filter operation (that requires that all overt noun phrases have abstract Case assigned) is dependent on both the inherent and structural Case assignment operations. That is, in any valid ordering the filter must be preceded by both operations.

[3] In their paper, Smith and Genesereth drew a distinction between 'static' and 'dynamic' ordering strategies. In static strategies, the conjuncts are first ordered, and then solved in the order presented. By contrast, in dynamic strategies the chosen ordering may be revised between solving individual conjuncts. Currently, the PO-PARSER employs a dynamic strategy. The ordering mechanism computes an ordering based on certain features of each structure to be processed. The ordering may be revised after certain operations (e.g., movement) that modify the structure in question.

[4] Obviously, there are many ways to implement such a selection procedure. Currently, the PO-PARSER uses a voting scheme based on the frequency of cues. The (unproven) underlying assumption is that the probability of a filter being a failing filter increases with the number of occurrences of its associated cues in a given structure. For example, the more traces there are in a structure, the more likely it is that one of them will violate some filter applicable to traces, such as the Empty Category Principle (ECP).

[5] It is possible to automate the process of finding structure cues simply by inspecting the closure of the definitions of each filter and all dependent operations. One method of deriving cues is to collect the negation of all conditions involving category features. For example, if an operation contains the condition 'not (Item has_feature intransitive)', then we can take the presence of an intransitive item as a possible reason for failure of that operation. However, this approach has the potential problem of generating too many cues. Although, it may be relatively inexpensive to test each individual cue, a large number of cues will significantly increase the overhead of the ordering mechanism. Furthermore, it turns out that not all cues are equally useful in predicting failure filters. One solution may be to use 'weights' to rank the predictive utility of each cue with respect to each filter. Then an adaptive algorithm could

be used to 'learn' the weighting values, in a manner reminiscent of Samuel (1967). The failure filter prediction process could then automatically eliminate testing for relatively unimportant cues. This approach is currently being investigated.

[6] If such a scheme can be found, then it can effectively replace the definition of the principle itself.

[7] We ignore the additional cost of reordering the sequence of operations once a failing filter has been predicted. The actual reordering can be made relatively inexpensive using various tricks. For example, it is possible to 'cache' or compute (offline) common cases of re-ordering a default sequence with respect to various failing filters, thus reducing the cost of reordering to that of a simple look-up.

[8] Obviously, there are many different ways to accomplish this. One method is to compute the 'distance' of potential failure filters from the current state of the parser in terms of the number of generators yet to be applied. Then the failing filter will be chosen on the basis of some combination of structure cues and generator distance. Currently, the PO-PARSER uses a slightly different and cheaper scheme. The failure filter is chosen solely on the basis of structure cues. However, the fronting mechanism is restricted so that the chosen filter can only move a limited number of positions ahead of its original position. The original operation sequence is designed such that the distance of the filter from the front of the sequence is roughly proportional to the number of (outstanding) operations that the filter is dependent on.

[9] So far, we have not encountered any linguistic filters that require either structure building or feature assignment. Operations such as θ-role and Case assignment are not considered filters in the sense of the definition given in the previous section. In the PO-PARSER, these operations will never fail. However, definitions that involve some element of 'modality' are potentially problematic. For example, Chomsky's definition of an *Accessible Subject*, a definition relevant to the principles of Binding theory, contains the following phrase '... *assignment to α of the index of β would not violate the (i-within-i) filter* $*[_{\gamma_i}...\delta_i...]$'. A transparent implementation of such a definition would seem to require some manipulation of indices. However, Lasnik and Uriagereka (1988, p. 58) point out that there exists an empirically indistinguishable version of *Accessible Subject* without the element of modality present in Chomsky's version.

[10] It turns out that there are situations where a filter operation (although side-effect free) could succeed more than once. For example, the linguistic filter known as the 'Empty Category Principle' (ECP) implies that all traces must be 'properly governed'. A trace may satisfy proper government by being either 'lexically governed' or 'antecedent governed'. Now consider the structure $[_{CP}$ *What$_1$ did you* $[_{VP}$ *read t$_1$]]$. The trace t_1 is both lexically governed (by the verb *read*) and antecedent governed (by its antecedent *what*). In the PO-PARSER the ECP operation can succeed twice for cases such as t_1 above.

[11] This behavior can be easily simulated using the 'cut' predicate in Prolog. We can route all calls to filter operations through a predicate that calls the filter and then cuts off all internal choice points. (For independent reasons, the PO-PARSER does not actually use this approach.)

[12] Obviously, the speedup obtained will depend on the number of principles present in the system and the degree of 'fine-tuning' of the failure filter selection criteria.

82   SANDIWAY FONG

REFERENCES

Chomsky, N.: 1981, *Lectures on Government and Binding: The Pisa Lectures*, Foris, Dordrecht, Holland.

Chomsky, N.: 1986, *Knowledge of Language: Its Nature, Origin, and Use*, Praeger Publishers, New York.

Correa, N.: this volume, 'Empty Categories, Chain Binding, and Parsing', pp. 83–121.

Johnson, M.: this volume, 'Parsing as Deduction: the Use of Knowledge of Language', pp. 39–64.

Kolb, H. and C. Thiersch: 1988, 'Levels and Empty Categories in a Principles and Parameters Approach to Parsing', unpublished manuscript, Tilburg University, Tilburg, The Netherlands.

Lasnik, H. and J. Uriagereka: 1988, *A Course in GB Syntax: Lectures on Binding and Empty Categories*, MIT Press, Cambridge, Massachusetts.

Samuel, A.: 1967, 'Some Studies in Machine Learning Using the Game of Checkers. II—Recent Progress', *IBM Journal* **11**, pp. 601–617.

Smith, D. and M. Genesereth: 1985, 'Ordering Conjunctive Queries', *Artificial Intelligence* **26**, 171–215.

Stabler, E.P., Jr: 1991 forthcoming, *The Logical Approach to Syntax: Foundations, Specifications and Implementations of Theories of Government and Binding*, MIT Press, Cambridge, Massachusetts.

MIT Artificial Intelligence Laboratory, Room 810,
545 Technology Square,
Cambridge, Massachusetts 02139, U.S.A.

NELSON CORREA

EMPTY CATEGORIES, CHAIN BINDING, AND PARSING

1. INTRODUCTION

In Government-Binding (GB) theory, the chief empirical effect of the principle Move-α is the definition of coindexing relations between nodes in phrase structure trees. This situation is explained by the extreme generality of the base component and several substantive constraints on transformations. The constraints on transformations, in particular Emonds' (1976) Structure Preserving Hypothesis, imply that the base may generate all S-structures of the core constructions of the language in question. The two conditions combine with a shift away from a grammatical model with both conditions on derivations, such as transformational rule ordering, and conditions on representations, such as the Subjacency condition on adjacent chain elements, to a grammatical model that favors representations.[1] It follows that the principal function of Move-α in the grammar is not reordering or otherwise rewriting of an input phrase marker for the derivation of S-structure, but rather the above noted establishment of coindexing relations between the nodes in the output representation. The relations in question are trace-antecedent relations. This trend in the role of Move-α in the grammar has been noted in the literature, especially by Koster (1978), Chomsky (1982), and Barss (1983). Koster proposes simplification of the class of grammars permitted in the Extended Standard Theory by eliminating the rule Move-α, reducing its empirical effect to a suitably extended theory of bound anaphora. Barss reformulates binding theory to remove inadequacies of the version in Chomsky (1981) in its account of clefts, relative clauses, questions, and topicalized constructions. Binding theory is generalized to constrain both argument and nonargument anaphoric relations, in particular those induced by application of the principle Move-α.

In this chapter we pursue the use of attribute grammars for the statement of computationally oriented instantiations of Government-Binding theory, exploiting the noted shift towards a representational

83

R. C. Berwick et al. (eds.),
Principle-Based Parsing: Computation and Psycholinguistics, 83–121.
© 1991 *Kluwer Academic Publishers. Printed in the Netherlands.*

model. We present an interpretive *Chain rule* for the identification of trace-antecedent relations. This rule is similar to that described in previous work (Correa, 1987), but differs from it in that the attribution statements in this case are oriented to bottom-up processing of the input string. We do not address in this chapter the problem of deriving a parsing program from the attribute grammar statement. This is a technical matter of great interest but no major linguistic relevance. It is partly addressed in the literature on programming languages and compiler construction; the reader is referred to Waite and Goos (1984), Kastens, Hutt, and Zimmermann (1982), and Watt and Madsen (1983). The new Chain rule is used in an English grammar written in the PLNLP language (Heidorn, 1972) and its operation may be observed in a bottom-up parallel parser generated automatically from the grammar by the PLNLP system.

This chapter is more explicit than Correa (1987) about the base generation and insertion of empty categories in phrase structure trees. The conditions assumed for classification of empty categories, as well as the correctness of the Chain rule proposed are assessed against the notion of Chain Binding proposed by Barss (1983). The chapter also addresses the recent trend in linguistic theory (especially within the GB framework) to specify natural language grammar in terms of extremely general generative rules, whose task is generation and annotation of syntactic structure, and whose output is subject to a variety of constraints or axioms that must be satisfied. As a case in point, we look at Barss' Chain Binding rule, an instance of this trend, and the Chain rule developed here. We suggest that Government-Binding theory, as currently proposed, is better viewed as an abstract specification of grammatical competence to which no psychological import is attached (insofar as processing is concerned). The translation of a competence grammar into computationally oriented mechanisms that satisfy the abstract specification is a difficult task, that has only recently begun to be addressed, and that should not be neglected since it explores another facet of the human language faculty.

The Chain rule may be evaluated in a direct way and is a crucial component of a performance model for Government-Binding theory. In contrast, transformations have proved to be the most significant obstacle for the formulation of analysis procedures for transformational grammar and the descendent GB theory . While transformations are useful grammatical devices, amenable to algorithmic implementation when viewed as generative devices—*i.e.*, in the sense of tree transduction—there is no general directed recognition procedure for the languages defined by transformational grammars. Thus, we find in Petrick (1965) and more recently Sharp (1985) recourse to a covering surface structure grammar and inverse transformations to implement a generate-and-test analysis procedure.

In this chapter we assume basic knowledge of Government-Binding theory and motivation for the grammatical principles assumed in it (Chomsky, 1981; van Riemsdijk and Williams, 1986). For readers interested in parsing, we also assume knowledge of compiler construction techniques from a given attribute grammar language definition (Waite and Goos, 1984).

The chapter is organized into eight sections as follows. In section 2 we sketch our assumptions about phrase structure and the manner in which empty categories arise. In section 3 we define attribute grammars and illustrate their use in the definition of core grammatical processes in Government-Binding theory, namely government and Case marking. Section 4 discusses the distribution of empty categories according to functional type and casts within the framework of attribute grammar alternatives about the determination of empty categories, according to whether their syntactic features are intrinsically, functionally, or freely determined (Lasnik and Uriagereka, 1988). Section 5 presents the bottom-up version of the Chain rule and illustrates its operation with an example. In section 6 we present Barss' (1983) Chain Binding algorithm and compare it to the Chain rule. We claim that the two rules are empirically equivalent, so the relation between them is that of program refinement. In section 7 we give a simple demonstration about the exponential complexity of the generate-and-test algorithm assumed in Barss' Chain Binding, compared with the linear complexity of the more directed Chain rule. This leads in section 8 to a distinction between grammars as definitions of a language, versus grammars as concrete mechanisms for the generation and analysis of strings in a language. This point is illustrated with the aid of an artificial language.

2. PHRASE STRUCTURE AND EMPTY CATEGORIES

We assume a base component that satisfies the principles of the $\overline{X}$ theory, a restricted form of context-free grammar (Chomsky, 1970). Pullum (1985) surveys the variants of $\overline{X}$ grammar. The principal notion that $\overline{X}$

theory captures is that of *head of a phrase*; in particular it requires that every syntactic category be a *projection* of a head. Adopting current conventions about $\overline{X}$ grammar, we assume a two-level system, in which zero-level categories are denoted by X, first-level projections by $\overline{X}$, and second-level or maximal projections by XP. Complements of a head are generated as sisters of the head, while specifiers and adjuncts are sisters of the first-level projection. The relative order of complements, specifiers, and adjuncts with respect to the head is a parameter of universal grammar. The base component in a GB grammar is thus defined by the maximally concise $\overline{X}$ production schema (1), assuming the parameter settings for English.

(1) (a) XP → YP $\overline{X}$

    (b) $\overline{X}$→ X YP

The zero-level categories in the grammar are comprised of the *lexical* categories (2a), whose extension is defined by the entries in the lexicon, and by the *nonlexical* categories (2b), that do not have lexically defined extensions, but rather are expanded into certain specified lexical formatives or the empty string. The schema (1) specify that in English specifiers precede their heads, while complements follow them. The schema are extended with (3) to provide an arbitrary number of positions for adjuncts, typically following the head (in English).

(2) (a) N(oun), A(djective), V(erb), P(reposition), Adv(erb), Q(uantifier), Art(icle), M(odal)

    (b) I(nflection), C(omplement)

(3) $\overline{X}$→ $\overline{X}$ YP

Attribute grammars define semantic and context-sensitive properties of a language in a *syntax-directed* manner; that is, by making direct reference to phrase structure rules for the statement of attribution rules and conditions. Accordingly, the base component that we assume is the explicit set of context-free productions defined by the schema (1) and (3). The $\overline{X}$ schema are overly general, though. They permit any maximal projection YP to appear as a complement, specifier or adjunct of a given head X. Typically, a head X allows only certain categories to appear in these positions. Subcategorization or thematic properties of the head may restrict the categories that appear as complements, but other lexical properties of a head do not in general determine the category of the specifiers or adjuncts that it allows. Here we assume that the $\overline{\text{X}}$ schema is supplemented with other devices (*e.g.*, a table) indicating the categories allowed at each position for each head X; Jackendoff (1977) addresses the issue at length.

The structure of projections of the nonlexical categories I and C is crucial in the statement of the Chain rule in section 5. The category I introduces tense, modal, and inflectional elements of a sentence and is the head of the sentence symbol IP.[2]. The category C provides a position for the clause complementizer in pre-IP position, and projects to the category CP for clause. Adopting current assumptions about clause structure (Chomsky, 1986), we identify the position for *Wh*-movement with the C-specifier position, rather than the complementizer position itself.[3] The specific phrase structure productions for projections of I and C appear in (4) and (5).

(4) (a) IP → NP $\overline{\text{I}}$

   (b) $\overline{\text{I}}$→ I VP

(5) (a) CP → (NP| PP| CP) $\overline{\text{C}}$

   (b) $\overline{\text{C}}$→ C IP

The nonlexical expansions of I and C are given by the productions (6). The first righthand side alternative in (6a) is redundant, but we show it explicitly for clarity.

(6) (a) I → ϵ| (M)(*have*)(*to*)(*be1*)(*be2*)

   (b) C → ϵ| *for* | *that* | *whether*

As implied by the $\overline{\text{X}}$ schema (1) and (3), most base productions are binary branching. Note that (6a) could easily be stated in binary form. We ignore certain details regarding the schema that are required to permit several constituents to be attached as complements, specifiers, or adjuncts of the same head. To illustrate, (1b) permits attachment of only a single constituent as complement of the head X. But for many languages most analyses assume that more than one such constituent may be attached. The 'abstract syntax' thus contains the nonbinary branching scheme (7) in place of (1b). The 'concrete syntax' may be captured succinctly by a binary-branching scheme with recursion on a category symbol, for example as in (8). Recursion is via the category X of the head; constituents are attached as sisters of this symbol, one at a time, until the subcategorization/thematic requirements of the head are satisfied. Binary branching rules have certain advantages over nonbinary ones, particularly describing free constituent order, optional constituents, and occurrence of nonarguments, such as adjuncts and parentheticals, between the complements of a head (Jensen, 1987). More traditional accounts of these phenomena assume unordered righthand sides of productions, unit productions, or construction-specific transformations, such as NP-shift.

(7) $\overline{X} \rightarrow X \, YP_1 \ldots YP_n$

(8) (a) $X \rightarrow X \, YP$

    (b) $\overline{X} \rightarrow X$

In addition to the productions implied by the schema (1) and (3), the base contains productions that rewrite a symbol X into the empty string ϵ, as in (9). The schema (9) has instances for X equal to C, I, V, NP, PP, CP, and possibly other categories. A phrase marker $[x \; \epsilon]$ derived by application of one such rule is called an *empty category* of category X.

(9) $X \rightarrow \epsilon$

An empty category generated by (9) is said to be *base generated*. In the model of transformational grammar, empty categories also arise due to the operation of transformations. Application of Move-α or Quantifier Raising (QR) leaves an empty category (a *trace*) at the extraction site and crucially induces a syntactic relation between the moved constituent and the trace. By the trace convention, the trace-antecedent relation is represented by coindexation of the two elements. The moved constituent together with the traces coindexed with it are said to form a *syntactic chain*. As noted in the introduction to this chapter, it is not crucial to the notion of trace-antecedent relations that they are transformationally defined. Instead, we pursue here the idea that they are anaphoric relations, established by an interpretive rule.

Base rules like (9) are also needed in a transformational model, assuming a strict version of Emonds' (1976) Structure Preserving Hypothesis. This constraint requires a target position $[x \; \epsilon]$ in the input phrase marker for movement of another phrase marker [$_X$ α]. Under this interpretation, Move-α is structure preserving, but Quantifier Raising is not.

3. ATTRIBUTE GRAMMARS

Attribute grammars are an extension of context-free grammars, originally developed for the formal specification of the semantics of programming languages and their compilers. Two closely related formalisms, developed with the same purpose in mind and at about the same time, are the Affix grammars of Koster (1971) and the Two-level grammars of van Wijngaarden (1969). Although the generative power of these formalisms is equivalent to that of unrestricted rewriting systems, they are of significant linguistic interest, in the sense used by Chomsky (1959), since they permit suitable structural descriptions to be associated with the strings they generate.[4]

The first formal characterization of attribute grammars is due to Knuth (1968), although the main ideas can be traced back to the syntax-directed compiler of Irons (1961). Attribute grammars appear related to the unification-based formalisms discussed by Shieber (1986) in one important respect: namely, the basic 'informational elements' in unification formalisms are attribute-value structures of the sort that appear in attribute grammars. Attribute-value structures are in turn an elaboration of the feature matrices used for phonological description. The two formalisms differ significantly, however, in the kinds of operations allowed to describe attribute values and in their separation of phrase structure from attribution structure. The characterization of attribute grammars in the present section is adapted from Waite and Goos (1984).

3.1. *Formal Definition of Attribute Grammars*

An *attribute grammar* is defined using a context-free grammar $G = (N, T, P, Z)$, where N and T are nonterminal and terminal vocabularies, respectively, P is a finite set of productions, and Z the start symbol. The grammar defines for each symbol $X \in N \cup T$ a set $A(X)$ of *attributes* or syntactic features, and a *type* or domain $dom(a)$ of possible values for each attribute $a \in A(X)$.

Each attribute represents a specific, possibly context-sensitive prop-

erty of symbol X. For each occurrence $X.a$ of the attribute in a derivation tree containing X, its value must be uniquely defined.[5] An *attribute
occurrence* is a single-assignment variable.

Attribute values are defined by *attribution rules* of the form $X_i.a \leftarrow$
$f(X_j.b, \ldots, X_k.c)$, associated with each production $p = X_0 \to X_1 \ldots X_n$
in the grammar, $0 \leq i, j, k \leq n$. The intent is that f is an effectively
computable applicative expression whose value depends only on the values of attribute occurrences associated with symbols in p. In particular,
f cannot perform any kind of tree traversals to compute its value.[6]
When p applies in a derivation, the attribution rule defines the value of
attribute occurrence $X_i.a$ in terms of the occurrences $X_j.b, \ldots, X_k.c$,
associated with other symbols in p. We let $R(p)$ denote the packet of
attribution rules associated with p.

In addition to attribution rules, the grammar may define *attribute
conditions* of the form $B(X_i.a, \ldots, X_j.b)$, for $0 \leq i, j \leq n$, on the attributes of symbols occurring in the production p. These conditions
are truth-valued functions that must be satisfied in derivation trees requiring application of the production, and thus contribute to the notion
of *grammaticality* in the language generated by the attribute grammar.
Otherwise plausible constructions may be ruled out by the violation of
one or more attribute conditions. We let $B(p)$ denote the packet of
attribute conditions associated with p.

The above remarks are summarized in definition (10):

(10) An *attribute grammar* is a four-tuple $AG = (G, A, R, B)$, where

    (a) $G = (N, T, P, Z)$ is a context-free grammar,

    (b) $A = \bigcup_{X \in V} A(X)$ is a finite set of *attributes*,

    (c) $R = \bigcup_{p \in P} R(p)$ is a finite set of *attribution rules* of the form
$X.a \leftarrow f(Y.b, \ldots, Z.c)$, and

    (d) $B = \bigcup_{p \in P} B(p)$ is a finite set of *attribute conditions* of the
form $B(X.a, \ldots, Y.b)$.

The underlying context-free grammar G assigns a derivation tree to
each sentence in $L(G)$. Each node X in the tree is annotated with the set
$A(X)$ of attributes associated with X. If the grammar is well-defined,
in the sense given below, then it is possible to evaluate each attribute
occurrence on the tree. A tree generated by G is *correctly attributed* if
upon attribute evaluation, all attribute conditions yield *true*. We define

the *language* generated by the attribute grammar, $L(AG)$, as the set of sentences in $L(G)$ that have at least one correctly attributed tree.[7]

For each production p in G, we let the set $AF(p) = \{X_i.a : X_i.a \leftarrow f(\ldots) \in R(p)\}$ be the set of *defining occurrences* of attributes associated with symbols in p. The attributes associated with a symbol X are classified according to the manner in which their values depend on attributes in the neighboring nodes. We say that attribute occurrence $X.a$ is *synthesized* if its value depends only on values of attributes on daughters of X, and possibly also other attributes of X. The attribute occurrence is *inherited* if its value depends on the values of attributes associated with the parent or sister nodes of X. Thus, synthesized attribute values result from consideration of the subtree dominated by the symbol X, while inherited attribute values depend on the local syntactic environment (parent and sisters) of X. This classification of attributes in a grammar is stated precisely in (11).

(11) Let $AG = (G, A, R, B)$ be an attribute grammar. An attribute $a \in A$ is *synthesized* if there exists a production $p = X \to \gamma$ such that $X.a \in AF(p)$. The attribute is *inherited* if there is a production $q = Y \to \alpha X \beta$ such that $X.a \in AF(q)$.

We let $AS(X)$ and $AI(X)$ denote the sets of synthesized and inherited attributes of X, as in (12).

(12) $AS(X) = \{X.a : \text{ for some } p = X \to \gamma \in P, X.a \in AF(p)\}$
$AI(X) = \{X.a : \text{ for some } p = Y \to \alpha X \beta \in P, X.a \in AF(p)\}$

We admit certain attributes, such as the lexical features of a lexical item, whose values are determined by the symbol with which they are associated. We call these attributes *intrinsic* or inherent, since their values are defined in the lexicon. This class, however, may be reduced to inherited and synthesized attributes without loss of generality.[8]

3.2. *Well-formedness of Attribute Grammars*

Nothing thus far prevents writing attribute grammars that yield improperly attributed trees. This happens when some occurrence of an attribute in a tree has its value defined multiple times (in possibly multiple ways), or does not have a value defined at all.

(13) An attribute grammar $AG = (G, A, R, B)$ is *consistent* if for each attribute occurrence $X.a$ in a derivation tree generated by

G, at most one attribution rule is applicable to compute its value. The grammar is *complete* if at least one such attribution rule is applicable.

To illustrate the notion of consistency, the *Case* value assigned to a noun phrase (NP) must be uniquely defined. If several mechanisms exist for Case assignment to a given NP position, at most one may apply. Thus, an embedded subject position may be Case-marked by *tense*, a *for* complementizer, or an exceptional Case marking verb. The interaction of these mechanisms must be such that at most one applies. If an attribute grammar is consistent, then for each symbol X in its vocabulary the sets $AS(X)$ and $AI(X)$ are disjoint: $AS(X) \cap AI(X) = \emptyset$. If the grammar is complete, then $A(X) = AS(X) \cup AI(X)$, for each X; we obtain a partition of the set of attributes associated with each symbol X into synthesized and inherited attributes (Waite and Goos, 1984).

Well-formedness of an attribute grammar also depends on the nature of the data dependencies between attributes. Let $X.a$ be an attribute occurrence whose value is defined by the attribution rule $X.a \leftarrow f(X_j.b, \ldots, X_k.c)$. In order to compute the value of $X.a$, we must know the values of attribute occurrences $X_j.b, \ldots, X_k.c$ upon which $X.a$ depends.[9] In this case we say that $X.a$ *directly depends* on $X_j.b, \ldots, X_k.c$. This situation is shown graphically in the directed graph (14), where the node set contains the attribute occurrences involved and the edge set contains the direct attribute dependencies.

(14) $X.a$

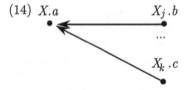

In general, given a structure tree τ with node set K and collection D of direct dependency relations between attributes, a *dependency graph* $DT(\tau) = \langle \bigcup_{X \in K} A(X), D \rangle$ is defined that records all the dependency relations arising from the attribution associated with the productions applied to derive the tree. We are now in a position to define a *well-defined* attribute grammar, as in (15).

(15) An attribute grammar is *well-defined* if and only if it is consistent, complete, and the dependency graph $DT(\tau)$ is acyclic for

each derivation tree τ corresponding to a sentence of $L(G)$.[10]

3.3. *Attributed Definition of Grammatical Processes*

Government-Binding is a modular theory in which phrase structure rules play only a limited, though basic role in the definition of a language. Following an argument by Stowell (1981), most current work assumes that the phrase structure component is eliminated—that is, reduced to the $\overline{X}$ schema (1), (3), and (9) (Lasnik and Uriagereka, 1988). Attribute grammars can be used to capture core grammatical processes, such as government and Case marking. Each process defines formally part of the overall attribution on the trees generated by the grammar.

3.3.1. *Government*

We consider government first. The core notion is the relation between the head of a phrase and each of its complements and specifiers, as defined in (16). The relation *m-command* (maximal command) used in (16ii) is defined in (17).

(16) α *governs* β if

  (i) α is a zero-level category; if α is I(nflection), then AGR has a non-*nil* value.

  (ii) α m-commands β.

  (iii) Each maximal projection dominating β also dominates α.

(17) α *m-commands* β if

  (i) Neither α nor β dominates one another.

  (ii) The first maximal projection dominating α also dominates β.

If the head in question is of category I, then the agreement element AGR must be present. Thus, the subject of a finite sentence is governed by the inflectional element, while the subject of an infinitival sentence is ungoverned (by that element). Condition (16i) must be carefully formulated. The agreement attribute AGR is in the attribution set of each category that exhibits agreement phenomena, as shown in (18a). The domain of AGR is (18b); it includes the value *nil*, which is taken by AGR when the category in question does not have 'any' agreement features.

(18) (a) AGR is in $A(X)$, for X =N, $\overline{\text{N}}$, NP, I, $\overline{\text{I}}$, V, $\overline{\text{V}}$, VP.

(b) $dom(AGR) = \{nil\} \bigcup \{ \langle P, G, N \rangle : P = 1, 2, 3, G = masc,$
fem, *neuter*, and $N = plural, sing\}$

By standard assumptions, only maximal projections may appear as complements, adjuncts, or specifiers of a head. It follows from condition (16iii) that only maximal projections may be governed. Current usage of the notion of government, however, assumes that if α governs XP, then α also governs the head X and the intermediate projection $\overline{\text{X}}$. The core notion (16) of government is extended as in (19).

(19) If α governs β , then α also governs the head of β and its intermediate projections.

By this extension, a node of any category may be governed. We assume an attribute *Gov* that is associated with all categories in the grammar. According to the definitions, a node may be governed in the core sense of (16) and (19) by only one other node. An appropriate domain for *Gov* is pointers to the annotated tree nodes defined by the grammar. The attribute evaluates to a pointer to the governor of the node that bears the attribute occurrence. If there is no governor for the node, then *Gov* evaluates to the special value *nil*. The core process of government is captured by the attribution in (20a–b), with direct reference to the $\overline{\text{X}}$ schema (1). If X is a symbol in a grammar rule, we use the notation $\uparrow$ X to denote a pointer to the record structure of the node corresponding to symbol X.[11] The attribute *head* in the attribution is associated with all nonzero level categories and its domain is pointers to record structures labeled by zero-level categories—*i.e.*, heads of phrases. (20c) shows the dependencies induced by government; similar dependency graphs may be drawn for attribution statements in the remainder of the chapter.

(20) (a) $\overline{\text{X}} \rightarrow$ X YP
attribution:
$\overline{\text{X}}.head \leftarrow \uparrow$ X
YP. $Gov \leftarrow \uparrow$ X
X. $Gov \leftarrow \overline{\text{X}}.Gov$

(b) XP $\rightarrow$ YP $\overline{\text{X}}$
attribution:
XP.$head \leftarrow \overline{\text{X}}.head$

$\text{YP.}Gov \leftarrow \overline{\text{X}}.head$
$\overline{\text{X}}.Gov \leftarrow \text{XP.}Gov$

(c)

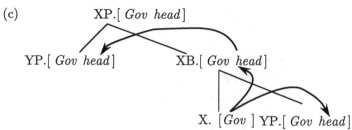

The category variable X in (20) ranges over lexical categories. For X equal to I(nflection), the attribution may not be obtained from the same schema. Instead, the attribution should be sensitive to the presence of the *AGR* attribute on the I node, as in (21). The agreement feature is propagated upwards from the I to the Ī node. If $\text{I.}AGR \neq nil$, then I governs the NP subject. If $\text{I.}AGR = nil$, however, condition (16i) of government does not obtain, and I does not govern. The Subject position may still be governed exceptionally, by a *for* clause complementizer, if present, or by the governor of the clause, if it is an exceptional Case marking (*ecm*) verb such as *want* or *believe*. The governor of the IP node is given by either of these two possibilities, or is *nil* otherwise. The attribution in (22) implements this assumption. The values of the *Gov* and *ecm* attributes of the CP node in (22b) are, in turn, determined by the context in which the node appears.

(21) (a) Ī→I VP
     attribution:
     $\overline{\text{I}}.head \leftarrow \uparrow\text{I}$
     $\overline{\text{I}}.AGR \leftarrow \text{I.}AGR$

     (b) IP→NP Ī
     attribution:
     $\text{NP.}Gov \leftarrow$ if $\overline{\text{I}}.AGR \neq nil$ then $\overline{\text{I}}.head$ else $\text{IP.}Gov$
     $\text{IP.}head \leftarrow \overline{\text{I}}.head$

(22) (a) $\overline{\text{C}}$→C IP
     attribution:

$$\text{IP}.Gov \leftarrow \text{if } C.forcomp \text{ then } \uparrow C$$
$$\text{else if } \overline{C}.ecm \text{ then } \overline{C}.Gov$$
$$\text{else } nil$$
$$\overline{C}.head \leftarrow \uparrow C$$

(b) $CP \rightarrow (XP) \ \overline{C}$

attribution:

$\overline{C}.Gov \leftarrow CP.Gov$

$\overline{C}.ecm \leftarrow CP.ecm$

$CP.head \leftarrow \overline{C}.head$

We have ignored proper government in this discussion, in particular government by a local antecedent. Given a suitable definition of this notion, the manner in which it by may expressed in an attributed definition seems clear, although it certainly may raise some questions. For example, subject position may be governed by a tensed inflection node, but properly governed only by an element in C-specifier position. It is necessary to identify the precise mechanism by which the relevant governor is chosen.

3.3.2. *Case Marking*

Grammatical Case is assigned to a noun phrase by a Case assigner structurally, under government, or inherently, in double-object constructions (Chomsky, 1981). The instances of structural Case assignment are: (i) assignment of nominative Case to an NP subject, if governed by a tensed I node (if the node is not tensed, subject position may still be Case-marked exceptionally, as detailed below); (ii) objective Case assignment by a verb; (iii) oblique Case assignment by a preposition; and (iv) genitive Case marking of an NP in N-specifier position.

Structural Case assignment is captured by the attributed definitions (23)–(24). The attribute *Case* is associated with NP, the categories of potential Case assigners, such as V and P, and several other categories that may intervene in the process, including CP and IP. The domain of the attribute is (25), which includes the special value *nil*. A node X is said to have 'no Case' if X.*Case* has the value *nil*.

(23) (a) $IP \rightarrow NP \ \overline{I}$

attribution:

$NP.Case \leftarrow \text{if } \overline{I}.tensed \text{ then } Nom \text{ else } IP.Case$

(b) $\overline{X} \to X$ YP
   attribution:
   YP.*Case*←X.*Case*

(c) NP→NP $\overline{N}$
   attribution:
   NP2.*Case*←*Gen*

(24) (a) $\overline{C} \to C$ IP
   attribution:
   IP.*Case*← if C.*forcomp* then *Oblq*
            else if $\overline{C}$.*ecm* then $\overline{C}$.*Case* else *nil*

(b) CP→(XP) $\overline{C}$
   attribution:
   $\overline{C}$.*Case*←CP.*Case*

(25) *dom*(*Case*) = *Nom, Acc, Dat, Oblq, ..., nil*

The attribution (23a) defines the first instance of structural Case assignment. It interacts with (24), which defines the mechanism of exceptional Case marking. Notice that CP deletion is not postulated, but rather that the categories CP, $\overline{C}$, and IP bear the *Case* attribute, and are instruments in propagating a Case value from an exceptional Case assigner to the exceptionally Case-marked NP. This formalization is similar to that of van Riemsdijk and Williams (1986), who assume that a maximal projection may be lexically marked 'transparent' to government and Case marking. (23b–c) cover the other instances of structural Case assignment. Inherent Case assignment, not covered by (23), may be added similarly, although the actual motivation for inherent Case marking is controversial.

The Case filter, a major constraint on NP distribution, is simply expressed by attribute condition (26). It is associated with all productions that expand NP.

(26) Case filter:
   if ¬NP.*empty* then NP.*Case*≠*nil*

4. DETERMINATION OF EMPTY CATEGORIES

In the interpretive model of grammar adopted here, all empty categories arise by base generation. The categories generated, however, exhibit different behavior, as they appear in different environments. Government-Binding theory distinguishes four types of empty category (of syntactic type NP): *Wh*-trace, NP-trace, PRO, and small *pro*. In a transformational account, the first two are instances of trace, and arise due to the operation of Move-α. The last two categories are base generated and behave like empty pronominals. Small *pro* does not occur in English, however.

The functional type of an empty category may be encoded with two attributes *anaphoric* and *pronominal*, as in (27), like the way overt nominals are partitioned. *Wh*-trace is nonanaphoric and nonpronominal (a referential expression); NP-trace is anaphoric and nonpronominal (a pure anaphor); and PRO is both anaphoric and pronominal (with no counterpart in overt nominals).[12]

(27)

	Wh-trace	NP-trace	pro	PRO
anaphoric	−	+	−	+
pronominal	−	−	+	+

An empty category's type may be functionally determined by the category's environment. Chomsky (1982) refers to the argument status of the position in which the category appears and to properties of its antecedent, if it has one. Thus *Wh*-trace is in argument position (A-position) and bound by an element in nonargument position ($\overline{A}$ position, $\overline{A}$-bound). NP-trace appears in argument position and is A-bound by an element in a position at which no thematic role is assigned ($\overline{\theta}$-bound). PRO is in argument position, and is optionally A-bound by an element with independent thematic role (θ-bound).

A crucial property of Chomsky's functional determination of empty categories is that it requires reference to the antecedent of the category, if it has one, before its type may be determined. In Correa (1987) a different set of contextual conditions is used to determine the functional type of an empty category without reference to its antecedent—that is, before chains are hypothesized. These conditions are the argument status of the position, government, and Case. Hence, a trace is (properly) governed, while PRO is not. Two instances of *Wh*-trace are recognized: variables and intermediate traces in C-specifier position.[13] Variables are in argument position and Case marked, while NP-trace is also in argument position, but not Case marked. A *Wh*-trace in C-specifier position is, by definition, in nonargument position. This yields the method (28) for functional classification of empty categories, according to the new conditions.

(28)

	A-position	Government	Case
Wh-trace (variable)	+	+	+
Wh-trace (C-spec)	−	+	−
NP-trace	+	+	−
PRO	+	−	−

The fact that (28) does not refer to antecedents to determine functional type is extremely useful for the formulation of interpretive analysis procedures for the grammar. It means that we may determine the type of a category without hypothesizing in advance the chain to which the category belongs. This avoids an inefficient generate-and-test approach for the interpretive computation of the chains present in a given surface string. Instead, once the relevant phrase structure is identified, it is sufficient to look at the argument status of the position, and whether it is governed and Case-marked—all three of which are conditions established independently of chain formation. The analysis (28) is a crucial element of the interpretive Chain rule in Correa (1987), and of the bottom-up version of the rule developed in the next section.

Before leaving this section, however, it is of interest to discuss alternatives for the determination of empty categories. An interpretation of the approach (28), and also that in Chomsky (1982), is that empty categories are base generated (or transformationally inserted) as categories of type NP, without instantiation of the values of the features that determine their functional type. That is, at generation time there is only one type of empty category: empty NP with unspecified functional type. Scheme (9) generates empty categories and may be augmented by the attribution (29), so that it defines the values of the attributes *anaphoric* and *pronominal*. The functional type of a category is determined when it is generated in a particular context. The attributes *anaphoric* and *pronominal* are synthesized by NP, but their values may not be determined until the values of the attributes *Apos*, *Gov*, and *Case* are instantiated. The latter are instantiated only when the NP is inserted in a particular context.[14]

(29) NP$\rightarrow \epsilon$

attribution:

NP.*anaphoric*←if NP.*Apos*='–' then '–'
      else if NP.*Gov*=*nil* then '+'
          else if NP.*Case*=*nil* then '+' else '–'
NP.*pronominal*← if NP.*Gov*=*nil* then '+' else '–'

A second interpretation of (28) is as a set of conditions on the contexts in which an empty category of a given type may be inserted. Under this approach, the type of an empty category is determined when it is generated. The attribution in (30) implements this approach. The attribution rules fix functional type and may be evaluated as soon as the production is applied, while the attribute conditions constrain the contexts in which the category may appear, and may be evaluated only once the context is established. This new attribution parallels the 'intrinsic' determination of empty categories assumed in Chomsky (1981) and discussed by Lasnik and Uriagereka (1988), and is completely equivalent to the attribution (29) in terms of the annotated trees it defines.[15]

(30) NP→ ϵ
    attribution:
    NP.*anaphoric*←x
    NP.*pronominal*←y, for x, y='+', '–'
    condition:
    NP.*anaphoric*=if NP.*A-pos*='–' then '–'
          else if NP.*Gov*=*nil* then '+'
             else if NP.*Case*=*nil* then '+' else '–'
    NP.*pronominal*=if NP.*Gov*=*nil* then '+' else '–'

In a transformational model, intrinsic determination of empty categories is problematic in the following case. The functional type of a category left by Move-α is presumably determined by lexical features of the moved phrase, since the structural description of Move-α does not indicate whether movement is to an argument or nonargument position. Otherwise two distinct movement transformations would need be posited. But then successive movement of the same phrase may leave two traces of different functional type, as in (31), which is NP-movement followed by *Wh*-movement. Thus, intrinsic determination is not possible in a transformational definition of chains, without unduly complicating the transformational component. Functional determination, as given by (28) or Chomsky (1982), must be assumed.

(31) Who$_i$ was [$_{\rm IP}$ [ϵ]$_i$ beaten [ϵ]$_i$]

A third alternative for the determination of empty categories is free-determination. As described in Lasnik and Uriagereka (1988), this is similar to functional determination in that there is only one 'type' of empty category at generation time, namely an empty NP with functional type unspecified. However, rather than having an algorithm that functionally determines the type of a category at insertion time, there is a simpler algorithm that 'freely' assigns types to categories (at some level of representation), while "independent principles will rule out the bad constructions" (Lasnik and Uriagereka, 1988, p. 66). In this respect, then, free determination is actually closer to intrinsic determination. The independent principles needed must include or subsume the contextual conditions (28) and those of Chomsky (1982). From a computational viewpoint there appears to be no important difference between free determination and the previous two approaches.

5. INTERPRETIVE CHAIN RULE

The base component generates all possible S-structures. Traces, as well as antecedents, are base generated in their surface positions. We refer to an S-structure in which trace-antecedent relations are not identified as a *surface structure*. Given a structure in this sense, the objective of the Chain rule is to identify interpretively the trace-antecedent relations that may be present in that structure. We assume an attribute *Chain*, associated with NP, whose domain is pointers to annotated tree nodes. The Chain rule evaluates the *Chain* attributes of the NPs in the given surface structure. Upon evaluation, if the attribute is associated with a node X, it points to the next element in the chain to which X belongs, or is *nil* if X is the last element of the chain. This is illustrated with a simple example in (32). Application of the Chain rule yields an S-structure.[16]

(32) [$_{\rm NP}$Who]$_{.Chain}$ does John think[$_{\rm CP}$[$_{\rm NP}\epsilon$]$_{.Chain}$Mary likes[$_{\rm NP}\epsilon$]$_{.nil}$]

The functional type of an empty category may be determined in advance of the application of the Chain rule, by the method of last section. We note that the method uniquely determines the type of the category, but that nonstructural ambiguity may be present regarding government and Case marking. For example, in (33) there is ambiguity regarding the type of the empty category in embedded subject position, depending on whether the matrix verb *want* exceptionally governs and Case marks the position. In (33a), *Wh*-trace and PRO are the only two possibilities. NP-trace is not feasible, since if the position is governed it is also Case-marked by *want*. The ambiguity between *Wh*-trace and PRO disappears once the Chain rule (or alternatively, well-formedness conditions on chains) applies. *Wh*-trace is not possible since it would lack an antecedent; PRO is the only possibility. In the closely related (33b), the situation is reversed. PRO is not possible, since this would leave a vacuous operator *who*; hence *Wh*-trace is the only alternative. In (33c), similar considerations indicate that NP-trace and PRO are both plausible, but only NP-trace satisfies all considerations.

(33) (a) John wants $[_{CP}\ [\epsilon]$ to do the dishes]

   (b) Who$_i$ does John want $[_{CP}\ [\epsilon]_i$ to do the dishes]

   (c) John$_i$ is wanted $[_{CP}\ [\epsilon]_i$ to do the dishes]

We distinguish three kinds of chains: elementary, argument, and nonargument. Elementary chains are a special instance of argument chains and contain a single NP element. If the NP is lexical, it must be in a position which is Case-marked and θ-marked. An expletive element is exceptional, since it requires no θ marking. If the NP is empty, it must be PRO and θ-marked. In general, argument chains consist of elements in argument position, and are characterized by the fact that their last element is a trace in a θ-marked position.[17] Since the element must be NP-trace, the position is Caseless. The θ-criterion and the Projection Principle imply that any other chain element, including the head, is in a non-θ-marked position. Thematic theory determines that subject position (of IP) is the only possibility for the other chain elements. If the chain is headed by a lexical NP, Case theory requires that exactly one position be Case-marked; Chomsky (1986) assumes that position is always the head.

   Nonargument chains are headed by an operator in C-specifier position or by a phrase in Topic position. Every other element of the chain, except the last, is a trace in C-specifier (nonargument) position. The last element is a trace in Case-marked argument position, and is either θ-marked, or the head of an argument chain. In section 6 we will discuss an additional locality condition on chain bindings.

In addition to the attribute *Chain* associated with NP, and corresponding to the two types of nonelementary chain, the Chain rule assumes a two pointer-valued attributes *A-Chain* and *AB-Chain* (corresponding to the linguistic notions of an A-chain and an $\overline{\text{A}}$-chain). These attributes are associated with the nodes CP, $\overline{\text{C}}$, IP, $\overline{\text{I}}$, VP, $\overline{\text{V}}$, PP, and $\overline{\text{P}}$, all of which may be in the c-command domain of NP, for some tree generated by the base.[18] It is sufficient to consider only these nodes for the propagation of chain links, since a computationally important property of movement, which follows in part from the Binding theory of Chomsky (1981), is that movement is always to a c-commanding position.

The Chain rule defines how the attributes *Chain*, *A-Chain*, and *AB-Chain* are evaluated locally in terms of each other and other properties of an S-structure tree. More abstractly, the Chain rule defines local constraints on the possible values of these attributes. The domain of evaluation is always limited to an elementary tree defined by a production in the grammar. From this observation, it is easy to see that the account of chains given by the Chain rule always reduces to simple relations between attribute occurrences in elementary trees. Informally, the steps of the Chain rule are as in (34). Note, however, that attributed definitions do not imply a particular ordering of attribute evaluation steps; (34) is a sketch of how evaluation might proceed.

(34) Chain rule (sketch)
      For each NP in the input structure,

    1. Determine the functional type of the NP.

    2. Assign the NP to a chain:
    Evaluate the *Chain* attribute of the NP, according to its functional type and other properties of the position it occupies, including θ-role.

    3. Start, propagate, or terminate a chain:
    Evaluate the *AB-Chain* and *A-Chain* attributes on the parent of the NP. The evaluation depends on properties of the NP and its position.

The attribution that defines the Chain rule is stated in (35), (37), and (38) below. (35) shows the schema for the productions that introduce complements of a head X. The predicates *Wh-trace* and *NP-trace* in (35a) evaluate to true, according to the type of the NP. If X is a symbol with several occurrences in a production, the notation X_i, for $i \geq 0$, denotes the i-th occurrence of X on the righthand side, or the symbol X on the lefthand side, if $i = 0$. We employ PLNLP notation in the attribute conditions, by which a Boolean test like $\neg X.a$ on attribute $X.a$ succeeds if $X.a=nil$. An important property of (35) and subsequent attribution statements is that attribute evaluation is local; that is, limited to attribute occurrences on the elementary tree defined by the production in question.

(35) (a) X→ X NP
        attribution:
        $NP.Chain \leftarrow nil$
        $X_0.AB\text{-}Chain \leftarrow$ if *Wh*-trace(NP) then $\uparrow$NP
                        else $X_1.AB\text{-}Chain$
        $X_0.A\text{-}Chain \leftarrow$ if NP-trace(NP) then $\uparrow$NP
                        else $X_1.A\text{-}Chain$
        condition:
        $\neg$ *Wh*-trace(NP) $\vee \neg X_1.AB\text{-}Chain$
        $\neg$NP-trace(NP) $\vee \neg X_1.A\text{-}Chain$

  (b) X→X YP (YP$\neq$NP)
        attribution:
        $X_0.AB\text{-}Chain \leftarrow$ if $YP.AB\text{-}Chain$ then $YP.AB\text{-}Chain$
                        else $X_1.AB\text{-}Chain$
        $X_0.A\text{-}Chain \leftarrow$ if $YP.A\text{-}Chain$ then $YP.A\text{-}Chain$
                        else $X_1.A\text{-}Chain$
        condition:
        $\neg YP.AB\text{-}Chain \ \vee \neg X_1.AB\text{-}Chain$
        $\neg YP.A\text{-}Chain \ \vee \neg X_1.A\text{-}Chain$

In (35a), independent attribution determines the functional type of the NP object. Setting to *nil* the *Chain* attribute of P, regardless of its type, captures concisely the fact that movement is never to object position (as implied by the θ-criterion). The attributes *A-Chain* and *AB-Chain* on the parent node X_0 are evaluated according to the type of the NP. Thus, if NP is *Wh*-trace, $X_0.AB\text{-}Chain$ is a pointer to NP ($\uparrow$NP); this signals the start of a nonargument chain. Otherwise, $X_0.AB\text{-}Chain$ evaluates to the value of the corresponding attribute occurrence on the daughter node X_1. This value is non-*nil* if a nonargument chain extends across this node.

The use in (35) of an $\overline{X}$ scheme recursive on X allows for attachment of multiple complements of a head. This subtle point was ignored in the attribution for government and Case marking, but it is of interest here. The recursive scheme was introduced in (8) above. Its application is shown in (36), where the complements of the head verb are attached as sisters one at a time. The symbol X on the righthand side in (35a–b) is either the lexical head of the phrase defined, or a phrase consisting of the lexical head and several complements already attached. Upon lexical insertion of a formative under a category X, the attributes *AB-Chain* and *A-Chain* of X are set to *nil*—that is, no chain propagates below this node.

(36) (a) John$_i$ was [$_V$ [$_V$ given [ϵ]$_i$] a book]

  (b) Who$_i$ did Paul [$_V$ [$_V$ give a book] to [ϵ]$_i$]

  (c) What$_j$ was John$_i$ [$_V$ [$_V$ given [ϵ]$_i$] [ϵ]$_j$]

  (d)*What$_j$ ... who$_i$ ... he [$_V$ [$_V$ gave [ϵ]$_i$] [ϵ]$_j$]

The attribute conditions in (35a–b) limit movement (of either kind, argument or nonargument) to only one extraction of each kind per phrase. By the first condition in (35a), for example, either NP is not a *Wh*-trace or there is no nonargument chain across the sister NP$_1$ node. Hence the examples (36a–c) are accounted for, but a configuration like (36d) may not be correctly attributed. An immediate consequence of this restriction on extractions is that the Chain rule does not account for parasitic gap constructions. The explanation of these constructions is controversial; we have not considered extension of the Chain rule to these cases.

The attribution for the productions that expand IP appears in (37). In (37a), the *Chain* attribute of the subject is immediately set to $\overline{\mathrm{I}}$.*A-Chain*, which is either *nil* or points to a lower element of an A-Chain. Several interesting facts are implied at once by this simple assignment. NPs in subject position will never appear as intermediate elements of $\overline{\mathrm{A}}$ chains. Since no condition is put on the functional type of this NP, it follows that PRO, overt NP, or *Wh*-trace may appear as head of an A-Chain. If there is no open A-Chain in the subtree dominated by $\overline{\mathrm{I}}$ ($\overline{\mathrm{I}}$.*A-Chain=nil*), this subject position will be the last element of a chain. The first attribute condition in (37a) limits to one the number of phrases that may be extracted from an IP phrase, per type of movement. The second condition, on external θ-role assignment by $\overline{\mathrm{I}}$, blocks chains with multiple θ-roles. The third condition requires a θ-role at the position or a link to an element with a θ-role. The condition rules out non-θ-marked $\overline{\text{A}}$ chains, as in $*What_i$ $[\epsilon]_i$ *seems that John is here.* The last two conditions thus contribute to the implementation of the θ-criterion.

(37) (a) IP→NP $\overline{\text{I}}$
   attribution:
   NP.$Chain$←$\overline{\text{I}}$.A-$Chain$
   IP.AB-$Chain$←if Wh-trace(NP) then ↑NP
                          else $\overline{\text{I}}$.AB-$Chain$
   IP.A-$Chain$←if NP-trace(NP) then ↑ NP
                          else *nil*
   condition:
   ¬ Wh-trace(NP) ∨ ¬$\overline{\text{I}}$.AB-$Chain$
   ¬$\overline{\text{I}}$.A-$Chain$ ∨ ¬$\overline{\text{I}}$.θ_E
   $\overline{\text{I}}$.A-$Chain$ ∨ $\overline{\text{I}}$.θ_E

(b) $\overline{\text{I}}$→I VP
   attribution:
   $\overline{\text{I}}$.AB-$Chain$←VP.AB-$Chain$
   $\overline{\text{I}}$.A-$Chain$←VP.A-$Chain$

The attribution for the productions that expand CP is in (38). Note that by the first attribute condition in (38a–b), presence of C-specifier position is directly correlated to whether an $\overline{\text{A}}$ chain is propagated across the $\overline{\text{C}}$ node (value of $\overline{\text{C}}$.AB-$Chain$). The implications of the attribution may be studied with the help of the previous two sets of rules, (35) and (37).

(38) (a) CP→$\overline{\text{C}}$
   attribution:
   CP.AB-$Chain$←$\overline{\text{C}}$.AB-$Chain$
   CP.A-$Chain$←$\overline{\text{C}}$.A-$Chain$
   condition:
   ¬$\overline{\text{C}}$.AB-$Chain$

(b) CP→NP $\overline{\text{C}}$
   attribution:
   NP.$Chain$←$\overline{\text{C}}$.AB-$Chain$
   CP.AB-$Chain$←if Wh-trace(NP) then ↑NP else *nil*
   CP.A-$Chain$←$\overline{\text{C}}$.A-$Chain$

condition:

$\overline{C}$.*AB-Chain*

Wh-trace(NP) ∨ operator(NP)

(c) $\overline{C} \rightarrow C$ IP

attribution:

$\overline{C}$.*AB-Chain*←IP.*AB-Chain*

$\overline{C}$.*A-Chain*←IP.*A-Chain*

The Chain rule just presented enforces attribute dependencies on the *Chain*, *A-Chain*, and *AB-Chain* attributes in S-structure trees. The attribution may be evaluated bottom-up in the trees defined by the grammar; *Chain* is inherited, but *A-Chain* and *AB-Chain* are synthesized, in contrast to the previous version of the rule (Correa, 1987). The operation of the rule is illustrated with the example (39) from Correa (1987).

(39)   Who does John seem $\left[\begin{smallmatrix}\end{smallmatrix}\right.$ ...

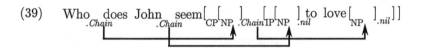

6. BARSS' CHAIN BINDING

The algorithm presented by Barss (1983) assumes the Linking theory of Higginbotham and is a representational characterization of nonargument chains. Rizzi (1986) presents a similar algorithm for argument chains. The framework assumed in this chapter is that of Chomsky (1981); thus we ignore the distinction between linking and coindexing (although in this section we use the linking terminology of Barss). Barss assumes that linking is not automatic under movement, and instead that free linking is carried out at S-structure. The representational characterization (40) of nonargument chains is a set of well-formedness conditions on the output of the free linking rule.[19]

(40) C is an $\overline{\text{A}}$-Chain if:

(i) $C = (a_1, \ldots, a_i, \ldots, a_n)$

(ii) a_n is θ-marked (or binds a θ-marked position)

(iii) a_i is in an $\overline{\text{A}}$ position, for all $i = 1, \ldots, n-1$

(iv) a_i links a_{i+1}, for $i = 1, \ldots, n-1$

(v) a_n is Case-marked; a_i is Caseless, for $i < n$

(vi) a_1 has semantic content

(vii) a_i is a *Wh*-trace, for $i = 2, \ldots, n$

(viii) For all i, j, category of a_i=category of a_j

This characterization of $\overline{\text{A}}$ chains is supplemented by the Locality Principle on Chains (LPC) (41). The notion *most local $\overline{A}$ position* in (41ii) is defined by Barss as in (42).

(41) Locality Principle on Chains (LPC):
Let $C = (a_1, \ldots, a_i, \ldots, a_n)$ be an $\overline{\text{A}}$- Chain. Then:

(i) a_i c-commands a_{i+1}, for $i = 1, \ldots, n-1$

(ii) a_i is the most local $\overline{\text{A}}$ position for a_{i+1}, for $i = 1, \ldots, n-1$

(42) X is *the most local $\overline{A}$ position* for Y if there is no $\overline{\text{A}}$ position Z (intervening between X and Y) such that Z is not in the same $\overline{\text{A}}$-Chain as a licensed position W, where W c-commands Y.

Scoping out the multiple negations in (42) we get the simpler (43).

(43) X is *a most local $\overline{A}$ position* for Y if for each $\overline{\text{A}}$ position Z (intervening between X and Y), there exists a licensed position W such that (i) Z is in the same $\overline{\text{A}}$-Chain as W, and (ii) W c-commands Y.

The Locality Principle on Chains is a close translation of Pesetsky's (1982) Path Containment Condition (PCC), not making use of the notion *path*. Condition (41ii) rules out overlapping but not nested *Wh*-movements, as in (44).

(44) (a) [What subject]$_i$ do you know [who$_j$ PRO
to talk to e$_j$ about e$_i$]

(b) Who$_j$ do you know [[what subject]$_i$ PRO
to talk to e$_j$ about e$_i$]

In (44a) the chains (*what subject*, e$_i$) and (*who*, e$_j$) satisfy the LPC since *what subject* and *who* are most local antecedent for e$_i$ and e$_j$, respectively. *Who* does not block the relation between *what subject*

and e_i since it is in the same $\overline{A}$ chain as e_j, which c-commands e_i.[20]
(44b) on the other hand is not well-formed, since (who, e_i) does not
satisfy the LPC. In spite of the close correspondence between the LPC
and Pesetsky's PCC, they do not completely overlap. The two may be
empirically distinguished, in favor of the LPC. The structures in question
are those in which a nonargument position X intervenes between a Wh-
trace and its antecedent. Consider (45a–b). The sentence is ambiguous,
depending on the extraction site of the Wh element $when$. However,
the sentence is disambiguated by an additional adverbial, as in (45c–d).
In this case, the only interpretation is (45c), with the second adverbial
attached to the lower clause. Wh-movement from the lower clause (45d)
is blocked by presence of the adverbial in the higher clause.

(45) (a) When$_i$ did you tell [$_{CP}$ Mary to leave [ϵ]$_i$]

(b) When$_i$ did you tell [$_{CP}$ Mary to leave] [ϵ]$_i$

(c) When$_i$ did you tell [$_{CP}$ Mary to leave yesterday] [ϵ]$_i$

(d)*When$_i$ did you tell [$_{CP}$ Mary to leave [ϵ]$_i$] yesterday

The LPC accounts for (45d), since the last adverbial is the most local
$\overline{A}$ position for the trace [ϵ]$_i$. Thus the chain ($when$, e_i) is ill-formed. The
PCC on the other hand does not distinguish between (45c) and (45d)
since there is only one $\overline{A}$ chain; it is satisfied trivially in both cases. The
LPC may be incorporated into the Chain rule by constraining values of
occurrences of the attribute $AB\text{-}Chain$. We omit the exact formulation
of this constraint.

It may be verified that the chains defined by the Chain rule satisfy
the Chain Binding conditions (40). The version of the rule defined here
does not allow multiple Wh-extractions, so it trivially satisfies the PCC.
See Correa (1987) for discussion of an extension that obeys Pesetsky's
PCC. The LPC may be easily accounted for as noted above.

7. COMPLEXITY OF CHAIN CONSTRUCTION ALGORITHMS

Barss interprets the chain conditions (40) and the LPC as elements of
a chain construction algorithm, acting as filters on the output of free
linking. The architecture of the algorithm is parallel to that of the
algorithm implicit in Chomsky's (1981) binding theory; it is a generate-
and-test algorithm.

In spite of the possibility of interpreting the chain binding conditions as an algorithm, we propose instead that they should be interpreted as a *specification* of the output of any chain construction algorithm. It is extremely unlikely that a blind generate-and-test algorithm is embodied in an actual performance grammar. The reason for this is clear: the runtime complexity of a generate-and-test algorithm for chain construction is (unnecessarily) related exponentially to the length of the input string being analyzed.

This may be verified by a simple argument. First we need note that the number of nodes in a syntactic tree (say S-structure) is at most linearly related to the length of the terminal string dominated, provided the tree satisfies $\overline{X}$ theory conditions. The following argument shows under what conditions this claim is true. By the succession property of $\overline{X}$ grammars (Kornai, 1983; Pullum, 1985), the length of any derivation employing unit productions alone is limited to the maximum bar level of the grammar. This number is two under our assumptions, and hence the number of tree nodes introduced by such derivations alone, before a branching or terminal node is produced, is bounded by the bar level to two. If the tree in question does not have any empty categories on its frontier, the original assertion follows easily. For if the minimum degree of branching of the tree is $k > 1$, then the number of nodes required is bounded above by $(n+k-2)/(k-1)$. If unit productions are considered, but constrained by $\overline{X}$ theory, then this bound is increased at most by a constant multiplicative factor, namely the bar level.

This condition on empty categories does patently not hold in a Government-Binding theory grammar. The base component may generate infinitely many trees that ultimately yield the empty string. For example, the tree (46), obtained by expansion of the symbol CP without recursion on any category symbol, provides a basic recursive building unit. Recursion is via the symbol CP. All leaves of the unit (C, NP, I, V, and CP) may be expanded into the empty string. We advance as a substantive claim, however, that the number of empty categories in a well-formed (correctly attributed) tree is at most linearly related to the number of overt terminals dominated. The substantive fact about (46) is that other components of the grammar require that at least one of its leaves be overt. Typically a verbal element is required and it may appear under the V, I, or C node. If the verb is interpreted elliptically, then some other leaf—*e.g.*, an argument NP—must be overt.[21]

(46) $[_{CP} \ldots C \; [_{IP} NP \; [_{I'} \; [_{VP} V \; CP \;]]]]$

Since each recursive unit (46) requires at least one overt element, the depth of the recursion in a structure generated from (46) is bounded by the number of overt elements generated. Furthermore, since the number of leaves in the unit is finite (bounded by the grammar), any structure built from (46) by recursion on CP will have a number of empty nodes bounded by the overt elements. Similar considerations may show that structures built by recursion on projections of lexical categories (NP, PP, and so forth) also have this property; typically an overt head is required. The reader is referred to Berwick and Weinberg (1984) for a similar argument to the one just presented. They show that the size of an annotated S-structure generated by a Government-Binding theory grammar is linearly related to the length of the input string.

Having established informally that the number of nodes in a tree generated by a GB grammar is at worst linearly related to the length of the terminal string dominated, the rest of the argument for the complexities of Chain Binding and the Chain rule follows easily. The cases of interest are those in which the number of (embedded) clauses present in the input is proportional to the length of the input. In these cases, and for fixed and small integer k, the number of NP nodes in a tree with $c \cdot n$ nodes is $c \cdot n/k$, where n is the length of the input. Assuming free linking, each NP node can be linked to any other NP node, or to none. Hence there are $c \cdot n/k$ possibilities for each NP, and the total number of candidate linkings generated is $(c \cdot n/k)^{c \cdot n/k}$ Assuming that the Chain Binding conditions (40) may be checked in constant time t_B for each candidate assignment, the running time of Chain Binding is $t_B \cdot (c \cdot n/k)^{c \cdot n/k}$, which is exponentially related to the length of the input string.

In contrast, the attribution associated with each production in the definition of the Chain rule may be evaluated in constant time. This may be verified by noting that the attribution associated with each production is strictly local, in the sense that it refers only to attribute occurrences in the elementary tree defined by the production. Furthermore, attribute values are not used to encode syntactic structure, so that the complexity of each value (*e.g.*, its size) is not related to input length and may be assumed to be constant.[22] Chain computation consists of the evaluation of the attributes *Chain*, *AB-Chain*, and *A-Chain* at each node in the tree and the conditions associated with them. Given a surface tree, the number of productions needed to derive it is linearly related to the input length. It follows that Chain rule application is linearly related to the same string.[23]

In the discussion above we have ignored questions of ambiguity and parsing of the input surface string. Both chain algorithms were compared according to the amount of work each would have to do to identify chains in the input string, assuming a suitable surface structure is available.

8. GRAMMAR AS SPECIFICATION AND GRAMMAR AS REALIZATION

The contrast we have noted between the Chain Binding algorithm and the Chain rule raises some questions about the status of grammatical descriptions like the Chain Binding conditions (40), or a suitably reduced version of the same conditions, and other similar components of GB theory, including Move-α and the Binding theory. The components of the theory are assumed to be elements of the language-particular grammars that describe an ideal speaker's intrinsic competence. However, one of the claims often associated with a linguistic theory is that it provides a description of the actual structure of mentally represented grammars. That is, the theory is claimed to be psychologically real in a rather strong sense. Chomsky (1980, p. 187) remarks "There is no reason for the linguist to refrain from imputing existence to this initial apparatus of mind [universal grammar] as well".

We propose that descriptions of grammatical competence of the sort advanced by GB theory have no psychological reality—they do not describe the actual structure of mentally represented grammars. Instead, the description provided by the theory is an abstract and neutral *specification* of the grammatical competence of the native speaker. Indeed, Chomsky (1980, p. 187) adds to his remark above that "Proposed principles of universal grammar may be regarded as an abstract partial specification of the genetic program that enables the child to interpret certain events as linguistic evidence". The fact that is obscured by assigning psychological reality to a theory of competence is that there may be a wide gap between the "abstract partial specification" provided by the theory and the actual "genetic program" embodied in the speaker. The gap may exist even under all speaker idealizations assumed by the theory, and the specification can in fact have numerous genetic realizations.

We turn to this issue below.

The manner in which an abstract specification is realized in a performance grammar that meets observed performance constraints has not been addressed to a significant extent in the linguistic literature. Recent work on Government-Binding parsing by Stabler (1987), Fong (this volume), Johnson (this volume), and Abney and Cole (1986) has faced the problem of obtaining procedural interpretations of the grammatical devices assumed in Government-Binding theory. Stabler exploits the principles of Government-Binding theory to develop a grammatical formalism, restricted logic grammar, suited especially for the statement of natural language grammars. He remarks on the problem of mapping from the abstract principles in the theory to a procedural interpretation "It is unfortunate that efficient implementation of these constraints [on movement] requires such careful attention to procedural details" (1987, p. 8).

Johnson axiomatizes part of GB grammar in first-order logic, and applies logic program transformation techniques (Tamaki and Sato, 1984) to obtain restatements of the grammar for which the procedural interpretation given by a Prolog interpreter yields a prototype parser. Thus, program transformations bridge with partial success the gap between the original specification and the grammar embodied in the runtime program. Abney and Cole use a model of distributed computation to formulate parsing procedures that satisfy the grammatical principles of Government-Binding theory. It appears that the work noted focuses on the interpretive derivation of syntactic representations that are transformationally defined in Government-Binding theory. That is, traces are hypothesized and coindexed with antecedents without using Move-α directly. The Chain rule differs from that work since the rule is a declarative definition of chain relations at S-structure. The procedural interpretation of the rule is assigned independently by an attribute evaluator.

The distinction between grammatical descriptions intended as language specifications and descriptions intended as more realistic models of how grammar is put to use in generation and understanding is seen clearly in the following example. Consider the *sorting language S* of strings over some finite subset **N** of the natural numbers. Each string has the property that it may be split into two substrings x and y, such that y is the sorted version of x:

(47) $S = \{xy : x, y \in \mathbf{N}^* \ \wedge \ \mathrm{sorted}(x, y)\}$

This simple language might be given a phrase structure description (48). A sample parse tree for the string '1 2' is shown in (48d). The left-recursive productions (48b–c) define the 'concrete syntax' that would commonly be given to a production $Z \rightarrow X^* \, X^*$ employing regular expression notation.

(48) (a) $Z \rightarrow X \, X$

    (b) $X \rightarrow \epsilon$

    (c) $X \rightarrow X \, t$, for each $t \in \mathbf{N}$

    (d)

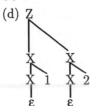

The phrase structure rules as defined clearly overgenerate; they generate $\mathbf{N}^*$. To see this, note that each string s in S may be split into two substrings x and y. The first constraint we may observe is the Ordering Constraint (49) on the second half of the string:

(49) Ordering Constraint (OC):
$^*s = xy$, unless y is ordered,
where $x = x_1 \ldots x_n$ is *ordered* if
$i < j$ implies $x_i \leq x_j$, for all $i, j = 1, \ldots, n$.

The further constraint (50) yields the language observed.[24]

(50) Permutation Constraint (PC):
$^*s = xy$, unless y is a permutation of x,
where x is a *permutation* of y if
(i) $x = y = \emptyset$, or
(ii) for each $x_i \in X$, $x_i \in y$, and
$x - x_i$ is a permutation of $y - x_i$.

The grammar consisting of (48), (49), and (50) is an abstract and concise description of the intended language. The constraints of the grammar, OC and PC, may be interpreted as components of an abstract algorithm for the generation and analysis of strings in the language.

However, it would be foolish to use the abstract algorithm for a practical purpose or, if the language defined were a natural one, to claim *a priori* that those principles are elements of a model for how strings in the language are processed by speakers of the language.

The principles (49) and (50) have the features of a good specification: they are precise, consistent, complete, and unbiased towards a particular realization of the sorting relation they define. Refinement of the specification (Jones, 1980) yields a realization or particular algorithm whose only relation to the specification is, ideally, logical equivalence. The sorting relation may be refined in several ways, to yield one of the known sorting algorithms. Performance is likely to be one of the criteria used in the selection of one refinement over another. The refinement may be done systematically, by applying one of several specification transformation schemes. Thus a sort-by-permutation logic program (Clocksin and Mellish, 1981) may be transformed into a more efficient form by application of the fold/unfold transformation (Tamaki and Sato, 1984). Johnson (this volume) uses this approach in the derivation of the more efficient of his PAD parsers. Typically, however, specifications must be refined in other creative ways, which follow no particular systematic pattern. The Quicksort algorithm of Hoare (1962) is an interesting example.

As the example of the sorting language S illustrates clearly, there may be a wide gap between the description of some linguistic phenomena and the mechanism that actually produces the phenomena. Marr (1977) argues that both levels of description, specification of what is to be computed and the particular algorithm that implements the computation, are important for a complete understanding of an information processing problem.[25] This calls for a distinction on principles of grammar, according to whether they may be taken only as *specifications* of linguistic phenomena (their primary function), or also as natural algorithms for dealing with the phenomena. It seems that only the former is the proper interpretation of the elements of grammar assumed in Government-Binding theory. From our point of view, the psychological claim that may be made about universal grammar is that it imputes existence to a mechanism that satisfies the abstract specification given, not to a mechanism with the 'specific internal organization' postulated. Questions about the 'physical reality' of the principles of a grammatical theory demand a precise procedural interpretation to be associated with them, and may be answered only by correlation of psycholinguistic observations with the predicted behavior of the theory for actual inputs.

9. CONCLUSION

This chapter has presented an interpretive Chain formation rule (*Chain rule*) and defined it explicitly in the formalism of attribute grammar. The formulation of the rule was influenced to a large extent by the rule Move-α and several other components in Government-Binding theory, including the thematic, Case, and government subtheories. While the Chain rule did not include an account of parasitic gaps and multiple *Wh*-extractions from a given phrase, it seems likely that the rule can be refined to cover all cases of trace-antecedent relation currently explained by Move-α. By contributing towards a theory a performance, the Chain rule argues indirectly for an interpretive theory of grammar. We note, however, that the work of Koster (1978), Rizzi (1986), and Barss (1983) also suggests an advantage of the interpretive approach over the transformational one, on grounds of descriptive and explanatory adequacy.

The principles of grammar assumed in Government-Binding theory are best seen as specifications of linguistic phenomena, and not as algorithms that deal with the phenomena. A significant gap exists between the principles given by the theory and the actual algorithms that may be used in human sentence processing. This view is consistent with the goal of linguistic theory to provide an abstract and neutral characterization of the knowledge of language possessed by native speakers.

ACKNOWLEDGEMENTS

Thanks are due to Robert C. Berwick for detailed comments on an earlier version of this article, Susumu Kuno for the reference to Barss (1983), and the Natural Language Processing group at IBM Research. Any shortcomings and inaccuracies are of course my own.

NOTES

[1] We assume intermediate traces left by application of Move-α are retained at S-structure. If traces are optionally left by Move-α, as in Lasnik and Saito (1984), then Subjacency must be taken as a condition on derivations.

[2] We identify I with the category AUX(iliary) of Steele *et al.* (1981).

[3] Notice that this changes the account that may be given of *that*-trace phenomena in terms of c-command. The C-specifier position c-commands subject position (I-

specifier), regardless of whether an overt complementizer element is dominated by C.

[4] Interest in the structural properties of natural language provided empirical motivation for the study of linguistic devices with more generative power that regular grammars and more special structure than unrestricted rewriting systems. Chomsky (1959) dismissed unrestricted grammars as devices of linguistic interest, since there is no adequate way to define for them a method for obtaining structural descriptions of the strings they generate.

[5] We write $X.a$ to denote *attribute occurrences* of attributes of symbol X. Thus $X.a \neq Y.a$, if $X \neq Y$, for all categories X and Y. By this convention, we distinguish the attribute occurrence *Case* associated with V ($V.Case$) from the attribute occurrence *Case* associated with NP ($NP.Case$).

[6] This intended characteristic of attribute grammars cannot be enforced in a vacuum, ignoring the *types* of attributes allowed. For when pointer types are permitted, as in the PLNLP system of Heidorn (1972), attribution functions may refer to attributes of nodes arbitrarily far away from the node of the attribute being defined.

[7] We do not impose any restriction on the degree of ambiguity of the underlying grammar G. In fact, it is easy to verify that the language-particular base grammars implied in current GB theory are infinitely ambiguous.

[8] Knuth (1968) shows that restriction of attribute grammar to just synthesized attributes does not change the class of attributions that may be defined on derivation trees or its formal descriptive power.

[9] If the implementation medium for attribute evaluation provides *unification* (Robinson, 1965), then evaluation of an attribution rule need not coincide with instantiation of the attribute value the rule defines. In general, evaluation of the attribution rule does not require knowing the values of all input arguments to the rule.

[10] This definition assumes *value semantics* for attribute evaluation.

[11] In the PLNLP language of Heidorn (1972), tree nodes are represented by record structures encoding the categorial information of the node and the attributes associated with it. In spite of the use of pointers, the attribution is strictly local. Each pointer value may be assumed to be a runtime-generated index, with the convention that a node's *node number* is the address at which the node is stored. The up-arrow notation in pointers does not bear any relation to the same notation in lexical-functional grammar.

[12] This partitioning of empty categories, well established in early GB literature, is questioned in more recent work. Aoun (1985), for example, proposes that a variable is both referential and anaphoric. This cross-classification cannot be achieved in terms of the attributes *anaphoric* and *pronominal* assumed in the earlier work.

[13] This distinction is not new. In Lasnik and Uriagereka (1988, p. 71), intermediate traces "are presumably not any of the empty categories we are considering [NP-trace, Wh-trace, and PRO]", and they bear no *anaphoric* and *pronominal* attributes. This view implies an elaboration of the transformational component since, among other things, it is now necessary to specify for each transformation which attributes of a moved phrase it retains and which it leaves. Within the attribute grammar framework assumed here, the set $A(X)$ of attributes associated with each category X is fixed.

[14] A closely related alternative is to associate the attribution in (29) with each

NELSON CORREA

production that has NP on the righthand side. This increases the size of the grammar, since the attribution is replicated in all such productions, but does not change the amount of computation required to determine functional type, compared with (29).
[15] As with the attribution (29), it is possible to move the attribute conditions in (30) to all productions with NP on the righthand side.
[16] Due to the use of pointer types rather than integers, the Chain rule presented here defines *linking* relations from antecedent to traces. This is an inessential feature of the rule, though. The coindexing relation assumed in Chomsky (1981) may be obtained by computing the reflexive and transitive closure of linking. Correa (1987) uses coindexation explicitly, but requires explicit enumeration of tree nodes.
[17] An exception exists, depending on the acceptability of expletive chains, as in *It$_i$ seems $[\epsilon]_i$ to be likely that John won the race.*
[18] These two attributes should make accessible also categorial, agreement, and Case information of the element they point to. $\overline{}$
[19] Barss does not intend (40) as a definition of $\overline{A}$ chains; some properties may follow from other principles in the grammar.
[20] Barss assumes reanalysis of the verb and adjacent preposition, so that e_j is object of the reanalyzed verb.
[21] This is a substantive claim for which I have no formal proof.
[22] Strictly speaking, we must allow that the representation of node indices or pointer values will grow logarithmically with the length of the input string. The point made is that our use of attribute-value structures differs significantly from the use of the same objects in other formalisms such as lexical-functional grammar. The present use is more consistent with the notion of *complex symbol* introduced in Aspects-type grammars.
[23] Taking into account the representation of pointers, evaluation of the Chain rule requires $O(n \cdot \log(n))$ steps.
[24] The Permutation Constraint subsumes a weaker constraint, the Equal Length Constraint (ELC), which asserts that a string s is not in the language S unless it splits into two substrings of equal length.
[25] I thank Bob Berwick for this observation.

REFERENCES

Abney, S. and J. Cole: 1986, 'A Government-Binding Parser', unpublished manuscript, Department of Linguistics and Philosophy, Massachusetts Institute of Technology, Cambridge, Massachusetts.

Aoun, J.: 1985, *A Grammar of Anaphora*, MIT Press, Cambridge, Massachusetts.

Barss, A.: 1983, 'Chain Binding', unpublished manuscript, Department of Linguistics and Philosophy, Massachusetts Institute of Technology, Cambridge, Massachusetts.

Berwick, R. and A. Weinberg: 1984, *The Grammatical Basis of Linguistic Performance*, MIT Press, Cambridge, Massachusetts.

Chomsky, N.: 1959, 'On Certain Formal Properties of Grammar', *Information and*

Control **2**, 137–167.

Chomsky, N.: 1970, 'Remarks on Nominalization', in R. Jacobs and P. Rosenbaum (eds.), *Readings in English Transformational Grammar*, Ginn and Co., Waltham, Massachusetts, pp. 184–221.

Chomsky, N.: 1980, *Rules and Representations*, Columbia University Press, New York.

Chomsky, N.: 1981, *Lectures on Government and Binding: The Pisa Lectures*, Foris, Dordrecht, Holland.

Chomsky, N.: 1982, *Some Concepts and Consequences of the Theory of Government and Binding*, MIT Press, Cambridge, Massachusetts.

Chomsky, N.: 1986, *Barriers*, MIT Press, Cambridge, Massachusetts.

Clocksin, W. and C. Mellish: 1981, *Programming in Prolog*, Springer-Verlag, New York.

Correa, N.: 1987, 'An Attribute Grammar Implementation of Government-Binding Theory', *Proceedings of the 25th Annual Meeting of the Association for Computational Linguistics*, Stanford University, Stanford, California, pp. 45–51.

Emonds, J.: 1976, *A Transformational Approach to Syntax*, Academic Press, New York.

Heidorn, G.: 1972, *Natural Language Inputs to a Simulation System*, Naval Postgraduate School, Technical Report No. NPS-55HD72101A, Alexandria, Virginia.

Hoare, C.: 1962, 'Quicksort', *Computer Journal* **5**, 10–15.

Irons, E.: 1961, 'A Syntax-directed Compiler for ALGOL 60', *Communications of the Association for Computing Machinery* **4**, 51–55.

Jackendoff, R.: 1977, $\overline{X}$ *Syntax: A Study of Phrase Structure*, MIT Press, Cambridge, Massachusetts.

Jensen, K.: 1986, 'Binary Rules and Non-binary Trees: Breaking down the Concept of Phrase Structure', in A. Manaster-Ramer (ed.), *Mathematics of Language*, John Benjamins, Amsterdam, pp. 65–86.

Johnson, M.: this volume, 'Parsing as Deduction: The Use of Knowledge of Language', pp. 39–64.

Jones, C.: 1980, *Software Development: A Rigorous Approach*, Prentice-Hall International, Series in Computer Science, Englewood Cliffs, New Jersey.

Kastens, U., B. Hutt, and E. Zimmermann: 1982, *GAG: A Practical Compiler Generator*, Lecture Notes in Computer Science, Springer-Verlag, New York.

Knuth, D.: 1968, 'Semantics of Context-free Languages', *Mathematical Systems Theory* **2**, 127–145.

Kornai, A.: 1983, '$\overline{X}$ Grammars', in J. Demetrovics, G. Katrona, and A. Salomaa (eds.), *Algebra, Combinatorics, and Logic in Computer Science*, vol. 2, North-Holland, Amsterdam, pp. 523–536.

Koster, C.: 1971, 'Affix Grammars', in *IFIP Working Conference on Algol 68 Implementation*, North-Holland, Amsterdam, pp. 95–109.

120   NELSON CORREA

Koster, J.: 1978, 'Conditions, Empty Nodes, and Markedness', *Linguistic Inquiry* **9**, 551–593.

Lasnik, H. and J. Uriagereka: 1988, *A Course in GB Syntax: Lectures on Binding and Empty Categories*, MIT Press, Cambridge, Massachusetts.

Lasnik, H. and M. Saito: 1984, 'On the Nature of Proper Government', *Linguistic Inquiry* **15**, 235–289.

Marr, D.: 1977, 'Artificial Intelligence: A Personal View', *Artificial Intelligence* **9**, 37–48.

Pesetsky, D.: 1982, *Paths and Categories*, Ph.D. dissertation, Department of Linguistics and Philosophy, Massachusetts Institute of Technology, Cambridge, Massachusetts.

Petrick, S.: 1965, *A Recognition Procedure for Transformational Grammars*, Ph.D. dissertation, Department of Linguistics, Massachusetts Institute of Technology, Cambridge, Massachusetts.

Pullum, G.: 1985, *Assuming Some Version of the $\overline{X}$ Theory*, Syntax Research Center, University of California at Santa Cruz, Santa Cruz, California.

Rizzi, L.: 1986, 'On Chain Formation', in H. Borer (ed.), *The Grammar of Pronominal Clitics—Syntax and Semantics, vol. 19*, Academic Press, New York, pp. 65–95.

Robinson, A.: 1965, 'A Machine-oriented Logic Based on the Resolution Principle', *Journal of the Association for Computing Machinery* **12**, 23–41.

Sharp, R.: 1985, *A Model of Grammar Based on Principles of Government and Binding*, M.S. dissertation, Department of Computer Science, University of British Columbia, Vancouver, British Columbia.

Shieber, S.: 1986, *An Introduction to Unification-based Approaches to Grammar*, CSLI Lecture Notes No. 4, University of Center for the Study of Language and Information, Stanford, California.

Stabler, E. P. Jr.: 1987, 'Restricting Logic Grammars with Government-Binding Theory', *Computational Linguistics*, **13**, 1–10.

Steele, S.: 1981, *An Encyclopedia of AUX: A Study in Cross-linguistic Equivalence*, MIT Press, Cambridge, Massachusetts.

Stowell, T.: 1981, *Origins of Phrase Structure*, Ph.D. dissertation, Department of Linguistics and Philosophy, Massachusetts Institute of Technology, Cambridge, Massachusetts.

Tamaki, H. and T. Sato: 1984, 'Fold/Unfold Transformation of Logic Programs', *Proceedings of the Second International Logic Programming Conference*, Uppsala University, Uppsala, Sweden, pp. 127–138.

Van Riemsdijk, H. and E. Williams: 1986, *An Introduction to the Theory of Grammar*, MIT Press, Cambridge, Massachusetts.

Van Wijngaarden, A. (ed.): 1969, 'Report on the Algorithmic Language ALGOL 68', *Numerical Mathematics* **14**, 79–218.

Waite, W. and G. Goos: 1984, *Compiler Construction*, Springer-Verlag, New York.

Watt, D. and O. Madsen: 1983, 'Extended Attribute Grammars', *The Computer Journal* **26**, 142–153.

Departamento de Ingeníeria Eléctrica, W-311,
Universidad de los Andes,
Apartado Aéreo 4976,
Bogotá, D.E., Colombia

MICHAEL B. KASHKET

PARSING WARLPIRI—A FREE WORD ORDER LANGUAGE

1. INTRODUCTION

An important challenge for natural language parsers is the phenomenon of free word order. In languages exhibiting this phenomenon—and it seems that all languages do have free ordering to some extent—the words in a sentence may swap about freely with little effect on meaning. It also appears that no language is completely free, so for a parser to properly handle this phenomenon, it must be able to accept sentences that vary where they may and that do not vary where they may not. In this chapter, I will present a parser that works well for a part of Warlpiri, an Aboriginal language from central Australia, that exhibits a great deal of free word order. It is believed that the same underlying mechanism will also handle more fixed word order languages like English.

Here is the outline of this chapter. First I will describe some Warlpiri to give the reader a concrete understanding of free word order in this language. Then I will discuss the failings of a standard parsing technology, context-free parsing, for handling this language, and more generally free word order. It should be noted that other parsers have dealt with the phenomenon with varying degrees of success, but none has done so perspicuously.[1] I will then present a solution to this problem and demonstrate the implemented parser on a sample Warlpiri sentence. Finally, I will outline a grammar for the corresponding fragment of English, demonstrating the cross-linguistic promise of the parser.

2. A VERY BRIEF WARLPIRI PRIMER

While there are over 3000 native speakers of Warlpiri, few of them will likely read this chapter. If you are fluent in Warlpiri, however, feel free to skip to the next section.

The parser's ability to handle free word order is demonstrated in example (1), a typical, simple declarative Warlpiri sentence.[2] For the sake of brevity, I will describe only the part of Warlpiri syntax needed to analyze this sample sentence.[3] The verb, *punta-rni*, like its English

123

R. C. Berwick et al. (eds.),
Principle-Based Parsing: Computation and Psycholinguistics, 123–151.
© 1991 *Kluwer Academic Publishers. Printed in the Netherlands.*

counterpart, takes three arguments, a subject, a direct object, and an indirect object. In this sentence, the subject, *ngajulu-rlu*, appears first; the direct object, *karli*, appears last; and the indirect object, *kurdu-ku*, appears fourth. The auxiliary word, roughly speaking the counterpart to the English auxiliary phrase, appears second.

(1) *Ngajulu-rlu ka-rna-rla   punta-rni   kurdu-ku karli.*
     I-*erg*   *imperf*-1s-3d take-*nonpast* child-*dat* boomerang
     'I am taking the boomerang from the child'

Grammatical functions (*e.g.*, subject, object, and indirect object) in Warlpiri are determined by Case marking suffixes. For example, *-rlu* of *ngajulu-rlu* indicates that *ngajulu-rlu* fills the subject grammatical function. This contrasts with a language like English in which grammatical function is determined by position (*e.g.*, the subject appears to the left of the verb). That the position of a Warlpiri noun phrase does not indicate its grammatical function is demonstrated in (2) through (4), which show equivalent ways of saying (1).[4] In these sentences the nouns move about freely. Notice that the verb, *punta-rni*, appears in different positions as well; although not demonstrated here, it may also begin the sentence.

(2) *Karli   ka-rna-rla   punta-rni   ngajulu-rlu kurdu-ku*
     boomerang *imperf*-1s-3d take-*nonpast* I-*erg*   child-*dat*
     'It is the boomerang I am taking from the child'

(3) *Kurdu-ku ka-rna-rla   ngajulu-rlu karli   punta-rni*
     child-*dat imperf*-1s-3d I-*erg*   boomerang take-*nonpast*
     'From the child I am taking the boomerang'

(4) *Ngajulu-rlu ka-rna-rla   punta-rni   karli   kurdu-ku*
     I-*erg*   *imperf*-1s-3d take-*nonpast* boomerang child-*dat*
     'I am taking the boomerang from the child'

There is also an ordering constraint, shown in these examples. The auxiliary word, *ka-rna-rla*, must appear in the second position.[5] Even given the fixed position of the auxiliary, these four permutations do not exhaust the possibilities for uttering this sentence. There are in fact 4!, or 24, different ways of saying the same thing.

3. A CRITERION FOR SUCCESS

In order to evaluate the success of a parser for dealing with free word order, it will be necessary to refine the problem beyond the description just given. What we noted about sentence (1) and its permutations was that, despite reordering of the words, they meant the same thing. Laughren (1987), for one, argues that argument noun phrases fill the same grammatical functions across permutations. Assuming Laughren's analysis, we arrive at a basic hypothesis: similarity in (this aspect of) meaning is reflected in similar structures in syntax. On the computational end of things, this hypothesis entails that a parser must assign the same syntactic structure to sentences that mean the same thing. In Warlpiri, permutations of a sentence must be assigned the same structure.

Consider (1). In part, this sentence means that the speaker is the agent of the taking, that the boomerang is what is taken, and that the child is the one from whom it is taken. These semantic roles are usually called *agent*, *theme*, and *source*, respectively. Syntactically, these semantic roles are associated with the grammatical functions, subject, object, and indirect object. The correspondence is shown below.

(5)

word	grammatical function	semantic role
ngajulu	subject	agent
karli	object	theme
kurdu	indirect object	source

This far in the analysis, it would seem that only a list associating lexical items with grammatical functions would be required for the syntactic structure of simple ditransitive sentences. However, it appears that there is more to the syntax than just a list. In fact, there is a basic asymmetry between subjects and other grammatical functions, as evidenced by a variety of constructions in many languages, including Warlpiri (see Laughren, 1987). The hypothesis here is that this asymmetry is properly represented in syntactic structure. The structure is taken to be a tree, and subjects are placed higher in the tree than objects, as shown in figure 1.

Now we have arrived at a concrete linguistic theory of the syntax of simple declarative sentences. Furthermore, we have provided an interpretation of the syntactic structures that seems to capture some of the meaning, especially the meaning that is invariant across the simple Warlpiri sentences under discussion. While this account is still informal, it is precise enough for us to judge the ability of parsers to handle free word order. Linguistically speaking, the above structures are what parsers must produce in order to be said to handle the phenomenon correctly.

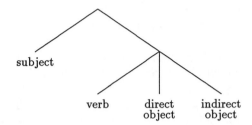

Figure 1: The syntactic structure of ditransitive sentences.

4. THE PROBLEM WITH CONTEXT-FREE PARSERS

In order to appreciate the problem of free word order for context-free parsers, we need not consider a sentence as complicated as (1). We can remove the auxiliary word, thereby eliminating the task of processing auxiliary-second phenomena. What remains, shown in (6), is actually ungrammatical,[6] but even handling this restricted subproblem eludes context-free parsers.

(6) *Ngajulu-rlu*   *punta-rni*   *kurdu-ku*   *karli*
    I-*erg*   take-*nonpast*   child-*dat*   boomerang
    subject   *indirect object*   *direct object*

A linguistically satisfying context-free grammar for sentences with ditransitive verbs is given in (7) (the subscripts on the NPs stand for 'subject', 'direct object', and 'indirect object'). Grammar (7) generates the tree structure presented in the previous section, with the subject in a higher position than nonsubjects. Note that this grammar will indeed generate pseudo-sentence (6).

(7) $S \rightarrow NP_s$ VP
    $VP \rightarrow V\ NP_i\ NP_d$

Of course, this grammar will not generate any of the permutations of the pseudo-sentence. Even if we were to allow permutation of the righthand side of the rules—thereby maintaining a common hierarchical structure across permutations of the sentence—the grammar would not generate all the valid ways of saying the sentence. For example (8) would not be generated. In general, this grammar would not generate sentences in which the subject noun phrase was interposed between elements of the verb phrase.

(8)   *Punta-rni*   *ngajulu-rlu*   *kurdu-ku*   *karli*
      take-*nonpast*   I-*erg*   child-*dat*   boomerang
                       subject   indirect object   direct object

This criticism of context-free parsing has not been meant as a dia-
tribe against the technique. Instead, we can learn from its failings in
order to improve the parser. In particular, it seems that the problem
with context-free grammars is that they are too constrained: they impose linear ordering between elements of righthand sides, even where no
such constraint exists in the utterance. This observation has led to the
reformulation of grammar that forms the linguistic basis of the parser.

5. THE LINGUISTIC THEORY

The linguistic theory of the parser is based on Chomsky's (1981) Government-Binding (GB) framework, though I have modified the theory
to some extent to provide for a better account of free word order. In
GB terms, the parser computes only the level of S-structure, leaving
aside the levels of D-structure, logical form and phonological form.[7] D-
structure is not computed because movement is not required to handle
free word order (this will be explained presently).[8] Let us focus, then,
on S-structure.

Consider as an example a partial S-structure of (1) (the structure
of the auxiliary has been omitted), shown in figure 2. In this structure there are four projections, one for the verb, and one for each of
the nouns. (Because the nominal projections in this sentence are simply nonbranching trees—the nouns do not take any arguments—I have
abbreviated the depiction of the nominal projections with only maximal
nodes.) Because *punta* means what it does, it takes three arguments,
hence the three nominal projections. This structure encodes more than
simply the argument relations, however; it also encodes the subject–
object asymmetry mentioned above. The subject, *ngajulu-rlu*, appears
as the sibling of $\overline{V}$, and the objects as siblings of V. I will assume that
the agent is the subject and that the other semantic roles fill the object grammatical functions. In fact, this seems to be a good descriptive
generalization for both Warlpiri and nominative-accusative languages in
general (Marantz, 1984).

One should be able to see that S-structures form a subset of context-
free trees.[9] That is, S-structures are context-free trees with two restric-

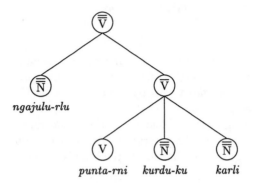

Figure 2: A partial S-structure of (1).

tions: first, lexical items correspond to projections (linear trees of height two) and second, projections may only be combined as siblings of non-maximal nodes of other projections. Unfortunately, as we saw above, context-free trees prove to be too constrained to represent free word order. Even if we were to allow arguments to appear to either side of their siblings in the head's projection—analogous to permuting the righthand sides of context-free rules—not all possible permutations of a particular sentence would be generated. Thus, S-structure is not appropriate for free word order languages.

The solution adopted here is to split the task of representing hierarchy and precedence into two structures, *syntactic structure* (SS) and *precedence structure* (PS). One can picture these levels as different views on the same sentence, in the autosegmental style.[10] By teasing apart hierarchy from precedence, we are no longer constrained to enforce both kinds of relations simultaneously as with standard S-structure. Instead, in syntactic structure we may represent unordered relations between elements that would normally cause a 'crossing of arcs', and in precedence structure, precedence relations where no unordered relations exist (this even more *avant garde* suggestion will be discussed below).[11] Let me explain the modified theory by first describing precedence structure, then syntactic structure, and then the mapping between the two.

5.1. *Precedence Structure*

The theory of PS is based on standard ideas in morphology (cf. Lieber, 1980), however, PS is used to represent linear precedence at any level, be it morpheme, word, or phrase. Every morpheme corresponds to a node in PS. Nodes may be combined by a simple rule (9). The result of combination is another node, which may be combined with other nodes recursively by the same rule. In this way, precedence structures may be built up to cover entire words or sentences.[12]

(9) *PS Rule of Combination*
Combine two adjacent nodes.

In order to fix the idea of combination, consider figure 3, the precedence structure of (1) (further details of PS will be given shortly). Each morpheme of the sentence, including the phonologically null absolutive Case marker, has entered PS as a single node bearing its category. The rule of combination has applied to the morphemes to produce nodes that dominate each word. However, the rule has not applied across words, because descriptively speaking there is no precedence among words in a Warlpiri sentence.

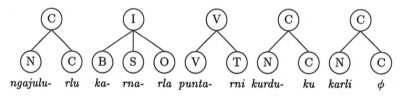

Figure 3: The precedence structure of sentence (1).

One might reasonably question the validity of the claim that this structure represents only precedence relations when the structures that compose it are obviously hierarchical. I term this structure 'precedence structure' because precedence relations are the primary relations of the structure. That is, precedence relations *determine* hierarchical relations in PS: all precedence relations correspond to a hierarchical relation and no hierarchical relation exists apart from a precedence relation. PS contrasts with the level of SS, where, as will be seen in the following section, hierarchical structure cannot be determined from linear precedence. SS can be thus be thought of as 'hierarchical' or 'unordered' structure.

As described thus far, PS is much too general, allowing for the combination of any node with any other. I will now cover a number of restrictions on the linear arrangement of Warlpiri elements for the purpose of refining the theory. These observations will lead to constraints on the application of the rule of combination. It should be noted that this theory is derived from Nash's (1986) work, a much broader study of Warlpiri.

One restriction concerns the category of the element to which an affix may be attached. In Warlpiri, Case markers may attach only to nouns, and tense elements may attach only to verbs. This can be seen from the examples in (10) and (11). In (10) suffixes have been attached to morphemes of an acceptable category, and the words are grammatical. In (11), on the other hand, suffixes have been attached to morphemes of the wrong category, and the words are ungrammatical.

(10) (a) *punta-rni*
        take-*nonpast*

   (b) *kurdu-ku*
        child-*dat*

(11) (a)**punta-ku*
        take-*dat*

   (b)**kurdu-rni*
        child-*nonpast*

Another restriction concerns the direction of combination. For example, a verbal morpheme may have a tense element following it, but not the other way around, as shown in (12). A similar situation holds for Case-marked nouns, such as *kurdu-ku*.

(12) (a) *punta-rni*
        take-*nonpast*

   (b)**rni-punta*
        nonpast-take

Lastly, there is the requirement that affixes affix. Tense elements and Case markers must appear as affixes to words and may not appear as words in their own right. Sentence (13) illustrates a pair of two-word sequences ruled out by this constraint.

(13) (a)*_punta rni_
          take _nonpast_

      (b)*_kurdu ku_
          child _dat_

These phenomena may be accounted for with a standard device in morphology, the _head_. A head is an element that dictates what may or may not be associated with it by virtue of its lexical information (which may either be assigned on an item-by-item basis or by rule). For inflected verbs, the head is the tense element; for declined nouns, the head is the Case marker. We take these elements and not, say, nouns and verbs, to be heads because this allows us to state the restrictions on linear arrangement in a fairly perspicuous manner, that is, with _parameters_ of PS.

One parameter, the direction of combination, applies on a language-wide basis, independent of the category of the combining participants. In Warlpiri, heads may combine with arguments to their right. (Though this may present a problem for the relatively rare prefix or for compounding, this choice does work for the range of phenomena considered here.) There are two parameters that depend on the category of the head. First, heads subcategorize for the category of the element to which they may be adjacent (the direction depending on the parameter above); Case markers take nouns and tense elements take verbs. Second, heads indicate the level at which the combination takes place, whether morpheme or word. Both tense elements and Case markers combine with their arguments morpheme-to-morpheme (_i.e._, they are affixes). One should be able to see that these parameters interact with the rule of combination to account for the grammaticality observations above.

There is a problem with this formulation. Observe that the rule of combination is optional, which means that constraints on its application will not necessarily be invoked to rule out ill-formed words. We can enforce this constraint with the well-formedness condition (14). This condition works by filtering out precedence structures that contain more than one root, and this may only occur when at least one pair of adjacent nodes may not be combined due to a violation of the restrictions placed on that combination (whether it be a direction, subcategorization, or level violation).

(14) *PS Well-formedness Condition*
PS must be fully connected.

However, this condition is too severe for all languages, especially for Warlpiri. In Warlpiri (that is, for the limited range of Warlpiri we are considering here) there are no ordering constraints between words, so to require a fully connected precedence structure across words would not be correct. We must indicate the level at which this condition applies. In Warlpiri, the precedence structure of words (but not sentences) must be fully connected. In English, where order is much more fixed, the condition seems to apply to both levels. This is the fourth parameter of PS. We may summarize this discussion of precedence structure with the following PS grammar for Warlpiri.

(15)

parameter	setting
direction of combination	right-to-left
connectedness	within words

parameter	category	setting
subcategorization	Case marker	noun
	tense element	verb
level	Case marker	within word
	tense element	within word

Before leaving the level of PS, I must take up a less principled part of the grammar that deals with the linear composition of the auxiliary. Following Nash (1986) and Simpson and Withgott (1986), it would appear that it is best accounted for in terms of a linear template, not a structure that is produced by the composition of adjacent morphemes. The template in (16) covers the simple auxiliaries being considered here. It should be noted that each element of the auxiliary may be omitted, though they are subject to various agreement requirements (cf. Hale, 1973).

(16) auxiliary → base subject-clitic object-clitic

5.2. *Syntactic Structure*

As mentioned at the beginning of this section, SS is S-structure but without any precedence encoded in it. The atoms of this level are projections (not single nodes as in PS), that may be combined by a simple rule (17).[13] Figure 2 can be viewed as a partial syntactic structure of (1), as long as one remembers that the linear order of the projections is of no importance.

(17) *SS Rule of Combination*
   Add a maximal projection as a sibling of a nonmaximal node (of another projection).

As with the PS rule of combination, there are constraints on its application. These constraints fall under the purview of *Case theory* and θ (theta or thematic theory), that I will describe in turn.

Case theory accounts for the distribution of Case. In sentence (1) for example, there are three nouns each marked with a different Case, ergative, absolutive, and dative. At the level of PS, Case relations obtain under adjacency, subject to the restrictions stated above. At SS, on the other hand, the relation between a *Case assigner* and a *Case recipient* obtains under *government*. A node governs its sibling projections and projections that are siblings of nodes higher in its projection.[14] Because Case assigners govern their Case recipients, they must project one level.[15] For example, figure 4 shows the syntactic structure for the Case-marked pronoun, *ngajulu-rlu*. *Rlu* is the Case assigner and *ngajulu* is the Case recipient. Observe that they do indeed stand in a relation of government.

Figure 4: The syntactic structure for *ngajulu-rlu*.

The relation of Case assignment represents how a noun phrase receives its Case, but it does not address the issue of why one noun phrase appears as subject (*i.e.*, the sibling of $\overline{V}$) and why others appear as objects (*i.e.*, siblings of V). While a deeper theory will probably be needed for a wider range of Warlpiri, we can use Hale's (1982) account of the relationship between Case and grammatical function, given in (18) and (19).[16] These rules refer to the *Case frame* of a verb that contains the number and type of arguments for which it subcategorizes. *Punta*, for example, subcategorizes for three arguments, ergative, absolutive, and dative.[17]

(18) Identify the subject function with the *erg* argument, if there is one, otherwise with the *abs* argument.

(19) Identify the object function with the *dat* argument, if there is one, otherwise with the *abs* argument (if this is not already identified as the subject).

We can now take the syntactic analysis of Case assignment along with the rules of argument placement to determine a more articulated syntactic structure of (1), as shown in figure 5.

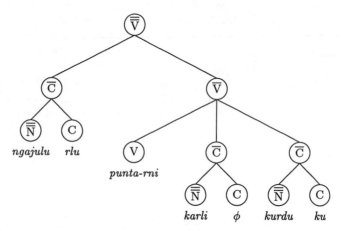

Figure 5: The syntactic structure (SS) of sentence (1).

The second set of constraints on the rule of combination comes from Theta theory, which accounts for the distribution of semantic or *thematic* roles (θ-roles). As should be clear by now, there is a very close relationship between the Case that a noun phrase bears and the semantic role it plays in its relationship with the verb. In fact, for the verb *punta* and similar verbs, there is a one-to-one mapping between the two, as shown below.[18]

(20) | θ-role | Case |
      | ------------- | ---------- |
      | agent | ergative |
      | theme | absolutive |
      | path | dative |

Cross-linguistically however, this rather constrained view of the mapping between Case and θ-roles seems too limited. Perhaps the most celebrated example that demonstrates the inadequacy of such a mapping is the English passive. In the active voice (for some simple sentences), the subject is assigned nominative Case and is interpreted as the agent, while the direct object is assigned accusative Case and is interpreted as the theme. In the passive voice, on the other hand, while the subject still receives nominative Case, it is interpreted as the theme; the agent, should it appear, is realized in a *by* phrase. This split argues for separate levels of analysis, one for Case and one for θ-roles.

In GB theory, θ-roles are assigned at the level of D-structure. Predicators (*e.g.*, verbs) license a certain number and type of arguments due to their meaning. *Punta*, for example, licenses three θ-roles, an agent, a theme, and a source. (This is a more formal statement of the licensing that was mentioned above when discussing a criterion for successful parsing.) Licensing the appearance of an argument in a syntactic structure is known as *assigning* a θ-role, which takes place under government as with Case assignment.[19]

While it seems that the two-level analysis is not mandated for the simple Warlpiri sentences being considered here, Laughren (1987), for one, argues that the level of D-structure is required in order to explain other Warlpiri phenomena. For the parser, the two-level analysis will be adopted, but in a slightly 'compiled' form. That is, SS will represent both Case and θ-relations, which is feasible since no movement is required.

Up to this point, we have discussed Case theory and its constraints on the rule of combination as well as θ theory and its constraints. These theories are not independent, however. Chomsky (1981) posited a rather strong connection between the two. His *Visibility Condition* requires an argument to be assigned Case in order to be assigned a θ-role. It is, in fact, this condition that underlies the Case-θ mappings given earlier.

According to this condition, a Case that did not correspond to a licensed θ-role or *vice versa* would be ill-formed.

Given the Visibility Condition, we can state a simple well-formedness condition on SS, shown in (21). Remember that in the current view of grammar, syntactic structure is built up with a rule of combination that is subject to both Case- and θ-constraints. Should a constraint not be satisfied, no combination may take place. This means that a fully connected syntactic structure must satisfy both the Case filter (Rouveret and Vergnaud, 1980) and the θ-criterion. To see why this is so, we need to examine the three cases. In the first case, we have a noun phrase that has not been assigned Case. Such a noun phrase would not be visible for θ assignment, and therefore its projection would not be attached to the predicator's projection because the rule of combination would be blocked. By the well-formedness condition, such a sentence would be ruled out. In the second case, the noun phrase has been assigned Case, but the Case does not correspond to a licensed θ-role. Again, by the Visibility Condition, the nominal projection would not be combined with the predicator's projection, and the sentence would be ruled out. In the last case, we have a noun phrase that has been assigned Case, which, furthermore, corresponds to a licensed θ-role. In this situation, the Case-assigned nominal projection would be combined with the predicator's projection, leaving a single tree. Such structures represent grammatical constructs and the well-formedness condition would allow it to pass.

(21) *SS Well-formedness Condition*
     SS must be fully connected.

What remains to be accounted for is the syntactic manifestation of the auxiliary. This aspect of the theory is borrowed almost directly from GB theory, where the auxiliary, *INFL* (Inflection), projects and takes the verb phrase as its complement. This form of licensing differs from the θ licensing between a verb and its arguments; the relation between INFL and its verbal complement is known as *functional* licensing (Abney, 1986). Unlike the more traditional accounts, INFL in Warlpiri does not project a second level because it does not assign nominative Case. Leaving aside the details of the relation between the auxiliary base and the verb, as well as the relations between the nominal agreement clitics and the noun phrase arguments, a more fully articulated syntactic structure of (1) would be as shown in figure 6.

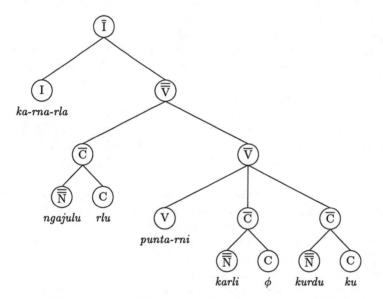

Figure 6: A more fully articulated syntactic structure of (1).

5.3. *The Mapping between PS and SS*

In the previous two subsections, I described the levels of PS and SS, which, nothing further said, exist independent of each other. In this section, I will discuss where the mapping between the two levels is constrained and, just as important, where it is not.

An important constraint between the levels concerns Case assignment. Following Stowell (1981), Case assignment is required to hold under adjacency. In the present theory, this relation obtains in SS in which no precedence is encoded. The ordered nature of Case assignment, however, is accounted for by the correspondence between the unordered relation of Case assignment in SS and the ordered relation of directed adjacency in PS. That this relation obtains between the elements of a single word is a further restriction for Warlpiri. In English, for example, the same ordered relation obtains between words. Thus, there is no need to appeal to a special theory of morphology for this phenomenon.

While Case assignment is an ordered relation, θ assignment is taken to be unordered. In terms of PS and SS, this is the null hypothesis: there is no connection between θ assignment in SS and any ordered relation in PS. It is this 'nonrelation' that accounts for free word order in Warlpiri: predicators assign θ-roles as with any other languages, but no ordering corresponds to this relation.

We have just seen a relation that has both PS and SS reflexes, and one that has only an SS reflex. It seems that there is also a relation that obtains only at PS (this is the *avant garde* suggestion mentioned earlier). In Warlpiri, the position of the auxiliary (Wackernagel's position, 1892) may properly be accounted for without reference to its syntactic representation: the auxiliary must appear to the right of any syntactic constituent.[20] Note that this linear requirement is not necessarily without explanatory force, which may be seen once one considers it from a phonological perspective. It seems that the position of the auxiliary determines the intonational envelope of a sentence, which, in turn, may be used in separating sentences in connected speech. So, while the position of the auxiliary may not have a syntactic manifestation (as does the English counterpart), it does enter into other areas of grammar. It is only from the limited perspective of this parser that the linear requirement on the auxiliary seems like an *ad hoc* stipulation.

6. THE PARSER

In this section, I will present the representations and algorithm of the parser, as based on the linguistic theory above. In the following section an extended sample 'run' will be given, clarifying this presentation.

6.1. *Representation*

The first part of a program specification concerns its input and output. The input to the parser is a sentence for which a substantial amount of preprocessing has been assumed. What is given is a list of words which are composed of lists of morphemes. The input corresponding to (1) is shown in (22).

(22) ((ngajulu rlu) (ka rna rla) (punta rni) (kurdu ku)
     (karli))

The output of the parser for an input sentence consists of a precedence structure and a syntactic structure. Both PS and SS are based on trees. Each node in a tree contains a category label, and data and actions particular to the level of representation. For example, in PS there are actions for combining adjacent nodes, and in SS there are actions for case assignment and θ assignment.

PS is actually represented as an ordered forest of ordered trees. Each tree represents parts of the input sentence where precedence is relevant, such as among the morphemes of a word. The relation between trees in the forest is not relevant to processing the sentence; however, the ordering is kept to mimic the order of the input sentence. Because words are not ordered with respect to one another, the precedence structures of Warlpiri sentences will not contain trees with more than one word in them; rather, there will only be one word per tree.

SS, on the other hand, is represented as an unordered forest of unordered trees. The need for a forest rather than a single tree is a bit subtle. Following the well-formedness condition that every syntactic structure be fully connected, we would expect grammatical sentences to correspond to a single structure in syntax. This is, indeed, a condition of grammaticality, and the parser checks this upon completion of the parse. However, a forest is required because during the parse there may be several unconnected trees corresponding to different parts of the input sentence. This is a key to processing free order phenomena. Consider (3), one of the permutations of (1); its input representation is given in (23).

(23) ((kurdu ku) (ka rna rla) (ngajulu rlu) (karli)
     (punta rni))

In the process of parsing this sentence, which is performed left-to-right, the parser will reach a stage where it has processed all but the last word, *punta-rni*. At this point it will have parsed the auxiliary word, as well as the three noun phrases. Because the verb has not yet entered the parse, there will be no way for the substructures to be connected (the parser operates in a bottom-up fashion). Instead, they must reside separately, as shown in figure 7. When the verb does enter the syntactic structure, the arguments may be connected by inserting them into the argument positions of the verb's projection.

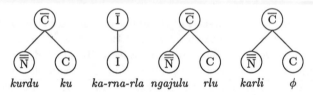

Figure 7: The syntactic structure of (3) after parsing four words.

6.2. *Algorithm*

The parser consists of two basic engines, one for PS and one for SS, that operate in a coroutine fashion to produce its two output structures; see figure 8 for a graphic depiction of the overall design. Input sentences are given to the PS parser that traverses them left-to-right and builds up precedence structure. Every time a morpheme is encountered, it is also sent to the SS parser for syntactic processing. The SS parser accepts the incoming unit, projects it according to its lexical information, and then enters the projection into syntactic structure. When finished, the SS parser returns control to the PS parser that consumes some more input. Upon completing the input sentence, the PS parser stops, and both output structures are returned.

I will now describe the PS parser and the SS parser in turn. The discussion will focus only on Case and θ processing, however. Readers

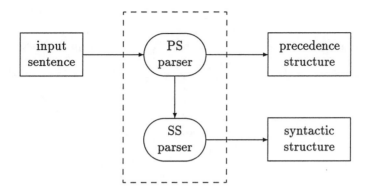

Figure 8: An overview of the parser's flow of control.

interested in the details of processing the auxiliary and other phenomena not covered here are once again invited to read the complete description in Kashket (1987).

6.2.1. *The PS Parser*

The PS parser is a recursive engine that operates on the three levels of input: sentences, words, and morphemes. The top level of the parser accepts an entire sentence as input. It calls on the word parser to parse each of the constituent words, and then performs sentential actions on the returned precedence structure. In a like manner, the word-level parser calls on the morphological parser, which is essentially a lexicon look-up routine, and then performs word-level actions. This is diagrammed in figure 9.

Each level of PS parsing uses the same engine. The basic algorithm is given below in (24). The first step of the algorithm is a loop that traverses the input from left to right. Each unit (morpheme or word) is sent to the subordinate parser for processing. The structure returned is then added to end of the precedence structure for the current level. At this point unexecuted PS actions are tried to see if they can apply. Note that only actions that pertain to the current level of parsing are considered.

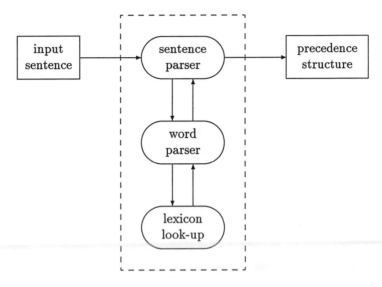

Figure 9: The recursive PS parser.

(24) 1.   Loop through constituents from left to right:
           a. call the subordinate parser, then
           b. execute applicable actions on adjacent trees.

     2.   Execute default actions.

     3.   Check well-formedness.

PS actions, following the PS rule of combination, act on adjacent elements in precedence structure. The two actions of concern here are select and inject. Executing a select action causes the combiner (*e.g.*, a Case marker) to become a sibling of the combinee (*e.g.*, a noun). This action also has a syntactic reflex: the SS projection corresponding to the combinee is assigned case by the SS projection of the combiner (which is executed by the SS parser, described below). The other action, inject, is similar to select, but the syntactic effect differs. Rather than making the SS projection corresponding to the combinee an object of the SS projection of the combiner, the syntactic information in the injector is added to (metaphorically speaking, 'injected into') the syntactic counterpart of the object. This action is used by tense elements to effect their syntactic merger with the verbs to which they are suffixed.

After the precedence structure of the current level has been built up from the structure of the next lower level, the parser performs default actions. Currently there is only one default PS action. This action inserts the phonologically null absolutive Case marker after otherwise unmarked nouns. If the word parser returns a structure that contains only a noun, a node for the absolutive Case marker is added and the PS parser is called once again to execute the actions of the newly inserted node. This null node is just like an overt Case marker except that it has no phonological content: it too projects one level in syntactic structure and contains a select action.

The last operation of the engine is to check the well-formedness of the parse. As discussed above, the well-formedness check may or may not be performed, depending on the parameter setting for the level. In Warlpiri, only the word level is checked. Should there be more than one tree for a word, an error is reported.[21]

6.2.2. *The SS Parser*

The SS parser is called whenever a unit of precedence structure becomes syntactically relevant. At such times, the PS parser calls the SS parser indicating what syntactic action should be performed. There are three actions that the PS parser may use: project, assign-case, and inject. Project is used for morphemes that have just entered the parse. This action projects the morpheme a certain number of levels (according to its category), and enters the projection into syntactic structure. Assign-case causes the argument projection to become a sibling of a node of the assigning projection, as an instance of the SS rule of combination. The third action, inject, is used to add the syntactic information of one element to that of another.

The execution of one of these actions constitutes only the first step of the SS parsing algorithm. In the second step, the parser loops over all unexecuted actions—of both new and existing projections—to see if any apply. This method will cover actions both introduced by and applicable to newly added projections. This loop must be reiterated should any actions have applied because the parser may have built new structure that enables further actions to apply. When all executable actions have been executed the SS parser stops and returns to the PS parser. We may summarize the process as follows:

(25) 1. Execute the action indicated by the PS parser.
2. Loop over every unexecuted action in SS, executing those that apply.
3. If any actions have fired, try the loop again.

There is a fourth action in the repertoire of the hierarchical SS parser, `assign-theta-role`, which is executed only in step two because θ assignment does not have a PS reflex. This action causes the argument projection to be added as a sibling of the assign projection if the argument projection has been assigned the corresponding Case (following the Case-θ mapping above). In the theory, this action is undirected. In the parser, this is reflected in the search for candidate projections for the execution of an action: all projections are considered. In fact, this parser cannot consider whether a projection is adjacent or not because that information is not represented at this level.

As with the PS parser, there are also routines for performing default actions and checking the well-formedness of the syntactic structure. However, unlike the PS parser, these computations are not performed at the end of the execution of the basic engine. Instead, these routines are called by the PS parser once it has completed the sentential level of processing.

The only default action of the SS parser is to supply an auxiliary word if one is not present in the input string. Such an auxiliary consists of the null base and null agreement clitics, that contain the default information of perfective aspect and third-person number, respectively. Note that placing the handler for the zero auxiliary in syntactic parser eliminates the need for the parser to guess where the auxiliary is to be placed in the input sentence: its linear position does not matter; only its syntactic effects concern the parser.

Like the PS parser, the SS parser reports an error if the resulting parse is not well-formed, *i.e.*, if there is more than one tree in the forest.

7. A SAMPLE PARSE

In this section, I will demonstrate the parser operating on sentence (1). This will be done by showing a few snapshots of the output structures as the parser traverses the input. Without further ado, let us join the

PS parser just after it has parsed the first word, *ngajulu-rlu*, as shown in figure 10. At this point, the loop of step one has completed, as no further actions are applicable. The default action is not triggered because the noun has been Case-marked. This word passes the well-formedness condition because it does indeed consist of a single precedence structure. Thus, the word parser finishes and returns this structure to the sentence parser.

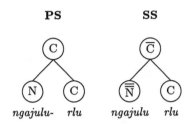

Figure 10: The parse after ((NGAJULU RLU)).

The sentence parser continues on its iteration of the main loop and calls the word parser to operate on the second word, *ka-rna-rla*. We will skip over this processing and pick up the parse in the middle of the third word, *punta-rni*. In particular, we will pick up the parse when the morpheme parser has looked up the verb stem *punta* and has called the syntactic parser indicating that the verb should be projected in syntactic structure. Figure 11 shows the state of the parse after the first step of the SS parser algorithm has executed.

At this point, the SS parser searches for applicable actions, and finds two. First, the INFL projection takes the verb's projection as an argument (via a hitherto unmentioned action, **argument**, that is the computational equivalent of functional licensing). Figure 12 shows the parse after this action has been executed.

The second action to be fired is **assign-theta-role** in the $\overline{V}$ node of the verb's projection. This action was placed in this node (rather than the zero-level node) in accordance with the mapping from Case to grammatical function, specifically, rule (18). Note that there is no ordering between this action and the **argument** action above; either rule could have fired first. This action fires and the nominal projection is attached to the verbal projection, as depicted in figure 13.

The **argument** and **assign-theta-role** actions having fired, there

PS **SS**

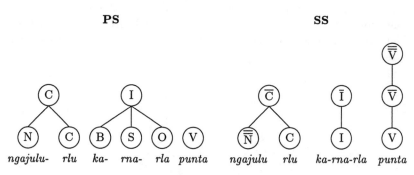

Figure 11: The parse at ((NGAJULU RLU) (KA RNA RLA) (PUNTA)).

PS **SS**

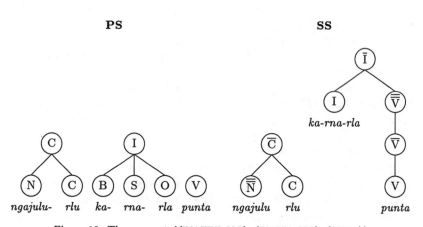

Figure 12: The parse at ((NGAJULU RLU) (KA RNA RLA) (PUNTA)).

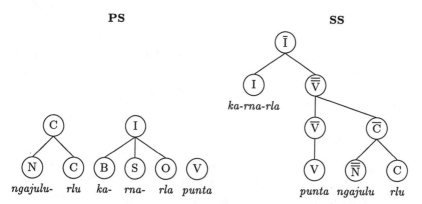

Figure 13: The parse at ((NGAJULU RLU) (KA RNA RLA) (PUNTA)).

is nothing more for the SS parser to do, so it returns control to the morpheme parser. The morpheme parser returns to the word parser and then the remainder of the verb is parsed. It should be clear how the parse will continue. Each Case-marked noun will be processed just like *ngajulu-rlu*—including *karli*, where the only difference will be that the default PS action will execute to enter the null Case marker into the parse. After the Case markers on each of these words have been processed by the PS parser, the corresponding Case projections will be visible to the θ-assigning actions of the verb and will be attached as was *ngajulu-rlu*. The only difference here is that, instead of the argument arriving before the predicator, the predicator has been added to syntactic structure before these later arguments. Because the loop in the SS algorithm is insensitive to the order of arrival of projections, the free ordering of the verb and its nominal arguments will be parsed properly.

8. CONCLUSION: A SKETCH OF ENGLISH

The bipartite representation of PS and SS should also handle a more fixed-order language such as English. Consider (26), roughly the English equivalent of (1).

(26) I am taking the boomerang from the child

The ordering between the subject, verb, and object is accounted for via Case-marking considerations as in Warlpiri. That is, in English, it is the tense element that marks nominative Case to its left. In this sentence, the tense element appears on the second word, *am*. The verb itself marks accusative Case to its right. Observing that tense is constrained to appear on the first element in the sequence of auxiliary verbs, we arrive at a theory of the SVO ordering that English typifies: this order arises due to the Case-marking of the subject and the object, coupled with the composition of the auxiliary.

Continuing further down the sentence, we find more evidence for the bipartite analysis. Prepositions, like verbs, assign Case to their right. *The child* receives dative Case from the preposition *from*. Nothing further need be said about this sentence (at this level of analysis). Of course, this leaves open the possibility that the prepositional phrase may precede the first part of the sentence, as the ordering between the two parts has not been constrained. In fact, this permutation is grammatical, and it means the same thing as the original; see (27).

(27) From the child I am taking the boomerang

This presentation has just scratched the surface of English grammar, but it should be clear that this sort of analysis has some promise for English. What this grammar fragment has demonstrated is that the grammar may be parameterized to allow for varying degrees of ordering. As far as the ordering of a verb and its arguments is concerned, this theory would claim that ordering exists when the verb is involved in Case-marking and that no ordering exists when other elements perform this grammatical task. Because the parameterization is relatively fine-grained, divisible down to the category level at least, it should allow for a whole range of ordering, from very fixed to very free. Fortunately for this account, it seems that languages of the world do indeed populate many points on the spectrum of word order.

NOTES

[1] See Kashket (1987) for a discussion of these systems.

[2] Example sentences are written in the standard orthography. In practice, hyphens are not used often, but they are included here to aid the novice reader. Note also that, in general, definiteness is not available from a single sentence and context must be used to provide this information. For simplicity, definite reference will be used. Finally, a note on the notation: '1s' stands for first-person, singular subject, and '3d' stands for third-person, singular dative object.

[3] There is a substantial and growing literature on Warlpiri. A good place to start is Nash (1986), which also contains perhaps the most nearly complete bibliography of Warlpiriana to date. See also Simpson (1983) and works by Hale and by Laughren, a few of which are cited below.

[4] There is some difference among the sentences, of course, but it concerns a change in focus, rather than a change in meaning. The first word is given a slight emphasis over the others. This subtle difference is mimicked in the English translations for the sentences.

[5] Actually, it may appear in the first position too. The details are rather complex, and the reader is referred to Kashket (1987) and the references therein for details

[6] In fact, there are null auxiliaries in Warlpiri. Roughly speaking, null auxiliaries indicate either intransitive or transitive verbs, third-person subjects and objects, and perfective aspect. Sentence (5) is ungrammatical because the null auxiliary does not correspond to the (dative) indirect object, nor to the first-person subject.

[7] The use of phonological information will not enter into this abridged discussion of the parser, so for present purposes, PF may be ignored. The parser presented in Kashket (1987), however, does use intonational phrasing for syntactic disambiguation.

[8] Alternatively, one could view the parser as computing D-structure precisely because no movement is involved.

[9] Admittedly, this is an incomplete statement of S-structure. However, in the full-blown structure that includes movement, as long as one kept to something like the Structure Preserving Hypothesis of Emonds (1976), S-structures would still constitute a subset.

[10] See Goldsmith (1979) for the original proposal of the autosegmental approach in the realm of phonology, and see van Riemsdijk (1982) on incorporating this view into syntax.

[11] It should be noted that this idea fits well with Marantz's (1984) grammar. Among other levels, he proposes an unordered S-structure that represents grammatical relations and a surface structure for relations between elements in the surface string. He did not discusses the details of surface structure as he focussed on other levels, but precedence structure might be a good candidate for that level.

[12] This view of grammar is similar to Abney's (1986) licensing grammar. His grammar is also reminiscent of SS, to be described presently.

[13] In a fuller account of S-structure, adjunction would also have to be allowed.

[14] This definition is based on Aoun and Sportiche's (1983) formulation.

[15] As mentioned earlier, the number of bar-levels for a projection is still under debate. For the parser, it is assumed that lexical categories (*e.g.*, nouns and verbs) project two levels and functional categories (*e.g.*, Case assigners), one. But this is mostly a matter of expediency.

[16] These rules really refer to the correspondence between nominal agreement clitics in the auxiliary and nominal arguments, at most two of which are registered in the auxiliary. In fact, a third rule is required to account for the object status of the absolutive argument of a ditransitive verb.

[17] There are four other verb paradigms in Warlpiri, involving only one or two arguments and some subset of these Cases. See Nash (1986) for a thorough account.

[18] This Case-θ mapping, however, is particular to but a few verbs in Warlpiri; in general, the mapping is more complicated. Nash (1986) provides a θ-role–Case mapping that seems to hold for all of the five verb paradigms in Warlpiri.
[19] Marantz (1984) argues that θ licensing and θ assignment are distinct relations. However, without loss of coverage of the sentences considered here, we may take them to be identical.
[20] As noted above, this constraint does not account for all placements of the auxiliary, but a more nearly correct analysis can be stated solely in terms of precedence. See Kashket (1987).
[21] In the event of an error, the parser immediately halts, returning the output structures extant at the time of the detection. Thus, the parser takes any ill-formedness to be fatal.

REFERENCES

Abney, S.: 1986, 'Licensing and Parsing', in *Proceedings of NELS* **17**, North Eastern Linguistic Society, University of Massachusetts, Amherst, Massachusetts, pp. 1–17.

Aoun, J. and D. Sportiche: 1983, 'On the Formal Theory of Government', *The Linguistic Review* **2**, 211–237.

Chomsky, N.: 1981, *Lectures on Government and Binding: The Pisa Lectures*, Foris, Dordrecht, Holland.

Emonds, J.: 1976, *A Transformational Approach to English Syntax*, Academic Press, London.

Goldsmith, J.: 1979, *Autosegmental Phonology*, Garland Publishing, New York.

Hale, K.: 1973, 'Person Marking in Walbiri', in S. Anderson and P. Kiparsky (eds.), *A Festschrift for Morris Halle*, Holt, Rinehart, and Winston, New York, pp. 308–344.

Hale, K.: 1982, 'Some Essential Features of Warlpiri Verbal Clauses', *Working Papers of the Summer Institute of Linguistics*, Australian Aboriginal Branch, series A, volume 6.

Jackendoff, R.: 1977, $\overline{X}$ *Syntax: A Study of Phrase Structure*, MIT Press, Cambridge, Massachusetts.

Kashket, M.: 1987, *A Government-Binding Based Parser for Warlpiri, a Free-Word Order Language*, Technical Report 993, Artificial Intelligence Laboratory, Massachusetts Institute of Technology, Cambridge, Massachusetts.

Laughren, M.: 1989, 'The Configurationality Parameter and Warlpiri', in L. Maracz and P. Muysken (eds.), *Configurationality*, Foris, Dordrecht, Holland, pp. 319–353.

Lieber, R.: 1980, *On the Organization of the Lexicon*, Ph.D. dissertation, Department of Linguistics and Philosophy, Massachusetts Institute of Technology, Cambridge, Massachusetts.

Marantz, A.: 1984, *On the Nature of Grammatical Relations*, MIT Press, Cambridge, Massachusetts.

Nash, D.: 1986, *Topics in Warlpiri Grammar*, Garland Publishing, New York.

Rouveret, A. and J.-R. Vergnaud: 1980, 'Specifying Reference to the Subject', *Linguistic Inquiry* 11, 97–202.

Simpson, J.: 1983, *Aspects of Warlpiri Morphology and Syntax*, Ph.D. dissertation, Department of Linguistics and Philosophy, Massachusetts Institute of Technology, Cambridge, Massachusetts.

Simpson, J. and M. Withgott: 1986, 'Template Morphology', in H. Borer (ed.), *Syntax and Semantics*, Academic Press, London, pp. 149–174.

Stowell, T.: 1981, *Origins of Phrase Structure*, Ph.D. dissertation, Department of Linguistics and Philosophy, Massachusetts Institute of Technology, Cambridge, Massachusetts.

Van Riemsdijk, H.: 1982, 'Locality Principles in Syntax and Phonology', in *Selected Papers from SICO: 1981*, Hanshin, Seoul, pp. 693–708.

Wackernagel, J.: 1892, 'Über ein Gesetz der indogermanischen Wortstellung', *Indogermanische Forschungen* 1, 333–436.

MIT Artificial Intelligence Laboratory, Room 823,
545 Technology Square,
Cambridge, Massachusetts 02139, U.S.A.

BONNIE JEAN DORR

PRINCIPLE-BASED PARSING FOR MACHINE TRANSLATION

1. INTRODUCTION

This chapter describes a syntactic parsing model that accommodates cross-linguistic uniform machine translation without relying on language specific context-free rules. Parsing systems typically use grammars that describe language with complicated rules that spell out the details of their application. ATN-based systems (Woods, 1970; Bates, 1978) have several hundred grammar arcs, each with detailed tests and actions; augmented phrase-structure grammars, as used in Diagram (Robinson, 1982), spell out the type, position, and probability of occurrence of constituents in a given phrase; and the GPSG approach (Gazdar et al., 1985) uses a 'slash-category' mechanism to incorporate long-distance relations directly into the grammar rules.[1] Such systems do not work in the context of translation across several languages: the rules of a given grammar are painstakingly tailored to describe a *single* language, thus forcing a loss of linguistic generalization and limiting the addition of new languages.[2]

An additional problem with rule-based systems is that the grammar size is typically quite formidable. For example, Slocum's METAL system (1984, 1985), developed at the Linguistics Research Center at the University of Texas, relies on thousands of context-free rules per language solely for parsing. Each parser operates unilingually and accesses an unwieldy number of language specific rules. Unfortunately, the grammar size of a parsing system makes a difference in processing time. As noted in Barton (1984), the Earley algorithm (1970) for context-free language parsing can quadruple its running time when the grammar size is doubled.

Another disadvantage of rule-based systems is that they fail to preserve the modular organization of new theories of grammar. Designing a system on the basis of a rule-based linguistic theory means that the grammar writer must keep track of hundreds of rules and the context in which each rule applies in order to do any system editing. Preserv-

R. C. Berwick et al. (eds.),
Principle-Based Parsing: Computation and Psycholinguistics, 153–183.
© 1991 *Kluwer Academic Publishers. Printed in the Netherlands.*

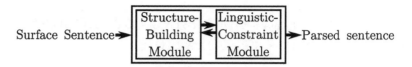

Figure 1: The parser takes on a coroutine design. The structure building module constructs skeletal syntactic structures; these are then modified by the linguistic constraint module according to the principles of GB. The two modules pass control back and forth until the sentence is completely parsed.

ing modularity allows general conditions to be factored out so that each system component is simplified and language descriptions are reduced in size. Furthermore, modularity allows several people to work on the same system without affecting one another, since each is working on an independent component of the system.

In this chapter I describe an implementation of a parser for a machine translation system called UNITRAN[3], which is based on subsystems of grammatical principles and parameters.[4] The parser follows a *coroutine* design: the structure building mechanism operates with access to linguistic constraints of Government-Binding (GB) theory as developed by Chomsky (1981, 1982). (See figure 1.) The structure building module assigns a skeletal syntactic structure to a sentence, and then this structure is eliminated or modified according to the principles of GB. This design is consistent with recent psycholinguistic studies that indicate that the human processor initially assigns a (potentially ambiguous or underspecified) structural analysis to a sentence, leaving other decisions for subsequent processing.[5] Furthermore, the parser is designed so that it applies uniformly across many languages, allowing the grammar writer to modify the parameters of the system to accommodate additional languages. Currently, UNITRAN operates bidirectionally between English and Spanish.[6] Some examples of the phenomena handled by the system are in figure 2.

Parsing uniformly across languages is difficult because the parser appears to require a massive amount of 'knowledge'. Not only must it be able to parse several types of phenomena (and their interaction effects) in a language, but it must also avoid giving ill-formed sentences the same status as well-formed sentences.[7] Consider (1):

(1) La vio a María

Phenomenon	Example
Null Subject	Vio a María (He/She saw Mary)
Clitic Doubling	Juan la vio a María (John saw Mary)
Free Inversion	Vio a María Juan (John saw Mary)
Verb Preposing	¿Qué vio Juan? (What did John see)
Subject-Auxiliary Inversion	Did John see Mary
Pleonastics	There is a man in the room

Figure 2: The phenomena handled by UNITRAN include Null Subject, Clitic Doubling, Free Inversion, Verb Preposing, Subject-Auxiliary Inversion, and Pleonastics. These phenomena are instrumental in understanding the parametric variations between Spanish and English.

'(He) saw Mary'

Although (1) appears to be simple, it is not simple from the viewpoint of uniform parsing since the equivalent sentence parses differently in other languages. The Spanish and English parse trees for (1) are in figure 3. Literally, the English translation for (1) is (2), which is ungrammatical:

(2) Her *e* saw to Mary

The *e* stands for a *null subject* that is realized as *he* in English.[8] (See section 3.3 for a discussion of the null subject phenomenon in Spanish.) The parsing implementation presented here rules out sentence (2) without sacrificing the ability to parse (1).

Perhaps a more important consideration than ruling out ungrammatical sentences is the requirement that the parser avoid assigning wrong interpretations to grammatical sentences. In a cross-linguistically applicable system, this requirement is difficult to satisfy. For example, it is conceivable that the system might parse a Spanish sentence incorrectly on the basis of the knowledge it has for parsing English sentences. Consider (3):

(3) Qué golpeó Juan
    'What did John hit'

If the parser were to use English parameter settings to parse this sentence, it would understand the sentence to mean *what hit john* (*i.e.*,

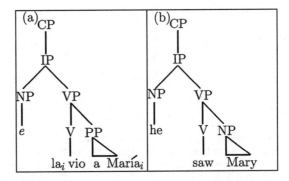

Figure 3: The Spanish and English parse trees for equivalent sentences are not always identical. For example, here the subject is not lexically realized in the Spanish parse tree, but it is overt in the English parse tree. (Subscripts are used for coreferring elements; thus, *la* (= her) refers to *María*.)

the *agent* and *goal* roles would be reversed). The parameter-setting approach allows incorrect interpretations such as this to be avoided in one language without affecting the processing of other languages.

The coroutine design differs from other GB parsing/translation systems (*e.g.*, Sharp, 1985) in that the linguistic principles are used for *online* verification during parsing rather than as well-formedness conditions on output. Furthermore, in Sharp's system, context-free rules (set up for English-like languages) are hardwired into the code rather than generated by the parser from principles of GB; thus, Sharp's system cannot handle languages (like German or Japanese) that do not have the same order of constituents as English, unless the code is modified. The root of the problem in Sharp's system is that the grammar writer has limited access to the grammatical principles of the system. The system described here allows the grammar writer to specify parameter values for the principles, thus modifying their effects from language to language.

The modularity imposed by the GB framework is an improvement over context-free based systems for several reasons. First, properties common to several languages are not specified directly in rules, but are abstracted into modularized principles. For example, the passive transformation that relates an active sentence to its passive counterpart used to look something like the following:

(4) NP_1 V $NP_2 \rightarrow NP_2$ be V+en by NP_1

Thus, the sentence *Susan beat John* is related by the passive transformation to *John was beaten by Susan*. Rule (4) is complicated and idiosyncratic. It relies heavily on the word choice and ordering requirements of English. Unfortunately, word choice and ordering do not necessarily carry over to other languages. In Spanish, there are three passive transformations:

(5) NP_1 V $NP_2 \rightarrow NP_2$ ser V+ido por NP_1
    NP_1 V $NP_2 \rightarrow$ se V a NP_2
    NP_1 V $NP_2 \rightarrow$ se le/les V

Only the first of the three Spanish passive transformations in (5) is the same as the one English passive transformation. Thus, the sentence *John was beaten by Susan* can be literally translated as *John fue golpeado por Susan*. However, the passive form may also be realized as *se golpeó a Juan* (here the subject is not specified) or *se le golpeó* (here the subject and object are not specified).

The abstraction of properties into modularized principles allows linguistic generalization to be captured. The system uses a general principle called Move-α rather than a detailed passive rule that changes from language to language. This movement principle allows a constituent (α) to be displaced to another position in the sentence, but the movement is constrained according to principles of Trace theory (to be discussed in section 3.3). Because these constraining principles are allowed to vary from language to language, we can account for the fact that Spanish passive NP-movement may involve realization of a pronoun *se*, whereas the English passive NP-movement does not allow such a realization. Thus, the passive rule is reduced to a small set of cross-linguistically applicable principles that are sensitive to parametric variation.

Another advantage to modularity is that multiplicative effects of linguistic constraints are not spelled out in the form of grammar rules. In a rule-based system, subject/verb agreement might use the following two rules:

(6) $S \rightarrow NP_{sg}$ VP_{sg}
    $S \rightarrow NP_{pl}$ VP_{pl}

These two rules work for parsing active sentences, but, to also parse passive sentences, subject/verb agreement has to be encoded in passive rules too:

(7) $S \rightarrow NP_{sg}$ be_{sg} VP_{+en}
    $S \rightarrow NP_{pl}$ be_{pl} VP_{+en}

Now, if another phenomenon (say, past/present tense alternation) were added, each of (6) and (7) would have to be multiplied out into additional rules. It is easy to see that the grammar can quickly become explosive. The more desirable approach is to use a simple (underspecified) grammar, and then superimpose separate modules that individually handle agreement and movement phenomena on the grammar. The elimination of multiplicative effects from the grammar rules allows grammar size (hence processing time) to be reduced.

Modularity has the further advantage that a separate description is not required for each language handled by the system. The grammar writer does not have the traditional task of constructing a set of complex language specific phrase structure rules; instead, the task of the grammar writer is to determine the parameter-settings for each language. For example, two rules accounting for the fact that a Spanish sentence does not require a subject are the following:

(8) $S \rightarrow NP$ VP
    $S \rightarrow VP$

Rather than specifying these two rules, the grammar writer need only set the *null subject* parameter (to be discussed in section 3.3) to T(rue) for Spanish. The parameter-setting approach facilitates the extension of the system to handle additional languages: adding a language reduces to changing the parameter-settings to suit that language.

Translation in UNITRAN is primarily syntactic; thus, there is no global contextual 'understanding' (the system translates each sentence in isolation).[9] Semantics is incorporated only to the extent of locating possible antecedents of pronouns (*e.g.*, linking *himself* with *he* in the sentence *he dressed himself*), and assigning semantic roles (*e.g.*, designating *he* as the *agent* in *he ate dinner*) to certain elements of the sentence, in particular, arguments of verbs.[10] It should be noted that determining the mapping between semantically equivalent verbs is not a trivial task. For example, although the Spanish verb *gustar* is semantically equivalent to the English verb *like*, the argument structures of these two verbs are not identical. The subject of the verb *like* is the *agent*, whereas the object of the verb *gustar* is the *agent*. In order to include such cases of thematic divergence, the argument structure of a

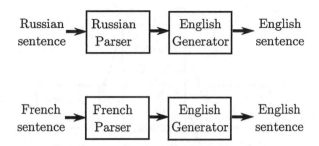

Figure 4: The direct approach, as found in GAT (1964), is a word-for-word translation scheme in which there is a parser and a generator for each source-target language pair.

source language verb must be matched with the argument structure of the corresponding target language verb before the two verbs are considered equivalent for the purposes of translation.

The following sections describe the UNITRAN system in more detail. Section 2 presents the underlying computational model; section 3 presents the underlying linguistic model; section 4 provides an overview of the system; section 5 provides an example of the parser in action; and section 6 provides a summary and discusses some of the shortcomings of the system.

2. UNDERLYING COMPUTATIONAL MODEL

The aim of this section is to present the computational framework for UNITRAN, and to put into perspective how the design of the system differs from and compares to other approaches. The distinction between rule-based (noninterlingual) and principle-based (interlingual) systems will be presented, and the advantages of the principle-based design over other designs will be discussed.

2.1. *Direct and Transfer Approaches: Rule-based Systems*

An early approach to machine translation (*e.g.*, the Georgetown Automatic Translation (GAT) system, 1964) was a *direct* word-for-word scheme in which there was a parser and a generator for each source-target language pair (see figure 4).[11] The primary characteristic of such an approach is that it is designed to translate out of one specific language

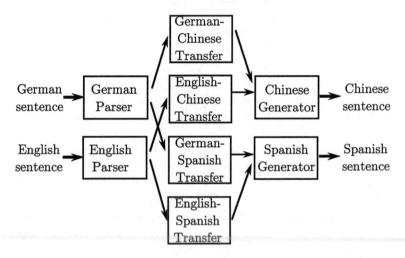

Figure 5: The transfer approach as found in METAL (1984) makes use of a set of transfer components, one for each source-target language pair. The source language sentence is first parsed into a source transfer form. This form is then mapped to a target transfer form that is used to generate the target language sentence.

into another.

Later approaches to machine translation (*e.g.*, the METAL system by Slocum, 1984) have taken a *transfer* approach, in which there is only one parser and one generator for each source and target language. In this approach, there is a set of *transfer* components, one for each source-target language pair (see figure 5). The transfer phase is actually a third translation stage in which one language specific representation is mapped into another. In contrast to the direct approach to translation, the transfer approach has been somewhat more successful, accommodating a variety of linguistic strategies across different languages. The METAL system currently translates from German into Chinese and Spanish, as well as from English into German.

The problem with the transfer approach is that, in general, each analysis component is based on language specific context-free rules. Although the type of grammar formalism is allowed to vary from language to language in a system such as METAL, each parser is nevertheless based on a large database of rules of a context-free nature. For example,

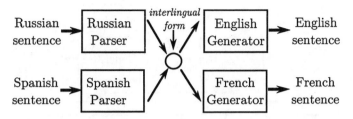

Figure 6: The interlingual approach taken by CETA (1961) and Sharp (1985) eliminates the need for a transfer component by providing a common underlying form. However, a language-dependent parser and a language-dependent generator are required for each language. Also, because language specific mechanisms are used by both systems, the grammar writer cannot easily add new languages to the system.

the German parser is based on phrase structure grammar, augmented by procedures for transformations, and the English parser employs a modified GPSG approach (see Gazdar *et al.*, 1985). Because the system has no access to universal principles, there is no consistency across the components; thus, each parser has an independent theoretical and engineering basis. Rather than abstracting principles that are common to all languages into separate modules that are activated during translation of any language, each parser must independently include all of the information required to translate that language, whether or not the information is universal. For example, agreement information must be encoded into each rule in the METAL system; there is no separate agreement module that can apply to other rules. Consequently, in order to account for a wide range of phenomena, thousands of idiosyncratic rules are required for each language, thus increasing grammar search time. Furthermore, there is no 'rulesharing'. All rules are language-dependent and cannot apply across several languages.

2.2. *Interlingual Approaches: Principle-based Systems*

The model described in this chapter moves away from the language specific rule-based design, and moves toward a linguistically motivated principle-based design. The translator is *interlingual*, (*i.e.*, the source language is mapped into a form that is independent of any language); thus, there are no transfer modules or language specific context-free rules. The interlingual approach to translation has been taken by CETA

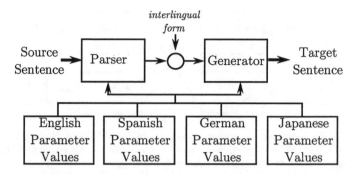

Figure 7: The interlingual approach taken by Dorr in UNITRAN uses the same parser and generator for all languages. The grammar writer may modify the parameters of the system in order to handle additional languages.

(Centre d'Etudes pour la Traduction Automatique),[12] and Sharp (1985). However, the CETA system is not entirely interlingual since there is a transfer component (at the lexical level) that maps from one language specific lexical representation to another. Sharp's system, although not rule-based, is also not entirely interlingual since context-free rules (set up for English-like languages) are hardwired into the code rather than generated on the fly using linguistically motivated principles; thus, languages (like German or Japanese) that do not have the same order of constituents as English cannot be handled by the system. The result is that the class of languages that can be translated is limited. The interlingual approach as embodied by CETA and Sharp is illustrated in figure 6. Note that there are no transfer components, but that there is a language-dependent parser and a language-dependent generator for each source and target language. The interlingual form is assumed to be a form common to all languages.

There are two problems with this incarnation of the interlingual approach. First, the grammar writer must supply a parser for each source language and a generator for each target language. Second, the grammar writer has limited access to the parameters of the system. For example, the *constituent order* parameter mentioned in note 4 is not available for modification in the interlingual approach as embodied by CETA and Sharp.

The approach taken for UNITRAN is still interlingual by definition (*i.e.*, the source language is mapped into a form that is independent of any language), but the design is slightly different from that of CETA and Sharp: the same parser and generator are used for all languages. Furthermore, the grammar writer is allowed to specify parameter values for the principles, thus modifying the effect of the principles from language to language. This more closely approximates a true universal approach since the principles that apply across all languages are entirely separate from the language specific characteristics expressed by parameter settings.[13] Figure 7 illustrates the design of the model. The parser and generator are programmable: all of the linguistic principles are associated with parameters that are set by the grammar writer. Thus, the grammar writer does not need to supply a source language parser or a target language generator since these are already part of the translation system. The only requirement is that the built-in parser and generator be *programmed* (via parameter settings) to process the source and target languages. For example, the grammar writer must specify that an English sentence requires a subject, but that a Spanish sentence does *not* require a subject. This is done by setting the *null subject* parameter to *yes* in Spanish; by contrast, this parameter must be set to *no* for English. (For details on the null subject parameter, see van Riemsdijk and Williams, 1986, pp. 298–303.) A dictionary for each language must also be supplied.

The translation process consists of three stages: First, the parser takes a morphologically analyzed input and returns a tree structure that encodes structural relations among elements of the source language sentence. (This structure is the interlingual representation that underlies both languages.) Second, substitution routines replace the source-language constituents with the thematically corresponding target language lexical entries. Third, the generator performs movement and morphological synthesis, thus deriving the target language sentence. An overview of the translation system is given in section 4.

3. UNDERLYING LINGUISTIC MODEL

The structure building and linguistic constraint components of figure 1 correspond to a bipartition of several underlying subsystems of grammar. The partition corresponding to the structure building component consists of the $\overline{X}$ subsystem, which imposes certain restrictions on the order and positioning of phrasal constituents. The partition corresponding

Module	Constraint Satisfaction	Constraint Violation
X̄	I saw the man.	* I the man saw.
Bounding	*Who* t saw the movie?	* *Who* do you wonder whether t saw the movie?
Trace	*Who* do you think that John will beat t?	* *Who* do you think that t will beat John?
Case	John seems to be happy.	* Seems John to be happy.
Binding	John felt that his friends liked him.	* John felt that his friends liked himself.
θ	La vio a María.	* La vio María.

Figure 8: Each GB module applies various constraints to the parses constructed by the structure building component. Any parse that violates a constraint is considered ill-formed, and any parse that does not violate a constraint is considered well-formed. All well-formed parses are returned.

to the linguistic constraint component consists of the Bounding, Trace, Case, Binding, and θ subsystems, each of which imposes restrictions on movement of constituents in a sentence.

Figure 8 summarizes the GB modules included in the system and shows the effects of each module on various English and Spanish sentences. For example, the Bounding module accounts for the contrast between the well-formedness of *Who saw the movie?* and the ill-formedness of *Who do you wonder whether saw the movie?* The interaction of these subsystems is precisely what is needed to gain the effects of complicated rule systems without stipulatory rules.

This section describes three of the GB subtheories (X̄ theory, θ theory, and Trace theory) that underlie the two components of the system. The principles and parameters of variation associated with these three theories are described. Also, the relevance of the parameters within the context of the parsing model is discussed. The goal is to incorporate the parameterized principles of GB into a single, cross-linguistically uniform parsing system.

3.1. $\overline{X}$ Theory Parameters: Choice of Specifiers and Constituent Order

There are two central notions associated with $\overline{X}$ theory. First, the dictionary (henceforth *lexicon*) specifies subcategorization frames for lexical items. For example, the frame for the verb *put* includes two arguments: a noun phrase and a prepositional phrase (*e.g.*, *put the car in the garage*). Second, phrase structure is expressed as a projection of a lexical head X (= N, V, P or A). Thus, in the sentence *he put the car in the garage*, the verb *put* projects the verb phrase *put the car in the garage*.[14] $\overline{X}$ theory assumes that phrase structures for English are derived by rules of the following form:

(9) $X^{max} \rightarrow$ (Specifier) X (Complement)

Here X^{max} is the maximal projection of the lexical head X (more commonly called XP). The Specifier of X is determined by a parameter setting associated with the $\overline{X}$ module, and the complement of X is determined by the subcategorization frame of the verb. For example, if X is a noun, then X^{max} is NP, a possible Specifier is a determiner, and a possible complement is a prepositional phrase (depending on whether this is specified in the lexical entry for the noun).

English requires that specifiers of all lexical categories occur before the lexical head and that complements follow the lexical head. However, this rule does not apply to all languages (*e.g.*, Navajo, German, Japanese). For example, consider the following Navajo sentence:

(10) ashkii at'ééd yiyiiłtsą
      'the boy saw the girl'

This sentence literally translates as *the boy the girl saw* since Navajo requires the complement to precede the head.[15] It is assumed that the constituent order of a language is determined by a parameter of variation (see note 4). Thus, as parsing proceeds, $\overline{X}$ phrases are attached relative to the head according to the constituent order of the language being parsed. This is crucial in the parsing model since many of the principles of other GB subtheories cannot apply until a valid licensed structure (with predetermined ordering restrictions) has first been built. In other words, $\overline{X}$ theory provides basic templates to which remaining parsing constraints can apply.

3.2. *θ Theory Parameters: Clitic Doubling*

$θ$ theory is the theory of thematic (or semantic) roles. A principle of this theory is the $θ$-criterion (Theta-criterion) which states that each noun phrase argument of a verb is uniquely assigned a semantic role (henceforth $θ$-role) and each $θ$-role is uniquely assigned to an argument. For example, the verb *ver* (= see) uniquely assigns a $θ$-role of *goal* to its direct object:

(11) (a) Juan vio el libro

      (b) Juan lo vio

In (11a) the *goal* $θ$-role is assigned to the noun phrase *el libro* (= book) and in (11b) the *goal* $θ$-role is assigned to the object pronoun *lo* (= him). In order for $θ$-roles to be assigned to arguments of a verb, there is a principle of $θ$-role transmission that maps $θ$-roles in the lexicon entry of the verb to the verbal arguments in the sentence.

In Spanish, the phenomenon of *clitic doubling* is relevant to parametric variation of the $θ$-role transmission principle. A *clitic* is a pronominal constituent that is associated with a verbal object. For example, the pronoun *le* in the following sentence is a clitic associated with *Juan*, the object of the verb *regalé*:

(12) Le regalé un libro a Juan
      'I gave a book to John'

In general, a pronominal clitic is associated with a lexical referential NP. Thus, clitic doubling is defined in terms of the pair ⟨*clitic, lexical NP*⟩ where the clitic must agree in number, person, and gender with the lexical referential NP. In (12) the clitic *le* actually stands for an NP that does not yet have a $θ$-role (namely, *Juan*).

In order to satisfy the $θ$-criterion, a parameter of variation is required for the principle of $θ$-role transmission. Jaeggli (1981) proposes that clitics supply $θ$-roles to object NPs that are doubled through a $θ$-role transmission principle:

(13) $[\text{CL} +Case_i +θ_j] \ldots [\text{NP} +Case_i] \Rightarrow$
      $[\text{CL} +Case_i +θ_j] \ldots [\text{NP} +Case_i +θ_j]$

This rule allows a doubled NP object to receive a $θ$-role as long as the clitic and NP have the same Case.[16] If a clitic is not present, a

θ-role is assigned, in the usual fashion, from the verb that contains the argument in its lexical entry. Thus, for languages that allow clitics, clitic doubling must be available as a parameter of variation to the θ-role transmission principle of θ theory. The θ-criterion can then be used as a well-formedness condition during parsing so that clitic doubling constructions will be ruled out unless (13) is allowed to fire. This is important in a parsing model since languages that allow clitics could not be parsed uniformly without such a parameter of variation.

3.3.   Trace Theory Parameters: Choice of Traces and Null Subject

Trace theory is another subtheory of GB that is important for uniform parsing across languages, in part because it explains the distinctions between languages that allow null subjects (like Spanish) and other languages. A trace is an empty position that is either base-generated or left behind when a constituent has moved. In this discussion we will talk only about NP traces. However, there may be other types of traces. Thus, the choice of traces for each language is specified as a parameter setting in the trace module.

According to the analysis of the null subject parameter introduced by van Riemsdijk and Williams (1986), the choice of whether or not sentences are required to have a subject is allowed to vary from language to language. In Spanish, as in Italian, Greek, and Hebrew, morphology is rich enough to make the subject pronouns redundant and recoverable. Thus, we can have this sentence:

(14) Hablé con ella
      '(I) spoke with her'

Since the inflection on the verb is first person singular, the subject pronoun *yo* (=I) need not be used.

The formulation of the *null subject* parameter by van Riemsdijk and Williams is motivated by the observation that subjects are missing in a variety of constructions, not just in cases like (14). In many other languages (*e.g.*, English), these constructions do not appear; thus, there must be some common factor that will account for the distinction between languages that allow subjects to be omitted and languages that do *not* allow subjects to be omitted. The null subject parameter, then, is a minimal binary difference that does or does not allow empty noun phrases to occupy subject position.[17] The parameter-setting approach is

Theory	Principles	Parameters
$\overline{\mathrm{X}}$	A phrasal projection (X^{max}) has a head (X), a specifier, and a complement	Constituent Order Choice of Specifiers
θ	[CL $+Case_i$ $+\theta_j$] ... [NP $+Case_i$] $\Rightarrow$ [CL $+Case_i$ $+\theta_j$] ... [NP $+Case_i$ $+\theta_j$] if language allows clitic doubling	Clitic Doubling
Trace	Subjects may be omitted in certain languages	Null Subject
	An empty position may occur where traces are allowed	Choice of traces

Figure 9: The principles of GB are modularized according to subtheories. Each principle may have one or more parameters associated with it.

more desirable than a rule-based approach since it accounts for several types of null subject constructions without requiring several independent rules.[18] The null subject parameter is important in the parsing model because it allows uniform parsing of null subject and overt subject languages, ensuring that sentences without a subject are ruled out unless the null subject parameter is set.

3.4. *Principles and Parameters*

Figure 9 summarizes the various subsystems of principles and parameters (grouped according to subtheory) relevant to the parsing model presented here. Because of space limitations, only those parameters that are relevant to a condensed description of the parser are shown. The actual implementation currently has 20 parameters. Figure 10 summarizes the parameter settings required for parsing Spanish and English.

4. OVERVIEW OF UNITRAN

At each of the three stages of translation, processing tasks are divided between the structure building module and the linguistic constraint module as shown in figure 11.

During the parsing stage, the structure building component applies

Theory	Parameters	Parameter Values	
		Spanish	English
$\overline{\text{X}}$	Constituent Order	spec-head-comp	spec-head-comp
	Choice of Specifiers	V: have-aux; N: det; I: N^{max}	V: have, do-aux; N: det; I: N^{max}
θ	Clitic Doubling	applicable and allowed	not applicable
Trace	Null Subject	yes	no
	Choice of traces	N^{max}, *Wh*-phrase, V, P^{max}	N^{max}, *Wh*-phrase, V, P^{max}

Figure 10: The parameter settings associated with the principles of GB are allowed to vary from language to language. Here are some of the parameter settings for Spanish and English.

Translation Stage	Structure Building Tasks	Linguistic Constraint Tasks
Parsing	Syntactic Parse	Phrase Structure: Agreement & Case filters; Argument Structure & θ-role checks
Substitution	Lexical Replacement	Lexical: Argument Structure & Thematic Divergence
Generation	Structural Movement & Morphological Synthesis	Structural and Morphological checks

Figure 11: The translation tasks of the structure building and linguistic constraint modules differ according to the stage of the translation. During parsing, the structure building module performs a syntactic analysis of the source language sentence, while the linguistic constraint module applies structural filters and checks well-formedness. During substitution, lexical replacement is performed by the structure building module, and tests are applied to predicate-argument structure by the linguistic constraint module. In the generation stage, the structure building module performs a syntactic synthesis of the target language sentence, while the linguistic constraint module applies structural filters and checks morphological well-formedness.

projection, attachment, and empty element prediction, while the linguistic constraint component enforces well-formedness conditions on the structures passed to it. The phrase structures that are built by the structure building component are underspecified, (*i.e.*, they do not include information about agreement, abstract case, θ-roles, argument structure, and so forth); the basis of these structures is a set of templates that are generated according to the $\overline{\text{X}}$ parameter settings (*e.g.*, constituent order, choice of specifiers) of the source language. The linguistic constraint component eliminates or modifies the underspecified phrase structures according to principles of GB (*e.g.*, agreement filters, Case filters, argument requirements, θ-role conditions).

Just prior to the lexical substitution stage, the source language sentence is in an *underlying form*, *i.e.*, a form that can be translated into any target language according to conditions relevant to that target language. This means that all participants of the main action (*e.g.*, *agent*, *patient*, ...) of the sentence are identified and placed in a 'base' position relative to the main verb. At the level of lexical substitution, the structure building module simply replaces source language words with their equivalent target language translations, subject to argument structure requirements and tests of thematic divergence (*i.e.*, tests for semantic mismatches as in the *gustar-like* example mentioned in section 1).

Generation consists of transformation of the sentence into a grammatically acceptable form with respect to the target language (*e.g.*, in English, the underlying form *was called John* would be transformed into the surface form *John was called*).

An example of how the structure building module operates in tandem with the linguistic constraint module is presented in the next section.

5. EXAMPLE

All three stages of translation have been implemented as discussed in Dorr (1987). However, the example provided in this section describes only the parsing portion of the translation process. The substitution and generation routines are not as elaborate as the parsing routines, and they do not handle all of the cases that the parser can handle due to problems concerning structural realization (*i.e.*, choosing the *syntactically* correct form to generate from the underlying form) and lexical selection (*i.e.*, choosing the *semantically* correct form to generate from the underlying form).[19]

Do until no more input:
1. Project phrase.
2. Do until no changes made:
   a. Attach completed phrase.
   b. Predict empty elements.

Figure 12: The algorithm for the parsing stage of the structure building process projects a lexical item up to the maximal $\overline{\mathrm{X}}$ level and then enters a complete-predict loop until no more actions can be taken. These structure building steps are executed for each word in the input.

The general algorithm for the parsing stage of the structure building process is shown in figure 12.

That is, for each word, the parser projects up to the maximal $\overline{\mathrm{X}}$ level, and then enters a complete-predict loop until the next word is 'ready to be parsed'.

Each one of the three structure building actions (1, 2a, and 2b) is associated with a set of linguistic constraint actions as shown in figure 13. While the structure building component provides both underspecified and overgenerative $\overline{\mathrm{X}}$ structures, the linguistic constraint component weeds out ill-formed parses and realizes possibilities unavailable to the structure building component. Note that most of the linguistic constraints are applied during attachment of completed phrases. This is because most of the constraints are not applicable to a phrase until it is complete (*i.e.*, all of the arguments of the phrasal head are present).

To clarify the above description of the parsing algorithm, we will look at the problem of parsing (1), repeated here as (15):

(15) La vio a María
     '(He) saw Mary'

We will see how the structure building module determines phrase structure for this sentence through projection of lexical elements, completion of phrases, and prediction of empty elements. At the same time, we will see how the linguistic constraint module processes clitics, assigns θ-roles, and predicts a null subject. Figures 14, 15, and 16 give snapshots of the parser in action. As each phrase is projected, it is pushed onto a stack. Only the top two stack elements are shown in the snapshots at any given time. (The stack 'grows' from left to right.) The final result

Action	Structure Building	Linguistic Constraint
1. Project phrases	Project maximal phrases from lexical elements	Instantiate features Determine arguments
2a. Attach completed phrases	Drop complete phrases into argument and non-argument positions	Percolate features Trace-antecedent Check Bounding Check Binding Check ECP Assign Case Assign θ-role Check θ-criterion
2b. Predict empty elements	Project empty feature holders and drop traces into argument positions	Determine legal traces and empty feature holders

Figure 13: Each one of the three structure building parsing actions (1, 2a, and 2b) is associated with a set of linguistic constraint parsing actions.

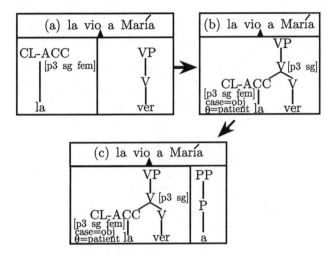

Figure 14: The first three snapshots of the parser in action show: (a) projection of the first two input words, *la* and *ver*, up to their maximal level; (b) attachment of the clitic to the verbal head; and (c) projection of the third input word *a* up to its maximal level. Note that the verb *ver* assigns *patient* θ-role to the object clitic *la* once the clitic has been attached. The stack grows from left to right.

will be a single parse tree in the top stack element.

First the structure building component projects a phrase (step 1) for each of the first two words, *la* and *ver*.[20] After the two phrases, CL-ACC (accusative clitic) and VP (verb phrase), have been projected, the linguistic constraint component instantiates the associated features (person, number, and gender). Snapshot 14(a) shows the result of the parse thus far.

At this point, the structure building component enters the complete-predict loop (step 2), and the clitic is associated with the verbal head.[21] Since a phrase has just been completed, the linguistic constraint component fires several constraints (step 2a). Among the linguistic actions taken are θ-role assignment and θ-criterion checking.[22] First, the system attempts to discharge the θ-roles associated with *ver* (the root form of *vio*). The lexical entry for *ver* is encoded as follows:

(ver: [ext: agent] [int: patient] V (english: see) ...)

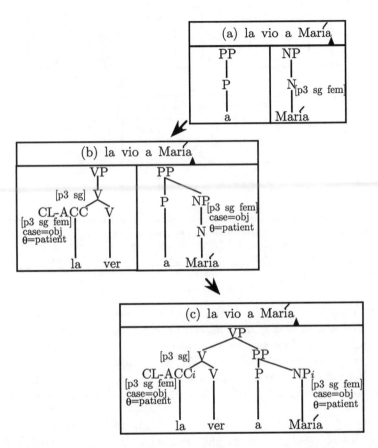

Figure 15: The second three snapshots of the parser in action show: (a) projection of the final input word *María* up to its maximal level; (b) attachment of the NP containing *María* as a prepositional object; and (c) attachment of the PP as a verbal object. Note that the clitic *la* is coindexed with its associated NP *María*, thus satisfying the θ-criterion.

From this entry, it is determined that the internal argument for the verb *ver* is assigned a θ-role of patient. In this case, the internal argument (*i.e.*, the constituent governed by the V node) is the clitic *la*; thus, the clitic is assigned a *patient* θ-role. Next, the linguistic constraint component checks the clitic doubling parameter as part of the θ-criterion. Spanish allows clitic doubling, but there is no corresponding NP to which the θ-role transmission principle (13) applies, so no further linguistic actions are taken. The result of the completed phrase is in snapshot 14(b).

Since no more structure building or linguistic constraint actions apply, the next word *a* is projected up to its maximal level, PP (step 1). The features of this newly projected lexical item are instantiated and the argument structure of the head is established. The head *a* takes an internal NP argument; however, no such argument is available yet. Snapshot 14(c) shows the parse at this point.

Again, no more structure building or linguistic constraint actions apply, so the parser exits the complete-predict loop and executes step 1. The final word *María* is projected up to its maximal NP level and its features are instantiated (see snapshot 15(a)). Now the complete-predict loop is re-entered. Since the NP is already complete, its head features are percolated up to the maximal level and it is attached by the structure building component under the PP (step 2a). This attachment is allowed only because the head *a* requires an NP object. Furthermore, the attachment of the NP to the *right* of the head (rather than to the *left* of the head) is established by means of the constituent order $\overline{X}$ parameter mentioned in section 3.1. Thus, the attachment of the NP is an example of how the linguistic constraint component is able to realize a possibility unavailable to the structure building component. Snapshot 15(b) shows the resulting structure.[23]

Because the PP is complete, it too can be attached (step 2a). Thus, the PP becomes the complement under the VP, positioned again according to the constituent order parameter. The attachment of the PP is legal only because the lexical item *ver* takes a PP internal argument (the structural realization of the *patient* θ-role). At this point the linguistic constraint module attempts to assign θ-role to the NP *María*. However, all of the θ-roles from the lexical entry of *ver* have already been assigned; thus, assigning a role from this element would be a violation of the θ-criterion. On the other hand, leaving the NP *María* without a role also violates the θ-criterion. Consequently, the constraint

module determines (via the clitic doubling parameter setting) that the
θ-role transmission rule (13) is applicable, and recognizes that the NP
María corresponds to the 'recorded' clitic preceding the verb *ver* (since
the two match in person, number, gender, and Case). Thus, a θ-role of
patient is transmitted to the NP *María*.[24] As a result of the application
of the θ-transmission rule, the clitic *la* and NP *María* are coindexed;
thus, these two constituents are interpreted as coreferential during the
stages following the parse. Note that the application of the θ-criterion
is an example of how the linguistic constraint component weeds out a
parse that is ill-formed, namely, the parse in which the verb *ver* has
an extraneous NP argument (the coindexation of the clitic with the NP
'combines' the two constituents into a single argument). The new state
of the parse is illustrated in snapshot 15(c).

Now the VP is complete and the linguistic constraint component per-
colates the features of the head (V) up to the maximal level (step 2a).
Next, the structure building component determines that an empty projection is required (step 2b).[25] Thus, an IP (Inflectional Phrase) is predicted, and the VP is attached to the right of the head (I) as its complement. The features from the VP are then percolated up to the head of
the IP as part of the linguistic constraint actions. (See snapshot 16(a).)

Next, the structure building component establishes that the IP has
an NP specifier (according to the choice-of-specifier parameter). Because there are no more input words to fill out this position, an empty
element must be predicted (step 2b). Just as in the case of the internal
argument attachment, the linguistic constraint component again realizes
a possibility unavailable to the structure building component: the null
subject parameter (see section 3.3) is accessed, and the parser establishes
that an empty element can be attached under the IP as a subject. The
pro(nominal) feature is associated with the node so the structure will
accommodate both null subject and overt subject target languages.[26]
A θ-role of *agent* is then assigned to the empty subject of the sentence
since the lexical entry of *ver* dictates that this verb requires an external argument with an *agent* θ-role.[27] The resulting parse is shown in
snapshot 16(b).

Finally, the structure building component determines that an empty
CP projection is required to the left of the IP in much the same way that
an empty projection was predicted for the VP (see note 25). After the
IP is attached as the complement of the head (C), the parse is complete
as shown in snapshot 16(c).

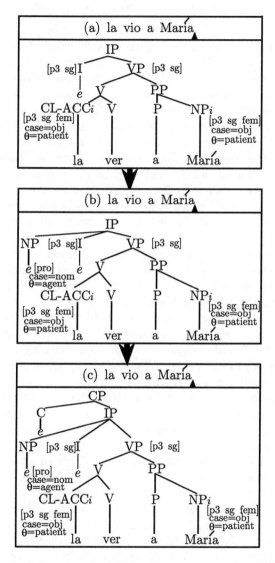

Figure 16: The final three snapshots of the parser in action show: (a) attachment of the VP as the complement of an empty I(nfl) node; (b) positioning of the null subject NP under the IP; and (c) attachment of the IP as the complement of an empty C(omp) node. Note that the null subject receives and *agent* θ-role by the verb *ver*.

6. SUMMARY AND LIMITATIONS

The system described here is based on modular theories of syntax which include systems of principles and parameters rather than complex, language specific rules. The contribution put forth by this investigation is two-fold: (a) from a linguistic point of view, the investigation allows the principles of GB to be realized and verified; and (b) from a computational perspective, descriptions of natural grammars are simplified, thus easing the programmer's and grammar writer's task. The model not only permits a language to be described by the same set of parameters that specify the language in linguistic theory, but it also eases the burden of the programmer by handling interaction effects of universal principles without requiring that the effects be specifically spelled out. Currently the UNITRAN system operates bidirectionally between Spanish and English; other languages could be supported by setting the parameters to accommodate those languages.[28]

An advantage to using the principle-based approach is that cross-linguistic generalization is captured. The parser operates uniformly across all languages by using general principles that are parameterized according to the language being parsed. A related benefit gained by using the principle-based approach is extensibility: the grammar writer has access to parameters associated with the system principles, thus enabling extension of the system to additional languages.

Another advantage of the principle-based approach is that the system preserves the modular organization of new theories of grammar. The coroutine design of the system divides the tasks of structure building and linguistic constraint application into two modules. The linguistic constraint module is further broken down into modules associated with each linguistic subtheory. The modularity imposed by the GB framework is an improvement over context-free rule-based systems because it allows general conditions to be factored out, thus simplifying each system component and reducing the complexity of natural language descriptions.[29] In summary, the principle-based parsing approach allows uniform parsing across languages, enables extensibility, and preserves modularity.

The primary limitation of the system as presented in this chapter is that it is almost entirely syntactic-based. The inclusion of θ-roles guides the processing of many semantically equivalent but structurally divergent source and target language predicates (*e.g.*, the *gustar-like* differences mentioned earlier). However, this syntactic-based approach is not adequate to handle a number of other types of structural divergences, nor is it adequate to account for semantic ambiguity. The system has recently been extended to include a more general method of translating between structurally distinct but semantically equivalent constituents (see Dorr, 1988, 1990). This new approach, based on lexical-semantic processing, eliminates many of the shortcomings of the entirely syntactic approach. Furthermore, it is expected that this approach will enable UNITRAN to handle certain types of semantic ambiguity in future versions.

ACKNOWLEDGEMENTS

This report describes research done at the Artificial Intelligence Laboratory of the Massachusetts Institute of Technology. Support for the Laboratory's artificial intelligence research has been provided in part by the Advanced Research Projects Agency of the Department of Defense under Office of Naval Research contracts N00014-80-C-0505 and N00014-85-K-0124, and also in part by NSF Grant DCR-85552543 under a Presidential Young Investigator's Award to Professor Robert C. Berwick. Useful guidance and commentary during this research was provided by Bob Berwick, Ed Barton, Michael Brent, Bruce Dawson, Ken Hale, Mike Kashket, and Patrick Winston.

NOTES

[1] Barton (1984) describes these rule-based systems in more detail.

[2] GPSG *does* make use of constraints that are claimed to be cross-linguistically applicable (see Gazdar *et al.*, 1985, p. 4). However, the universals used by GPSG (for example, the Exhaustive Constant Partial Ordering constraint on linear precedence in grammar) follow as a consequence of the grammatical formalism itself; they do not necessarily follow from empirical data. Thus, the constraints of GPSG differ from Government-Binding (GB) theory in that they are not developed on the basis of observation of natural language phenomena, but they are derived from formal statements of the grammatical metalanguage. Furthermore, the cross-linguistic applicability of GPSG is not as readily observable as that of GB since there is no notion of parameterized linguistic principles; instead, there are many complex and idiosyncratic grammar rules that are difficult to decode without understanding the intent of the grammar writer.

[3] The name UNITRAN stands for UNIversal TRANslator; that is, the system serves as the basis for translation across a variety of languages, not just two languages or a family of languages.

[4] For example, there is a *constituent order* parameter associated with a universal principle that requires there to be a language-dependent ordering of constituents with respect to a phrase. The parameter is set by the grammar writer to be *head-initial* for a language like English, but *head-final* for a language like Japanese. This

is discussed in section 3.1.

[5] Frazier (1986) provides recent psycholinguistic evidence that there is a temporal sequence of parsing consistent with the GB-based model presented here. However, the issue of psycholinguistic reality of the model will not be addressed in this chapter.

[6] The latest version of UNITRAN also operates on German (see Dorr, 1990).

[7] Partial sentences are ignored here. A system that performs question-answering allows partial sentences to be parsed as well-formed structures. The system described here analyzes sentences in isolation. Thus, incomplete sentences are considered ill-formed.

[8] Here the subject has been translated as *he*, but any third-person singular pronominal (*e.g.*, *he* or *she*) is an acceptable translation. The system returns all translation possibilities in such cases of ambiguity.

[9] This is not to say that semantic issues should be ignored in machine translation; on the contrary, semantics may be the next step in the evolution of the translation system presented here.

[10] In general, an *argument* of a verb is either a subject or an object of the verb. For example, in the English sentence *I read the book*, the external argument (agent) of *read* is *I*, and the internal argument (theme) is *book*.

[11] Slocum and Bennett (1985) describe the GAT system in more detail.

[12] The CETA system was developed at Grenoble University, France in 1961. See Slocum and Bennett (1985) for a more detailed description.

[13] The approach is 'universal' only to the extent that the linguistic theory is 'universal'. There are some residual phenomena not covered by the theory that are consequently not handled by the system in a principle-based manner. For example, the language specific English rules of *it-insertion* and *do-insertion* cannot be accounted for by parameterized principles, but must be individually stipulated as idiosyncratic rules of English. Happily, there appear to be only a few such rules per language since the principle-based approach factors out most of the commonalities across languages.

[14] The lexical representation used in the parser presented here is based on the input representation required by the morphological analyzer. It includes the root forms of words and pointers to applicable affixes. Root verbs are stored with their argument structure specifications and θ-role assignment possibilities. The lexicon is discussed in Dorr (1987, 1990) but will not be emphasized in this chapter.

[15] Hale (1973) describes how this and several other phenomena in Navajo reveal parametric variation of linguistic principles.

[16] Case theory is not described here. See Chomsky (1981).

[17] For details on the null subject (or *pro-drop*) parameter, see van Riemsdijk and Williams (1986, pp. 298–303).

[18] A rule-based approach (*e.g.*, Gazdar *et al.*, 1985) would require a separate rule for every possible null subject construction allowed in a null subject language including free subject inversion, relative clauses, *that*-trace constructions, resumptive pronouns, *etc.* (See van Riemsdijk and Williams, 1986, for a discussion of these constructions.) Although GPSG provides a metarule formalism for handling more 'top-level' phenomena (*e.g.*, passivization), no generalization is made for closely related phenomena. Furthermore, metarules force the grammar to grow rapidly, thus induc-

ing additional slowdowns during parsing. The parameter-setting approach obviates the need for independent treatment of closely related phenomena without causing a grammar blow-up.

[19] The latest version of UNITRAN relies on a lexicon-driven processing module in order to tackle the problems of lexical selection and structural realization. For a more detailed description of this approach, see Dorr (1988, 1990).

[20] The verb *vio* has been changed to the infinitive form *ver* (with person, tense, and number features) via a morphological analysis stage that will not be discussed here.

[21] The association of the clitic with the verbal head is determined by an adjunction parameter setting associated with $\overline{X}$. This parameter will not be discussed here.

[22] In addition, objective Case is assigned by the verb to the clitic. This process is not described here.

[23] Note that objective Case has been assigned to the NP containing María by the governing preposition *a*. This takes place after the PP phrase has been completed. Assignment of objective Case is necessary for the θ-role transmission principle to discharge a θ-role to the NP at a later point in the parse (see snapshot 15(c)). The details of this Case assignment are not described here.

[24] Note that the θ-role *patient* is assigned to the NP *María*, not to the PP *a María*; in general, the structural entity that is assigned θ-role is an NP, regardless of the type of phrase containing it.

[25] Empty feature projections are established by means of a Trace theory parameter setting. These projections, which I call empty-feature-holders, are similar to the functional selectors discussed in Abney (1986) in that they require certain complement constructions for proper licensing. In Spanish (and also in English), the empty-feature-holder I(nfl) requires a VP complement, and the empty-feature-holder C(omp) requires an IP complement.

[26] For example, Italian and Hebrew do not require an overt subject, but English and French do; thus, when the target language is generated (during a later stage), e[pro] will either be left as is, or lexicalized to a pronominal form (*e.g.*, *he* or *she* in English) that agrees with the main verb.

[27] θ-role assignment of the null subject takes place only after the NP has received nominative Case from the I(nfl)[p3 sg] node. Again, the Case assignment process is not described here.

[28] The latest version of UNITRAN also operates on German (see Dorr, 1990). Experiments with Warlpiri (a native aboriginal language of Australia) and other 'nonstandard' languages are expected to be carried out in future versions.

[29] There is a subtle difference between the modularity provided by a linguistic formalism and that provided by a programming language. In a modular linguistic system, the surface effects of a change may range far beyond the original source of the change. However, changing a single module does not affect the way other modules *operate*; it only affects the way the modules *interact*. For example, changing principles that determine constituent order does not affect the principles that relate pronouns to their referents, and *vice-versa*; on the other hand, the direction of pronominal-reference will indeed change from language to language according to how the constituent order parameter is set. Understanding the distinction between the *operation* of principles and the *interaction* of principles is crucial for full appreciation of linguistic modular-

182   BONNIE JEAN DORR

ity. The point is that a modular linguistic system allows different aspects of natural language to be dealt with independently, thus avoiding the task of having to think about the multiplicative surface effects of linguistic principles during the development of the system.

REFERENCES

Abney, S.: 1986, 'Functional Elements and Licensing', unpublished paper presented at GLOW (Generative Linguists of the Old World) Conference, Gerona, Spain.

Barton, E.: 1984, *Toward a Principle-Based Parser*, MIT Artificial Intelligence Laboratory Memo 788, Massachusetts Institute of Technology, Cambridge, Massachusetts.

Bates, M.: 1978, 'The Theory and Practice of Augmented Transition Network Grammars', in L. Bolc (ed.), *Natural Language Communication with Computers*, (Lecture Notes in Computer Science, 63), Springer-Verlag, New York, pp. 191–254.

Chomsky, N.: 1981, *Lectures on Government and Binding: The Pisa Lectures*, Foris, Dordrecht, Holland.

Chomsky, N.: 1982, *Some Concepts and Consequences of the Theory of Government and Binding*, MIT Press, Cambridge, Massachusetts.

Dorr, B.: 1987, *UNITRAN: A Principle-Based Approach to Machine Translation*, MIT Artificial Intelligence Laboratory Technical Report 1000, Massachusetts Institute of Technology, Cambridge, Massachusetts.

Dorr, B.: 1988, *A Lexical Conceptual Approach to Generation for Machine Translation*, MIT Artificial Intelligence Laboratory Memo 1015, Massachusetts Institute of Technology, Cambridge, Massachusetts.

Dorr, B.: 1990, *Lexical Conceptual Structure and Machine Translation*, Ph.D. dissertation, Department of Electrical Engineering and Computer Science, Massachusetts Institute of Technology, Cambridge, Massachusetts.

Earley, J.: 1970, 'An Efficient Context-Free Parsing Algorithm', *Communications of the Association for Computing Machinery* 14, 453–460.

Frazier, L.: 1986, 'Natural Classes in Language Processing', unpublished paper presented at the Cognitive Science Seminar, Cognitive Science Center, Massachusetts Institute of Technology, Cambridge, Massachusetts.

Gazdar, G., E. Klein, G. Pullum, and I. Sag: 1985, *Generalized Phrase Structure Grammar*, Basil Blackwell, Oxford, England.

Hale, K.: 1973, 'A Note on Subject-Object Inversion in Navajo', in B. Kachrue, R. Lees, J. Malkiel, A. Pietrangeli, and F. Saporta, *Issues in Linguistics: Papers in Honor of Henry and Renee Kahane*, University of Illinois Press, Urbana, Illinois, pp. 300–309.

Jaeggli, A: 1981, *Topics in Romance Syntax*, Foris, Dordrecht, Holland.

Robinson, J.: 1982, 'DIAGRAM: A Grammar for Dialogues', *Communications of the Association for Computing Machinery* 25, 27–47.

Sharp, R.: 1985, *A Model of Grammar Based on Principles of Government and Binding*, M.S. dissertation, Department of Computer Science, University of British Columbia, Vancouver, British Columbia.

Slocum, J.: 1984, *METAL: The LRC Machine Translation System*, paper presented at the ISSCO Tutorial on Machine Translation, Lugano, Switzerland, Linguistics Research Center, University of Texas, Austin, Texas.

Slocum, J.: 1985, 'A Survey of Machine Translation: Its History, Current Status, and Future Prospects', *Computational Linguistics* 11, 1–17.

Slocum, J. and W. Bennett: 1985, 'The LRC Machine Translation System', *Computational Linguistics* 11, 111–121.

Van Riemsdijk, H. and E. Williams: 1986, *Introduction to the Theory of Grammar*, MIT Press, Cambridge, Massachusetts.

Woods, W.: 1970, 'Transition Network Grammars for Natural Language Analysis', *Communications of the Association for Computing Machinery* 13, 591–606.

Department of Computer Science,
3157 A. V. Williams Building,
University of Maryland at College Park,
College Park, Maryland 20742, U.S.A.

SAMUEL S. EPSTEIN

PRINCIPLE-BASED INTERPRETATION OF NATURAL LANGUAGE QUANTIFIERS

1. INTRODUCTION

The interpretation of quantifiers is one of the central problems of natural language understanding. Quantifiers include expressions such as *everyone, many students*, and *the professor that skates*. Given a suitably general notion of 'quantifier', few natural language sentences contain no quantifiers. On some accounts, all natural language sentences contain quantifiers. This chapter describes a working prototype, called *QSB* (Quantifier Scopes and Bindings), that determines possible relative quantifier scopes and pronoun bindings for natural language sentences, with coverage of a variety of problematic cases.[1]

QSB parses a significant fragment of English and translates it into an enriched predicate logic. The computational techniques that it employs may find wider application.

(1) Every professor expects several students to read many books

is an example of a sentence with several possibilities for relative quantifier scope. To take one possibility, the 'several-every-many' reading, there can be a particular set of several students such that every professor expects each of those students to read many books, where for each choice of student and professor, there may be a different set of many books. The other possibilities for (1) are 'every-several-many' and "every-many-several".[2]

(2) Every professor that knows a student that owns a computer covets it

and

(3) Every professor that knows every student that owns a computer covets it

illustrate pronoun binding.[3] *A computer* can bind *it* in (2), but not in (3). Studies of relative quantifier scope and of pronoun binding have examined a great variety of examples from a variety of languages and have

185

R. C. Berwick et al. (eds.),
Principle-Based Parsing: Computation and Psycholinguistics, 185–198.

demonstrated the apparent complexity of these phenomena, but have also made impressive progress toward finding underlying regularities.[4]

QSB follows a principle-based approach to language processing. Principle-based grammars are a recent development in linguistic theory. They are particularly associated with the Government-Binding (GB) theory of syntax.[5] Principle-based grammars characteristically contain a small number of heterogeneous principles, rather than a large number of homogeneous rules. Ideally, principles are uniformly valid for all natural languages. Variation among natural languages is a matter of setting parameters, like *head initial* or *head final*, and supplying a lexicon. On the classical conception, principles constrain freely generated linguistic structures. Structures that conform to all the parameterized principles of a grammar belong to the language associated with the grammar. The modularity, simplicity, and substantial shared content of principle-based grammars offer strong advantages for natural language processing. However, it is necessary to confront some apparent problems for principle-based language processing, as discussed in section 3 below.

For purposes of exposition, QSB may be decomposed into three modules: a parser module, a scope module, and a binding module. The scope and binding modules directly implement aspects of a principle-based grammar. The parser module does not. The next three sections describe these modules in turn. This chapter emphasizes computational techniques for efficient implementation of principle-based grammars. Because of space limitations, its discussion of other aspects of the prototype is very brief.

2. PARSER MODULE

The QSB parser module produces usable surface structure parses for the scope and binding modules. The other QSB modules could be made to work with a parser of different design and functionality, providing that this other parser correctly analyzed certain phenomena. The QSB parser is not among the chief points of interest of this work. It will eventually be replaced by a parser that directly implements grammatical principles. However, the current parser's analyses do include some information that most other parsers fail to derive.

The QSB parser is basically a recursive descent parser with a data-driven component. While it is not principle-based in any strong sense, its analyses conform to Government-Binding theory, particularly to an elaboration of Government-Binding theory proposed in Aoun and Li (forthcoming). It finds only a single constituent structure analysis for each sentence that it parses, hypothetically corresponding to a preferred reading. In addition to finding constituency relationships among overt categories, the parser posits certain empty categories (*Wh*-trace, NP-trace, and PRO) and associates these empty categories with the categories that bind them. The parser also sets pointers from determiners to their noun phrase complements, or *restrictions*. QSB includes a facility for bit-mapped displays of parse structures, with various links between nodes ('control', and so on) indicated by various kinds of line (for example, 'chains' look like chains).

The current parser produces correct results for a subset of English that exhibits the following phenomena, among others: coordination, relativization, raising, obligatory control, and exceptional case marking. For example, it produces an accurate parse for:

(4) Every student that admires a dean that every professor seems to respect wants to read many books and some instructor expects many students to read several books that every professor likes and many professors love

in 0.12 seconds (Symbolics 3645, Release 7.1).

3. SCOPE MODULE

The scope module is based on an account in Aoun and Li (to appear), as adapted in Aoun and Epstein (1988). Aoun and Li explain data from several languages concerning relative quantifier scope and relative scope of quantifiers and *Wh* operators (such as *who*). Their entirely general and principle-based exposition covers a great variety of syntactic constructions, including, for example, the cases discussed in Hobbs and Shieber (1987).

Following May (1977), Aoun and Li base their treatment on a rule of *Quantifier Raising* that is used to derive *Logical forms* (LF's) from *Surface structures* (SS's). Aoun and Li formulate alternative accounts of quantifier raising. In the adapted account of Aoun and Epstein (to appear), LF's are obtained from SS's by raising determiners. Well-formed LF's conform to the following four principles, stated here as they apply in the scope module of QSB:

(I) (Phrasal-node-adjunction) Determiners are raised only to phrasal nodes (such as noun phrase nodes, verb phrase nodes, and sentence nodes).

(II) (Non-theta-adjunction) Determiners are never raised to theta (thematic) positions (argument positions within verb phrases, such as direct object positions).

(III) (Opacity) Determiners are never raised outside their opaque domains. (The *opaque domain* of a determiner is roughly speaking the smallest clause that contains the determiner and either a subject or a tensed verb.)

(IV) (Minimal Binding Requirement, or MBR) A determiner's 'landing site' cannot dominate the 'launch site' of another determiner unless it also dominates the landing site of that other determiner.

Principles (I)–(IV) have independent linguistic motivation. Given a well-formed LF, possible relative quantifier scopes are determined by the *Scope Principle* which states in effect that a quantifier Q1 may have scope over a quantifier Q2 in case the lowest phrasal node that dominates the landing site of the determiner of Q1 also dominates the determiner of Q2 or a trace associated with Q2. Traces are empty (nonovert) categories. For example, in:

(5) Every student seems to admire some professor

the subject of the infinitive clause *to admire some professor* is a trace associated with *every student*. When *some professor* raises to the top of its opaque domain (the clause *to admire some professor*) it is 'higher' than the trace of *every student*, and so by the Scope Principle, *some professor* can have scope over *every student*. Note that LF's do not disambiguate sentences with respect to quantifier scope. The set of possible quantifier scope readings for a sentence is the union of possible scopings over the set of its well-formed LF's.

This is a principle-based account of relative quantifier scope. As with other principle-based accounts, a simple-minded implementation is computationally hopeless. For example, assuming quantifier raising applies without any of the constraints (I)–(IV), (5) has 70 candidate LF's.

(6) Some dean seems to expect several professors to want every student to read many books

has 50830 candidate LF's. Even for a moderately long sentence like (6), generating each candidate and testing it against (I)–(IV) is absurdly impractical. This absurdity might be compounded by applying the Scope Principle to candidate LF's before filtering them. There thus may appear at first glance to be a trade-off between the simplicity and modularity of principle-based grammars and the computational expense of running the generate-and-test model that they seem to incorporate. One method of confronting this apparent trade-off is to write a language processor that produces outputs that correspond to well-formed structures according to a principle-based grammar, but which makes no use of principles itself. It is not clear how a processor that is not itself principle-based can be made to share advantages of principle-based grammars.

According to one ideal, efficient language processors would be compiled from the declarative specifications of principle-based grammars. Berwick (1987, 1991 forthcoming) and Johnson (this volume) discuss some very preliminary ideas along these lines. This is an ambitious goal with no immediate prospect of achievement. Grammatical principles vary greatly in their forms and in how they interact. Use of general-purpose theorem-proving technology does not (yet) offer a practical solution to this problem.

The quantifier scope module of QSB follows a third broad approach to the implementation of principle-based grammars. The implementation directly mirrors the principle-based grammar. Principles apply as function calls. Effective use of some programming strategies permits highly efficient processing. The implementation retains advantages of a principle-based approach. Extensions and alterations are entirely straightforward.

More specifically, the quantifier scope module of QSB obtains efficiency primarily through six strategies:

1. Easier-Earlier Strategy
Principles whose applications require less work apply earlier.

2. Maximal Filtering Strategy
Principles that filter more representations apply earlier.

3. Wholesale Filtering Strategy

Filters apply to classes of representations (where possible), rather than to single representations.

4. Schematic Representation
Principles apply to schematic representations (where possible).

5. Minimal Construction Strategy
Principles apply to components of representations prior to construction of representations (where possible); only representations whose components pass filters are constructed.

6. Partitioning
Representations are partitioned (or quasi-partitioned) to minimize domains of application of principles (where possible).

Accumulation of experience may lead to the formalization and eventual automation of these techniques. The examples that follow illustrate their application in the scope module of QSB.

As an example of the Easier-Earlier strategy, consider Non-theta-adjunction and the MBR. Non-theta-adjunction is a very simple check on landing sites. The MBR must consider interactions among members of sets of (determiner, landing-site) pairs. It is more expensive computationally than Non-theta-adjunction, and should thus apply only after Non-theta-adjunction has reduced its domain of application. If the MBR is ordered before Non-theta-adjunction, processing of (6) requires 0.05 seconds for application of Non-theta-adjunction and 0.14 seconds for application of the MBR. If Non-theta-adjunction is ordered before the MBR, following the Easier-Earlier strategy, processing of (6) requires 0.07 seconds for application of Non-theta-adjunction, but only 0.06 seconds for application of the MBR. The total amount of time required for application of these two filters is thus reduced by approximately one-third.[6]

As an example of the Maximal Filtering strategy, consider Opacity and Non-theta-adjunction. In order to make a reasonable comparison of the relative filtering power of these two principles, suppose that both principles apply after Phrasal-node-adjunction and before the MBR.[7] When a sentence contains a single opaque domain, Opacity does little work. The more opaque domains a sentence contains, the more candidate LF's are filtered by Opacity. For (5), with two opaque domains, Non-theta-adjunction applying after Phrasal-node-adjunction passes 15 candidate LF's to Opacity and the MBR. Opacity applying after Phrasal-node-adjunction passes 6 candidate LF's to Non-theta-adjunction and the MBR. For (6), Non-theta-adjunction applying after Phrasal-node-adjunction passes 1701 candidate LF's to Opacity and the MBR. Opacity applying after Phrasal-node-adjunction passes 150 candidate LF's to Non-theta-adjunction and the MBR. Given a policy of optimizing average-case performance (not to mention a policy of avoiding very bad worst-case performance), the Maximal Filtering Strategy would seem to require ordering Opacity before Non-theta-adjunction.[8]

Applications of Opacity, Non-theta-adjunction, and Phrasal-node-adjunction in the scope module of QSB all illustrate the Wholesale Filtering strategy. For example, for (6), any candidate LF where *many* is raised to its closest dominating phrasal node violates the principle of Nonthetaadjunction. It is possible to eliminate all these candidate LF's with a single application of Non-theta-adjunction. With this kind of wholesale filtering, the total number of applications of Non-theta-adjunction necessary to process (6) is 15. With Non-theta-adjunction correctly ordered after Opacity and Phrasal-node-adjunction and before the MBR, but without Wholesale Filtering, the number of applications of Non-theta-adjunction for (6) is 203.

Schematic linguistic representations abstract away what is irrelevant to the purposes at hand. Their use corresponds to a radical sort of structure-sharing. For example, given a full representation of the Surface Structure of a sentence, each candidate LF for the sentence can be represented as a set of (determiner, landing-site) pairs, with one pair for each determiner in the sentence. Properties of candidate LF's can be read off their schematic representations in association with the SS. It is thus possible to apply (I)–(IV) and the Scope Principle without ever computing full LF's. The notion of schematic representation is related to the notion of 'use of knowledge' of structures in Johnson (this volume).

The Minimal Construction strategy reduces the number of representations that get constructed, and thus reduces the amount of time and space expended on the construction of representations. Minimal construction is similar to lazy evaluation. For example, constructing a set of schematic representations of LF's for a sentence requires constructing for each determiner d in the sentence a set of pairs of the form $(d$, landing-site), and then taking the Cartesian product of these sets of pairs. Opacity, Phrasal-node-adjunction, and Non-theta-adjunction apply directly to landing sites. Following the Minimal Construction strategy, these three principles apply to reduce the size of the set of candidate landing sites for each determiner prior to the construction of schematic representations of LF's. For (6), the number of candidate LF's constructed is thereby reduced from 50830 to 64.

The technique of partitioning linguistic representations applies readily to the problem of computing relative quantifier scopes. It follows from Opacity (and may be observed independently) that relative quantifier scope relationships never arise across coordination boundaries. It is therefore possible to compute relative quantifier scopes one coordinate at a time. For example, in

(7) Every dean read few books and many students read several reports

the question of relative scope for *few books* and *many students* does not arise. In order to analyze (7), it is sufficient to analyze *every dean read few books* and *many students read several reports*, and then 'multiply' the analyses. Thus rather than considering 4! = 24 possible relative quantifier scopings, it is necessary only to consider 2 possible scopings in the first conjunct, and 2 in the second. Similarly, quantifiers in a relative clause (for example) can only enter into direct relative quantifier scope relationships inside the relative clause or with its head. In,

(8) Every dean that many professors admire reads few books

the question of relative scope for *few books* and *many professors* does not arise. In order to analyze (8), it is sufficient to consider ordering possibilities for *every dean* and *few books*. *Many professors* inside the relative clause must have narrower scope than *every dean*.

Examples like (1) require 'quasi-partitioning'. Rather than analyze (1) as a single structure it is possible to divide this sentence into the slightly overlapping quasi-partitions *every professor expects several students* and *several students to read many books*. Quasi-partitioning may proceed top-down as follows: (i) Find all quantifiers that lie within the clause in question but no lower clause. (ii) Find the lowest clause that contains a member of the chain of one of these quantifiers. This lowest clause, with all intermediate clauses, is included in the quasi-partition. ((5) in its entirety is thus included in a single quasi-partition.) (iii) If the next lower clause is an infinitive and has a subject, also include this subject in the quasi-partition. Given possible relative quantifier scope orderings within quasi-partitions for a sentence, the possible orderings for the entire sentence are those orderings which are consistent with possible orderings within quasi-partitions.

(Quasi-)partitioning can yield dramatic performance advantages.[9] Consider

(9) [1 Every professor expects [1 several students]0 to want [2 few deans]1 to expect [3 some freshman]2 to read many books]3

which divides into quasi-partitions as indicated. Sentence (9) has 5 quantifiers, with 8 possible relative quantifier scope orderings. Without quasi-partitioning, it is necessary to consider $5! = 120$ possible orderings. If processing is set up to follow strategies (1)–(5) but not (quasi-)partitioning, 50 seconds are required to compute relative quantifier scope orderings for (9). With the (quasi-)partitioning technique, 0.45 seconds are required, an improvement of two orders of magnitude. (Quasi-)partitioning may be viewed as a special case of the very general strategy of divide-and-conquer. It seems likely that an analog of (quasi-)partitioning plays a role in human language processing.

Strategies (1)–(6), working in concert with the application of some additional programming practices, permit highly efficient computation of relative quantifier scope possibilities. Given the output of the parser module, the scope module computes the 3 relative scope possibilities for sentence (4) (which has $9! = 362880$ candidate orderings) in 0.16 seconds (Symbolics 3645, Release 7.1).

4. BINDING MODULE

I describe the binding module in a forthcoming paper. Space limitations permit only a brief summary here. The binding module computes possible quantifier antecedents for pronouns. For example, it determines that *a donkey* can bind *it* in both

(10) Every man that owns a donkey that loves every child that feeds it is content

and

(11) Every man that owns a donkey beats it

(10) exhibits top-down propagation of binding scope, while (11), a proto-typical 'donkey' sentence, exhibits both top-down and bottom-up prop-agation of binding scope. Chomsky (1981) and Reinhart (1983) dis-cuss top-down propagation of binding scope, using other terminology. Hintikka and Carlson (1979), Kamp (1981), Heim (1982), and Barwise (1986) discuss examples like (11). Johnson and Klein (1986) discuss an implementation of aspects of Kamp's account.

The binding module of QSB is based on a new account of pronom-inal bound variables that recognizes bottom-up propagation of binding scope, subject to localized requirements of existence and uniqueness. For example, the binding scope of *a donkey* in

(12) Pat owns a donkey, and Terry covets it

can propagate up to the main clause and then down to *it*. However, such propagation is blocked by the *negation operator* in,

(13) Pat doesn't own a donkey, and Terry covets it

because of the localized existence requirement on bottom-up propaga-tion. On a reading of (13) where the negation operator has higher scope than *a donkey*, the assertion of the existence of a donkey is not in force for the second conjunct. Karttunen (1969) discusses a variety of exam-ples that illustrate the localized existence requirement.

(14) Pat owns every donkey, and Terry covets it

where binding is impossible, illustrates the localized uniqueness require-ment on bottom-up propagation of binding scope. No singled-out donkey is available for association with *it* in (14). Note that binding is possible in

(15) Pat owns every donkey, and Terry covets them

but not in

(16) Many men own several donkeys, and Terry covets them

on a reading where there can be different sets of several donkeys for different men, and where *them* is intended to identify a particular set of several donkeys owned by one man. *Every* in (15) in effect introduces a single level of multiplicity that is accommodated by the plural pronoun *them*. *Many* in (16) introduces a second level of multiplicity beyond the level introduced by *several*, and blocks the binding of the plural pronoun *them*. Similarly, binding of *it* by *a computer* is possible in (2) above, but not in (3). Note that bottom-up propagation of binding scope also works intersententially, as in

(17) Pat owns a donkey
  Terry covets it

Determination of possibilities for pronominal bound variables requires prior determination of possible relative quantifier scopes. For this and other reasons, the QSB binding module works on logical translations of natural language sentences. The current target language for translation is an enriched predicate logic. The next prototype will use a target language that more adequately captures meanings of natural language expressions. Binding scopes propagate bottom-up and top-down, from left to right. Binding is subject to agreement constraints, and to the following constraint, discussed in varying forms in Keenan (1974), Chomsky, (1981) and Hintikka and Kulas (1983): a quantifier cannot bind a pronoun and another variable within the minimal complete functional complex of the pronoun. This constraint disallows binding in such examples as

(18) Every man admires him

The current binding module handles intrasentential binding of singular pronouns by universal and existential quantifiers. It finds binding possibilities with one pre-order pass through each logical translation. Total elapsed time for parsing and computation of normalized logical translations for

(19) Some pony expects every child to pet it and every man that knows every woman that owns a donkey covets it or some horse loves every child that feeds it

with all possible pronoun bindings indicated, is 0.47 seconds (Symbolics 3645 Release 7.1). Of this time, 0.09 seconds is attributable to the parser module, 0.05 seconds is attributable to the scope module, and 0.04 seconds is attributable to the computation of binding possibilities.

SAMUEL S. EPSTEIN

ACKNOWLEDGEMENTS

This chapter grew out of my ongoing collaboration with Joseph Aoun of the University of Southern California. I have also benefited greatly from interactions with Steven Abney, David Ackley, George Collier, Michael Kashket, Madhur Kohli, and Maria Slowiaczek at Bellcore. I received valuable comments on aspects of this work at the CUNY Human Sentence Processing Conference and during visits to MIT, Stanford, SRI, XEROX PARC, USC, and UCSD. Responsibility for errors that remain is entirely mine.

NOTES

[1] QSB is implemented in Common Lisp on Symbolics, Release 7.1.

[2] QSB does not yet deal explicitly with the possibility of branching quantifiers.

[3] *Bind* has distinct technical meanings recognized by different communities of researchers. Its meaning here is fairly close to the standard in logic.

[4] Good (although not up-to-date) bibliographies of relevant work are included in May (1985) (relative quantifier scope); and in Heim (1982), van Riemsdijk and Williams (1986), and Brennan, Friedman, and Pollard (1987) (pronoun binding).

[5] Chomsky (1981) is the seminal work on Government-Binding theory. Van Riemsdijk and Williams (1986) is a textbook introduction. Berwick (1987, 1991 forthcoming) discusses the computational exploitation of principle-based grammars.

[6] In order to isolate the effects of the Easier-Earlier strategy in this case, it is necessary to suspend the Wholesale Filtering strategy. With both the Easier-Earlier and Wholesale Filtering strategies in effect, processing of (6) requires 0.007 seconds for application of Non-theta-adjunction and 0.06 seconds for application of the MBR.

[7] In practice the Wholesale Filtering strategy stipulates that neither Opacity nor Non-theta-adjunction applies to individual LF's. In addition, the Maximal Filtering strategy requires ordering Phrasal-node-adjunction after Opacity but before Non-theta-adjunction, subject to reservations noted below.

[8] As optimal ordering for application of principles varies from sentence to sentence, orderings might be adjusted based on simplified preliminary analyses of sentences. For the principles implemented in the scope module of QSB, such case by case adjustment does not appear to save computational resources overall.

The Easier-Earlier strategy and the Maximal Filtering strategy may conflict. For example, Opacity is a more complex principle than Phrasal-node-adjunction, but for long sentences it filters more LF's. I am not aware of any general method that resolves conflicts between ordering strategies. In this case, it seems advantageous to order Opacity first.

[9] Barton, Berwick, and Ristad (1987) discuss some other computational applications of linguistic locality principles.

REFERENCES

Aoun, J. and A. Li: to appear, *The Syntax of Scope*, MIT Press, Cambridge, Massachusetts.

Aoun, J. and S. Epstein: 1988, 'Relative Quantifier Scope', paper presented at *CUNY Conference on Human Sentence Processing*, City University of New York, New York.

Barwise, J.: 1986, *Noun Phrases, Generalized Quantifiers, and Anaphora* Report number CSLI-86-52, CSLI, Stanford University, Stanford, California.

Barton, E., R. Berwick, and E. Ristad: 1987, *Computational Complexity and Natural Language*, MIT Press, Cambridge, Massachusetts.

Berwick, R.: 1987, 1991 forthcoming, 'Principle-Based Parsing', in T. Sells, S. Shieber, and T. Wasow (eds.), *Foundational Issues in Natural Language Processing*, MIT Press, Cambridge, Massachusetts. Also MIT Artificial Intelligence Laboratory, Technical Report Number 972, Massachusetts Institute of Technology, Cambridge, Massachusetts.

Brennan, S., M. Friedman, and C. Pollard: 1987, 'A Centering Approach to Pronouns', *Proceedings of the 25th Annual Meeting of the Association for Computational Linguistics*, pp. 155–162.

Chomsky, N.: 1981 *Lectures on Government and Binding*, Foris, Dordrecht, Holland.

Heim, I.: 1982, *The Semantics of Indefinite and Definite Noun Phrases*, Ph.D. dissertation, Department of Linguistics, University of Massachusetts, Amherst, Massachusetts.

Hintikka, J. and L. Carlson: 1979, 'Conditionals, Generic Quantifiers, and Other Applications of Subgames', in F. Guenthner and S. Schmidt (eds.), *Formal Semantics and Pragmatics for Natural Languages*, D. Reidel, Dordrecht, Holland, pp. 1–36.

Hintikka, J. and J. Kulas: 1983, 'Definite Descriptions in Game-Theoretical Semantics', in J. Hintikka and J. Kulas (eds.), *The Game of Language*, Reidel, Dordrecht, Holland, pp. 137–160.

Hobbs, J. and S. Shieber: 1987, 'An Algorithm for Generating Quantifier Scopings', *Computational Linguistics*, **13**, 47–63.

Johnson, M.: this volume, 'Parsing as Deduction: The Use of Knowledge of Language', pp. 39–64.

Johnson, M. and E. Klein: 1986, 'Discourse, Anaphora, and Parsing', *Proceedings of the 11th International Conference on Computational Linguistics*, International Committee on Computational Linguistics, pp. 669–675.

Kamp, H.: 1981, 'A Theory of Truth and Semantic Representation', in J. Groenendijk, T. Janssen, and M. Stokhof (eds.), *Formal Methods in the Study of Language*, Part 1, Mathematisch Centrum, Amsterdam, Holland, pp. 277–322.

Karttunen, L.: 1969, 'Discourse Referents', in J. McCawley (ed.), *Notes From the Linguistic Underground*, Academic Press, New York, pp 363–385.

Keenan, E.: 1974, 'The Functional Principle: Generalizing the Notion "Subject Of" ', in M. LaGaly, R. Fox and A. Bruck (eds.), *Papers from the Tenth*

Regional Meeting of the Chicago Linguistic Society, Chicago Linguistic Society, Chicago, Illinois, pp. 298–309.

May, R.: 1977, *The Grammar of Quantification*, Ph.D. dissertation, MIT Department of Linguistics and Philosophy, Massachusetts Institute of Technology, Cambridge, Massachusetts.

May, R.: 1985, *Logical Form: Its Structure and Derivation*, MIT Press, Cambridge, Massachusetts.

Van Riemsdijk, H. and E. Williams: 1986, *Introduction to the Theory of Grammar*, MIT Press, Cambridge, Massachusetts.

Bell Communications Research,
445 South Street,
Morristown, New Jersey 07962-1910, U.S.A.

EDWARD P. STABLER, JR.

AVOID THE PEDESTRIAN'S PARADOX

1. THE PARADOX

Mark Steedman (1989) has suggested that each of the following assumptions about human language understanding is appealing, but that they lead to a paradox when taken together:

1. *Incremental comprehension:* Human natural language understanding is serial and incremental: the words of a sentence are interpreted rapidly as they are heard or read.

2. *Right-branching syntactic structures:* English, like other SVO and SOV languages, has predominantly right-branching syntactic structures.

3. *Strong competence hypothesis:* The principles of the competence grammar are directly used by the human language processor in constructing a syntactic structure and interpreting it.

The problem is that the first complete, interpretable phrase containing the first word of a sentence may contain many words, and yet there is abundant introspective and experimental support for the view that an interpretation of the first words is available almost immediately. Steedman concludes that one of the three assumptions must be abandoned. Similar arguments have played a prominent role in psycholinguistic disputes before (see section 4 below), but never have they been so crisply stated.

Since the empirical support for the first assumption is so overwhelming, the other two assumptions become suspect. The strong competence hypothesis is often rejected, but this makes the prospects for adequate performance and acquisition models seem rather bleak. If the human parser does not use the linguists' grammar, then the psychologist is left with the problem of saying what rules the human parser *does* use and how *those* rules are acquired.[1] Given the complexity of our phonological, syntactic, and semantic abilities, this is a formidable task. Another less

199

R. C. Berwick et al. (eds.),
Principle-Based Parsing: Computation and Psycholinguistics, 199–237.
© 1991 *Kluwer Academic Publishers. Printed in the Netherlands.*

common response to the paradox, recently championed by Steedman and others, has been to adopt a left-branching syntax, even for languages like English. This option is unappealing, though, until we have disarmed the constituency arguments that support right-branching accounts.

So we seem to be faced with the the most challenging kind of paradox: we do not want to reject any of the assumptions of the argument. In his famous essay on paradoxes, Quine (1961, p. 5) takes particular delight in puzzles like this, and points out the only alternative to rejecting an assumption: "some tacit and trusted pattern of reasoning must be made explicit and henceforward avoided or revised". This is the response I want to urge: *the assumptions are not inconsistent.* A tacit and eminently discardable assumption plays an essential role in the argument that there is a paradox here. Once this tacit assumption is revealed, we see that assumptions (1)–(3) are not only logically compatible, but there is not even any tension among them that should worry us. Furthermore, once this is granted, we see that the strong competence hypothesis has been rejected too quickly by many psychologists and philosophers. Many of the arguments against the strong competence hypothesis ultimately rest on essentially the same implausible assumption that generates Steedman's paradox.

2. REJECTING THE PEDESTRIAN'S ASSUMPTION

The suggested problem is that in right-branching languages, words are not generally rightmost in the interpretable phrases containing them, and yet interpretation develops almost continuously, word-by-word or even more quickly than that (Marslen-Wilson, 1987; 1989; Marslen-Wilson and Tyler, 1980; etc.). In left-branching constructions like that in figure 1, this problem would not arise because each word completes a constituent.

The problem is that, on standard syntactic accounts, languages are not restricted to structures of this form. Even in predominantly left-branching languages, some right-branching constructions occur, and yet there is no psychological support for the idea that a right-branching construction disrupts incremental interpretation. Steedman suggests that this is a problem for any performance model in which the rules of the grammar correspond to processing steps. The reasoning here is presumably that if the grammar has rules defining the interpretation of syntactic constituents, the parser cannot deliver syntactic constituents

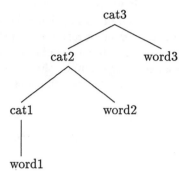

Figure 1: A left-branching constituent structure. Each word completes a constituent in this kind of phrase structure, making word-by-word interpretation straightforward.

for interpretation on a word-by-word basis, because many words do not complete (nonlexical) constituents. A different performance model that defines some special kind of interpretable 'partial constituents' would not be a strong competence model since it would need these special representations and rules defined over them.

The fallacy arises in this last step. Once we suppose that understanding involves the two steps of identifying a syntactic constituent and interpreting it, it is a mistake to think that we must finish the first step before beginning the second. Let's call this the pedestrian's assumption. Notice that this perfectly reasonable idea about walking is not a reasonable idea about, say, preparing and serving a dinner. It is true that the food must be prepared before it is served, but only the most inexperienced chef would *finish* the preparation before beginning the serving. The salad can go in the bowl before the steak is done cooking. We still perform both steps, preparing and serving, literally and completely, and completing the second depends on having completed the first. Furthermore, in a clear sense, we do not need to be engaged, at any given instant, in doing two things at once. Some sort of parallel processing is a possibility for expert and ambidextrous chefs, but the essential point is that each step consists in performing a number of subtasks, and so we can perform all and only these subtasks using a strategy that intermingles them. Once this is allowed as a possibility, it offers another way out of the paradox. Not only is this a *possible* way to avoid the paradox, but this way out is demanded by the evidence.

Computer scientists are fond of noting that we can define the alphabetization of a list as a permutation or reshuffling of the original list that respects the alphabetic ordering, but it would be silly to use this as a recipe for alphabetizing lists. For example, the definition might suggest that we could alphabetize a list with the following procedure:

(1) Reshuffle the items in the list,

(2) Check to see if the new list is alphabetic. If it is, we are done; if not, go to step 1.

To help us remember just how inefficient this is, Knuth (1973) recommends that we commit to memory the fact that a 10 element list has about $3\frac{1}{2}$ million permutations. As every filing clerk knows, all of the reasonable alphabetizing procedures, in effect, interleave the reshuffling step with the ordering checks. Computational linguists have similar points to keep in mind. Church and Patil (1982) have argued that because of the attachment ambiguity in English, an English sentence with 10 prepositional phrases and relative clauses, a sentence like

I put the bouquet of flowers that you gave me for Mother's Day in the vase that you gave me for my birthday on the chest of drawers that you gave me for Armistice Day.

can have 4,862 different syntactic trees (even if it has no other kind of syntactic ambiguity). And Langendoen (1987) has argued that a sentence with 10 coordinate expressions can have 103,049 different structures. He found the following example in his corpus:

Combine grapefruit with bananas, strawberries and bananas, bananas and melon balls, raspberries or strawberries and melon balls, seedless white grapes and melon balls, or pineapple cubes with orange slices.

Local ambiguities can be even more numerous than global ambiguities like these. So if these observations are close to right, the *parse first, then interpret* strategy is infeasible, and would still be so even if we had no reason to believe the first of the three assumptions of the purported paradox. That is, the mere fact that you can successfully manage a filing task or a comprehension task tells us something about how you must be doing it: you cannot be using a hopelessly pedestrian strategy in either case.[2]

No one seriously proposes pedestrian approaches to language understanding according to which *sentences* are fully parsed and then interpreted. So what could make the three assumptions with which we began seem paradoxical? It is just the idea that, although we do not need to have complete sentence structures before interpretation begins, we do at least need complete syntactic constituents, such as phrases. But why keep this assumption? The structures of phrases are complex (*i.e.*, composed of a number of elements), as are the structures of sentences, so we can perfectly well assume that the constituent parts of phrase structures become available for interpretation as soon as syntactic analysis formulates them. Furthermore, since the interpretation of a syntactic constituent is definitionally and procedurally complex, typically involving the interpretation of subconstituents, these subtasks can be intermingled with the parsing subtasks, *without making any modification at all in our definition of what each task involves*. Similarly for later stages of processing.

I will call a language processing system *pedestrian* just in case semantic processing of syntactic structures begins only when the input syntactic constituents are complete, and assessment of reference and truth values does not begin until completed constituents of semantic form are available. What Steedman's paradox really shows is that no one should seriously propose pedestrian approaches to language understanding, according to which *phrasal constituents* of *any* category must be fully parsed before their interpretation starts.[3] Once the nonpedestrian alternatives are noted, Steedman's three assumptions can all be embraced at once.

3. A SIMPLE NONPEDESTRIAN PARSER

The idea of nonpedestrian parsing is not new, but we do not need to look at large, complex natural language understanding systems to illustrate the approach. A little example suffices to show that nonpedestrian parsing is a very natural option, requiring no special rules about partial trees or any such thing. I will present in complete detail a little example of a nonpedestrian parser that respects the strong competence hypothesis (with respect to a little context-free grammar) and provides incremental interpretation (and even incremental referential assessment) on a word-by-word basis. It is clear that the same basic ideas apply to applications of arbitrarily complex grammars to arbitrary linguistic tasks. (Anyone willing to accept the existence of simple examples of this sort can skip to section 4 without losing the main thread of the argument.)

In this example, we represent syntactic, semantic, and interpretive rules as directly as possible in standard first-order logic, adding *nothing* special for our nonpedestrian use of those rules. Since the rules are represented as directly as possible, and since they are used by a sound and complete deductive strategy, there can hardly be any worry about adherence to the strong competence hypothesis in this case. We will explain the nonpedestrian proof strategy (and a complete implementation of it is provided in appendix A). Since the grammar is represented and used in the most direct way, there would also be no obstacle to the use of an acquisition theory for these grammars, if one were available (as we hope there will be in the natural language case). The key advantage of using a transparent *logical* representation is roughly that we have a well-developed proof theory that can be used to guarantee that various proof techniques are sound and complete, as we will see below. We could of course consider models that differ from the one presented here along many dimensions: interactive vs. noninteractive, top-down vs. bottom-up, parallel vs. serial, but these distinctions are irrelevant to defusing the purported paradox. It happens though, that our example is interactive, top-down, and serial. These choices were made for simplicity of exposition, and none of them is essential to the argument.

The syntax of our example is trivial but definitely right-branching, our semantic rules apply to the specified syntactic constituents, and our assessment of reference and truth is, in turn, based on constituents of the semantic representation. Nevertheless, the formulation of logical form and the assessment of reference and truth can be done in a very elegant way on a word-by-word basis, using simple deductive reasoning. This by itself would defuse the paradox, but the example is so simple and natural that we see that there is truly no tension at all among the three assumptions that Steedman has drawn to our attention. The nonpedestrian strategy is nothing more than a very simple proof technique: we use a natural principle to decide the order in which steps of the proof are to be taken.

3.1. *Syntax*

In this notation, predicates and function symbols begin with lower case letters, while variables begin with upper case letters, the sentences are all universally closed, and we write material conditionals of the form $(p \wedge q) \to r$ as $r \leftarrow q \wedge r$. We will represent a simple rewrite rule like the following:

$ip \to np\ vp$

with the following sentence of first-order logic:

$ip(L0, L) \leftarrow np(L0, L1) \wedge vp(L1, L).$

The two arguments of each grammatical predicate represent the string to which the predicate applies; it is the string that remains when a list L, given as the second argument, is removed from the end of the list $L0$ given as the first argument. Using the notation $L0 - L$ ($L0$ minus L) to mean the string that results from removing list L from the end of list $L0$, our logical sentence can be read, 'for all $L0$ and L, the string $L0 - L$ is an inflectional phrase (*i.e.*, a sentence or IP) if the string $L0 - L1$ is a noun phrase and the string $L1 - L$ is a verb phrase'. With this interpretation of grammatical predicates, it is no surprise that lexical rewrite rules have a slightly different appearance. Using the notation $[the|L]$ to represent the string that begins with 'the' and ends with the list L, it is clear that $[the|L] - L$ is simply the word 'the', and so the rewrite rule,

$d \to the$

is represented by the logical sentence

$d([the|L], L).$

In other words, 'the' is a determiner, no matter what string L follows it. This logical representation of the grammar not only expresses just what the grammar does, but there is an isomorphism between derivations of strings from the grammar and deductions of results about strings from the logical representation of the grammar.[4]

Since we are interested in parsing, rather than merely recognizing or generating strings, a slight elaboration of these logical sentences is required, again along the lines suggested by Pereira and Warren (1980).

We simply add an extra argument to each grammatical predicate to hold the derivation tree that is, in effect, dominated by that predicate. We represent trees like,

with the term a/[b,c]. The '/' represents the 'immediately dominates' relation which holds between a node and the ordered list of subtrees of which it is the parent. Then the two rules shown above are elaborated as follows:

$$ip(L0, L, ip/[NP, VP]) \leftarrow np(L0, L1, NP) \wedge vp(L1, L, VP). \quad (S1)$$
$$d([the|L], L, d/[the]). \quad (S2)$$

Sentence (S1) now says, for example, that (for all $L0, L, NP, VP$) $L0 - L$ is a sentence with structure $ip/[NP, VP]$ if $L0 - L1$ is a noun phrase with structure NP and $L1 - L$ is a verb phrase with structure VP. To complete our simple syntax we add just 9 more rules:

$$np(L0, L, np/[D, N]) \leftarrow d(L0, L1, D) \wedge n(L1, L, N). \quad (S3)$$
$$np(L0, L, np/[D, N, CP]) \leftarrow d(L0, L1, D) \wedge n(L1, L2, N) \wedge \quad (S4)$$
$$cp(L2, L, CP).$$
$$cp(L0, L, cp/[C, IP]) \leftarrow c(L0, L1, C) \wedge ip(L1, L, IP). \quad (S5)$$
$$vp(L0, L, vp/[V, A]) \leftarrow v(L0, L1, V) \wedge a(L1, L, A). \quad (S6)$$
$$n([joke|L], L, n/[joke]). \quad (S7)$$
$$n([argument|L], L, n/[argument]). \quad (S8)$$
$$c([that|L], L, c/[that]). \quad (S9)$$
$$v([is|L], L, v/[is]). \quad (S10)$$
$$a([funny|L], L, a/[funny]). \quad (S11)$$

The language generated by this grammar includes noun phrases with arbitrarily deep center embeddings:

the joke is funny
the argument is funny
the joke that the argument is funny is funny

the argument that the joke that the argument is funny is funny is funny

...

Using standard resolution proof techniques, it is a straightforward matter to use this theory in a parser, obtaining the parse trees from the substitutions used in the proofs that the strings are in the language. For example, a (pure) Prolog proof (which is a perfectly sound logical deduction) suffices to prove that there is a parse tree for the string *the joke is funny:*[5]

$$\leftarrow ip([the, joke, is, funny], [\,], Tree)$$

by $(S1)$: $\leftarrow np([the, joke, is, funny], L1, NP) \wedge vp(L1, [\,], VP)$

by $(S3)$: $\leftarrow d([the, joke, is, funny], L2, D) \wedge n(L2, L1, N) \wedge$
$\qquad\qquad vp(L1, [\,], VP)$

by $(S2)$: $\leftarrow n([joke, is, funny], L1, N) \wedge vp(L1, [\,], VP)$

by $(S7)$: $\leftarrow vp([is, funny], [\,], VP)$

by $(S6)$: $\leftarrow v([is, funny], L1, V) \wedge a(L1, [\,], A)$

by $(S10)$: $\leftarrow a([funny], [\,], A)$

by $(S11)$: $\square$ $Q.E.D.$

We can collect from this proof the instance of the variable *Tree* that was shown to be the parse of the string:

$$ip/[np/[d/[the], n/[argument]], vp/[v/[is], a/[funny]]].$$

The graphical depiction of this tree is much more readable:

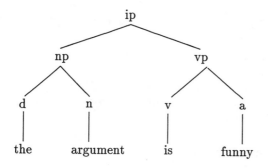

It is a simple matter to demonstrate that a similar proof is available for all and only the strings in the language generated by the rewrite grammar that corresponds to our axioms in the obvious way (Stabler, 1991 forthcoming). Note that the first complete noun phrases can be arbitrarily long, and so the language has the appropriate right-branching structure.

3.2. *Logical Form*

The logical form component for our trivial context-free grammar can be similarly trivial. We can adopt a naive approach to definite descriptions like 'the joke' and treat them as functions. Thus, 'the joke' is a joke we will call $joke(0)$. Intuitively, it does not matter what this joke is about, so let's simply call the subject of the joke '0'. A simple predication, saying that this joke is funny, is sometimes represented as $funny(joke(0))$ or $\lambda X funny(X)joke(0)$ or $joke(0) \in funny$ or $funny \in joke(0)$, but we will use the following simple notation to signify that the object $joke(0)$ satisfies the predicate $funny$:

$sat(joke(0), funny)$.

Then the joke that the joke is funny can be represented as the function,

$joke(sat(joke(0), funny))$.

In other words, this is the joke about $sat(joke(0), funny)$ which is, in turn, the joke's being funny. To map the syntactic structures into these logical forms the following rules do the trick:[6]

$$i\_ip([ip/[NP|VP]], sat(Subj, Pred)) \leftarrow i\_np([NP], Subj) \wedge \qquad (I1)$$
$$i\_vp(VP, Pred).$$
$$i\_np([np/[D|N1]], I\_N) \leftarrow i\_d([D], the) \wedge i\_n(N1, I\_N). \qquad (I2)$$
$$i\_cp([cp/[C|IP]], I\_IP) \leftarrow i\_c([C], that) \wedge i\_ip(IP, I\_IP). \qquad (I3)$$
$$i\_cp([\,], 0). \qquad (I4)$$
$$i\_vp([vp/[V|A]], I\_VP) \leftarrow i\_v([V], is) \wedge i\_a(A, I\_VP). \qquad (I5)$$
$$i\_d([d/[the]], the). \qquad (I6)$$
$$i\_n([n/[joke]|CP], joke(Subj)) \leftarrow i\_cp(CP, Subj). \qquad (I7)$$
$$i\_n([n/[argument]|CP], argument(Subj)) \leftarrow i\_cp(CP, Subj). \qquad (I8)$$
$$i\_c([c/[that]], that). \qquad (I9)$$
$$i\_v([v/[is]], is). \qquad (I10)$$
$$i\_a([a/[funny]], funny). \qquad (I11)$$

Rule (I1) says, for example, that the interpretation of an IP structure is $sat(Subj, Pred)$ where $Subj$ is the interpretation of the subject NP and $Pred$ is the interpretation of the main VP. Notice that the role of the interpretation rules for d, c, and v is really insignificant, since we are restricting ourselves to just one determiner, complementizer, and verb. This simplifies the example enormously. According to this theory, the tree displayed above has the logical form,

$$sat(argument(0), funny)),$$

and the following simple Prolog proof demonstrates this fact:

$$\leftarrow i\_ip([ip/[np/[d/[the], n/[argument]], vp/[v/[is],$$
$$a/[funny]]]], sat(argument(0), funny)))$$

$by\ (I1):\quad \leftarrow i\_np([np/[d/[the], n/[argument]]], argument(0)) \wedge$
$\qquad\qquad i\_vp([vp/[v/[is], a/[funny]]]], funny)$

$by\ (I2):\quad \leftarrow i\_d([d/[the]], the), i\_n([n/[argument]], argument(0)) \wedge$
$\qquad\qquad i\_vp([vp/[v/[is], a/[funny]]]], funny)$

$by\ (I6):\quad \leftarrow i\_n([n/[argument]], argument(0)) \wedge$
$\qquad\qquad i\_vp([vp/[v/[is], a/[funny]]]], funny)$

$by\ (I7):\quad \leftarrow i\_cp([\ ], 0) \wedge i\_vp([vp/[v/[is], a/[funny]]]], funny)$

$by\ (I4):\quad \leftarrow i\_vp([vp/[v/[is], a/[funny]]]], funny)$

$by\ (I5):\quad \leftarrow i\_v([v/[is]], is) \wedge i\_a([a/[funny]], funny)$

$by\ (I10):\quad \leftarrow i\_a([a/[funny]], funny)$

$by\ (I11): \square \quad Q.E.D.$

3.3. The World Model

Given a logical form, a hearer may want to assess it with respect to knowledge of the world. What do the terms of the logical form denote, and are the predications true? It is a bit artificial to do this with such a simple language, but it may help illustrate the point that the system can not only parse and interpret on a word-by-word basis, but can also begin assessing the denotations of terms and the truth of predications. Steedman suggests that not only is interpretation incremental, but so is 'reference', in the sense that a hearer can begin making judgments about what in the world the interlocutor is talking about almost as soon as the words are uttered.

So let's assume that the joke that is relevant to this example is a strange logician's joke, a joke about an argument about itself—the sort of joke that Raymond Smullyan might make. To be more precise, suppose that all of the jokes that can be mentioned in this language are the same. The joke, the joke about the argument, the joke about the argument about the joke, all of these are the same joke. Every noun phrase in our language denotes this same joke, and at LF, the denotation of joke(X) is this same joke for all X. And let's suppose that this joke is, in fact, funny.

In order to get some contrasting cases, let's make rather different assumptions about the arguments. Let's suppose that no two different noun phrases beginning with 'the argument...' refer to the same argument. Let 'the argument' denote a serious argument, an argument about arms control or something, and it is not at all funny. And let 'the argument that the argument is funny' be a different argument, but one that is similarly not funny. But let 'the argument that the joke is funny' be a funny argument about a joke. Notice that all of the complex argument noun phrases in our language are either of the form:

$[_{np}$the argument that ... the argument is funny$]$,

or of the form:

$[_{np}$the argument that ... the joke is funny$]$.

Let's suppose that all of the arguments denoted by noun phrases of the first form are funny, but none of the arguments denoted by noun phrases of the latter form are funny. If we call the deepest sentence (ip) in an noun phrase the 'kernel', then the rule can be intuitively expressed as follows: argument noun phrases with a joke in their kernel all denote funny arguments, argument noun phrases with an argument in their kernel all denote arguments that are not funny, and the argument noun phrase with no kernel denotes an argument that is not funny.

The following rules assign truth values to logical forms according to the scheme just described:

$truth(sat(joke(X), funny), true).$ (M1)

$truth(sat(argument(A), funny), Value)$ (M2)
$\leftarrow argument\_kernel(A, Value).$

$argument\_kernel(0, false).$ (M3)

$argument\_kernel(joke(A), Value)$ (M4)
$\leftarrow joke\_kernel(A, Value).$

$argument\_kernel(argument(A), Value)$ $(M5)$
                   $\leftarrow argument\_kernel(A, Value).$
$argument\_kernel(sat(A, X), Value)$ $(M6)$
                   $\leftarrow argument\_kernel(A, Value).$
$joke\_kernel(0, true).$ $(M7)$
$joke\_kernel(joke(A), Value) \leftarrow joke\_kernel(A, Value).$ $(M8)$
$joke\_kernel(argument(A), Value)$ $(M9)$
                   $\leftarrow argument\_kernel(A, Value).$
$joke\_kernel(sat(A, X), Value)$ $(M10)$
                   $\leftarrow joke\_kernel(A, Value).$

According to the interpretation described above, the logical form

$$sat(argument(0), funny))$$

expresses a false proposition, and (M1)–(M10) accordingly entail

$$truth(sat(argument(0), funny), false).$$

We can demonstrate this entailment with the following simple proof:

$$\leftarrow truth(sat(argument(0), funny), false)$$
$$by\ (M2): \leftarrow argument\_kernel(0, false)$$
$$by\ (M3): \square\ \ Q.E.D.$$

On the other hand,

$$sat(joke(sat(argument(0), funny)), funny)$$

expresses a true proposition, and (M1)–(M10) accordingly entail

$$truth(sat(joke(sat(argument(0), funny)), funny), true).$$

With this definition of a world model, we can let our system assess the truth value of the sentences of our little language.

3.4. *The Proof Strategy*

We can now try to prove from our theory that

$$\exists Tree, LF, Value\ ip([the, joke, is, funny], [\ ], Tree) \wedge$$
$$i\_ip([Tree], LF) \wedge truth(LF, Value).$$

This can be done with a simple proof strategy that proves each conjunct in order, completing the proof of the first conjunct before starting on the proof of the second conjunct, and completing the second before starting the third. In effect, this simply amounts to doing the three proofs shown in the previous three sections one after the other, and this is essentially what Prolog does. However, we need not proceed in this way. At each step we are faced with proving a conjunction $p_1 \wedge p_2 \wedge \ldots p_n$, and, as even beginners in logic would expect, at each point in the proof, one can work on any one of the conjuncts. What is more remarkable is that the particular choice about the order in which steps are taken will not have any substantial effect on the length of the proof, even though it can have a dramatic influence on the difficulty of *finding* a proof, for a wide class of proof systems.[7] Computer scientists have been interested in this result because it allows us to choose a selection rule that is optimally efficient. Especially given the observations we made about alphabetizing lists, it is no surprise that optimal selection strategies are often nonpedestrian (Naish, 1987). It is easy to describe a nonpedestrian strategy for our simple parser.

In the notation we have used to represent our proofs, each line can be regarded as a conjunction of atomic predications, each atom of which must be eliminated by a resolution step. In all the proofs shown above, each step involves eliminating the leftmost atom. If we proceed in the same way given

$$\leftarrow ip([the, joke, is, funny], [\,], Tree) \wedge$$
$$i\_ip([Tree], LF) \wedge truth(LF, Value),$$

we end up with a pedestrian system. It is easy to define an alternative strategy, though, based on the idea that we should use the LF and world model predicates as soon as they receive the needed information from the parse predicates. Let's be more precise. Call all the predicates that occur in (M1)–(M10) the *model* predicates; call all the predicates that occur in (I1)–(I11) the *LF* predicates; and call all the predicates in (S1)–(S11) the *syntax predicates*. In the extremely modular theory we have presented, there is no overlap among these sets.[8] In the first line of our proof, then, we have one model predicate, one LF predicate, and one syntax predicate:

$$\leftarrow ip([the, joke, is, funny], [\,], Tree) \wedge$$
$$i\_ip([Tree], LF) \wedge truth(LF, Value).$$

It would be a mistake to begin the proof with the model or LF predications here because the arguments of these predicates do not yet contain any information about the input string. As the syntax predications are resolved upon, these arguments will become instantiated to nonvariable terms, and then they can be used. So, at each step of the proof, let's use the following rule:

> If there is one, choose the first model predication whose leftmost argument τ is not a variable and either $\tau = sat(t_1, t_2)$ where t_1 is a nonvariable term, or else $\tau \neq sat(t_1, t_2)$. Otherwise, if there is one, choose the first LF predication whose first argument is a (list containing a) tree structure whose leftmost leaf is not a variable. Otherwise choose the first predication.[9]

We are guaranteed that this selection rule gives us a sound and complete resolution system (since *every* selection rule does). The result in this case is a nonpedestrian language processing system: it develops its interpretation incrementally, beginning before phrases are complete, and yet it obviously respects the strong competence assumption. A brief consideration of a couple of examples illustrates the nonpedestrian online performance of this system.

3.5. *Runtime Analyses*

Consider the example,

>   *the joke is funny.*

We can attempt to find a parse tree $Tree$, a logical form LF and a truth value $Value$ for this string by beginning a proof with the following line, in which we have underscored the predication that our selection rule tells us to choose:

$$\leftarrow \underline{ip([the, joke, is, funny], [], Tree)} \wedge$$
$$i\_ip([Tree], LF) \wedge truth(LF, Value).$$

The first argument of the model predication is a variable, so we cannot work on it. The first argument of the LF predication is also a variable, so we cannot use it either. Subjecting each step to such consideration yields the 17-step proof shown in appendix B. The point to note, which should be obvious even without consulting the appendix, is that we interpret each word as soon as it is placed into the parse tree. In the case of *the joke is funny*, this means that the system, in effect, figures out what you are talking about as soon as it sees the noun *joke*, and since there is only one predicate, the system immediately and justifiably assumes that the sentence is true at this point, on condition that the remainder of the string satisfies the syntactic and LF constraints. (In the appendix it is easy to see that the truth assessment is begun and completed in the 8th step, before the LF analysis of the initial noun phrase is complete, and before the syntactic analysis of the verb phrase has even begun.)

The same proof strategy applied to the example,

> *the argument that the joke that the argument is funny is funny is funny*

yields an interestingly different proof. In particular, although the LF and referential analysis is still done on a word-by-word basis, we cannot know what the denotation of the initial noun phrase is until we have seen all of it. Accordingly, although our model is constructing its representation of the denotation of the initial noun phrase on a word-by-word basis, that representation is not complete until the whole noun phrase has been completely analyzed at the syntactic and LF levels, and consequently the truth assessment for the sentence is delayed until the whole noun phrase is processed. Since we have presented our processing model in full detail, the reader can easily explore its behavior on a range of other examples. Interpretation is incremental in all of them. In some cases, the proof system can make incorrect guesses about syntactic structure and interpretation (and undo them by backtracking, or abandon them if they are found in parallel).

4. INCREMENTAL INTERPRETATION: COMPLEX LANGUAGES AND BOTTOM–UP PARSERS

Stepping back from the details, how is the incremental parsing achieved in the example of the previous section? One way of looking at the matter is this. A simple proof strategy finds a parse tree in standard top-down left-to-right order, and builds the corresponding parts of the LF form in the same order. For example, the string *the argument is funny* has the parse tree shown in figure 2, and the LF representation can similarly be represented as a kind of tree, as in figure 3.[10]

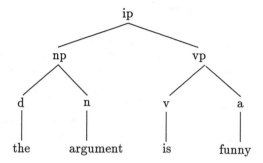

Figure 2: The parse tree for the sentence *the argument is funny*.

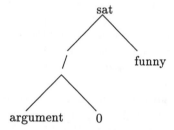

Figure 3: The corresponding LF for the sentence *the argument is funny*.

The property of these representations that was exploited was simply that as the syntactic tree was built from left-to-right on a word by word basis, we were able to build the LF 'tree' from left-to-right. This observation might raise some worries, though, about whether an approach of this kind could be extended to more complex languages, and about whether it could be extended to bottom-up parsing strategies. Let's very briefly consider each of these in turn. The point is not to propose any particular theory of human language processing, but simply to show that a wide variety of processing strategies are compatible with incremental interpretation.

4.1. *Extending the Semantics (Slightly)*

A full syntax and semantics for natural languages is fortunately beyond the scope of this brief note, but one might think that even in very simple fragments of English, the strategy used in our little example will not work. Let's consider just one simple problem which might occur to a semanticist from the generalized quantifier tradition. Suppose that we regard NPs as sets of properties, or, equivalently as functions from properties to truth values. Then a simple sentence like *john reads* might be represented as *john(reads)*, that is, the value of the function corresponding to *john* applied to the property corresponding to *reads*. It is clear that we could begin to construct the LF form *john(reads)* as we constructed the parse tree for the sentence *john reads*. Similarly, we could construct the form *some(man)(reads)* as we built the parse tree for *some man reads*, indicating that *some* maps the property *man* into a function which maps the property *reads* to a truth value. However, in most semantic theories that use LF representations like these, the functors are not always assumed to precede their arguments in the syntax. For example, a nominal PP might be interpreted as a function that maps the property corresponding the the head noun into another property. Then the meaning of *some man with some hat reads* might be represented as *some(with(some(hat))(man))(reads)*. Or if we regard direct objects as functions that map binary relations into properties then *john likes mary* might be represented as *john(mary(likes))* (cf. Keenan, 1989; Keenan and Faltz, 1985).

These last two logical forms present a problem: they cannot be incrementally specified from left-to-right as the parse tree is constructed because the parse tree sometimes specifies arguments before it specifies the corresponding functors. The problem is perhaps clearer if we regard the LF forms as trees. There is no problem with incrementally building the LF form of *john reads* as the parse is built:

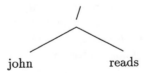

As soon as the first leaf of the parse tree is specified, the first leaf of this LF tree can be specified. With the sentence *john likes mary*, though, the relation between the parse tree and the LF form is more complicated:

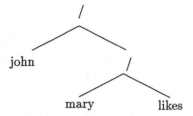

The problem is that, if we build our tree from left-to-right, we will be unable to place the property name corresponding to the verb into this LF until the direct object is fully parsed, so we do not obtain incremental interpretation.

Once stated, though, it is easy to see that this problem is just an artifact of an inessential aspect of the LF notation. The inessential aspect is simply the convention that functors are specified before their arguments. The problem does not arise if we use a slightly different notation. Suppose we adopt a bit of notation from categorial grammar, and use the forward slash to indicate the application of a functor to its argument (as already done in the LF trees displayed above),

$functor/argument$

and a backward slash to indicate the provision of an argument to a functor,

$argument \backslash functor.$

Then the LF of *john likes mary* is $john/(likes \backslash mary)$, and the LF of *some man with some hat reads* is

$(some/(man \backslash (with/(some/hat))))/reads.$

These LF trees have the property that their n'th leaf can be specified as soon as the n'th leaf of the parse tree is specified.

4.2. *Incremental Interpretation with Bottom-Up Parsing*

The incremental deductive processor described in section 3 is top-down. Abney (1989, p. 130) has proposed that although top-down parsing can allow incremental interpretation, this is not possible with bottom-up parsing:

> ...LR parsers cannot model the incrementality of human pars-
> ing. Namely, in right-branching structures, LR parsers build no
> structure until all the input has been read...By contrast, people
> clearly build structure before the end of the sentence and pass it
> incrementally to the semantic processor.

The idea here is similar to the one in the previous section. If we use a bottom-up LR parser on the string *the joke is funny*, structure is built by 'reduce' operations, and these precede from left-to-right and bottom-up. That is, the parser first discovers that d dominates *the*, then that n dominates *joke*, then that np dominates the previously formed d, n, and so on. Abney's suggestion is that this makes incremental interpretation of the sentence impossible, since the parser does not even begin to build the tree for ip until the whole string has been read.

After the previous section, it is easy to see that this problem is similarly an artifact of inessential formal details. The problem depends on the assumption that the only syntactic structure that can be interpreted is one that has the root ip, but this assumption is mistaken. Notice that our notation for trees in previous sections is top-down oriented in the sense that the root is specified first:

$$ip/[np/[d/[the], n/[joke]], vp/[v/[is], a/[funny]]],$$

but there is no need to specify trees in this form. We can just as well specify the very same trees with their components in the order that they are found by an LR parser:

$$[d/[the], n/[joke], np/[D, N], v/[is], a/[funny], vp/[V, A],$$
$$ip/[NP, VP]].$$

Under the obvious interpretation, this latter representation defines exactly the same tree as the former, and so it serves perfectly well as the output of a syntactic processor.

Notice that the LF theory of section 3.2 specifies interpretations for every syntactic constituent, but it uses a top-down oriented notation for both the syntactic constituents and for the LF forms. Given the new notation for our syntactic structures, it is natural to use a bottom-up notation for our LF representations as well. Instead of using the form

$sat(joke(0), funny)$

let's use

$[joke, 0, INP/ICP, funny, sat(INP, IVP)].$

These LF representations have the desired relation to the LR syntactic representations: the order of elements in LF is exactly the same as the order of the corresponding elements in the syntactic representation. Consequently, it is clear that a proof strategy that does truth assessment and LF interpretation as soon as the requisite parts of the syntactic form are specified will provide incremental interpretation. The theories of syntax, LF, and the world model remain completely modular, and the syntax remains right-branching. The only change is the use of a new tree notation in both the syntax and the LF, and the use of a different parsing strategy.[11] In sum, LR parsing is perfectly compatible with incremental interpretation

5. PREVIOUS REJECTIONS OF THE PEDESTRIAN ASSUMPTION

Various versions of the pedestrian hypothesis have been embraced and rejected before this response to Steedman (1989) and Abney (1989). In response to Tyler and Marslen-Wilson (1977) and Tyler (1980), Berwick and Weinberg (1983, pp. 7–8) make the point very clearly:

> The logic of Tyler and Marslen-Wilson's argument must assume that a grammar adhering to the autonomy of syntax thesis is compatible with one and only one derivational model (the model of noninteracting components usually associated with the *logical* organization of a [transformational grammar]) ...We will show that even under [the strong competence hypothesis], the autonomy thesis says nothing about the flow of information between components. Rather, it spells out the types of information that can form the representations of each component.[12]

Although the possibility of beginning the interpretation of partially built phrases was not explicitly considered by Berwick and Weinberg, the basic idea in this passage is essentially the same.[13] As noted above, once we grant that nothing blocks the interpretation of subsentential

220   EDWARD P. STABLER, JR.

constituents, the same reasoning shows that nothing blocks the interpretation of subphrasal constituents, even in models that conform to
the strong competence hypothesis. Under the strong competence hypothesis, linguistic theory places substantial constraints on performance
models all right, but it still leaves the whole range of purely procedural
issues open. A logical formulation of grammar makes this point obvious:
the steps of parsing and interpretation can be interleaved and structured
in any way.

To use processing data to support claims about the grammar, psychologists are faced with the prospect of sorting through the large range
of possible processing assumptions. As J.D. Fodor (1988; 1991 forthcoming) has pointed out, this makes good arguments from on-line performance to the grammar rather hard to come by, and in fact she fingers
the nonpedestrian parsing possibilities with modular grammars as one
of the main obstacles:

> Two distinct components of the grammar might be integrated be-
> fore or during parsing, so that the absence of a processing distinc-
> tion does not entail the absence of a distinction in the grammar.
> (Fodor, 1988, p. 127)

This appears to be our rejection of the pedestrian assumption in yet
another guise. However, although Fodor rejects the pedestrian's argument from distinctness in the grammar to distinctness in processing, she
accepts the converse argument:

> ... evidence for nonsynchronous application during sentence pars-
> ing of two (or more) different kinds of linguistic information con-
> stitutes indirect evidence for modularity within the mental gram-
> mar. If two kinds of information are integrated in the knowledge
> base, it is difficult to see how they could be systematically sep-
> arated by the parser and applied at different times to an input
> sentence. Hence we can reasonably infer a grammatical distinc-
> tion from a processing distinction. (Fodor, 1988, p. 127)

Fodor (1988) quickly qualifies this claim,[14] but let's briefly consider
why some qualification is necessary here. In the first place, there is
some vagueness here about what counts as a distinction of the relevant
sort. In the little example of the previous section, there were three au-
tonomous modules that had no predicate in common: these were called

the syntax, the semantics and the world model. Does this organization rule out processing models which apply different parts of one module at different times? Certainly not: we can and do apply information about the immediate constituents of noun phrases at one point, delaying other syntactic information such as the constituency of verb phrases, but these two parts of the syntax are in the same module and, in a clear sense, cannot be separated. That is, noun phrases can include verb phrases, and conversely, and so our account of the syntax of one necessarily involves the syntax of the other. This *linguistic argument* for a modularity claim is very strong, but does not begin to suggest that all syntactic information must be applied at once. This point applies quite generally: whenever one module, one rule or one principle, tells you two things, in a sense that allows those two things to be checked at different times, we can design a processing system that does check those two things at different times. The point can be put more abstractly: if we represent ϕ and ψ with a single representation γ, we can still apply ϕ at a different time from ψ in a processing task if we can (easily) compute both ϕ and ψ from γ. Consequently, it seems that processing distinctions do not imply grammatical distinctions in any interesting sense.

Fodor (1988, 1991 forthcoming) considers the following argument (among others). Suppose that we discovered evidence that subcategorization constraints associated with lexical items are not enforced as early as possible in human sentence processing. (For present purposes, the question of whether there really is such evidence is not relevant; we are interested in the significance that evidence of this kind would have.) It is suggested that this would be relatively difficult to reconcile with Government Binding (GB) theories in which phrase structure rules have been eliminated because of their redundancy with lexical subcategorization and other parts of the grammar. Apparently the idea is that, in the absence of phrase structure rules, a transparent GB parser would use lexical subcategorization to guide tree construction in parsing, and consequently it is hard to make sense of delaying this information. Fodor suggests that the delay of subcategorization information might be more easily handled in realizations of a certain kind of GPSG grammar, one in which phrase structure rules are separate from lexical subcategorization information.[15]

We can now see that this is a pedestrian assumption. There is no reason at all to suppose that a parser should use all lexical information at once: it is perfectly natural to suppose that certain key structural information (the principal syntactic category of the words specified in the lexicon, together with $\overline{X}$ restrictions, etc.) is used first, leaving sub-categorization information (also specified in the lexicon) and other less central information to later. Not only is a nonpedestrian processing story possible in this case, but it is very natural and straightforward. The reason for assuming that various kinds of information are represented in the lexicon is that the information is lexical-item-specific. From a linguistic perspective, it is natural to group item-specific information together in the lexicon, even if it rather diverse. From a computational perspective, it is also natural to suppose that the lexicon is accessed (or perhaps, activated) once, to provide a variety of item-specific information. Evidence that subcategorization information is not applied immediately does not disconfirm these accounts.

This is not to say that psychological evidence about what information is used when could never have any bearing at all on questions about what grammar is being used. It is perhaps possible (though it seems very unlikely to happen) that we will find two quite different grammars such that each has strong and roughly equal empirical support, but where only one of them represents some particular aspect of the language in a distinct module with distinct principles. In this case, if psychological evidence showed that information about this aspect of the language has a distinctive role in processing, then this might provide some weak support for the grammar that segregates the information. The evidence would be weak because there could well be an independently motivated nonpedestrian processing story to explain the psychological evidence for the nonmodular account. And the situation seems unlikely to arise in any case because it is hard to imagine that there would not be more direct linguistic arguments to address such a basic difference between two such grammars.

The psychological evidence about when in a processing task each type of information is used tells us just that. This by itself is something we want to know! How is the immense wealth of information in a grammar and lexicon brought to bear in linguistic tasks? The psychological studies mentioned, and many others, show that this problem can be addressed even before the linguists have settled all disputes about what information, exactly, is in the grammar and lexicon, and in what form. There is some consensus among linguists about what information must be there, and that there is lots of it, even though none of the prominent grammars comes very close to getting everything right for every language (or even for a single language, even at the most superficial, 'descriptive' levels of analysis). Even if significant headway is made on what information is used when, I think it is a mistake to expect that this will tell us very much about how that information must be represented. Although there are certainly inappropriate representations for computational problems, typically the range of suitable representations is quite wide.[16]

However, as discussed above, the question of how and when each piece of information is deployed can have a dramatic effect on performance. This is again just another formulation of our rejection of the pedestrian assumption. To sort a longish list, we really must start using our ordering information while we are still using the information about what constitutes a permutation. In our little deductive parser, or in any similar deductive reasoning, the best strategies reduce the needed search by (roughly) selecting subproblems with relatively small search spaces at each step. From any reasonable perspective, the study of the order in which subproblems are tackled in human language processing is of more direct and immediate interest than such questions as whether the some propositions ϕ and ψ are represented by a single representation in a single part of the grammar or with distinct representations possibly in distinct parts of the grammar.

6. CONCLUSION

Natural processing models can provide incremental left-to-right analysis and interpretation of left-branching structures. The more general and important point is that even in performance models that have no other information about a language than the grammar provides, even in models that assign structure strictly according to deductive reasoning from the grammar, there is a huge range of processing options. There are many possible ways to bring the grammatical constraints to bear in any particular linguistic task. Getting reaction time studies to bear on the grammar is consequently quite difficult in our present state of ignorance about language processing. For example, if psychologists discover that humans initially assign incorrect structures to certain locally ambiguous constructions, there are other options to consider than the common idea that extra-grammatical heuristic principles are being used to assign structure. The evidence might instead reflect on the way that the space of grammatical structures is being explored on the basis of the local, incomplete information.[17]

However, far from removing the interest of results about what is used when, the rejection of the Steedman's paradox comes with the insight that the order of application of linguistic information, though not determined by the grammar, is fundamental to finding a feasible performance model. The other fundamental requirement for a descriptively adequate model is, of course, that we get a correct account of what the linguistic information is, a correct grammar, but reaction time studies are not the most direct approach to this problem.

APPENDIX A: A PROLOG IMPLEMENTATION OF THE NONPEDESTRIAN PARSER

To get a complete Prolog implementation of the nonpedestrian language processor described above, most Prologs will require only a minor change in the notation of (S1)–(S11), (I1)–(I11), and (M1)–(M10). Simply change ← to : −, and change ∧ to a comma. These axioms then can be used by the *demonstrate* predicate given here. For further discussion of proof predicates like *demonstrate* see Pereira and Shieber (1987) and Stabler (1990).

```
%%%% the non-pedestrian metainterpreter: demonstrate(Goal)
% For example, run
% ?- demonstrate(s([the,joke,is,funny],[],Tree))
% All demonstrate proofs use the following rule to select the next step:
% If the first model literal has a first arg with a nonvar leftmost leaf,
%       select it; otherwise
% If the first lf literal has a first arg with a nonvar leftmost leaf,
%       select it;
% otherwise select the first literal

demonstrate([]) :- !. % nothing left to prove - finished!
demonstrate(Goal) :- % otherwise select next literal L from Goal...
% nl,itemize(Goal),nl, % for tracing only
( select(Position,Goal,[L],Rem),model(L),leaved(L) -> true
; select(Position,Goal,[L],Rem),lf(L),leaved(L) -> true
; Position=s(0), select(Position,Goal,[L],Rem)
),
% write('Next literal: '),write(Position),write('.'),nl,
% for tracing
clause(L,Body),
and_to_list(Body,NewLiterals),
select(Position,NewGoal,NewLiterals,Rem),
```

```prolog
demonstrate(NewGoal).

% specify the lf and model predicates:
lf(i_ip(_,_)). lf(i_np(_,_)). lf(i_d(_,_)). lf(i_n(_,_)).
lf(i_cp(_,_)). lf(i_vp(_,_)).
lf(i_v(_,_)). lf(i_a(_,_)).   lf(i_c(_,_)).

model(truth(_,_)). model(argument_kernel(_,_)).
                        model(joke_kernel(_,_)).

% check if leftmost leaf of term is not a variable
leaved(Arg) :- atomic(Arg), !.
leaved(_/L) :- !, leaved(L). % to check left branch of trees
leaved(joke(_)) :- !. % a special leaf for model preds
leaved(argument(_)) :- !. % a special leaf for model preds
leaved(Term) :- arg(1,Term,Arg),nonvar(Arg),leaved(Arg).
                                    % check leftmost arg of other
                                    % terms

% to avoid arithmetic probs, we use s(0)=1, s(s(0))=2, s(s(s(0)))=3,...
select(s(0),Result,Insert,Remainder) :- append(Insert,Remainder,Result).
select(s(Position),[H|Result],Insert,[H|T])
                    :- select(Position,Result,Insert,T).

append([],L,L).
append([H|L1],L2,[H|L3]) :- append(L1,L2,L3).

% convert a conjunction of goals to a list of goals
and_to_list((L,Ls),[L|Rest]) :- !, and_to_list(Ls,Rest).
and_to_list(true,[]) :- !.
and_to_list(L,[L]).

% itemize is just for tracing display
itemize([],_).
itemize([H|T],N) :- M is N+1,write(M),tab(3),write(H),nl,itemize(T,M).
```

APPENDIX B. A NONPEDESTRIAN PROOF

Using the selection rule of appendix A, a rule that always prefers model predicates to LF predicates to syntactic predicates, but can only evaluate predicates whose leftmost argument is sufficiently instantiated, we get the following *incremental, word-by-word* proof that *the joke is funny* has a parse tree IP, a logical form LF and a truth value $Value$:

$$\leftarrow ip([the, joke, is, funny], [\,], IP)\wedge$$
$$i\_ip([IP], LF)\wedge$$
$$truth(LF, Value).$$

$by(S1):$

$$\leftarrow np([the, joke, is, funny], S1, NP)\wedge$$
$$vp(S1, [\,], VP)\wedge$$
$$i\_ip([ip/[NP, VP]], LF)\wedge$$
$$truth(LF, Value).$$

$by(S3):$

$$\leftarrow d([the, joke, is, funny], S2, D)\wedge$$
$$n(S2, S1, N)\wedge$$
$$vp(S1, [\,], VP)\wedge$$
$$i\_ip([ip/[np/[D, N], VP]], LF)\wedge$$
$$truth(LF, Value).$$

$by(S2):$

$$\leftarrow n([joke, is, funny], S1, N)\wedge$$
$$vp(S1, [\,], VP)\wedge$$
$$i\_ip([ip/[np/[d/[the], N], VP]], LF)\wedge$$
$$truth(LF, Value).$$

$by(I1):$

$$\leftarrow n([joke, is, funny], S1, N)\wedge$$
$$vp(S1, [\,], VP)\wedge$$
$$i\_np([np/[d/[the], N]], Subj)\wedge$$
$$i\_vp([VP], Pred)\wedge$$
$$truth(sat(Subj, Pred), Value).$$

by $(I2)$:

$$\leftarrow n([joke, is, funny], S1, N) \wedge$$
$$vp(S1, [\,], VP) \wedge$$
$$i\_d([d/[the]], the) \wedge$$
$$i\_n([N], Subj) \wedge$$
$$i\_vp([VP], Pred) \wedge$$
$$truth(sat(Subj, Pred), Value).$$

by $(I6)$:

$$\leftarrow n([joke, is, funny], S1, N) \wedge$$
$$vp(S1, [\,], VP) \wedge$$
$$i\_n([N], Subj) \wedge$$
$$i\_vp([VP], Pred) \wedge$$
$$truth(sat(Subj, Pred), Value).$$

by $(S7)$:

$$\leftarrow vp([is, funny], [\,], VP) \wedge$$
$$i\_n([n/[joke]], Subj) \wedge$$
$$i\_vp([VP], Pred) \wedge$$
$$truth(sat(Subj, Pred), Value).$$

by $(I7)$:

$$\leftarrow vp([is, funny], [\,], VP) \wedge$$
$$i\_cp([\,], X) \wedge$$
$$i\_vp([VP], Pred) \wedge$$
$$truth(sat(joke(X), Pred), Value).$$

by $(M1)$:

$$\leftarrow vp([is, funny], [\,], VP) \wedge$$
$$i\_cp([\,], X) \wedge$$
$$i\_vp([VP], funny).$$

by (*I*4) :

$$\leftarrow \frac{vp([is, funny], [\ ], VP) \wedge}{i\_vp([VP], funny).}$$

by (*S*6) :

$$\leftarrow \frac{v([is, funny], S3, V) \wedge}{a(S3, [\ ], A) \wedge}$$
$$i\_vp([vp/[V, A]], funny).$$

by (*S*10) :

$$\leftarrow \frac{a([funny], [\ ], A) \wedge}{i\_vp([vp/[v/[is], A]], funny).}$$

by(*I*5) :

$$\leftarrow a([funny], [\ ], A) \wedge$$
$$\frac{i\_v([v/[is]], is) \wedge}{i\_a([A], funny).}$$

by(*I*10) :

$$\leftarrow \frac{a([funny], [\ ], A) \wedge}{i\_a([A], funny).}$$

by (*S*11) :

$$\leftarrow \frac{i\_a([a/[funny]], funny).}{}$$

by (*I*11) :

$$\square \quad Q.E.D.$$

$$IP = ip/[np/[d/[the], n/[joke]], vp/[v/[is], a/[funny]]]$$
$$LF = sat(joke(0), funny)$$
$$Value = true$$

APPENDIX C. AN INCREMENTAL LR PARSER

In section 3 a logical representation of the following grammar was used:

(1) ip → np vp

(2) np → d n

(3) np → d n cp

(4) cp → c ip

(5) vp → v a

(6) d → the

(7) n → joke

(8) n → argument

(9) c → that

(10) v → is

(11) a → funny

There is a mechanical method for constructing the LR table for such a grammar. As usual, $ is the end-of-string symbol. (See, *e.g.*, Aho and Ullman (1977) for a description of these tables and their use.) With the simple grammar above, we get the following table:

state	$	argument	funny	is	joke	that	the
0							sh5
1							re9
2				re2		sh1	
3		sh10			sh9		
4							sh5
5		re6			re6		
6				sh11			
7				re4			
8				re3			
9				re7		re7	
10				re8		re8	
11			re10				
12	re11			re11			
13			sh12				
14	re5			re5			
15	re1			re1			
16	acc						

State	a	c	cp	d	ip	n	np	v	vp
0				3	16		6		
1									
2			4	8					
3						2			
4				3	7		6		
5									
6								13	15
7									
8									
9									
10									
11									
12									
13	14								
14									
15									
16									

We always begin in state 0, and then take the action specified for our current state and the next input symbol. For example, beginning in state 0 with *the* as the next word of the input, we see that the prescribe action is *sh5*, *i.e.*, shift the next word of the input into the stack and go into state 5. In state 5 with *joke* as the next word of the input, the prescribed action is *re6*, reduce using production 6. This reduce action pops *the* off the stack, taking us back to state 0. So now we are in state

0 and about to put push a *d* onto the stack. Using the far right of the table, we see that from state 0, on creation of a *d*, we go to state 3. We continue in this way until we get to the action *acc*, accepting the string, or else we get to an error condition in which no action is prescribed.

The steps in parsing and incrementally interpreting *the joke is funny* with this LR table are as on the following page.

stack: 0
input: the joke is funny
action: sh5
tree:
lf:
truth:

stack: 5 the 0
input: joke is funny
action: re6
tree:
lf:
truth:

stack: 3 d 0
input: joke is funny
action: sh9
tree: d/[the]
lf:
truth:

stack: 9 joke 3 d 0
input: is funny
action: re7
tree: d/[the]
lf:
truth:

stack: 2 n 3 d 0
input: is funny
action: re2
tree: d/[the] n/[joke]
lf: joke
truth:

stack: 6 np 0
input: is funny
action: sh11
tree: d/[the] n/[joke] np/[A,B]
lf: joke 0 A/B
truth: true

stack: 11 is 6 np 0
input: funny
action: re10
tree: d/[the] n/[joke] np/[A,B]
lf: joke 0 A/B
truth: true

stack: 13 v 6 np 0
input: funny
action: sh12
tree: d/[the] n/[joke] np/[A,B] v/[is]
lf: joke 0 A/B
truth: true

stack: 12 funny 13 v 6 np 0
input: $
action: re11
tree: d/[the] n/[joke] np/[A,B] v/[is]
lf: joke 0 A/B
truth: true

stack: 14 a 13 v 6 np 0
input: $
action: re5
tree: d/[the] n/[joke] np/[A,B] v/[is]
a/[funny]
lf: joke 0 A/B funny
truth: true

stack: 15 vp 6 np 0
input: $
action: re1
tree: d/[the] n/[joke] np/[A,B] v/[is]
a/[funny] vp/[C,D]
lf: joke 0 A/B funny
truth: true

stack: 16 ip 0
input: $
action: acc
tree: d/[the] n/[joke] np/[A,B] v/[is]
a/[funny] vp/[C,D] ip/[E,F]
lf: joke 0 A/B funny sat(C,D)
truth: true

ACKNOWLEDGEMENTS

The basic idea of this chapter is more carefully developed and applied to natural language processing in Stabler (1991 forthcoming). I am grateful to Robert Berwick, Janet Dean Fodor, Ed Keenan, and Mark Johnson for helpful discussions of this material.

NOTES

[1] It is not perfectly clear what counts as the direct use of a grammar by a processor, but this vagueness will not obscure the main point of this discussion. I will describe some examples that respect the strong competence hypothesis, but I think that my examples will all be uncontroversial. They directly use explicit and complete representations of the grammar, with no other structure-defining principles. Cf. Matthews (1988), Stabler (1984), Berwick and Weinberg (1984), Stabler (1983), Bresnan and Kaplan (1982) for discussions about what strong competence hypothesis we need, exactly, to obtain the desirable compatibility with the competence and learning theory.

[2] Obviously, the conclusion that you are using a nonpedestrian technique does not follow if you are not doing the task. In particular, the conclusion can be drawn about the human parser only on the assumption that humans do, in fact, resolve all the structural ambiguities in such cases, computing a single, definite syntactic structure.

[3] It is puzzling that Steedman does not notice this point, that once we allow interpretation to begin before the sentence is complete (as is done in Winograd (1972) and Bobrow and Webber (1980), cited by Steedman), we can just as well allow interpretation to begin before any phrase is complete.

[4] This isomorphism between context-free derivations and SLD-resolution refutations was implicit in VanderBrug and Minker (1975), Pereira and Warren (1980) and following work, but has been made completely explicit in Stabler (1991 forthcoming).

[5] Strictly speaking, this, and the other proofs shown below, are refutations, proofs by contradiction. Furthermore, all the proofs use the single inference rule: SLD resolution. See Lloyd (1987) for a presentation of this proof technique. It is sound and complete for the theories considered here, since they are all 'Horn theories'. That is, they have a special syntactic property which allows the use of especially simple proof methods. Stabler (1991 forthcoming) points out that most linguistic theories are not Horn, and consequently more powerful proof methods must be used.

[6] Although my strategy here is, I hope, intuitively clear, a logician will notice some tricky business, tricky but perfectly sound and natural. In the LF language, I am using *sat* as both a predicate and as a function. There are no other LF predicates, and the other LF functions and constants are *joke, argument,* 0 and *funny*. However, the LF language is itself an object language relative to the language of the following axioms. That is, the following axioms use terms identical to the expressions of the LF language to denote expressions of the LF language, in order to define the proper relation between syntactic trees and LF expressions.

[7] The completeness of particular selection functions in linear resolution and similar methods was established independently by several researchers, including Reiter

(1971); Kowalski and Kuehner (1971); and Loveland (1972). Completeness for *arbitrary* selection functions was established by Reiter and by Kowalski and Kuehner. The results on the lengths of the shortest proofs in these systems is explored by Kowalski and Kuehner. The result most directly relevant to Prolog is elegantly presented in a recent text by Lloyd (1987) as the 'independence of the computation rule' for Horn clause SLD-resolution. The origin of the result for SLD resolution is not discussed by Lloyd, but Kowalski (1979, p. 71) credits Edinburgh University technical memos by F.M. Brown (1973) and R. Hill (1974).

[8] Note that the modularity I mention here is not a modularity in processing, an 'informational encapsulation' of the sort that is often discussed in the psycholinguistic literature. I do not like calling it a 'representational modularity' either, because it is a property of the language rather than a property of our representation of the language. That is, the language itself is such that we can easily define its syntactic properties without reference to LF, and LF without reference to syntax. One can imagine languages (perhaps English) in which it is difficult or impossible to completely disentangle the specifications of different kinds of properties.

[9] A complete Prolog implementation of a proof predicate that uses this proof strategy can be defined with only a few lines. One is presented in appendix A.

[10] We use the forward slash / as a node label in this tree simply to indicate that *argument*(0) is to be constructed from the two pieces *argument* and 0. This use is different from our previous use of the slash in terms denoting trees. The motivation for this notation will become clear in the following paragraphs.

[11] For readers who want to see a few more of the computational details, see appendix C.

[12] I have replaced Berwick and Weinberg's abbreviation 'TG' by '[transformational grammar]', and their "such Type Transparency assumptions" by our term "[the strong competence hypothesis]".

[13] Berwick and Weinberg have been criticized for their claim that their particular parsing model is a transparent realization of a transformational grammar (Stabler, 1984; J.D. Fodor, 1985). But even if these critiques are sound (and their soundness is controversial: Berwick and Weinberg, 1985a; 1985b), the main point of the quoted passage remains untouched.

[14] Fodor (1988, p. 131) says "Other implementations are certainly imaginable...It does seem justified, as an initial step, to assume the most straightforward implementation of each type of grammar, and on that basis I think it can be agreed that evidence of nonsynchronous application of ... two kinds of information would be easier for [a theory with corresponding modules] to accommodate than for [a theory that does not separated the two kinds of information]." Similar remarks are made in Fodor (1989). My points are, first, that pedestrian implementations are *rarely* the most straightforward implementations, if they are feasible at all, and second, that better evidence for or against modularizing a particular aspect of the language is usually available.

[15] Fodor (1988, 1991, forthcoming); Clifton and Frazier (1986); Frazier, Clifton, and Randall (1983); and many others use essentially similar arguments in in application to many other points. Evidence that control information is delayed in parsing (were there any) is supposed to favor theories that segregate principles of control from

phrase structure and movement relations, as both GB and GPSG do. Evidence that movement relations (and such things as subjacency enforcement) are handled differently from other phrase structure constraints is supposed to favor theories like GB over theories like GPSG in which movement relations are handled with special features.

[16] Computer scientists sometimes express this by saying that basic complexity results remain invariant under any of the 'standard encodings' of a problem. A standard encoding does not have excessive amounts of redundancy or 'padding'; it does not keep most frequently needed information in a structure from which it can be derived only by extensive computation; etc.

[17] In our example, a deductive system could perfectly well explore the possibility that an NP has the structure D N before exploring the possibility that the structure is D N CP. This kind of behavior is perfectly familiar from the simplest context free parsing strategies, and does not reflect the use of any extragrammatical structure-defining principles.

REFERENCES

Abney, S.: 1989, 'A Computational Model of Human Parsing', *Journal of Psycholinguistic Research* **18**, 129–144.

Aho, A. and J. Ullman: 1977, *Principles of Compiler Design*, Addison-Wesley, Menlo Park, California.

Berwick, R. and A. Weinberg: 1983, 'The Role of Grammars in Models of Language Use', *Cognition* **13**, 1–62.

Berwick, R. and A. Weinberg: 1984, *The Grammatical Basis of Linguistic Performance: Language Use and Acquisition*, MIT Press, Cambridge, Massachusetts.

Berwick, R. and A. Weinberg: 1985a, 'Deterministic Parsing and Linguistic Explanation', *Language and Cognitive Processes* **1**, 109–134.

Berwick, R. and A. Weinberg: 1985b, 'The Psychological Relevance of Transformational Grammar: A Reply to Stabler', *Cognition* **19**, 193–204.

Bobrow, R. and B. Webber: 1980, 'Knowledge Representation for Syntactic/Semantic Processing', *Proceedings of the First Annual Conference on Artificial Intelligence*, Morgan-Kaufmann Publishers, Los Altos, California, pp. 316–323.

Bresnan, J. and R. Kaplan: 1982, 'Introduction: Grammars as Mental Representations of Language', in J. Bresnan (ed.), *The Mental Representation of Grammatical Relations*, MIT Press, Cambridge, Massachusetts, pp. xvii–lii.

Church, K. and R. Patil: 1982, 'Coping with Syntactic Ambiguity', *American Journal of Computational Linguistics* **8**, 139–149.

Clifton, C. and L. Frazier: 1986, 'The Use of Syntactic Information in Filling Gaps', *Journal of Psycholinguistic Research* **15**, 209–224.

Fodor, J.D.: 1988, 'On Modularity in Syntactic Processing', *Journal of Psycholinguistic Research* **17**, 125–168.

Fodor, J.D.: 1991 forthcoming, 'Sentence Processing and Mental Grammar', in P. Sells, S. Shieber, and T. Wasow (eds.), *Foundational Issues in Natural Language Processing*, MIT Press, Cambridge, Massachusetts.

Frazier, L., C. Clifton, and J. Randall: 1983, 'Filling Gaps: Decision Principles and Structure in Sentence Comprehension', *Cognition* **13**, 187–222.

Keenan, E.: 1989, 'Semantic Case Theory', In R. Bartsch, J. van Bentham, and R. van Emde-Boas (eds.), *Semantics and Contextual Expression*, Dordrecht, Foris, Groningen-Amsterdam Studies in Semantics (GRASS) Volume 11, pp. 33–57.

Keenan, E. and L. Faltz: 1985, *Boolean Semantics for Natural Language*, Reidel, Boston, Massachusetts.

Knuth, D.: 1973, *The Art of Computer Programming, Volume 1: Fundamental Algorithms*, Addison-Wesley, Reading, Massachusetts.

Kowalski, R.: 1979, *Logic for Problem Solving*, North-Holland, New York.

Kowalski, R. and D. Kuehner: 1971, 'Linear Resolution with Selection Functions', *Artificial Intelligence* **2**, 227–260.

Langendoen, T., A. Koslow, and C. Neff: 1988, 'The Syntax and Semantics of Co-ordinate Compounding in English', unpublished manuscript, City University of New York, New York.

Lloyd, J.: 1987, *Foundations of Logic Programming, Second Edition* Springer-Verlag, New York.

Loveland, D.: 1972, 'A Unifying View of Some Linear Herbrand Procedures', *Journal of the Association for Computing Machinery* **19**, 366–384.

Marslen-Wilson, W. and L.K. Tyler: 1980, 'The Temporal Structure of Spoken Language Understanding', *Cognition* **8**, 1–21.

Marslen-Wilson, W.: 1987, 'Functional Parallelism and Spoken Word Recognition', *Cognition* **25**, 71–102.

Marslen-Wilson, W.: 1989, 'Access and Integration: Projecting Sound onto Meaning', in W. Marslen-Wilson (ed.), *Lexical Representation and Process*, MIT Press, Cambridge, Massachusetts, pp. 3–24.

Marslen-Wilson, W.: 1989, (ed.), *Lexical Representation and Process*, MIT Press, Cambridge, Massachusetts.

Matthews, R.: 1988, 'Psychological Reality of Grammars', Unpublished paper presented at the conference on *The Chomskyan Turn*, Tel-Aviv and Jerusalem, April, 1988.

Naish, L.: 1986, *Negation and Control in Prolog*, Springer-Verlag, New York.

Pereira, F. and D.H.D. Warren: 1980, 'Definite Clause Grammars for Natural Language Analysis', *Artificial Intelligence* **13**, 231–278.

Quine, W.V.: 1961, 'The Ways of Paradox', in W.V. Quine, *The Ways of Paradox and other Essays*, Harvard University Press, Cambridge, Massachusetts, pp. 1–18.

Reiter, R.: 1971, 'Two Results on Ordering for Resolution With Merging and Linear Format', *Journal of the Association for Computing Machinery* **18**, 630–646.

Stabler, E.P. Jr.: 1983, 'How Are Grammars Represented?', *Behavioral and Brain Sciences* **6**, 391–421.

Stabler, E.P. Jr.: 1984, 'Berwick and Weinberg on Linguistics and Cognitive Psychology', *Cognition* **17**, 155–179.

Stabler, E.P. Jr.: 1990, 'Representing Knowledge with Theories about Theories', *Journal of Logic Programming* **9**, 105–138.

Stabler, E.P. Jr.: 1991 forthcoming, *The Logical Approach to Syntax: Foundations, Specifications, and Implementations of Theories of Government and Binding*, MIT Press, Cambridge, Massachusetts.

Steedman, M.: 1989, 'Grammar, Interpretation and Processing From the Lexicon', in W. Marslen-Wilson (ed.), *Lexical Representation and Process*, MIT Press, Cambridge, Massachusetts, pp. 463–504.

Tyler, L.: 1980, *Serial and Interactive Parallel Theories of Syntactic Processing*, Occasional Paper No. 8, Cambridge, Massachusetts, MIT Center for Cognitive Science.

Tyler, L. and W. Marslen-Wilson: 1977, 'The On-line Effects of Semantic Context on Syntactic Processing', *Journal of Verbal Learning and Verbal Behavior* **16**, 683–692.

VanderBrug, G. and J. Minker: 1975, 'State-space, Problem-reduction, and Theorem-proving—Some Relationships', *Communications of the Association for Computing Machinery* **18**, 107–115.

Winograd, T.: 1972, *Understanding Natural Language*, Academic Press, New York.

Department of Linguistics,
University of California at Los Angeles,
Los Angeles, California 90024, U.S.A.

RICK KAZMAN

PARSING WITH CHANGING GRAMMARS: EVALUATING A LANGUAGE ACQUISITION MODEL

1. INTRODUCTION

The use of parsing in creating and evaluating models of language development has not received a great deal of attention from theoretical linguists and language development researchers in the past. The attention that it has received has largely concentrated on the use of a parser to help to create a language model. Attempts of this sort can be found in Berwick (1985), Selfridge (1980), and Anderson (1975), for example. Each of these efforts consists of an acquisition system that attempts to modify its grammar in response to failed parses.

In this chapter, I will be concentrating on a different use of parsing in a language acquisition model: the use of a parser as a tool for evaluating the formal claims of hypothesized models in a controlled, consistent fashion.

In a parameterized theory of syntax, such as Government-Binding theory (as described in Chomsky, 1981; Chomsky, 1986; and elsewhere), certain principles of grammar are held to be universal and innately held—the principles of c-command, government, and the θ-criterion are examples of postulated universals. The differences between the world's languages are held to be expressible by parameterizing *other* facets of the grammar—word order is a typical example.

One school of language acquisition research has investigated the claim that acquisition is nothing more than a process wherein the child has to learn the settings of parameters for their particular language[1]. (see, for instance, Hyams, 1987; and Roeper and Williams, 1987). Although an instantaneous parameter-setting model does not adequately describe the *process* of language acquisition, this model can be profitably used to empirically test claims about the state of a child's grammar at a given stage of development, and to delineate the time period during which a parameter can be said to be 'acquired'.[2] Just such an approach will be adopted here.

The claims which will be tested in this manner are those made in Kazman (1988), regarding the acquisition of Case marking and agree-

R. C. Berwick et al. (eds.),
Principle-Based Parsing: Computation and Psycholinguistics, 239–256.

ment in the child's grammar. These claims are tested by processing samples of the spontaneous speech of two children between the ages of 24 and 29 months under different parameterizations of Gibson's parameterized parser (Gibson, 1987; Gibson and Clark, 1988). As a result of running these experiments, it appears that the predictions made by the acquisition model are well substantiated. The results indicate that the acquisition model correctly predicts the parametric changes accounting for the changing grammaticality (by adult standards) of a child's utterances.

The results obtained further suggest that Gibson's parsing model lends itself to the type of parameterization needed to characterize stages in the acquisition of syntax. This does not imply, however, that a parameterized parsing model, by itself, has anything to say about the process of acquiring the proper parameter settings. The parser is seen here purely as a testbed for the claims of a parametric language acquisition theory.

1.1. *The Acquisition Model*

The model of language acquisition being evaluated here makes certain predictions concerning the child's grammatical competence during the null subject stage of language acquisition (typically around the age of 24–36 months). If these predictions are correct then they should be empirically verifiable. The method of testing and verifying these predictions advocated here is to encode the relevant parameters into the parsing model, and to see whether, by setting the parameters to different values—including, but not limited to, the ones predicted by the theory of acquisition—a significant portion of a child's utterances at various stages of their acquisition of English can be accounted for. If the acquisition theory makes proper predictions, then the parametric changes hypothesized by the theory should most closely approximate the child's performance of all possible parameter settings.

In effect, each different combination of parameter settings defines a new hypothesized model of the child's grammar.[3] If a particular parameter setting adequately describes the child's production competence (by correctly parsing a significant portion of his spontaneous utterances), then it can be taken to be a descriptively accurate model of their linguistic competence. This is no different from our criteria of success for an adult parsing model, with the exception that the target is a moving one.

It is assumed here that a child *always* utters grammatical utterances, according to their own personal grammar. There is no stage of 'lawlessness' in language acquisition, only an apparent stage of permissiveness: the child's grammar is quite different from the adult grammar at the earliest stages of acquisition in that it is significantly less restrictive. For instance, it allows verb arguments to be optionally dropped. The child's grammar approaches the adult state over time. Consequently, one of the problems for the language acquisition researcher is to correctly characterize a child's grammar in order to account for their spontaneous utterances, while not positing any special-purpose mechanisms which would 'poison' their later grammar and have to be unlearned. If achieved, this model may be taken to be descriptively adequate. Furthermore, if the model accurately predicts the order and type of parameter settings that the child undergoes, then it may be claimed to be a psychologically accurate model as well.

In particular, I predict that the child's grammatical competence during the null-subject stage can be characterized by four parametric differences from the adult grammar. These are as follows:

(1) The basic unit of utterance is a small-clause phrase, rather than a sentence, since the child has not yet developed the notion of Infl (Inflection) as a distinct $\overline{X}$ node,[4] and a small-clause phrase can adequately express the thematic relations in the child's speech.[5] This is evidenced by the omission of most material which is typically analyzed as residing in Infl: modals, auxiliaries, infinitive-marking *to*, and agreement and tense features. This parameter will be denoted as [±Infl-present], where [−Infl-present] is the initial state and [+Infl-present] is the adult state.

(2) Case marking and the Case filter are not operational. That this parameter is not yet set in the child's grammar is evidenced by the omission of several morphemes that serve to indicate case assignment. For example, the *'s* morpheme in genitives is not present at this stage, and so, e.g., *Mommy's coffee* is produced as *Mommy coffee*. Similarly, the preposition *of*, which is a pure Case marker, is not used at this stage, and so *piece of cake* is produced as *piece cake*. This parameter will be denoted as [±Case-marking], where [−Case-marking] is the initial state and [+Case-marking] is the adult state.

(3) The child initially analyzes its language as morphologically uniform (and morphologically simple). That is, the child does not
initially attend to verbal morphology, and so treats his language
as though it were Chinese, where there is no verb-argument
agreement at all. This idea was first proposed by Jaeggli and
Safir (1987) as a way of linking the presence and regularity of
verbal morphology with the ability to drop subjects. The applicability of this parameter to learnability issues has been discussed
by Hyams (1987). Essentially, the idea is that the content of
dropped subjects can be recovered where there is sufficiently rich
agreement, or where there is no agreement at all. In either case,
the inflectional paradigm is uniform—always unambiguously inflected for person and number, or never inflected. In the former
case, when the verb uniquely agrees with its subject, the subject may be freely dropped, since its content is fully specified by
the verbal inflection; in the latter case, where there is no verbal
morphology at all, the content of a dropped subject is specified
by a discourse determined topic. In Kazman (1988) it is argued
that the morphological uniformity parameter (MUP) extends to
all verb arguments, and not just subjects.[6] The initial setting of
the MUP to [+uniform] captures the empirical observation that
children in the null subject stage typically omit verbal inflection
completely. In the adult stage, the MUP is set to [−uniform] (for
English speakers).

(4) In the child's grammar, agreement is not obligatory. This is
manifested most noticeably in Infl by the lack of subject-verb
agreement features, but it is common throughout the child's linguistic competence. For instance, children typically pay little
attention to the agreement between a determiner and its head
noun, using an incorrect determiner or omitting the determiner
altogether. Children lack agreement in other areas of grammar
as well, such as between auxiliaries and main verbs. This parameter will be denoted as [±Agreement], where [−Agreement]
is the initial state and [+Agreement] is the adult state. This
characterization of agreement is obviously an oversimplification.
Agreement is closely tied to lexical acquisition—the child cannot
make a noun such as *feet* agree in number if the child believes the
correct lexical entry to be *foots*. The parsing model can help to

determine when agreement has a significant impact on the child's grammar, but this must be coupled with a model of lexical acquisition to account for the specific details of the child's agreement phenomena—both erroneous and precocious acquisition.

I claim then, following Kazman (1988), that the child's speech during this stage can be largely characterized by positing the above parametric changes from the adult's grammar of English.[7] In Kazman (1989) I claim that the settings of the MUP, [±Infl-present], [±Case-marking], and [±Agreement] are all induced by the child's acquisition of morphology, but I will not delve into this argument here.

1.2. The Parsing Model

The parser that was used in the experiments described in this chapter is an implementation of a parallel parsing model. This parser is called the Constrained Parallel Parser (CPP). The CPP model is a modular parser based on the principles of Government-Binding theory. Unlike traditional parsing models, CPP has no grammar rule module. Instead, it has a built-in core grammar consisting of Government-Binding theory principles along with a number of parameters. Each of these parameters can be changed to account for language variation. Structures are built based upon the given core grammar and the values of its parameters.

The CPP model contains two data structures: the *stack* and the *buffer*. The buffer consists of a single cell that contains a set of tree structures, each of which is a different representation of the same segment of the input string. The stack has the same structure as the buffer, but may be more than one cell deep. Structures are built in this framework by making attachments between the buffer and the top cell of the stack. Allowable attachments are defined by the principles of Government-Binding theory and are constrained by CPP parsing principles.

For example, $\overline{\text{X}}$ theory in the CPP model is as defined in Chomsky (1986): each tree structure must have a head below it and each head must have a maximal projection above it. These principles interact with other Government-Binding theory principles (*e.g.*, the θ-criterion, the Extended Projection Principle, Case theory) to determine the positions of arguments, specifiers, and modifiers with respect to the head of a given structure. As a result, a specifier may only appear as a sister to the one-bar projection below a maximal projection, and the head must appear below the one-bar projection along with its arguments. The structure for categories in English is shown on the left below, with a modifier attachment on the right below.

For each word in an input sentence, the CPP model constructs maximal projections for each of the word's lexical entries. This set of maximal projections is placed in the buffer. Attachments are then attempted between the buffer and the stack. If no attachments are possible, the contents of the buffer are pushed onto the stack, and the next word in the input string is read.

Successful attachments are subject to the parsing constraints outlined below:

Exclusive Attachment Constraint: If an attachment is possible between two structures (one on the stack, one in the buffer), then it is made. All nodes in parallel that do not take part in attachment, either on the stack or in the buffer, are pruned.

Case filter and θ-criterion:[8] After attachments between the stack and the buffer are completed, if a structure A directly receives a necessary property (e.g., a thematic role or abstract Case for a lexical noun phrase), then prune all representations in which structure A appears but does not directly receive that property. For example, if a certain lexical noun phrase NP_1 receives Case in one representation, then all representations are pruned in which NP_1 does not receive Case.

Lexical Requirement Constraint: If an attachment is possible that satisfies the lexical requirements of some head, then make that attachment and all others that also satisfy lexical requirements. If no such attachment is possible, then make any other possible attachments satisfying other constraints.

As a model of human sentence processing, the CPP model correctly predicts a number of observed psycholinguistic effects, such as difficulty with garden-path sentences and slowdowns in processing with ambiguous input (see Gibson, 1987; and Gibson and Clark, 1988).

Since the Constrained Parallel Parser models adult sentence processing and is based on the principles of Government-Binding Theory, it is reasonable to use it as a test of the acquisition theory presented in Kazman (1988).[9] As a result of these considerations, the CPP model was considered an excellent vehicle for the experiments reported here.

2. THE CHILD DATA

A number of typical examples of a child's speech exhibiting some of the phenomena listed in section 1.1 are given below:[10]

(1a)   put on there
(1b)   no wheels in slide
(1c)   this coffee
(1d)   want piece paper
(1e)   I get Patsy pocketbook
(1f)   Jenny is going to eat this blocks
(1g)   Jenny play with Jenny
(1h)   I'm open it
(1i)   no lamb have a chair either

Sentence (1a) is missing a subject and the direct object argument of *put*, as a result of the MUP being set to [+uniform]. Sentences (1b) and (1c) are missing a copula, as a result of the settings: [–Infl-present] and [–Case-marking]. In sentence (1d) the preposition *of* is missing in the partitive *piece of paper*, as a result of Case marking being nonfunctional, and in (1e) the genitive morpheme, *'s*, was not inserted after *Patsy* for the same reason. Sentences (1f–h) demonstrate that agreement is not mandatory in the child's grammar. Sentences (1f–g) demonstrate incorrect Specifier-Head agreement, between *this* and *blocks* in (1f) and between *Jenny* and *play* in (1g), while (1h) shows incorrect Head-Head agreement. Sentences (1b) and (1c) demonstrate that Infl has not been hypothesized at this stage in the child's grammar, and so the child does not get the negative particle properly ordered with respect to the rest of the sentence.

Utterances taken from the post null-subject stage (2a–f), by comparison, show a marked improvement. Sentential subjects are used in most obligatory contexts (2a–e), the copula is fully productive (2a–d), overt abstract Case is being assigned regularly (2d–f), *to* is being used to mark infinitives (2c), and auxiliaries are beginning to be used (2b–c, e–f). The child does make some ungrammatical utterances under the new parameter assignment however—I will deal with approaches to characterizing the child's ungrammatical utterances in section 7.

(2a)   this is a car
(2b)   they are going shopping
(2c)   I am going to take this blocks
(2d)   that's Patsy's pills
(2e)   I can't reach it
(2f)   I am putting the rest of them

3. OBJECTIVES

The main objectives in carrying out this experiment are twofold: to empirically test the predictions made by the above parametric model, and to test the generality of the parsing model. The acquisition model should ideally describe the child's production competence at each stage of development. By parsing the child's spontaneous utterances, the accuracy of this model can be empirically tested, both before and after the parameters are believed to have been set. Furthermore, the generality of the parsing model is tested by observing the effects of parameterization on the parser's performance.

It is hypothesized that when the above four parameters are given their initial settings, the parser should be able to successfully parse a significant portion of the child's spontaneous utterances from the null subject stage, but relatively few utterances from the post null-subject stage,[11] and when the parameters are switched to the adult settings, the parser should successfully parse relatively few utterances from the null-subject stage, but a significant number of utterances from the post null-subject stage. The reverse is not exactly analogous. Since the child's parameter settings represent a less constrained grammar than the adult settings, it is reasonable to expect that a large number of the post null-subject stage utterances will be parsable with the initial parameter settings. The crucial point here, however, is that some of the child's utterances from the latter stage will not be parsable, and it is these utterances that provide positive evidence for the child that one cannot use the earlier settings. For instance, if the child utters a sentence such as *I will do it*, the child cannot parse this sentence without first having [±Infl-present] set to [+Infl-present]. If it is set to [−Infl-present] then the child has no means of analyzing the auxiliary *will* without postulating some special, ad hoc mechanism, which would have to be later unlearned—clearly an undesirable result. Consequently, the analysis of auxiliaries provides the child with the positive evidence that he needs to set [±Infl-present] to [+Infl-present].[12]

4. PROCEDURE

For this experiment, four sets of approximately 50 sentences each from Peter and four sets of data from Nina were parsed, each taken from samples made at intervals of approximately four weeks. Each of the samples was parsed using three different sets of parameter values—one in which each of the parameters listed above was given its initial setting (the setting hypothesized for the child's earliest stages), that is [+uniform, −Infl-present, −Case-marking, −Agreement], one in which each of the parameters was given its target (adult) setting, that is [−uniform, +Infl-present, +Case-marking, +Agreement], and finally one in which all parameters but Agreement are given their adult setting, that is [−uniform, +Infl-present, +Case-marking, −Agreement]. This third setting was used to attempt to isolate the contribution of agreement to the child's growing mastery of the language.

It is not necessary, and, indeed, not meaningful to test *all* possible parameter combinations because many of them are not empirically justified. The initial setting must be tested because this is the state of the child's early grammar, by hypothesis. This setting turns out to be well substantiated, as will be seen in section 6. Similarly, the adult state must be tested because it is the eventual state which all language learners will attain. Some parameter settings do not justify testing, however, since they represent incompatible parameter settings. For instance, the combination of −Infl-present and +Case-marking would conflict, because Case is assigned to the subject of a sentence by a tensed Infl. Furthermore, it must be noted that most parameters represent a more-restrictive to less-restrictive dichotomy. By testing the child's utterances with the adult setting, we are testing the most restrictive combination of parameters. I believe that testing intermediate settings would not offer any significant insight into the child's progress towards the adult state.[13] Intermediate parameter settings did not highlight any rational changes in the children's grammars.

Finally, the initial parameter setting was tested with differing assumptions about the lexical items. In one instance, contractions (such as *I'm* and *wanna*) were not expanded, while in the other test they are expanded. The justification for this is given in section 5.

5. ASSUMPTIONS

I have made a number of important assumptions and limitations to the scope of this experiment, in order to focus the field of inquiry. They are as follows:

–In general, only simple sentences are being considered. I have not pruned any sentences on the grounds of complexity (such as depth of embedding), however, the sentences spontaneously produced by the subjects around the null-subject stage were quite simple, lacking subordinate clauses, relative clauses and complex noun phrases, and so this type of pruning was not necessary.

–Due to parser limitations, I have not attempted to consider several types of sentences: those containing *Wh*-questions (because gap positing was not implemented in the parser at the time of the experiment); those containing verb-particle constructions; and sentences utilizing colloquialisms (which are relatively rare in the data that was considered).

–I have eliminated subjectless imperatives from this investigation since, to a parser lacking a pragmatic context for these sentences, they are indistinguishable from null-subject sentences.

–Two types of repetition have also been excluded from study—exact, or near exact repetition of an adult's utterance and immediate repetition of the same constituent by the child. I believe, following Pinker (1984), that repetition of an adult's utterance is not instructive of the child's grammatical knowledge, and that immediate repetition of a constituent (*e.g.*, *Good boy. Good boy. Good boy Jenny. Good boy.*) is simply a speech act that is more properly addressed in a theory of pragmatics.

–All contractions have been entered into the parser's lexicon in two ways—as single syntactic units and as their proper expansions— either an auxiliary and a subject or an auxiliary and a negative marker. So, for instance, *I'm* is entered as the single lexical unit *I'm* and as a combination of *I* and *am*. The latter entry is made under the assumption that the grammatical function of a contraction in the adult grammar is equivalent with the function of its subparts, and that the contraction is just a speech act. The former entry is made under the assumption that many lexical entries are initially misclassified by the child, and are not used productively. Bellugi (1967) notes this phenomenon in the acquisition of negation—specifically the acquisition of the apparent negated auxiliaries *can't* and *don't*. She notes that the equivalent auxiliaries *can* and *do* have not been acquired by the child at the time that they are using *can't* and *don't*, and concludes that these auxiliaries are actually being analyzed as negative markers by the child. By the current account, since the child in the null-subject stage does not have Infl as a distinct category, the child cannot analyze auxiliary verbs that reside in Infl, and so must analyze contracted elements as some other category. So, for instance, when Peter says things like *I'm write too* or *I'm do it*, he seems to be using *I'm* as an unanalyzed lexical subject.

–All utterances where there is no obvious predication have been removed from consideration. For example, if the child simply said *a block*, in response to the question *What are you playing with?*, then the child's utterance, by itself, contains no apparent predication (the predication is pragmatically determined). Once again, this type of utterance is not a simple grammatical phenomenon, and thus has been removed from consideration.

–Conjunctive structures have not been considered, since they are not yet implemented in the parser, and, more importantly, they shed no light on the questions being investigated. Consequently, a sentence such as *I see Nana and Bill* would be shortened to *I see Nana* for this study, without loss of generality.

In addition, I do not consider phonological problems alone to indicate ungrammaticality. So, for instance, when Peter says *a egg*, I treat that as a grammatical utterance.

RICK KAZMAN

6. RESULTS

The results are presented in table I for Peter and table II for Nina. Each line of the table shows, for each child, the number of sentences parsed correctly out of the total number of sentences in the sample at a given age and given parameter settings. The columns refer to the different parameter settings in the parser: the initial setting is [+uniform, −Infl-present, −Case-marking, −Agreement]; 'initial without contraction' refers to the initial settings, as above, but with contracted elements being expanded—that is, *I'm* would be expanded to *I am*, irrespective of the setting of [±Infl-present]; the adult setting is [−uniform, +Infl-present, +Case-marking, +Agreement]; 'adult without agreement' refers to the adult settings, except that [±Agreement] is set to [−Agreement].

Table I

Results for Peter

Age	Initial Setting	Initial w/o Contraction	Adult Setting	Adult w/o Agreement
2-1-18	50/50 (100%)	45/50 (90.0%)	7/50 (14.0%)	13/50 (26.0%)
2-3-3	50/53 (94.3%)	21/53 (39.6%)	34/53 (64.2%)	42/53 (79.2%)
2-4-15	47/53 (88.7%)	23/53 (43.4%)	30/53 (56.6%)	38/53 (71.7%)
2-5-22	45/51 (88.2%)	15/51 (29.4%)	41/51 (80.4%)	47/51 (92.2%)

Table II

Results for Nina

Age	Initial Setting	Initial w/o Contraction	Adult Setting	Adult w/o Agreement
2-0-24	56/56 (100%)	40/56 (71.4%)	16/56 (28.6%)	30/56 (53.6%)
2-1-15	53/57 (92.9%)	37/57 (64.9%)	29/57 (50.8%)	38/57 (66.7%)
2-2-14	64/67 (95.6%)	43/67 (64.2%)	20/67 (29.9%)	33/67 (49.3%)
2-3-18	45/52 (86.6%)	30/52 (57.7%)	36/52 (69.2%)	43/52 (82.7%)

7. DISCUSSION

These results suggest that the parameterized acquisition model and the parsing model that has been presented adequately account for the child data facts. With the initial setting of the parameters, we are able to parse 100% of the children's early utterances, and progressively fewer of the subsequent files. This suggests that the initial parameter settings adequately characterize the children's early utterances, but are progressively less and less appropriate for parsing their later utterances. This is mainly due to the child's use of material residing in Infl: auxiliaries, copulas and infinitive-marking *to*. With the initial setting of the parameters there is no way of parsing these phenomena, since they cannot be assigned a representation.

When we disallow contractions from being treated as single lexical units, the inappropriateness of the initial settings becomes significantly more marked. It seems reasonable to treat contractions as complex lexical units by the second data file (when Peter is 2-3-3 and Nina is 2-1-15) and thereafter. This is because by this time, auxiliaries, copulas, and *to* are being used very frequently and with significant productivity. Analyzing, for instance, *can't* or *they're* as single lexical items appears to be inconsistent, since, by this time the child is productively using other material in Infl, such as *can* and *are*. For example, the following sentences are taken from Peter at 2-3-3:

(3a)   I can put it to my head
(3b)   these are tapes
(3c)   this is not a toy
(3d)   I want to blow

As expected, then, when we disallow contractions from being treated as single lexical items in the data samples, the degradation in the performance of the initial settings becomes quite marked for Peter, dropping from 90.0% at 2-1-18 to a 39.6% success rate at age 2-3-3. At the same time, however, Peter's success rate of parsing with the adult settings increases significantly, from 14% in the initial sample to 64.2% in the next sample, climbing to 80.4% in the final sample.

The changes for Nina are not quite as dramatic[14] but they are still highly significant, ranging from 71.4% at 2-0-24 to 57.7% at 2-3-18 for the child settings with contractions disallowed. Similarly, her performance with the adult settings improves dramatically, from 28.6% at 2-0-24 to 69.2% at 2-3-18.

The changes between the first two samples for both children are, however, the most striking, since they appear to coincide with a parametric change in the child's knowledge of the structure of his language. The utility of the adult settings increases dramatically—from 14% to 64.2% for Peter and 28.6% to 50.8% for Nina. In fact, Peter shows a statistically significant jump in performance in just three weeks (in a data sample not reported here). This argues that the changes are, in fact, parametric, since a simple developmental theory would predict a smooth increase in linguistic abilities, lacking dramatic discontinuities in performance.

Considering the initial assumption that a child will always produce grammatical utterances, it must explained why the children produce significant numbers of ungrammatical utterances with the adult parameter settings, even *after* the child has apparently begun to switch to these settings. At first, I considered the possibility that the differences in grammaticality were due to agreement problems. This is evidently not the case, since toggling the [±Agreement] parameter produced increases in grammaticality of 11.8–19.4% throughout all the samples. That is, relaxing the restriction on agreement does not seem to favor one stage of acquisition over another. Given that the agreement process does not appear to develop independently of the other parameters, several other possible scenarios remain: that parameters are models of probabilistic processes, rather than on/off switches; that syntactic acquisition is too tightly intertwined with lexical acquisition to be able to distinguish the effects of each; or that the parametric model has not characterized the child's grammar to a sufficient level of granularity. So, for instance, when Peter utters the sentences *I making it* and *I'm taping this* in quick succession, one must determine whether this inconsistency is best modeled as a lexical misclassification, as a syntactic parameter setting with probability of < 1.0, as a phonological problem, or as some other parametric change.

Just as Chomsky (1965) claims that an instantaneous model of acquisition (one in which the learner evaluates all possible grammars together and chooses the best one) is a scientific idealization, so too we claim that the instantaneous setting of a single parameter must be an idealization. It is unreasonable to expect a child to acquire even a single grammatical phenomenon at a particular instant in time, and from that moment onwards use it correctly and consistently, in all contexts, concurrent with acquiring other parameters and large numbers of new lexical items. Children are acquiring all of language—syntax, semantics, phonetics, lexicon—in parallel, and so misclassifications, over- and undergeneralizations and uncertain behavior are bound to occur. When viewed in this light, a probabilistic model of parameter setting (and of lexical acquisition) seems unavoidable. The parametric model can, of course, be simultaneously refined, but the requirement that simple on/off parameters account for 100% of the child's language at any given moment of acquisition is unreasonably stringent.

This is seen more clearly when the data is examined closely: Nina, for instance, consistently misclassifies certain pronouns, using *my* for *I*, *her* for *she*, and *him* for *he*. This accounts for a significant portion of her ungrammatical utterances at age 2-2-14 and 2-3-18.

8. CONCLUSIONS AND FUTURE DIRECTIONS

I believe that the value of a parsing model for empirically testing the claims of acquisition models is well attested by the results presented here. The parsing model serves two purposes: to determine whether a proposed parametric configuration can account for a child's spontaneous utterances at some stage of development and to determine whether the change from one setting to another occurs quickly enough to be thought of as a parametric change. The results of this experiment indicate that both the model of parsing and the model of language acquisition are empirically justified, in that they correctly predicted and modeled the types and timing of changes in grammaticality which the child would undergo.

Certainly, more work is needed along these same lines. I am currently investigating the use of this model with other languages, for instance. Furthermore, other claims for parametric acquisition could easily be modeled by this approach—for example, the acquisition of binding theory.

Furthermore, other changes may be modeled which have not received a significant amount of attention as parametric phenomena. For example, the agreement parameter may be broken down into subparameters, such as Specifier-Head vs. Head-Head agreement, or tense vs. number vs. person (as has been suggested by Shlonsky, 1989). In this way, it may be determined whether agreement is acquired parametrically (if a significant increase in mastery of one parameter can be demonstrated), or whether it is simply an item by item lexical acquisition process (in which one would expect more gradual increases in the child's proficiency).

Finally, the parsing model of acquisition must be examined in connection with a model of lexical acquisition, to account for the data that slips between the cracks (I discuss this possibility in Kazman, 1989). It appears that the parametric approach, while accounting for a significant amount of the acquisition data in a highly principled fashion, has no detailed explanation of the data that does not fit. If, after all, a parameter is supposed to be acquired at a certain point in time, why do children universally show some proclivity to produce 'ungrammatical' utterances (that is, utterances that are not predicted under the new parameter setting) for a significant amount of time thereafter? The answer lies, I believe, in a detailed model of lexical acquisition.

NOTES

[1] Of course, other facets of language must be learned, but it is proposed that the core grammar of any language can be described by a particular parameter setting.

[2] The precise meaning of acquiring a parameter is not treated in this chapter. For the purposes of this exposition parameters are idealized as Chomsky has suggested. In outlining the cognitive machinery necessary for acquisition, Chomsky admits that what he has described is "an idealization in which only the moment of acquisition of the correct grammar is considered" Chomsky (1965, p. 202). I claim that even to speak of a 'moment of acquisition' is an idealization: acquisition can be better characterized as a series of successive approximations to an ideal: the adult state of competence. This idea is explored in some detail in Kazman (1989). In that paper, I suggest an alternative model for the acquisition of parameters, which more exactly models the gradual acquisition of grammatical phenomena.

[3] The model described by these parameter settings is simply a model of the child's linguistic performance, and should not be taken be a model of its linguistic competence, which typically exceeds production capabilities.

[4] In Kazman (1989), I follow Pollock (1989) and Chomsky (1989) in assuming that the information contained in Infl is better characterized as two distinct $\overline{X}$ nodes, T(ense) phrase and Agr(eement) phrase. For the purposes of the exposition here, however, little hinges on the distinction.

[5] I take thematic relations to be the underlying structure of the child's utterances, in the same way that D-structure represents the base structure of utterances in the adult's grammar. In fact, it may be argued that the child's mapping from D-structure to S-structure is simply the identity relation.

[6] The higher observed frequency of dropped subjects, relative to objects, may be due to prosodic constraints, as suggested by Gerken (1989).

[7] This characterization is not complete because it does not take into account the acquisition of the lexicon.

[8] The Case filter states that a lexical noun phrase must receive abstract Case. The θ-criterion states that all arguments must receive exactly one thematic role and that all thematic roles must be assigned.

[9] It was, in fact, simple to implement the parameters suggested in Kazman (1988):

since CPP is a modular parser, toggling a parameter needs only to be effected in the module appropriate to it. Setting a Case assignment parameter, for example, needs only to be done in the Case module.

[10] The data used in this study was taken from the CHILDES database (see MacWhinney and Snow, 1985). In particular, the utterances of Peter, taken from the Bloom study (Bloom, 1973), and the utterances of Nina, taken from the Suppes study (Suppes, 1973) were used.

[11] The post null-subject stage, it should be noted, does not necessarily coincide with the adult grammar. This is because the child has not yet set all relevant parameters, and the lexical acquisition process is far from complete. It does, however, seem to be a watershed—at this stage the child has mastered the basic form of his language—word order, Case marking, agreement and pro-drop facts.

[12] This analysis does not explain *why* auxiliaries are acquired at this point, but simply accounts for the observed fact of their acquisition in a principled way.

[13] This was confirmed in independent tests (not reported here).

[14] Although Nina appears to have been a slightly more advance language learner in some respects, her parametric change occurred more slowly than did Peter's.

REFERENCES

Anderson, J: 1975, 'Computer Simulation of a Language Acquisition System: a First Report,' in R. Solso, (ed.), *Information Processing and Cognition: The Loyola Symposium*, Lawrence Erlbaum, Washington, D.C.

Bellugi, U.: 1967, *The Acquisition of Negation*, Ph.D. dissertation, Department of Psychology and Social Science, Harvard University, Cambridge, Massachusetts.

Berwick, R.: 1985, *The Acquisition of Syntactic Knowledge*, MIT Press, Cambridge, Massachusetts.

Bloom, L.: 1973, *One Word at a Time*, Mouton, The Hague.

Chomsky, N.: 1965, *Aspects of the Theory of Syntax*, MIT Press, Cambridge, Massachusetts.

Chomsky, N.: 1981, *Lectures on Government and Binding*, Foris, Dordrecht, Holland.

Chomsky, N.: 1986, *Barriers*, MIT Press, Cambridge, Massachusetts.

Chomsky, N.: 1988, 'Some Notes on Economy of Derivation and Representation', in I. Laka and A. Mahajan (eds.), *MIT Working Papers in Linguistics 10: Functional Heads and Clause Structure*, Department of Linguistics and Philosophy, Massachusetts Institute of Technology, Cambridge, Massachusetts, pp. 43–74.

Gibson, E. and R. Clark: 1988, 'A Parallel Model for Adult Sentence Processing', unpublished manuscript, Carnegie Mellon University, Pittsburgh, Pennsylvania.

Gerken, L.: 1989, 'A Prosodic Account of Children's Subjectless Sentences', *Proceedings of the 20th Annual Meeting of the New England Linguistics Society (NELS)*.

Gibson, E.: 1987, 'Garden-path Effects in a Parser with Parallel Architecture', in A. Miller and J. Powers (eds.), *Proceedings of the 1987 Eastern States Conference*

256   RICK KAZMAN

on Linguistics, Ohio State University Press, Ohio State University, Columbus, Ohio, pp. 88–99.

Hyams, N.: 1987, 'The Setting of the Null Subject Parameter: A Reanalysis', paper presented at the *Boston University Conference on Child Language Development*, Boston University, Boston, Massachusetts.

Jaeggli, O. and K. Safir: 1987, 'The Null Subject Parameter and Parametric Theory', in O. Jaeggli and K. Safir (eds.), *The Null Subject Parameter*, Reidel, Dordrecht, Holland, pp. 1–44.

Kazman, R.: 1988, 'Null Arguments and the Acquisition of Case and Infl', paper presented at the *Boston University Conference on Child Language Development*, Boston University, Boston, Massachusetts.

Kazman, R.: 1989, 'The Induction of the Lexicon and the Early Stages of Grammar', unpublished manuscript, Carnegie Mellon University, Pittsburgh, Pennsylvania.

MacWhinney, B. and C. Snow: 1985, 'The Child Language Data Exchange System', *Journal of Computational Linguistics* **12**, 271–296.

Pinker, S.: 1984, *Language Learnability and Language Development*, Harvard University Press, Cambridge, Massachusetts.

Pollock, J.: 1989, 'Verb Movement, Universal Grammar, and the Structure of IP', *Linguistic Inquiry* **20**, 365–424.

Roeper, T. and E. Williams (eds.): 1987, *Parameter Setting*, Reidel, Dordrecht, Holland.

Selfridge, M.: 1980, 'A Computer Model of Child Language Learning', *Proceedings of the 1st Annual Conference of the American Association for Artificial Intelligence*, pp. 224–227.

Shlonsky, U.: 1989, 'Representing Agreement in Syntax', paper given to the University of Pittsburgh Department of Linguistics, University of Pittsburgh, Pittsburgh, Pennsylvania.

Suppes, P.: 1973, 'The Semantics of Children's Language', *American Psychologist*, 103–114.

Software Engineering Institute,
Carnegie Mellon University,
Pittsburgh, Pennsylvania 15213-3890, U.S.A.

STEVEN P. ABNEY

PARSING BY CHUNKS

1. INTRODUCTION

I begin with an intuition: when I read a sentence, I read it a chunk at a time. For example, the previous sentence breaks up something like this:

(1) [I begin] [with an intuition]: [when I read] [a sentence],
    [I read it] [a chunk] [at a time]

These chunks correspond in some way to prosodic patterns. It appears, for instance, that the strongest stresses in the sentence fall one to a chunk, and pauses are most likely to fall between chunks. Chunks also represent a grammatical watershed of sorts. The typical chunk consists of a single content word surrounded by a constellation of function words, matching a fixed template. A simple context-free grammar is quite adequate to describe the structure of chunks. By contrast, the relationships *between* chunks are mediated more by lexical selection than by rigid templates. Co-occurrence of chunks is determined not just by their syntactic categories, but is sensitive to the precise words that head them; and the order in which chunks occur is much more flexible than the order of words within chunks.

The work I would like to describe is an attempt to give content to these intuitions, and to show that parsing by chunks has distinct processing advantages, advantages that help explain why the human parser might adopt a chunk-by-chunk strategy.

2. CHUNKS

There is psychological evidence for the existence of chunks. Gee and Grosjean (1983) examine what they call *performance structures*. These are structures of word clustering that emerge from a variety of types of experimental data, such as pause durations in reading, and naive sentence diagramming. Gee and Grosjean argue that performance structures are best predicted by what they call ϕ-phrases. ϕ-phrases are

257

R. C. Berwick et al. (eds.),
Principle-Based Parsing: Computation and Psycholinguistics, 257–278.
© 1991 *Kluwer Academic Publishers. Printed in the Netherlands.*

created by breaking the input string after each syntactic head that is a content word (with the exception that function words syntactically associated with a preceding content word—in particular, object pronouns—group with the preceding content word). The chunks of sentence (1) are ϕ-phrases.

Unfortunately, Gee and Grosjean must make some undesirable syntactic assumptions. For example, they assume that prenominal adjectives do not qualify as syntactic heads—otherwise, phrases like *a big dog* would not comprise one chunk, but two. Also, Gee and Grosjean do not assign syntactic structure to chunks. To remedy these deficiencies, I assume that a chunk has syntactic structure, which comprises a connected subgraph[1] of the sentence's parse-tree, and I define chunks in terms of *major heads*. Major heads are all content words except those that appear between a function word f and the content word that f selects.[2,3] For example, *proud* is a major head in *a man proud of his son*, but *proud* is not a major head in *the proud man*, because it appears between the function word *the* and the content word *man* selected by *the*.

The parse tree segments associated with some sample chunks are illustrated in (2).

(2)

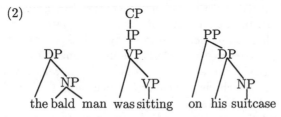

They are determined as follows. Let h be a major head. The root of the chunk headed by h is the highest node in the parse tree for which h is the *s-head*, that is, the 'semantic' head. Intuitively, the s-head of a phrase is the most prominent word in the phrase. For example, the verb is the s-head of a sentence, the noun is the s-head of a noun phrase or prepositional phrase, and the adjective is the s-head of an adjective phrase. The s-head is not necessarily the same as the syntactic head. In Government-Binding (GB) theory, for example, an abstract element Infl (Inflection), not the verb, is taken to be the head of the sentence, and the complementizer (C) is often taken to be the head of an embedded sentence (CP). (See Chomsky, 1986, for example.) P is generally taken to be the head of PP, not the noun. And under the DP-analysis (Abney

1987), which I adopt, the determiner is the head of the noun phrase, and a degree element, not the adjective, is the head of the adjective phrase. S-heads can be defined in terms of syntactic heads, however, as follows. If the syntactic head h of a phrase P is a content word, h is also the s-head of P. If h is a function word, the s-head of P is the s-head of the phrase selected by h.

The parse tree T_C of a chunk C is a subgraph of the global parse tree T. The root r of T_C is the highest node whose s-head is the content word defining C. For example, in (2), *man*, *sitting*, and *suitcase* are the major heads. $r = $ DP is the highest node whose s-head is *man*; $r = $ IP is the highest node whose s-head is *sitting*; and $r = $ PP is the highest node whose s-head is *suitcase*. T_C is the largest subgraph of T dominated by r that does not contain the root of another chunk. In (2), the parse tree of *man*'s chunk is the subtree rooted in DP. The parse tree of *sitting*'s chunk is the subtree rooted in CP (*i.e.*, the entire global parse tree) with the subtrees under DP and PP excised. The parse tree of *suitcase*'s chunk is the subtree rooted in PP.

There is a single special case. Terminal nodes are excluded from a chunk if their inclusion would cause the chunk to have a discontinuous frontier. Examples of such 'orphan nodes' are complementizers, where the subject intervenes between the complementizer and the rest of the verb chunk, and some prepositions, where they are separated from the rest of the noun chunk by an intervening possessor. For example:

(3)

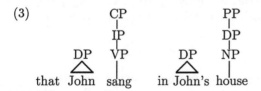

ϕ-phrases are generated from chunks by sweeping orphaned words into an adjacent chunk. As a consequence, ϕ-phrases, unlike chunks, do not always span connected subgraphs of the parse tree. In (3), for example, *that John* constitutes a ϕ-phrase; but syntactically, the phrase *that John* contains two unconnected fragments. The correspondence between prosodic units and syntactic units is not direct, but mediated by chunks. ϕ-phrases are elements in a prosodic level of representation. Chunks and global parse trees are elements of two different levels of syntactic representation. Global parse trees and ϕ-phrases are both calculated from chunks, but neither global parse trees nor ϕ-phrases are calculated from the other.

A final issue regarding the definition of chunks is the status of pronouns. On the one hand, we would like a clean division between the grammar of chunks and the grammar of interchunk relations. Since pronouns function syntactically like noun chunks—in particular, they can fill subject and object positions—we would like to consider them chunks. On the other hand, they are generally stressless, suggesting that they not be treated as separate chunks (we did not treat them as separate chunks in (1), for example). A reasonable solution is to consider them to be lexical noun phrases, and assign them the same status as orphaned words. At the level of chunks, they are orphaned words, belonging to no chunk. At the level of ϕ-phrases, they are swept into an adjacent chunk. And at the level of syntax, they are treated like any other noun phrase.

We are now in a position to be more specific about *which* adjacent chunk orphaned words are swept into. If the orphaned word takes a complement, it is swept into the nearest chunk in the direction of its complement (*i.e.*, the following chunk). Otherwise it is swept into the nearest chunk in the direction of its syntactic governor. For example, pronouns are function words that do not take complements. (To the best of my knowledge, they are the only function words that do not take complements.) Subject pronouns are swept into the following chunk, and object pronouns are swept into the preceding chunk.

The reader can verify that the units marked in (1) are ϕ-phrases (not chunks), in accordance with the definitions given in this section.

3. STRUCTURE OF THE PARSER

A typical natural language parser processes text in two stages. A tokenizer/morphological analyzer converts a stream of characters into a stream of words, and the parser proper converts a stream of words into a parsed sentence, or a stream of parsed sentences. In a *chunking parser*, the syntactic analyzer is decomposed into two separate stages, which I call the *chunker* and the *attacher*. The chunker converts a stream of words into a stream of chunks, and the attacher converts the stream of chunks into a stream of sentences.

The attacher's name is derived from the manner in which it assembles chunks into a complete parse tree. It *attaches* one chunk to another by adding missing arcs between parse tree nodes. In (2), for example, the attacher must add an arc from the IP node to the DP node dominating *the bald man*, and it must add an arc from the lower VP node to the PP node.

To illustrate the action of these three stages, the following are the streams output by each when parsing the sentence,

> *The effort to establish such a conclusion of course must have two foci, the study of the rocks and the study of the sun.*
> (taken from Williams, 1986)

Words:

{[Det the]} {[N effort]} {[Inf-To to] [P to]} {[V establish]} {[Predet such] [Det such] [Pron such]} {[Det a]} {[N conclusion]} {[Adv of course]} {[N must] [V must]} {[V have]} {[Num two]} {[N foci]} {[Comma ,]} $\cdots$

Words are sets of *readings*. Readings, but not words, have unique syntactic categories, feature-sets, and so forth. There is no one-one correspondence between words and pieces of text separated by whitespace. For example, we permit words with embedded whitespace, such as *of course*.

Chunks:

[DP [Det the] [NP [N effort]]]
[CP-Inf [IP-Inf [Inf-To to] [VP [V establish]]]]
[DP [Predet such] [Det a] [NP [N conclusion]]]
[CP [IP [AdvP [Adv of course]] [Modal will] [VP [V have]]]]
[DP [NP [Num two] [N foci]]]
[Comma ,]
[DP [Det the] [NP [N study]]]
[PP [P of] [DP [Det the] [NP [N rocks]]]]
$\cdots$

Lexical ambiguity is often resolvable within chunks, as seen here. Single-word chunks represent a common exception. A single word does not provide enough context to resolve lexical ambiguity.

Parse: [CP [IP [DP the effort [CP-Inf to establish
                              [DP such a conclusion]]]
          [VP of course must have [DP two foci]]
          [Appos [DP [DP the study [PP-of of the rocks]]
                 [Conj and]
                 [DP the study [PP-of of the sun]]]]]]]

I have omitted chunk-internal nodes that are not themselves the roots
of chunks, to make it clear what structure the attacher itself has built.
In fact, though, there is no distinction in the final parse between nodes
built by the chunker and nodes built by the attacher.

4. CHUNKER

The chunker is a nondeterministic version of an LR parser (Knuth, 1965)
employing a best-first search. I first give a brief description of LR parsing, for those unfamiliar with it. (A much more detailed discussion can
be found in Aho and Ullman 1972; see also Stabler, this volume.)

4.1. *LR Parsing*

An LR parser is a deterministic bottom-up parser. It is possible to
automatically generate an LR parser for any of a large class of context-
free grammars. The parser *shifts* words from the input string onto the
stack until it recognizes a sequence of words matching the right-hand
side of a rule from the grammar. At that point, it *reduces* the sequence
to a single node, whose category is given in the left-hand side of the rule.
    For example, consider the grammar,

Rule 1.   S → NP VP
Rule 2.   NP → Det N
Rule 3.   NP → N
Rule 4.   VP → V NP

Suppose the input is N V N. The parser shifts the first N onto the stack.
It recognizes the right-hand side of rule 3, and reduces N to NP. It
continues as follows:

Stack	Input	Action
[ ]	N V N	SH N
[N]	V N	RE NP→N
[NP]	V N	SH V
[NP V]	N	SH N
[NP V N]		RE NP→N
[NP V NP]		RE VP→V NP
[NP VP]		RE S→NP VP
[S]		Accept

Control is mediated by *LR states*, which are kept on a separate control stack.[4] LR states correspond to sets of items. An item is a rule with a dot marking how much of the rule has already been seen. An example of an item set is:

$$(4) \quad \begin{bmatrix} VP \to V \bullet NP \\ VP \to V \bullet S \\ NP \to \bullet Det\ N \\ NP \to \bullet N \\ S \to \bullet NP\ VP \end{bmatrix}$$

The kernel of an item set is the set of items with some category preceding the dot. In (4), the kernel is [VP → V•NP, VP → V•S]. The rest of the item set can be generated from the kernel, by adding items for every expansion of every category after a dot. In (4), we add NP → •N, NP → •Det N because of the NP after the dot in VP → V•NP. N and Det, which follow the dot in the new items, generate no new items, because they are terminals. VP → V•S generates the item S → •NP VP. The NP after the dot generates the items NP → •N, NP → •Det N, but since they are already present, nothing changes.

Item sets control the computation as follows. If a terminal symbol follows the dot in some item, a shift on a word of that category is legal. For example, if (4) is at the top of the control stack, we may shift on either Det or N. Suppose we shift an N. The kernel of the new item set is determined by stepping over the N in any item in which an N follows the dot. In this case, the new kernel is [NP → N•]. (Since there are no nonterminals following any dot, this kernel happens to be the entire item set.)

When the dot is at the end of some rule, a reduction is permitted on that rule. To continue our example, the item set [NP → N•] calls for reduction of N to NP. We pop n elements off both the control stack and the parse tree stack, where n is the number of children in the recognized rule. In this case, $n = 1$. This brings (4) back to the top of the control stack. Now we build an NP and push it onto the parse tree stack, and we determine the kernel of the new state by stepping over NP in any items in (4) with an NP after the dot. The new kernel is [VP → V NP•, S → NP•VP]. We push the corresponding state onto the control stack. The configuration now is:

	Control Stack		Parse Stack
$\begin{bmatrix} \text{VP} \to \text{V•NP} \\ \text{VP} \to \text{V•S} \\ \text{NP} \to \text{•Det N} \\ \text{NP} \to \text{•N} \\ \text{S} \to \text{•NP VP} \end{bmatrix}$		$\begin{bmatrix} \text{VP} \to \text{V NP •} \\ \text{S} \to \text{NP•VP} \\ \text{VP} \to \text{•V NP} \\ \text{VP} \to \text{•V S} \end{bmatrix}$	V NP

Now we have a conflict: we may either reduce by rule VP → V NP (because of the item VP → V NP•), or shift a V (because of the items VP → •V NP and VP → •V S). In this case, lookahead decides the conflict. We shift if the next word is a V, and reduce if there is no input left. In other cases, lookahead does not resolve the conflict, and we have a genuine next-action conflict. The *LR grammars* are those context-free grammars that do not generate next-action conflicts; they can be parsed deterministically by an LR parser.

4.2. *Grammar*

In the current implementation, I am using the (toy) grammar for chunks shown in figure 1.

The lexicon includes *'s* and possessive pronouns in category D (Determiner). Modals and *to* are in category Infl. Certain selectional constraints are imposed, though they are not represented in (5). For example, Aux imposes restrictions on its complement, and we must also guarantee that a DP whose determiner is *'s* does not appear in a PP chunk.

Grammar (5) is obviously incomplete; I present it here mostly for illustrative purposes. However, in its defense, it does contain the most common structures. Even though it represents only a small portion of a complete grammar for chunks, spotchecks of random text samples indicate that it covers most chunks occurring in natural text.

(5)

PP	$\rightarrow$ P DP
DP	$\rightarrow$ Predet? D? NP
DP	$\rightarrow$ QPPron
NP	$\rightarrow$ (Num | QP)? (AP (Comma? Conj? AP)*)? N^0
AP	$\rightarrow$ AdvP? A^0
QP	$\rightarrow$ AdvP? Q
QPPron	$\rightarrow$ AdvP? QPron
DegP	$\rightarrow$ AdvP? Deg AP
		AdvP? Deg AdvP
AdvP	$\rightarrow$ Adv? Adv
CP	$\rightarrow$ IP
IP	$\rightarrow$ (AdvP? Infl)? (VP | AuxP)
AuxP	$\rightarrow$ AdvP? Aux (VP | AuxP)
VP	$\rightarrow$ AdvP? V
PtcP	$\rightarrow$ AdvP? (Ing | En)
N^0	$\rightarrow$ N^0_{3sg} * N
N^0_{3sg}	$\rightarrow$ (A | Ing | En | Num | N_{3sg}) Hyphen N_{3sg}
A^0	$\rightarrow$ ((N_{3sg} | Adv) Hyphen)? (A | Ing | En)

Figure 1: The simple grammar for chunks used in the current implementation.

4.3.   *Nondeterminism in the Chunker*

The chunker is a nondeterministic version of the LR parser just described. There are two sources of nondeterminism in the chunker. First, the points at which chunks end are not explicitly marked in the word stream, leading to ambiguities involving chunks of different lengths. Second, a given word may belong to more than one category, leading to conflicts in which the chunker does not know *e.g.*, whether to shift the following word onto the stack as an N or as a V. As a result, if we graph the computation path of the chunker on a given input—that is, let each node be a snapshot of the chunker, and each arc be a parsing action—the result is not a line, but a tree. The chunker performs a best-first search through this tree of legal computations.

The aim of using best-first search is to approach deterministic parsing without losing robustness. The success of the Marcus parser and similar deterministic natural language parsers (*e.g.*, the Fidditch parser, Hindle, 1983) gives one cause to believe that a deterministic or near-deterministic parser for English is possible. However, Marcus-style deterministic parsing has two related drawbacks. First, the complexity of grammar development and debugging increases too rapidly. I believe this results partly from the use of a production-rule grammar format, and partly from the fact that grammatical and heuristic information are folded together indiscriminately. Second, if the parser's best initial guess at every choice point leads to a dead end, the parser simply fails. It is much preferable to separate heuristic information from grammatical information, and use a nondeterministic architecture. As heuristics improve, we approach deterministic parsing on non-garden path sentences. At the same time, sentences that are either genuine garden paths, or garden paths according to our imperfect heuristics, do not cause the parser to fail, but merely to slow down.

Nondeterminism is simulated straightforwardly in the chunker. A *configuration* is a snapshot of a computation. From each configuration, there are some number of possible next actions. The chunker builds one *task* for each possible next action. A task is a tuple that includes the current configuration, a next action, and a *score*. A score is an estimate of how likely it is that a given task will lead to the best parse. Tasks are placed in a priority queue according to their score.

For example, suppose we have the simple grammar

Chunk → NP
Chunk → VP
NP → N
VP → V

If the first word in the sentence is *water*, the chunker creates two tasks:

$(([\ ], [\ ], 0), [SH\ water_N\ [NP → N\bullet]], s_1)$

$(([\ ], [\ ], 0), [SH\ water_V\ [VP → V\bullet]], s_2)$

The first element in each task is the current configuration, $([\ ], [\ ], 0)$—*i.e.*, the control and parse stacks are empty and the current word is word 0. The second element is the action to be performed: either shift *water* onto the stack as an N and go to state $[NP → N\bullet]$, or shift *water* onto the stack as a V and go to state $[VP → V\bullet]$. The final element is the task's score. The two tasks are placed on the queue, with the best task first in the queue.

The chunker's main loop takes the best task from the queue, and makes that task's configuration be the current configuration. It executes the task's next action, producing a new configuration. Then a new set of tasks are computed for the new configuration, and placed on the priority queue, and the cycle repeats.

To continue our example, executing the first task yields configuration $([[NP → N\bullet]], [N], 1)$. There is only one possible next action, $[RE\ NP→ N]$, producing a single new task. Assuming its score is better than s_2, the new queue is:

$(([[NP → N\bullet]], [N], 1), [RE\ NP→ N], s_3)$

$(([\ ], [\ ], 0), [SH\ water_V\ [VP → V\bullet]], s_2)$

The parser will execute the reduction task next.

Scores for tasks are determined by the following factors:

1. Lexical frequencies

2. General category preferences: *e.g.*, prefer present participle to A, prefer N-N modification to adjectival modifier

3. LR-conflict resolution (*e.g.*, prefer shift to reduce)

4. Agreement: disagreement does not produce ungrammaticality, but dispreference

A score is a vector of length 4, one position for each factor. Values range from 0 to negative infinity, and represent log frequency, for the lexical frequency factor, and number of violations, for the other factors. The natural order on scores is a partial order: $s_1 < s_2$ iff $f_i(s_1) < f_i(s_2)$, for every factor $f_1 \ldots f_4$. This partial order can be embedded in a total order by assigning weights to each factor: $s_1 < s_2$ iff $\sum_i w_i f_i(s_1) < \sum_i w_i f_i(s_2)$. The weights are currently assigned arbitrarily, though a method for fixing them empirically is clearly desirable.

As is desirable for best-first search, scores decrease monotonically as the parse proceeds. This guarantees that the first solution found is a best solution. Namely, each task represents a tree of possible computations. By making the scoring function monotonic decreasing, we assure that solutions derivable from some task t have scores no better than t's score. Since the first solution found has a score at least as good as that of any task still on the queue,[5] and every task on the queue has a score at least as good as any solution derivable from it, the first solution found has a score at least as good as that of any other solution.

4.4. *Deciding Where a Chunk Ends*

There is a problem with deciding where a chunk ends, inasmuch as the ends of chunks, unlike the ends of sentences, are not marked in text. Given that, in general, a single chunk will not cover the entire input, we would like to return the most highly-valued chunk that covers some prefix of the input. A straightforward way to do that is to pretend that every word has an alternate reading as an end-of-input marker. (LR parsers treat end-of-input as a grammatical category, albeit a special one.)

Hallucinating end-of-input markers at every position in the string sounds absurdly expensive, but in fact it is not. One piece of information that we must keep with a task, whether we hallucinate end-of-input marks or not, is which subset of the readings of the lookahead word the task is legal on. For example, suppose we have just shifted the word *many* onto the stack as a Q, and the current configuration is:

(6) [[QP → Q•]], [Q], 1

(That is, [QP →Q•] is the sole LR state on the control stack, Q is the sole category on the parse stack, and the next word in the input is word 1.) The next word is *are*, let us say, which has two readings. It has a very common reading as a verb, and a very rare reading as a noun (a unit of measure of area). There is only one legal next action from configuration (6), namely, Reduce QP → Q. (This QP will ultimately be a modifier of the head noun *are*.) However, that reduction is legal only if the next word is a noun. Since the noun reading of *are* is rare, we should disprefer the task T calling for reduction by QP → Q. But we only know to disprefer T if we keep track of which subset of readings of the lookahead word T is legal on.

If we keep sets of lookahead readings with each task, we can slip fake end-of-input markers in among those lookahead readings. The only operations we perform which we would not have performed anyway are reductions that are legal *only* if the lookahead is a fake end-of-input marker. If we score such reductions relatively low (that is, if we prefer longer chunks to shorter chunks), it turns out that hallucinating end-of-input markers everywhere causes us to execute only a few tasks that we would not have executed otherwise.

The same technique is used for error recovery in the attacher. If it is not possible to get a parse for the entire sentence, the most highly-valued parse for some prefix of the input is returned. Since sentences often contain structures that were not anticipated in the grammar, and since we want to get as much information as possible even out of sentences we cannot completely parse, error recovery of this sort is very important.

5. ATTACHER

5.1. *Attachment Ambiguities and Lexical Selection*

The attacher's main job is dealing with attachment ambiguities. In basic construction, it is identical to the chunker. It simulates a nondeterministic LR parser, using the four heuristic factors given earlier. But in accordance with the importance of attachment ambiguity resolution, the attacher has two additional factors in its scores:

5. Prefer argument attachment, prefer verb attachment

6. Prefer low attachment

These factors are used to rate alternative attachment sites. Finding an attachment as argument is more important than finding an attachment as verb, so potential attachment sites are ranked as follows: attachment as verb argument (best), attachment as argument of nonverb, attachment as verb modifier, attachment as modifier of nonverb. The second factor is relative height of attachment sites, counted as number of sentence (IP) nodes below the attachment site in the rightmost branch of the tree at the time of attachment.

The attacher also has special machinery, in addition to the basic machinery that it shares with the chunker. Unlike the chunker, the attacher must deal with words' selectional properties. (Indeed, the fact that lexically-specified complements are frequently optional is precisely the source of most attachment ambiguities the attacher faces.) The lexical selectional properties of a head determine which phrases can co-occur with that head. A given word has a frameset, that is, a set of subcategorization frames. Each frame contains a list of slots, representing the arguments the head takes. There is a good deal of freedom in the order in which arguments appear, but there are also some constraints. For example, direct objects must appear first, and sentential complements must appear last. The current implementation of the attacher recognizes two positional constraints, namely, 'only appears first' (annotation on slot: <) or 'only appears last' (>). Arguments are also marked as obligatory (no extra annotation), optional (?), or iterable (*). For example, a typical subcategorization frame would be [DP<?, PP*, CP>], meaning that the word in question takes an optional direct object (which must be the first complement, if it appears at all), any number of PP's, and an obligatory final embedded clause.

In addition to frames, a frameset contains a specification of the adjuncts that can appear with the head in question. A 'fleshed-out' frame includes each of those adjuncts, in addition to the slots explicitly stored with it.

It is possible to convert a set of subcategorization frames into a set of context-free rules of the form XP → Y <args&modifiers>. Y is a specific lexical item of category X, and <args&modifiers> is some permutation of some fleshed-out frame of Y that does not violate any of the slot constraints.[6] Where there are n arguments and modifiers, there are 2^n such sequences, less those that violate some constraint. Thus, for a given word with m frames, there correspond $m \cdot 2^n$ context-free rules, less the ones that violate a constraint. In the worst case, we would have $p \cdot m \cdot 2^n$ such rules, where p is the number of words in the dictionary.

The actual number is much smaller, because words do fortunately group themselves into classes with respect to their subcategorization frames. However, even if the grammar that results from this approach is substantially smaller than $p \cdot m \cdot 2^n$, it almost certainly represents a larger grammar than is practical. It appears a better space-time tradeoff in this case to process subcategorization frames at run time, not at compile time. For this reason, in addition to LR machinery for handling rules that are insensitive to subcategorization, the attacher also has special facilities for dealing with subcategorization frames at run time.

Those facilities are as follows. Consider a word w with subcategorization frames. When we shift a chunk headed by w onto the stack, we suspend processing and look for complements of w. The general idea is to build a subgrammar on the fly that is looking for any category that could be the first complement of w, and parse that subgrammar. When we finish parsing the subgrammar—that is, when we execute an Accept action—the top node on the stack will be w's first complement. We attach it to w. Then we calculate the set of possible categories for the next complement of w, build another subgrammar, and parse it to get the next complement. We continue in this manner until there are no more potential complements, or until we (nondeterministically) decide to quit collecting complements. Then we resume where we had left off before collecting w's complements.

In more detail, we first calculate *frameset-first*(f), where f is w's frameset. *Frameset-first*(f) is the set of categories that can be the first category in some frame in f. For example, if w's frames are [DP<? PP*] and [PP* CP>?], *frameset-first*(f) = {DP, PP, CP}. We push a new initial LR state onto the stack, of the form [Start → •X_1, ..., Start → •X_n], where the X_i are the categories in *frameset-first*(f). If all frames contain only optional constituents, we also include an item Start → •. In our example, the new initial state is

$$(7) \quad \begin{bmatrix} \text{Start} \rightarrow \bullet \text{DP} \\ \text{Start} \rightarrow \bullet \text{PP} \\ \text{Start} \rightarrow \bullet \text{CP} \\ \text{Start} \rightarrow \bullet \end{bmatrix}$$

After pushing (7) onto the stack, we continue parsing. When we come to the point of executing an Accept action, the configuration is of form:

control: ...suspended parse... [Start → •X_i] [Start → X_i•]
parse: ... w X_i

At this point, instead of accepting, we attach X_i to w. That is, we pop X_i and w from the stack, make a copy of w that differs only in having X_i as new rightmost child, and push the copy of w back on the stack. We pop the top two states from the control stack, bringing us back to the configuration we were in before we suspended parsing to collect w's complements. Then we push a new initial state onto the stack that is generated as follows.

First, we calculate *frameset-next*(f, X_i), that is, a new frameset representing what remains of the frames after the slot of category X_i has been filled. We consider one frame at a time. If there is no slot for X_i in the frame, the frame is removed. If there is a slot, and it is not iterable, it is removed from the frame; if it is iterable, it remains in the frame. After the first slot is filled, all initial slots are removed. If a final slot is filled, the frame becomes empty. In our example, *frameset-next*(f, PP) = {[PP*], [PP*, CP>?]}, *frameset-next*(f, DP) = {[PP*]}, and *frameset-next*(f, CP) = {[ ]}.

After calculating the new frameset f', we build a new initial state from *frameset-first*(f') as before, and push it on the stack. For example, if we have just attached a DP to w, w's new frameset is [PP*], and the new initial state is [Start → •PP, Start → •].

When the new frameset contains only empty frames, or if we choose to Close (that is, reduce by Start → e), we are finished collecting w's complements. Instead of pushing a new initial state on the stack, we resume the parse we had suspended.

Attachment ambiguities show up as Shift-Close conflicts. Suppose we are parsing a sentence of form DP VP DP PP, where the PP may be attached either to the immediately preceding DP, or to the VP. At the point of conflict, the configuration is:

(8)   ctrl: ... [IP → DP•VP] [Start → •DP, •] [Start → •PP, •]
       parse: VP   DP

The conflict is whether to Close the DP, or to Shift the following PP. In general, Close is dispreferred, with the effect that low attachments are preferred. In certain cases, however, a higher attachment is preferred. For example, if VP's frameset permits a PP after the DP, Close is the preferred action from configuration (8), inasmuch as attachment to a verb is preferable to attachment to a noun. In general, to determine whether there is a more preferable high attachment, we need only look back through the stack for initial states. If the node corresponding to an initial state is a legal attachment site, and a more highly valued attachment site, then Close is preferred to Shift.

5.2. Attachment Ambiguities in the Chunker

I have asserted that the extra machinery for dealing with lexical selection and attachment ambiguities is only needed by the attacher. However, there are apparent examples of attachment ambiguity that arise within chunks, and it is important to explain why they do not require the machinery I have developed for the attacher.

For example, noun compounds have the property that any binary tree over the string of nouns is a valid parse, as far as syntactic constraints go. This is a hallmark of attachment ambiguities (cf. Church and Patil, 1982). Also, conjunction of prenominal adjectives can lead to similar ambiguities. However, these cases differ from interchunk attachment ambiguities in an important way. The chunker can simply treat noun sequences and adjective conjunction as iterative structures, e.g., [$_{DP}$ a [$_{NP}$ [$_{N+}$ cherry picker exhaust manifold]]], and leave it to the semantics to figure out the interrelationships. (The treatment of noun compounds in grammar (5) above is only slightly more elaborate.) The phrase [$_{N+}$ cherry picker exhaust manifold] represents the set of possible binary trees over the four nouns, but the ambiguity is a semantic ambiguity; the syntactic representation is unambiguous.

It may appear that the attacher could do the same for e.g., PP attachment. For example, if we are concerned only about VP's of the form V NP PP*, we could assume a flat VP expansion, generating structures like

[$_{VP}$ [place] [the ball] [in the box] [on the table] ...]

Such a structure could be interpreted as representing every possible binary tree over the bracketed phrases (as suggested by Church and Patil, 1982). But unfortunately, the ambiguity cannot be localized to a single VP. Consider *John met the woman he married in Italy*. To avoid a decision on the attachment of *in Italy*, we must assume a structure like

[$_{IP}$ John [$_{VP}$ [met] [$_{NP}$ the woman] [$_{CP}$ he married] [$_{PP}$ in Italy]]]

In order to guarantee a syntactically unambiguous, flat structure, we must assume that embedded VP's (*married*, here) expand only to V. If we group [CP he married] and [PP in Italy] in the semantics, as in the first tree in (9), we interpret *in Italy* as a modifier of married. If the grouping in the semantics is as in the second tree in (9), we interpret *in Italy* as a modifier of *met*.

(9)

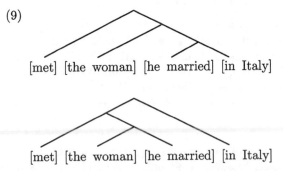

[met] [the woman] [he married] [in Italy]

[met] [the woman] [he married] [in Italy]

However, this approach is unsatisfactory, because virtually all chunks following the matrix verb are in fact left unassembled, and a considerable amount of syntactic information that constrains the assembly of those chunks is ignored. That is, unlike with noun compounds, it is not true that every binary tree over the chunks in (9) is syntactically admissible. In particular, the relative clause cannot be a modifier of the verb, and the PP cannot be a modifier of the NP. In effect, by pushing ambiguity out of the syntax and into the semantics, we also end up requiring the semantics to do much of the work of the syntax. Concisely, there is an intermingling of syntactic and semantic constraints in interchunk relations that is not found within chunks.

6.   COMPARISON TO RELATED MODELS

6.1.   *The Chunker and Chart Parsing*

An issue I have skirted to now is ambiguity in the output of the chunker. There are at least two sorts of ambiguity that arise that cannot be satisfactorily resolved by the heuristics we have discussed. First, it is possible for the same stretch of words to be analyzed as a chunk in more than one category. This arises especially with single-word chunks. For example, *described* may represent either a single-word VP or a single-word participle (PtcP), and the ambiguity can be resolved only in context. In this case, both readings are passed to the attacher.

A more difficult type of ambiguity arises when it is not clear where to end a chunk. Consider the following sentences:

In Manhattan apartments with low rent are in great demand

In Manhattan apartments with low rent, rats are a serious problem

Neither is a hopeless garden path like *the horse raced past the barn fell*, so we would like the parser to be able to handle either. However, it is not possible to decide whether the first PP chunk ends before or after *apartments* using only immediate context. We must pass both possibilities to the attacher, and let it choose based on right context.

As a consequence, the output of the chunker is actually not a stream, properly speaking. Reading from the chunker at a given position yields a set of chunks, along with the positions at which they end. In the attacher, the input pointer for a configuration after a shift is not necessarily one greater than the previous input pointer.

This invites comparison to a chart. One of the advantages cited for a chart is that it does not require that all competing readings in cases of ambiguity cover the same segment of the input string. In effect, the chunker as revised outputs chart edges. I think that is a profitable way of viewing the architecture of the parser I have described. A chart parser introduces a cache point for every partial parse tree constructed, to avoid duplication of effort. Often, though, the added overhead involved in caching and checking caches is greater than the savings from avoiding repeated construction. In the parser I have described, chunks, and only chunks, are 'cached'—in the sense that separate branches of the attacher's nondeterministic calculation can use the same chunks, without duplicating the effort of constructing them. This appears to be a good intermediate position between caching all trees, whether they are likely to be reused or not, and caching no trees.

6.2.   *The Chunker and the Sausage Machine*

A brief note is in order comparing the chunker to Frazier and Fodor's Sausage Machine (Frazier and Fodor, 1978). Apart from having two levels, there is actually little similarity between a chunking parser and the Sausage Machine. Processing in both stages of the Sausage Machine is identical, whereas in a chunking parser, only the attacher is powerful enough to deal with lexical selection and attachment ambiguities. The 'chunks' that the first-stage processor builds, in the Sausage Machine, are determined entirely by what fits in an input buffer of arbitrarily-chosen size. In a chunking parser, by contrast, chunks have a detailed syntactic definition, which can be defended on syntactic grounds alone (cf. Abney, to appear). For the same reason, the correspondence between chunks and ϕ-phrases is lacking in the Sausage Machine model. Again, because of the heterogeneity of Sausage Machine 'chunks', there is no basis for supposing that they constitute particularly good cache points in a nondeterministic parse. (In fact, the Sausage Machine model is deterministic, so the question does not arise.)

In brief, virtually none of the advantages of a chunking parser, which I summarize in the next section, accrue to the 'chunks' produced by the Sausage Machine.

7. CONCLUSION

By way of conclusion, I would like to reiterate the advantages of a chunking parser. First, one of the most difficult problems for context-free parsing techniques is attachment ambiguities. But within chunks, (syntactic) attachment ambiguities do not arise, and simple context-free parsing techniques are very effective. By having separate chunker and attacher, we can limit the use of expensive techniques for dealing with attachment ambiguities to the parts of grammar where they are really necessary—*i.e.*, in the attacher.

Another motivation is modularity. Since the chunker is insensitive to the state of the attacher, we can develop and debug it separately from the attacher. The chunker also simplifies the task that the attacher faces: many lexical ambiguities can be resolved within chunks, relieving the attacher of that task, and there is less clutter to deal with at the level of chunks than at the level of words.

A related motivation is that the chunker-attacher division keeps attachment ambiguities from being multiplied with chunk ambiguities. The chunker evaluates chunks as well as it can on its own, instead of making decisions relative to one or another branch of the attacher's nondeterministic computation.

As we have seen, there is also some psychological evidence for chunks. Gee and Grosjean argue that the 'performance structures' that emerge from a range of diverse experiments are best predicted by what they call ϕ-phrases. Apart from their structure, that is, seen simply as strings, chunks and ϕ-phrases are nearly identical.

A fifth motivation is related to Gee and Grosjean's work. They show that ϕ-phrases are a good predictor of intonation. Given the correspondence between ϕ-phrases and chunks, there is a possibility of using the chunker in determining intonation, for speech synthesis.

And last, but not least, we can account for a range of otherwise inexplicable syntactic constraints if we assume the existence of chunks. For example, we can explain why *the proud of his son man is odd, by observing that it involves a chunk, *of his son*, embedded in another chunk, *the proud man*. (See Abney, to appear.) If the chunks are produced in a stream, it is not possible to interleave them.

NOTES

[1] A chunk's structure is in fact a tree, but it is not necessarily a subconstituent of the global parse tree. In particular, the chunk's root node may have some descendants in the global tree that are absent from the chunk's parse tree.

[2] I consider the relation between a function word (*e.g.*, determiner) and associated content-word head (*e.g.*, noun) to be one of selection. See Abney (1987) for arguments.

[3] There is one case that this definition does not handle. We wish to say that a pronoun that heads a prepositional phrase is a major head, despite being a function word, not a content word. I have no more elegant solution at present than to add a disjunctive clause to the definition of major head: 'a major head is any content word that does not appear between a function word f and the content word f selects, OR a pronoun selected by a preposition'.

[4] In fact, the standard LR parser has only a control stack. Instead of building a parse tree, it outputs a string of rule-numbers, one for each reduction. Such a string encodes a parse tree: reversed, it specifies a rightmost derivation of the input string. 'LR' stands for 'Left-to-right, Rightmost derivation'.

[5] A solution's score is the same as the score of the 'Accept' task that generated it.

[6] Actually, it is more complicated than a simple sequence of categories, because of the presence of iterative categories in frames. However, the complications introduced by iterative categories do not compromise he argument made here, so I ignore them.

REFERENCES

Abney, S.: 1987, *The English Noun Phrase in Its Sentential Aspect*, Ph.D. dissertation, Department of Linguistics and Philosophy, Massachusetts Institute of Technology, Cambridge, Massachusetts.

Abney, S.: to appear, 'Syntactic Affixation and Performance Structures', in D. Bouchard and K. Leffel (eds.), *Views on Phrase Structure*, Kluwer, Dordrecht, Holland.

Aho, A. and J. Ullman: 1972, *The Theory of Parsing, Translation, and Compiling*, in two volumes, Prentice-Hall, Inc., Englewood Cliffs, New Jersey.

Chomsky, N.: 1986, *Barriers*, MIT Press, Cambridge, Massachusetts.

Church, K. and R. Patil: 1982, 'Coping with Syntactic Ambiguity or How to Put the Block in the Box on the Table', *American Journal of Computation Linguistics* **8**, 139–149.

Frazier, L. and J.D. Fodor: 1978, 'The Sausage Machine: A new two-stage parsing model', *Cognition* **6**, 291–325.

Gee, J. and F. Grosjean: 1983, 'Performance Structures: A Psycholinguistic and Linguistic Appraisal', *Cognitive Psychology* **15**, 411–458.

Hindle, D.: 1983, *User Manual for Fidditch, a Deterministic Parser*, Naval Research Laboratory Technical Memorandum #7590-142, Office of Naval Research, Arlington, Virginia.

Knuth, D.: 1965, 'On the Translation of Languages From Left to Right', *Information and Control* **8**, 607–639.

Williams, G.: 1986, 'The Solar Cycle in Precambrian Time', *Scientific American* **255** no.2, 88–97.

Bell Communications Research,
445 South Street,
Morristown, New Jersey 07962-1910, U.S.A.

PAUL GORRELL

SUBCATEGORIZATION AND SENTENCE PROCESSING

In this chapter I will discuss two issues concerned with the relationship between lexical information associated with verbs and syntactic processing. By syntactic processing, I mean that aspect of human sentence comprehension that recovers a syntactic structure for a given word string. First, I will examine two structural ambiguities in Mandarin (Gorrell and Chen, 1988) and discuss how they can be successfully parsed within the framework of minimal commitment parsing models (Marcus, Hindle, and Fleck, 1983; Berwick and Weinberg, 1985). I will then turn to a discussion of some recent experimental work investigating structural ambiguity in English and relate this to the Mandarin examples. This discussion will turn on the availability of subcategorization information associated with ambiguous verbs.

Finally, I will discuss the issue of the parser's use of subcategory information in the initial stages of processing. I will argue against recent models which postulate a delay in the parser's use of subcategory information.

1. STRUCTURAL AMBIGUITY

I will take as my starting point a brief discussion of three current approaches to how the parser responds to structurally ambiguous word strings. A given word string is structurally ambiguous if it is compatible with more than one syntactic structure. These approaches are sketched in (1).

(1) (a) Serial Models:
A single 'preferred' structure is computed for an ambiguous string. If this structure is incompatible with subsequent material, reanalysis is required.

(b) Parallel Models:
Multiple structures are computed for an ambiguous string. At points of disambiguation in the parse, incompatible structures are abandoned.

279

R. C. Berwick et al. (eds.),
Principle-Based Parsing: Computation and Psycholinguistics, 279–300.

(c) Minimal Commitment Models:
   Commitment to a particular analysis is postponed until the
   appearance of disambiguating information.

Serial parsing models (*e.g.*, Frazier and Rayner, 1982; Ford, Bresnan, and Kaplan, 1982) utilize various decision procedures for determining a preferred syntactic analysis at the onset of the ambiguity. If subsequent lexical material is incompatible with this analysis, then an additional process of reanalysis is required. Parallel models (*e.g.*, Chodorow, 1976; Kurtzman, 1985) compute multiple syntactic analyses for ambiguous word strings, abandoning those that are incompatible with subsequent information. Minimal commitment models delay commitment to a particular analysis either until a specified lookahead space is exhausted, or until disambiguating material is encountered. The intent of this delay is to allow a deterministic parse, where *deterministic* is defined in the sense of Marcus (1980). All three models assume the parser structures incoming material as it is received, rather than waiting until a clause boundary is encountered or some specified amount of lexical material has been received (see Fodor, Bever, and Garrett, 1974, for discussion).

1.1. *Minimal Commitment Parsing*

Our discussion of structural ambiguity in Mandarin assumes three properties of minimal commitment parsers: (i) hierarchical structure analysis uses the predicate dominates rather than directly dominates; (ii) an empty operator that is not part of the final syntactic analysis may be posited so long as it is not coindexed with an element in an argument position; (iii) no lookahead device is used.

The first property allows a deterministic parse of temporary ambiguities in English such as (2).

(2) John knew the old woman ...

Here, the NP *the old woman* may function either as the direct object of the verb knew (*e.g.*, *the old woman quite well*) or as the subject of an embedded clause (*e.g.*, *the old woman was ill*). The structural realizations of these two readings are shown in (3).

(3) (a) [$_{VP}$ knew [$_{NP}$ the old woman] quite well]

(b) [$_{VP}$ knew [$_{\bar{S}}$ [$_{S}$ [$_{NP}$ the old woman] was ill]]]]

At the point at which the NP *the old woman* is encountered, the parser commits itself only to the analysis that the VP dominates the NP. If subsequent lexical material, *e.g.*, the predicate *was ill*, proves the NP to be further embedded within the VP, then additional domination statements are added (*e.g.*, VP dominates S, S dominates NP).

The second property allows a deterministic parse of ambiguities involving parasitic gaps such as (4).

(4) Which article did you discuss without reading?

Following Chomsky (1986), I take the structure of (4) to be (5).

(5) [Which book$_1$ [$_s$ did you discuss t_1 without
 [$_{Comp}$ O$_1$ [reading e_1]]]]]

In (5), the *parasitic gap e* is bound by the empty operator O in the embedded Comp. As first noted by Fodor (1985), the fact that a parasitic gap is optional in sentences such as (4) poses serious problems for a deterministic parser. If we assume that parasitic gap constructions involve an empty operator which binds the gap, the specific problem that arises is that a deterministic parser, in order to avoid postulating structure which is not part of the final syntactic analysis, must posit an empty operator only if the embedded clause does, in fact, contain a parasitic gap. But without resorting to a lookahead device, it cannot know this until after it must decide on the presence or absence of an empty operator.

Nor is it possible for the parser to simply wait until the embedded clause is parsed and rely upon local subcategorization information, and then decide whether or not to place an operator in Comp. To understand why this is so, we must examine sentences such as (6) and (7) from the viewpoint of a deterministic parser such as the one proposed in Berwick and Weinberg (1984).

(6) What did you say [that Bill would eat tonight?

(7) Did you say [that Bill would eat tonight?

The problem for the parser is to insert a gap following *eat* in (6) but not to do so in (7). The Berwick and Weinberg parser will only postulate a gap if there is an available antecedent for it. The search space for an antecedent is the left context subjacent to the potential trace position.

In order to insure that an available antecedent is within this domain, the parser will place a trace in the embedded Comp that serves as the antecedent for the gap. The decision to place this intermediate trace in the embedded Comp is based on the presence of the *Wh*-phrase in the matrix Comp. Thus in (7), no trace is inserted into the embedded Comp and no gap is postulated after the verb *eat*.

The problem which parasitic gaps pose for such a parsing model is that the presence of an overt *Wh*-phrase does not ensure the existence of a parasitic gap. This is because a parasitic gap is bound by a nonovert, or empty, operator. The solution proposed by Berwick and Weinberg (1985) is to define determinism in such a way that an empty operator may be posited even if it may end up not binding a parasitic gap.

The proposed solution is as follows: the Berwick and Weinberg parser is a two-stage device. The first stage involves structure building, the second stage concerns indexation. Thus, an empty operator may be posited by the first-stage device without receiving an index. If the clause, in fact, contains a gap, then the second-stage device will coindex these elements. This coindexation will associate the empty operator with a theta-role (via the gap which is in a theta position) and cause it to be visible for semantic interpretation (cf. Chomsky, 1981). If no gap is present in the clause, then, clearly, coindexation will not occur. In this case, the empty operator will lack both semantic features (because it is not associated with a theta-role) and phonetic features (because it lacks phonetic content) and play no part in the final analysis of the sentence. In this way, its presence does not violate determinism.

1.2.   *Structural Ambiguity in Mandarin*

Having sketched our initial assumptions concerning minimal commitment parsing, I turn now to a discussion of structural ambiguity in Mandarin (Gorrell and Chen, 1988). Consider the ambiguity represented in (8):

(8) wo renshi ni zuotian kanjian de ren
     I know you yesterday see REL men
     'I know the men who you saw yesterday'

Although this type of structure does not cause a conscious garden path, a temporary ambiguity arises because the relative clause marker de occurs to the right of the clause. Thus, at the point at which it is initially encountered, the NP *ni* is a potential direct object of the verb *renshi*. Given the parsing model I am assuming, the parser may safely assert that this NP is dominated by the VP headed by *renshi* because this does not entail that it is *directly* dominated by the VP. As subsequent lexical material is encountered, additional domination statements can be made, embedding *ni* within the larger NP, *ni zuotian kanjian de ren*. Crucial to this analysis is the fact that the original assertion remains true of the final structure.

If the original dominance assertion had not been supplemented by additional assertions, *i.e.*, if *ni* were, in fact, the direct object of *renshi*, then this assertion would be interpreted as direct domination (see Marcus, Hindle, and Fleck, 1983).

Thus, our analysis of the Mandarin ambiguity represented in (8) parallels the one given for the English ambiguity in (2). Each ambiguity is parsed without a garden path effect, and each can be parsed deterministically, given that the initial structure does not involve the predicate direct domination.

The second ambiguity in Mandarin is illustrated in (9).

(9) Zhangsan shuo Lisi bu renshi (ta)
     Zhangsan said Lisi not know him
     'Zhangsan said that Lisi didn't know him'

In (9), the object in the embedded clause may be phonetically empty. I will assume, following Huang (1984, 1987) that the structure underlying the string with the empty embedded object is (10). That is, the empty object is a variable bound by an empty operator in TOPIC position.

(10) $[_{TOP}$ O_1 [Zhangsan shuo [Lisi bu renshi e_1]]]

This analysis is motivated, in part, by the observation that, unlike an overt pronominal object, the empty object may not refer to *Zhangsan*. This would follow if the empty object were a variable that cannot be *A-bound*, as is true of the *Wh*-trace in the embedded clause in (11).

(11) [Who$_1$ [did John say [e_1 [Mary knew e_1]]]]

Assuming Huang's analysis of (9), we are presented with an ambiguity that is similar to that posed by parasitic gaps in English. That is, the presence or absence of a gap in (9) cannot be determined by the presence or absence of an overt antecedent. As with the *parasitic gap* structure (5), the solution is to allow the parser to posit an empty operator which will play no part in the final analysis of the sentence unless it is coindexed with a gap.

Although Huang's analysis of this example does not include an intermediate trace in the embedded Comp, such a trace would be required by the Berwick and Weinberg parser as an available antecedent must exist within the parser's search space. Interestingly, Ni (1987) proposes such an analysis for independent reasons.

At this point it is important to note that the type of parsing model outlined here does not predict a complete absence of garden path effects. Rather, it predicts that garden path effects will only arise in those cases where the parser is forced to withdraw or alter an assertion concerning the computed structure. Consider (12), which produces a conscious garden path.

(12) Zhangsan yi   du   shu   jiu   diao le
     Zhangsan as soon as read book then fall ASP
     'As soon as Z. (began to) read the book fell'

The garden path effect occurs because the parser, at the point in the parse when *shu* appears, apparently asserts that this NP is dominated by the VP headed by *du*. Thus far, the parse is proceeding in a fashion similar to (8). The difference is that in (12), this assertion turns out to be incorrect. This requires that the assertion be altered and a conscious garden path results.

Although it may seem natural to offer an account of the garden path effect in terms of incorrect assertions by the parser, we have yet to account for the existence of such assertions. Specifically, if the parsing model incorporates a property that permits delay, why doesn't this property insure that the parser will never be garden-pathed?

What I would like to suggest is that there exists a tension between the need to quickly structure incoming material so that it does not tax short-term memory resources, and the desire to delay commitment in order to avoid being garden pathed. The task, then, of an efficient parser is to commit itself to as detailed a structure as possible while minimizing the need for reanalysis. For example, a recent proposal by Clark and

Gibson (1988) requires that incoming NPs be licensed either by receiving a theta-role or abstract Case in the sense of Chomsky (1981). Similarly, the parsing model outlined in Pritchett (1988, this volume) requires that the theta-criterion be satisfied at each point in the parse.

If we consider (12) from this perspective, we see that the NP *shu* can only be licensed if it receives a theta-role and Case from the verb. Locality constraints on theta-role and Case assignment require the NP to be within the VP. A garden path effect occurs when subsequent material casts this assertion into doubt. Interestingly, unlike its English counterpart, there is a grammatical structuring of the word string which is consistent with this initial assertion. Consider the structures in (13) and (14).

(13) Zhangsan yi   du   e   shu   jiu   diao le
     Zhangsan as soon as read (it) book then fall ASP
     'As soon as Zhangsan began to read it, the book fell'

(14) Zhangsan yi   du   shu   e   jiu   diao le
     Zhangsan as soon as read book (it) then fall ASP
     'As soon as Zhangsan began to read the book, it fell'

Unlike English, Mandarin permits empty subjects and empty objects. Thus, either (13) or (14) represent grammatical structures for the word string. What is of note here, is that the initial analysis of *shu* as the object of *du* does not force the reading represented in (14), thus allowing a deterministic parse and avoiding a conscious garden path.

Native-speaker intuitions suggest that the parse sequence is as follows: (i) *shu* is analyzed as the object of *du*; (ii) as processing of the next clause begins, there is conscious uncertainty as to the correct analysis; (iii) here we find that speakers diverge, some resolve the ambiguity as (13), some as (14). Although more research is needed, what may cause the conscious uncertainty is a conflict of otherwise automatic routines, that is, routines governed by the grammatical imperative of licensing NPs and parsing routines that attempt to determine the position of empty categories.(See the chapter by Pritchett.)

Putting aside this issue of how the ambiguity in (13) and (14) is resolved, one might conclude from the analysis of (8) and (9) that our assumptions concerning minimal commitment parsing allow for a unified account of structural ambiguity resolution in English and in Mandarin. Unfortunately for this unified account, there is experimental evidence in

English that the parser computes multiple analyses in parallel for the structural ambiguity illustrated in (2). I turn now to an examination of this evidence.

1.3. *Evidence for Parallel Processing in English*

Using a technique originally due to Wright and Garrett (1984), Gorrell (1988a, 1989) reports experimental results which indicate that for certain ambiguities, the parser computes multiple analyses in parallel. Wright and Garrett found that syntactic context exerted a robust influence on the recognition time for lexical decision targets. Specifically, they found that only targets belonging to syntactic categories predicted by the syntactic context produced faster reaction times. Extending this line of research, Gorrell (1988b) found that obligatory targets (*i.e.*, targets belonging to syntactic categories predicted by the context) produced RTs significantly slower than RTs for optional targets (*i.e.*, targets belonging to grammatically permissible categories not required by the context). In turn, optional targets were significantly faster than ungrammatical targets.

I have used this technique to investigate the parser's response to structurally ambiguous syntactic contexts. Consider the contexts in example (15).

(15) (a) Bill said that he discussed the answer to the
        problem VERB

     (b) Bill said that he found out the answer to the
        problem VERB

     (c) Bill said that he was happy the answer to the
        problem VERB

As with (2), (15b) contains a predicate (*found out*) which is ambiguous. Thus, when the parser encounters the NP the answer to the problem, it may be analyzed either as the object of the verb or as the subject of an embedded clause. Sentences (15a) and (15c) represent unambiguous controls corresponding to the two readings of the ambiguity in (15b). In (15a), the answer to the problem can only be analyzed as the object of the verb. In (15c), it can only be analyzed as the subject of an embedded clause.

Numerous studies (*e.g.*, that by Frazier and Rayner, 1982) have demonstrated that the preferred resolution of the ambiguity in (15b)

TABLE I

Results from Gorrell (1988a)
RTs and Percent Correct for Context/targets Pairs
(Verb Targets)

Context	NP/S Complement Ambiguity
Simple (15a)	733 (99%) *
Ambig. (15b)	693 (99%) **
Complex (15c)	682 (99%) **

is to analyze the NP following found out as its object. If this is the only analysis computed by the parser, or if the parser delays in committing to an analysis, then we would expect that lexical decision times for verb targets would be the same for (15a) and (15b). Because the context (15c) requires a verb, we would expect faster reaction times to verb targets with this context. Conversely, if the parser computes both readings of the ambiguity in (15b), then we would expect reaction times for verb targets to be the same for (15b) and (15c), with RTs for (15a) being significantly longer. The results are given in Table I.

The results confirm the prediction of the parallel hypothesis and argue against both the serial and delay hypotheses. This is because contexts such as (15b) and (15c) patterned together, both producing RTs significantly faster than contexts such as (15a). Only the parallel hypothesis would predict that the ambiguous context would produce faster RTs for verb targets, because it is only this hypothesis which predicts that the parser will compute an analysis which would predict the appearance of a verb. Recall that both ungrammatical and optional targets produce significantly slower RTs than predicted targets. A delay model would predict a verb continuation for unambiguous strings such as (15c), but not for the ambiguous (15b).

Given these experimental results, we are now in a position where we must attempt to reconcile the apparent success of minimal commitment parsing models in accounting for cross-linguistic ambiguity resolution, with contradictory evidence for parallel processing.

1.4. *Structural Ambiguity and Syntactic Information*

If we look again at the ambiguity studied in Gorrell (1988a), we see that
the parser is able to compute multiple readings based on the subcategorization frames of the ambiguous verb. Verbs such as know or find out
are compatible with either nominal or sentential complements. In section 2 I will present experimental evidence that the parser makes rapid
use of subcategory information in computing syntactic analyses.

In section 1.2 above I suggested that the parser responds to ambiguities such as (8) in Mandarin by asserting only that the NP *ni* is
dominated by the VP headed by *renshi*. This has the effect of delaying
commitment to a particular analysis. Yet in the previous section I argued that for English examples such as (2) and (15b), the parser does
not delay in its commitment, but rather pursues a strategy of computing
multiple analyses in parallel.

This apparent contradiction can be overcome if we look at these
ambiguities from the perspective of what type of information is available
to the parser at the onset of an ambiguity. As noted, for the English
examples, the subcategorization information of the verb is available,
and analyses based on this information are pursued. In the Mandarin
example (8), at the point at which the NP *ni* is encountered, there is
no information available which would justify analyzing it as embedded
within a larger NP. This information, in the form of the relative clause
marker, comes later in the parse.

Returning to our example (12) and its English counterpart, it appears that the parser would have access to the information that *du* may
occur with or without an object, yet it appears that only one analysis is
pursued. A plausible explanation for this is that it is only the reading
where the NP *shu* is analyzed as the direct object which licenses this NP,
i.e., under this reading it can receive a theta-role and case. Similarly,
the Clark and Gibson parser will only pursue analyses in which the NP
is licensed.

The picture which emerges is one in which the parser pursues all
analyses for which it has specific lexical or syntactic information, but
delays commitment in those cases where sufficient information is not
available.

1.5. *The Parser's Response to Structural Ambiguity*

We can summarize our conclusions as follows.

(16) (a) Minimize the need for reanalysis

(b) Compute multiple analyses based on available lexical and syntactic information

(c) Delay commitment to a unique analysis if sufficient information is unavailable

(d) Do not postpone a commitment if it leaves lexical material unlicensed (or unstructured)

The parser minimizes the need for reanalysis by quickly and efficiently using lexical and syntactic information to build a structure (or structures) compatible with the word string. Multiple syntactic analyses are computed only when the available information indicates which analyses to build. If an ambiguity is encountered but the necessary information for computing multiple analyses is lacking, the parser delays commitment to a particular structure. Clearly, more work is needed to give a more precise indication of what constitutes necessary information. One speculation would be that it is syntactic information listed in the lexicon.

Finally, there is a constraint on the parser's delay capability which ensures that the parser will not respond to ambiguity by simply assembling a series of phrases (or lexical items) dominated by the root S. That is, phrasal categories must be licensed as they are processed. It is this latter constraint which may lead to conscious garden path effects.

Although many issues still need to be addressed (*e.g.*, attachment preferences for adjunct phrases do not follow from licensing requirements), the parsing design I have outlined here constrains both the parser's capacity for computing multiple analyses as well as it's capacity for delaying commitment to a particular analysis.

2. SUBCATEGORY INFORMATION

An important issue in the construction of models of human syntactic processing is the relationship between information associated with individual lexical items and general principles of syntactic well-formedness. For example, the fact that (in English) direct object noun phrases occur to the right of verbs follows from general syntactic principles, whereas the presence or absence of a direct object follows from idiosyncratic properties (the *subcategorization frames* of Chomsky, 1965) of individual verbs.

Within the psycholinguistic literature, numerous studies have focused on the processing of verb-complement structures. For example, in one of the earliest investigations into the effects of verbal complexity on sentence processing, Fodor, Garrett, and Bever (1968) concluded that the subcategory information associated with a verb was crucial for the rapid recovery of a sentence's deep structure. Further, they concluded that processing complexity was a function, in part, of the number of distinct complement types a verb permits.

Janet Fodor's (1978) Lexical Expectation Model of Gap Detection assumes that subcategory information is available for use in determining the potential locations of Wh-traces in a sentence, and extends this concept to include not simply a list of the permissible complement structures, but also some representation of the relative likelihood of their occurrence. Clifton, Frazier, and Connine (1984) have offered experimental support for this model. Mitchell and Holmes (1985) offer evidence for a Verb Dominance Principle that extends the Lexical Expectation Model to the processing of complement structures in declaratives.

The well-known proposal of Ford, Bresnan, and Kaplan (1982) for the use of lexical preferences in parsing also depends upon the efficient use of subcategory information. Until quite recently there has been a near-consensus view that syntactic processing involves the rapid use of subcategory information in computing a structural analysis for a given word string.

For example, Clifton, Frazier, and Connine (1984) argue that subcategory information is used at an early stage of processing, prior to any semantic or pragmatic influences. This is based on the observation that performance on a secondary task suffered when the lexical item following a verb conflicted with the verb's preferred complement structure.

Mitchell and Holmes (1985) also argue for the early use of subcategory information. Using a self-paced reading paradigm, they found that garden path effects could be induced or prevented simply by changing the verb in a particular sentence. For example, they point to the intuitive distinction between the comparatively natural (17a) and the awkward (17b).

(17) (a) The groundsman chased the girl waving a stick in his hand

　　 (b) The groundsman noticed the girl waving a stick in his hand

More recently, Mitchell (1987) argues that syntactic processing involves two distinct stages: one in which a preliminary structure is computed without the use of subcategory information; and a second stage in which this information serves to confirm or disconfirm the initial analysis.

For example, consider the sentence fragments in (18), where (18a) contains a transitive verb and (18b) an intransitive verb.[1] The claim is that for (18a) and (18b) the parser will initially compute the structures in (18c) and (18d), that is, with the following noun phrase analyzed as the direct object of the verb.

(18) (a) The new owners bought NP

    (b) The new owners slept NP

    (c) The new owners [VP bought NP]

    (d) The new owners [VP slept NP]

Thus the first-stage device makes use of category information (*e.g.*, verb vs. noun) but ignores or does not have access to subcategory information. To test this hypothesis that the use of subcategory information is delayed, Mitchell used a phrase-by-phrase self-paced reading task and compared sentences in which a noun phrase followed either an intransitive verb or an ambiguous verb (optionally transitive or intransitive). The phrase-by-phrase self-paced reading task proceeds in this way: there is an initial prompt on the screen of the monitor. The subject presses the space bar which calls up the first display and starts a timer. The subject is instructed to read the display and press the space bar as soon as it has been read. This second key press signals the end of the reading time for the first display, and starts the timer for the reading of the second display. The subject presses the space bar as soon as the second display has been read. For example, (19a) shows the two displays for a sentence containing an ambiguous verb, while (19b) contains an intransitive verb.

(19) (a) After the child had visited the doctor [DISPLAY 1]
      prescribed a course of injections   [DISPLAY 2]

    (b) After the child had sneezed the doctor [DISPLAY 1]
      prescribed a course of injections   [DISPLAY 2]

The results are presented in Table II. Reading times for the first display were significantly longer with phrases containing intransitive verbs, as compared to their transitive counterparts.[2] But for the second display, the effect was reversed, with reading times for the phrases containing

TABLE II

Results from Mitchell (1987)
(Reading Times in msec.)

	Intransitive	Transitive	Difference
DISPLAY 1	3449	2770	+709
DISPLAY 2	2354	3346	−992
TOTAL	5803	6087	

transitive verbs significantly longer than the phrases with intransitive verbs.

Mitchell interpreted this pattern as follows. The DISPLAY 1 phrases with intransitive verbs such as (19b) produce longer reading times because the parser initially misanalyzes the intransitive verb-noun phrase sequence as a VP. But this initial analysis is disconfirmed by the second-stage processor which makes use of subcategory information to check the output of the first-stage. At this point, reanalysis is required, and it is the process of reanalysis which takes time, producing the longer reading times.

However, the additional time taken for reanalysis is offset by the fact that the string in the second display is consistent with this reanalyzed structure. Hence the comparatively fast reading times for this display with the intransitive examples.

For the optionally transitive cases, as in (19a), the parser's initial reaction to the first display is the same as for the intransitive cases. That is, the verb-noun phrase sequence is analyzed as a VP. This initial hypothesis is confirmed by the second-stage processor, which has access to the information that visit may take a noun phrase complement. Hence, there is no need for reanalysis, and reading times for the first display are fast compared to the intransitive cases. Unfortunately, the string presented as the second display is incompatible with the computed structure and reanalysis is required. This increases the reading time for the second display. Mitchell's proposed parse sequence for each sentence type is outlined in (20), where DO is direct object.

What is important to note here is that Mitchell's explanation for the pattern of reading times given in Table II crucially relies on the fact that the availability of subcategory information is delayed, requiring the first stage device to build a structure which may be grammatically ill-formed.

However, given the relative experimental insensitivity of the phrase-by-phrase reading task, it is difficult to determine the locus of the processing difficulty resulting in the reading time asymmetries. For example, another plausible explanation for the pattern shown in Table II is that, for the intransitive cases, reading times are long for DISPLAY 1 because subjects do make rapid use of subcategory information and are confused by the apparent oddity of strings such as *After the child sneezed the doctor.* An explanation along the lines suggested by Mitchell for the transitive cases may be correct. But here there appears to be little motivation for positing a processing stage prior to the use of subcategory information.

(20) Proposed Parse Sequence (Mitchell, 1987)

	Intransitives	Transitives
DISPLAY 1	assign DO structure. DO structure disconfirmed reanalysis required.	assign DO structure. DO structure confirmed no need for reanalysis.
DISPLAY 2	string is consistent with reanalyzed structure. no need for reanalysis	string is incompatible with DO structure. reanalysis required.

It is clear we would prefer a more sensitive measure of whether or not the use of subcategory information is delayed in syntactic processing. Below I describe an experiment making use of the lexical decision paradigm (Wright and Garrett, 1984) that I argue will serve as a useful test of Mitchell's delay hypothesis.

In terms of the use of subcategory information in syntactic processing, the delay hypothesis predicts the parser will initially treat all verbs as transitive. Thus we should observe comparable lexical decision times for nouns occurring after both transitive and intransitive verbs. If, however, the parser makes rapid use of subcategory information and this information is represented in the syntactic structure computed prior to the appearance of the lexical decision target, then RTs for noun targets will be significantly longer following intransitive verbs than transitive verbs.

Method

Subjects

Twenty-four students from the University of Maryland participated in the study. All were native speakers of English with normal or corrected vision. Subjects were randomly divided into four subject groups. Subjects received partial course credit for their participation.

Materials

Twelve quadruples such as (21) were constructed. Targets are indicated by capitals, although in the experiment they appeared in lowercase letters.

(21) (a) The committee wanted the chairman to permit DOORS

(b) The committee wanted the chairman to permit UNDER

(c) Susan told us that she had voted to remain DOORS

(d) Susan told us that she had voted to remain UNDER

Each quadruple consisted of a pair of context strings crossed with a pair of target words. One member of each target pair ended in a transitive verb and the other ended with an intransitive verb. Infinitive forms of verbs were used throughout to avoid any category ambiguity. Targets were either nouns or prepositions. Items were counterbalanced so that each subject saw equal numbers of each context/target pair.

The entire stimulus set consisted of 106 sentences, with equal numbers of word and nonword targets.

Design and Procedure

Each subject was seated before the CRT of an AST Premium 286 computer. Response keys were indicated by colored stickers. A YES response key was positioned on the righthand side of the keyboard and a NO response key was symmetrically positioned on the lefthand side of the keyboard. During stimulus presentation, subjects kept their index fingers resting lightly on the response keys.

Subjects were instructed to press the YES key if the target item was a word of English or to press the NO key if the target item was not a word. Subjects were instructed to make prompt decisions. The interval between sentences was self-paced by use of the space bar. Subjects used their thumb for the space bar.

Sentences appeared from left to right across the computer screen, with all words remaining on the screen until a response key was pressed. Each new word appeared 350 msec after its predecessor. Each context/target pair was a maximum of 80 characters long (including spaces) and was presented on one line. Before each trial, an inverted triangle appeared at the left margin of the computer screen and flashed three times to signal the start of a sentence. The triangle disappeared with the appearance of the first word of the sentence.

The target string of letters was distinguished from the words of the context string in two ways: (i) it appeared in green whereas the context appeared in off-white; (ii) it appeared 100 msec. after the final word of the context string (instead of the normal 350 msec.).

The subjects were given a practice session of ten sentences during which they were urged to make prompt responses. There was no mention that some of the targets might 'fit' the context while others might not. If subjects asked about this after the practice session, they were told to simply make lexical decisions for the target items. Presentation of the lexical decision target triggered a timer with an accuracy of $+/-$ 2 msec. Response times and responses were recorded by the computer.

Results and Discussion

Mean reaction times are presented in Table III. Overall percent error was 2 percent. Analyses of variance treating subjects and items as the random variable were performed. Main effects for context and for target were non-significant. There was a significant context × target interaction for both the subjects analysis (F1 (3,23) = 22.22; p < .01) and for the items analysis (F2 (3,23) = 3.43; p < .04). Planned t-tests reveal that noun targets produced faster RTs when they followed transitive verbs than when they followed intransitive verbs. There was no significant difference for the preposition targets.

The results are not consistent with the delay hypothesis. Subcategory information is apparently used quite early in the parse sequence. The response pattern for the preposition targets may be due to the fact that transitive verbs in English do not require an adjacent lexically realized NP. For example, in Heavy-NP Shift constructions such as (22) the direct object has been displaced to the right.

(22) The committee did not want the chairman to permit, under any circumstances, vandalism in the public schools

TABLE III

Mean Reaction Time (msec.) as a Function of
Target Category and Context-Final Verb Subcategory

	LEXICAL DECISION TARGET	
Context-final Verb	NOUN	PREP
Transitive	762	799
Intransitive	824	774
Difference	62	25

But the results for the noun targets clearly indicate that the parser is making rapid use of subcategory information. These results are consistent with those of previous studies, *e.g.*, Clifton, Frazier, and Connine (1984), as well as recent work using a cross-modal lexical decision task (Nicol, 1989).

3. CONCLUSION

The results of the present study disconfirm the hypothesis that the use of subcategory information is delayed until a later stage of processing. This finding is consistent with the view that lexical access makes available to the subsequent processors all information associated with a given lexical item. Thus we would expect that if the syntactic processor receives the information that a lexical item is a verb, it also receives information concerning the type of verb and (presumably) selectional information as well.

Frazier (1987) has recently argued for a processing model in which general syntactic information (*e.g.*, that objects follow verbs in English) is precompiled in the form of phrase structure rules. As in Chomsky (1965), these phrase structure rules represent dominance and precedence relations among syntactic categories but do not represent subcategory or selectional information. Frazier's proposal, in many ways quite similar to Mitchell's, is that the syntactic processor uses category information supplied by the lexical processor to trigger the application of phrase structure rules in the computation of an initial structure. A separate processor would then apply subcategory information as a checking device.

Frazier assumes a principles-and-parameters grammar (roughly along the lines of Chomsky, 1981) in which the information traditionally encoded in the form of phrase structure rules is separated out into numerous distinct modules (*e.g.*, Case theory, $\overline{\text{X}}$-theory). Although they do not address the important general issues which Frazier raises, the results presented here do argue against the specific proposal to separate category and subcategory information.

It must be noted that the present results do not establish that both category and subcategory information are used in the construction of the initial phrase marker. They clearly argue for the rapid use of subcategory information, but the experiment described here did not include a condition directly contrasting category and subcategory information. As is often the case, it may be that a more sensitive measure will show a processing distinction between these two types of information. At present however, there are no experimental results which would cause us to conclude that there is a temporal distinction in their application.

In addition, the parser makes use of subcategory information to build multiple syntactic structures for word strings containing ambiguous verbs. When such information is lacking, as in the Mandarin examples discussed above, the parser delays commitment to a particular analysis.

Both the computation of multiple analyses and the postponement of attachment decisions are constrained by the interaction of information availability and the parser's responsibility to grammatical principles.

NOTES

[1] For present purposes I will put aside the question of whether the class of intransitive verbs should be further divided into *accusative* or *unaccusative*, following work by Perlmutter (1978) and Burzio (1986). This distinction is important but is outside the scope of this chapter. Therefore, I will treat all verbs that do not permit a following lexically realized direct object simply as 'intransitives'. In addition, I should point out that, although I will refer to subcategory information, I do not distinguish here between argument structure and subcategory information (see Shapiro, Zurif, and Grimshaw, 1987 for discussion).

[2] Following Mitchell I will use *transitive* to refer to ambiguous verbs.

REFERENCES

Berwick, R. and A. Weinberg: 1985, 'Deterministic Parsing: A Modern View', *Proceedings of NELS 15*, Brown University, Providence, Rhode Island, p. 15–33.

Burzio, L.: 1986, *Italian Syntax*, Reidel, Dordrecht, Holland.

Chodorow, M.: 1976, *Experimental Studies of Syntactic and Lexical Processes in Language Comprehension*, Ph.D. dissertation, Department of Psychology, Massachusetts Institute of Technology, Cambridge, Massachusetts.

Chomsky, N.: 1965, *Aspects of the Theory of Syntax*, MIT Press, Cambridge, Massachusetts.

Chomsky, N.: 1981, *Lectures on Government and Binding: The Pisa Lectures*, Foris, Dordrecht, Holland.

Chomsky, N.: 1986, *Barriers*, MIT Press, Cambridge, Massachusetts.

Clark, R. and E. Gibson: 1988, 'A Parallel Model For Adult Sentence Processing', *Proceedings of the Tenth Annual Conference of the Cognitive Science Society*, pp. 270–276

Clifton, C., L. Frazier, and C. Connine: 1984, 'Lexical Expectations in Sentence Comprehension', *Journal of Verbal Learning and Verbal Behavior* 23, 696–708.

Fodor, J.A., T. Bever, and M. Garrett: 1974, *The Psychology of Language*, McGraw-Hill, New York.

Fodor, J.A., M. Garrett, and T. Bever: 1968, 'Some Syntactic Determinants of Sentential Complexity II, Verb Structure', *Perception and Psychophysics* 3, 453–461.

Fodor, J.D.: 1978, 'Parsing Strategies and Constraints on Transformations', *Linguistic Inquiry* 9, 427–473.

Fodor, J.D.: 1985, 'Deterministic Parsing and Subjacency', *Language and Cognitive Processes* 1, 3–42.

Ford, M., J. Bresnan, and R. Kaplan: 1982, 'A competence based theory of syntactic closure', in J. Bresnan (ed.), *The Mental Representation of Grammatical Relations*, MIT Press, Cambridge, Massachusetts, pp. 727–796

Frazier, L.: 1987, 'Against Lexical Generation of Syntax', unpublished manuscript, University of Massachusetts, Amherst, Massachusetts.

Frazier, L. and J.D. Fodor: 1978, 'The Sausage Machine: A New Two-stage Parsing Model', *Cognition* 6, 291–325.

Frazier, L. and K. Rayner: 1982, 'Making and Correcting Errors During Sentence Comprehension: Eye Movements in the Analysis of Structurally Ambiguous Sentences', *Cognitive Psychology* 14, 178–210.

Goodman, G., J. McClelland, and R. Gibbs: 1981, 'The Role of Syntactic Context in Word Recognition', *Memory and Cognition* 9, 580–586.

Gorrell, P.: 1987, *Studies in Human Syntactic Processing: Ranked-Parallel Versus Serial Models*, Ph.D. dissertation, Department of Linguistics, University of Connecticut, Storrs, Connecticut.

Gorrell, P.: 1988a, 'Lexical Decision and Structural Ambiguity', unpublished manuscript, Department of Linguistics, University of Maryland College Park, College Park, Maryland.

Gorrell, P.: 1988b, 'Evaluating the Heads-of-Phrases Hypothesis', unpublished manuscript, Department of Linguistics, University of Maryland College Park, College Park, Maryland.

Gorrell, P.: 1989, 'Establishing the Loci of Serial and Parallel Effects in Syntactic Processing', *Journal of Psycholinguistic Research* **18**, 61–73.

Gorrell, P. and Q. Chen: 1988, 'Minimal Commitment Parsing: Two Examples from Mandarin', *Proceedings of the 1988 Eastern States Conference on Linguistics*, Ohio State University Press, Columbus, Ohio.

Huang, J.: 1984, 'On the Distribution and Reference of Empty Pronouns', *Linguistic Inquiry* **15**, 531–574.

Huang, J.: 1987, 'Remarks on Empty Categories in Chinese', *Linguistic Inquiry* **18**, 321–337.

Kurtzman, H.: 1985, *Studies In Syntactic Ambiguity Resolution*, Ph.D. dissertation, Department of Psychology, Massachusetts Institute of Technology, Cambridge, Massachusetts. Distributed by Indiana University Linguistics Club, Bloomington, Indiana.

Lukatela, G., A. Kostic, L. Feldman, and M. Turvey: 1983, 'Grammatical Priming of Inflected Nouns', *Memory and Cognition* **11**, 59–63.

Marcus, M.: 1980, *A Theory Of Syntactic Recognition For Natural Language*, MIT Press, Cambridge, Massachusetts.

Marcus, M., D. Hindle, and M. Fleck: 1983, 'D-theory: Talking about Talking about Trees', *Proceedings of the 21st Annual Meeting of the Association for Computational Linguistics*, Morristown, New Jersey, pp. 129–136.

Mitchell, D.: 1987, 'Lexical Guidance in Human Parsing: Locus and Processing Characteristics', in M. Coltheart (ed.), *Attention and Performance XII: The Psychology of Reading*, LEA Publishers, Hillsdale, New Jersey, pp. 601–618.

Mitchell, D. and V. Holmes: 1985, 'The Role of Specific Information about the Verb in Parsing Sentences with Local Structural Ambiguity', *Journal of Memory and Language* **24**, 542–559.

Nicol, J.: 1989, 'What the Parser Knows about the Grammar: Psycholinguistic Evidence', *Proceedings of West Coast Conference on Formal Linguistics VIII*, pp. 289–302.

Ni, W.: 1987, 'Empty Topics in Chinese', *University of Connecticut Working Papers in Linguistics*, Volume 1, University of Connecticut, Storrs, Connecticut, pp. 81–86.

Perlmutter, D.: 1978, 'Impersonal Passive and the Unaccusative Hypothesis', *Proceedings of the Berkeley Linguistics Society*, 4, pp. 157–189.

Pritchett, B.: 1988, 'Garden Path Phenomena and the Grammatical Basis of Language Processing', *Language* **64**, 539–576.

Pritchett, B.: this volume, 'Subjaceny in a Principle-Based Parser', pp. 301–345.

Shapiro, L., E. Zurif, and J. Grimshaw: 1987, 'Sentence Processing and the Mental Representation of Verbs', *Cognition* **27**, 219–246.

Wright, B. and M. Garrett: 1984, 'Lexical Decision in Sentences: Effects of Syntactic Structure', *Memory and Cognition* **12**, 31–45.

Department of Linguistics,
University of Maryland at College Park,
College Park, Maryland 20742, U.S.A.

BRADLEY L. PRITCHETT

SUBJACENCY IN A PRINCIPLE-BASED PARSER

1. INTRODUCTION:
SUBJACENCY AND LANGUAGE PROCESSING

Recent wide-spread shifts in the conception of grammar from a system of rules to a system of constraints on representation has raised the possibility that a similar refocusing might also be appropriate with respect to performance and in particular natural language processing. This chapter explores certain empirical and theoretical issues relevant to principle-based approaches to parsing with special attention to the processing of long-distance dependencies.

> Parsing programs are typically rule-based; the parser, in effect, mirrors a rule system and asks how these rules can assign a structure to a string that is analyzed word-by-word. The examples given above, and many others, suggest that a different approach might be in order. Given a lexicon, structures can be projected from heads by virtue of the projection principle, $\overline{X}$ theory, and other subsystems of UG that are involved in licensing elements, which are associated with one another by these principles in the manner already illustrated. Perhaps parsers should not be based on rules at all but should rather be based on lexical properties and principles of UG that determine structures from them. Rule-based parsers are in some respects implausible. For one things, complexity of parsing increases rapidly as rules proliferate; for another, since languages appear to differ substantially if viewed from the perspective of rule systems, they will require quite different parsers if the latter are rule-based—an unlikely consequence. The entire question merits substantial rethinking, so it appears. (Chomsky 1986a, p. 151)

Specifically, I will argue that an independently motivated principle-based theory of parsing provides an account of the island constraints (cf.

R. C. Berwick et al. (eds.),
Principle-Based Parsing: Computation and Psycholinguistics, 301–345.
© 1991 *Kluwer Academic Publishers. Printed in the Netherlands.*

Ross, 1967), which are therefore not to be considered ungrammatical as long maintained but will instead be shown to exceed the capacity of the human sentence processor to perform certain structural analyses during parsing. Through a defense of this hypothesis that island violations are amenable to a processing-theoretic analysis, additional aspects of the structure and functioning of the human sentence processing mechanism will be explored. In turn, the characterization of island constraint violations in terms of processing will have implications for grammatical theory since principles such as subjacency will have no grammatical status if the data they attempt to characterize represent instead epiphenomena of performance. It is important to distinguish this claim from one that holds that Subjacency is a grammatical constraint whose functional motivation is to be found in the structure of the parser. (See, for example, discussion in Marcus, 1980; Berwick and Weinberg, 1984). Analyses of this latter sort continue to maintain that Subjacency violations are ungrammatical but that the syntax proper must incorporate such a constraint given the parser's intrinsic (possibly deterministic) structure (see Fodor, 1985 for critical discussion). This contrasts with the hypothesis defended here that the global representations associated with island violations are themselves grammatical, but locally lead to processing breakdown. This approach is potentially stronger in that it must account for the empirical data involving island violations rather than simply motivate a grammatical constraint which in turn accounts for the empirical facts.

It is probably not an exaggeration to say that contemporary linguistic theory is founded on the distinction between grammatical and ungrammatical utterances. In the simplest case, sentences are both grammatical and interpretable:

(1) I think John likes Bill

As has long been recognized, however, not all grammatical sentences are interpretable nor all ungrammatical strings uninterpretable. In addition, there exists a class of sentences that is neither interpretable nor grammatical:

(2) Bitten leg the the the on was cat dog

—a class of ungrammatical sentences that are nevertheless quite understandable:

(3) I going beat you over head

—and finally a class of sentences that are grammatical but nevertheless uninterpretable. Well-known examples of this last class include both multiple center-embeddings:

(4) The mouse (which) the cat (which) the dog chased ate died

as well as traditional garden path sentences:

(5) (a) The horse raced past the barn fell

(b) The doctor persuaded the patient that he was having trouble with to leave

While such unprocessable sentences have received relatively little attention within syntactic theory, these grammatical but virtually un-parsable sentences have proven rich territory for psycho- and computa-tional linguists interested in issues concerning natural language process-ing. For reasons that are quite familiar—*i.e.*, the existence of parallel structures that are perfectly grammatical:

(6) (a) The man (who) Bill chased fled

(b) Everyone (that) someone (who) I know likes died

(7) The horse ridden past the barn fell

(8) The doctor persuaded the patient who he was having trouble with to leave

it has long been recognized as both unnecessary and undesirable to ac-count for the deviance of such sentences within the grammar:

> The parser associates structural descriptions with expressions; the I-language generates structural descriptions for each expres-sion. But the association provided by the parser and the I-language will not in general be the same, since the parser is as-signed other structure, apart from the incorporated I-language. There are many familiar examples of such divergence: garden path sentences, multiple self-embedding, and so on. [...] Fur-thermore, so-called ungrammatical or deviant sentences are of-ten quite readily parsable and are even perfectly intelligible, and quite properly used in appropriate circumstances...(Chomsky, 1988, p. 15)

As Chomsky implies, in order to avoid potential complications in the construction of a theory of grammar, it is crucial to recognize whether a certain class of linguistic data is unacceptable for reasons involving grammar or performance, and the need to distinguish (at least) these two types of unacceptability: ungrammaticality and unprocessability, has long been recognized.

The principle of Subjacency (Chomsky, 1973), which was introduced in part to provide a putatively more unified account of the island constraints, exhibits two characteristics that make its status as a grammatical condition somewhat suspect. First, Subjacency arguably applies to a rather limited subset of movement (primarily *Wh*-movement) and as such could be viewed as a remnant of a nonmodular and construction specific approach to syntax. Second, and more important, Subjacency constrains such movement only in the mapping from D-structure (DS) to S-structure (SS)—but fails to apply to identical movement from SS to Logical form (LF) (Chomsky, 1986a; Huang, 1982; Lasnik and Saito, 1984, 1990). This suggests that what is relevant is the actual overt displacement of the *Wh*-word rather than the resulting representation, which is identical whether the movement occurs at SS or LF. This is rather surprising since Subjacency as a result stands alone as the sole remaining syntactic constraint on a rule (of movement) rather than on a representation.

It is not my intention to argue in detail against previous grammatical analyses of such illicit extraction—analyses that have obviously yielded many of the findings discussed here. Instead, what I wish to do is suggest an approach to these same phenomena that incorporates many of these previous insights in a somewhat different fashion and raise the possibility that this alternative analysis may in its own turn have interesting ramifications for grammatical as well as processing theory. Specifically, I would like to argue that an island violation is a type of garden path (GP) sentence—an unacceptable sentence that results from the combination of (a) local parsing decisions that ultimately prove not to be consonant with a global grammatical representation, and (b) the parser's inability to perform the structural reanalyses necessary to obtain a grammatical representation. The initial incorrect parsing decision is frequently, but not necessarily, the result of a local ambiguity in the input string. In other words, GPs are the result of unrecoverable parsing errors. (As in previous work, I employ the term garden path in a narrower sense than some researchers for whom condition (a) alone is sufficient.) Before attempting to demonstrate that island violations are garden paths, it is first necessary to introduce the particulai principle-based processing theory assumed throughout—a theory that itself necessarily makes crucial use of principles of grammar.[1]

2. THE STRUCTURE OF THE PARSER

Pritchett (1987, 1988a) defends the hypothesis that the human language processor operates by admitting structure which maximally satisfies the principles of Government and Binding (GB) theory locally at every poin: during a parse, and that the constraints on syntactic reanalysis during processing are also derived from grammatical theory. For example, the following principle is instrumental in steering the parser:

(9) θ- (thematic) attachment: The θ-criterion attempts to be satisfied at every point during processing given the maximal θ-grid.

Additional licensing principles, such as Case theory and Specifier-Head (Spec-Head) agreement are also crucially relevant. Since their effects often (but by no means always) overlap with that of θ-attachment, I will continue to employ the latter term where it is intended to suggest not only the local application of the theta criterion but also other grammatical principles that license argument structure. (Principles solely related to interpretation rather than argument structure, such as certain aspects of the Binding theory, are not as obviously relevant and for the most part will not be considered. Berwick, 1988, argues toward a similar conclusion in an interesting discussion of the computational tractability of an approach to parsing based on the local application of grammatical principles.)

θ-attachment in its wide sense is intended to insure that phrasal categories are projected only when a head is encountered in the input string and that phrases are attached into the parse tree only when locally licensed by global grammatical principles. Projecting a category before the occurrence of its head is by definition not possible in a strictly principle-based parsing model since the relevant features of the head that determine its categorical identity and license its arguments are not present until the head is encountered. With θ-attachment as its control structure, the processor may display both strictly data driven/bottom up behavior (the occurrence of a prenominal adjective does not cause the projection of an NP before the nominal head is encountered), as well as hypothesis driven/top down behavior (a complement position may be projected before the overt occurrence of the complement given the Theta- and Case assigning properties of a previously encountered head). Given this reliance on the occurrence of heads, the linear and structural position of that lexical constituent will be the primary locus of cross-linguistic variation in the operation of the parser—variation that is attributable to the syntax itself rather than to distinct parsing rules or differences in some fundamental cognitive ability, such as memory capacity.

Consider then how a simple sentence is processed within this model (for discussion of other principle-based parsing approaches see Abney, 1988; Berwick, 1987, 1991 forthcoming; Gibson, 1987; Johnson, this volume; Pritchett, 1987, 1988a; Wehrli, 1988; and references therein):

(10) Vampires bit those boys

(a) *Vampires* is encountered in the input string, its category N identified, and, as it is a head, an NP projected: $[_{NP} [_{\bar{N}} [_N \text{vampires}]]]$. Since no determiner has occurred in the input string and since *vampires* assigns no θ-role, no specifier or complement position is included in the projection. As no θ-role assigner has been processed, the NP must be left locally roleless. This is an unavoidable, and hence harmless local violation of the θ-criterion. No higher structure, including IP (Inflectional Phrase), is projected as no relevant heads have been admitted. Notice that given the existence of sentence fragments, the alternative hypothesis that an S is immediately projected makes precisely the wrong predictions.

(b) *Bite* is identified as a V, its θ-assigning properties recognized and a VP is projected that includes a complement position to which both a θ-role and Case may be assigned. Furthermore, an IP is also projected by virtue of the verb's possessing the features of INFL (Inflection). Whether this is by virtue of V raising or I lowering in languages where INFL is the head of S is not directly relevant here. If there are languages in which V is the head of S, no such features will be required in those languages, cf. Whitman (1987). *Vampires* may now be attached into the projected Spec of IP position where the requirements of Case and θ theory are satisfied to the maximum degree possible in the local string—both with respect to the target NP which requires these features and the head that must discharge them. (I will leave open for now the question of whether the θ-role and Case of (certain) IP subjects is obtained through a chain with its head in Spec of IP and its tail in Spec of VP.)

(c) *Those* is identified in the input string; its lexical category, Det (Determiner), is identified, but no further action can be taken. No NP is projected since no attachment could be licensed as this point: the NP would have no head whose features could license the Spec. As attachments are made solely based on the local application of global grammatical principles, the parser would gain nothing with respect to attachment of the determiner and a locally unlicensable NP node would have been created. If *those* is considered the head of a determiner phrase (DP) (cf. Abney, 1987; Stowell, 1989) the analysis will have to be extended in obvious ways with a DP being projected at this point, as will be discussed in section 4.2. I will ignore here certain aspects of lexical categorical ambiguity—such as the possibility that those is initially interpreted as an NP rather than a Determiner. Such reanalysis is not predicted to be costly within this model (see Pritchett, 1987).

(d) *Boys* is identified and an NP projected as in step (a). The unattached *those* is integrated into the parse tree via attachment as specifier, now licensed via Spec-Head agreement. The entire NP, rather than being left locally roleless and Caseless, is attached into the available Case and θ-marked complement position within the VP. The sentence then terminates, yielding the final parse.

The fundamental operation of the processor is thus quite straightforward: a parse results from the local application of global grammatical principles as driven by phrasal heads.

3. THE TREATMENT OF GARDEN PATH PHENOMENA

It is of course possible that in the processor's attempt to maximally satisfy the requirements of the grammar online, local attachments may be made that prove to be globally untenable. This is the well-known problem of local ambiguity in natural language processing. Consider the contrast between the following two sentences:

(11) After Steve drank *the soup* proved to be poisoned

(12) Steve knew *the boy* hated salmon

In each case when the italicized NP is encountered, grammatical principles will be maximally satisfied by attaching that NP as the complement of the immediately preceding verb allowing it to receive both a θ-role and Case. What is initially puzzling, however, is that though sentence (11) proves to be strikingly difficult to process (cf. Frazier and Rayner, 1982), example (12) is completely unproblematic. Clearly, not all local misattachments lead to processing difficulty. Pritchett (1987, 1988a) attempts to demonstrate the existence of a unified constraint on syntactic reanalysis during parsing that is itself dependent on grammatical notions:

(13) Theta Reanalysis Constraint (TRC): Syntactic reanalysis that reinterprets a Theta-marked constituent as outside of its current θ domain and as within an existing θ domain of which it is not a member renders a sentence unacceptable.

(14) Theta (θ) domain: α is in the γ theta domain (θ domain) of β iff α receives the γ θ-role from β or α is dominated by a constituent that receives the γ θ-role from β.

Together, θ-attachment and the TRC correctly account for and cross-classify a wide range of unprocessable garden path structures with respect to the source of the initial error and the subsequent reanalysis required, including:

(15)¿The horse raced past the barn fell

(16)¿The doctor persuaded the patient he was having trouble with to leave

(17)¿After Steve ate the soup proved to be poisoned

(18)¿Without her contributions would be impossible

(19)¿Mary warned her mother went home

(The symbol ¿ marks sentences that are unacceptable for reasons related to processing rather than grammar.) Principle (13) is essentially a constraint on the possible deformation of previously built argument structure and correctly accounts for the contrast in processing difficulty between sentence (11) and (12), both of which involve a local subject–object ambiguity. Consider the relevant aspects of their respective parses. (For the time being I will ignore certain ambiguities concerning the complement of the initial PP—details are discussed in example (28) below.)

(20)¿After Steve ate the soup proved to be poisoned

(a) *Steve* is identified as an N and an NP projected that at this point can receive no θ-role since no Theta-assigner has been encountered. This is an unavoidable local violation of the θ-criterion and is not costly.

(b) *Eat* is identified as a verb, its θ-grid recovered, and a VP, IP, and CP projected.[2] The verb may assign an external and an internal role. As both a role and target are locally available the previously projected NP is attached as the specifier of IP in order to receive the θ-role and Case.

(c) *The soup* is identified as an NP and in accord with θ-attachment is attached into the parse tree so as to be assigned by *eat* the available internal role as well as Case. Leaving the NP roleless would constitute an avoidable local violation of the θ-criterion and Case theory and is hence not pursued.

(d) *Prove* is encountered, projecting a VP, IP, and CP. The verb is found to possess an external role and Case that it must discharge onto Spec-IP. As English lacks any empty elements that could occur in this position, the only potential subject is the *soup*, that has already been attached as object. The resulting reanalysis must reinterpret that NP as outside of the internal θ domain of *eat*—it ceases either to receive that role from *eat* or to dominated by a constituent that receives that role. Furthermore *the soup* enters the external θ domain of *prove*, a domain of which it was not previously a member. This violates the Theta Reanalysis Constraint and is consequently predicted to be costly—to yield an unacceptable sentence, a garden path.

It is crucial to recognize that it is not simply the initial misattachment of an NP as object and its subsequent reanalysis as subject in the above example that yields the severe processing difficulty (*i.e.*, we make no claims for strict determinism). Contrast sentence (12), repeated below, that also involves a subject object ambiguity and a similar local misattachment (irrelevant details again suppressed):

(21) Steve knew the boy hated salmon

(a) *Steve* is identified as an NP but at this point can receive no θ-role or Case. No IP is projected as its head has not been encountered.

(b) *Know* is identified as a V, its maximal θ-grid recovered, and a VP, IP, and CP projected. This verb assigns two roles. *Steve* is attached as the Spec of IP to receive a role and Case locally.

310 BRADLEY L. PRITCHETT

(c) *The boy* is identified as an NP and assigned the internal role in accord with θ-attachment.

(d) *Hate* is identified and a VP, IP, and CP projected. No NP is available to serve as the verb's subject and hence syntactic reanalysis must occur, reinterpreting *the boy* as the subject of *hate* rather than the object of *know*. However, in contrast to the previous example, reanalysis in this case is not problematic. While in (20), the restructuring reinterpreted an NP, *the soup*, as outside of the internal domain of *eat* and within the external domain of *prove*, here the reanalyzed NP, *the boy*, though it does enter the external domain of *hate*, remains within the internal θ domain of *know*. Although the NP itself no longer receives its original internal role from *know*, it remains dominated by a constituent (CP) that receives that role and hence the Theta Reanalysis Constraint is not violated. *The boy* comes to be the subject of a clause that is itself the object of *know*. Such a reanalysis lies within the capabilities of the processor according to the TRC and the sentence is correctly predicted to be perfectly acceptable.

I will henceforth adopt this processing model and attempt to demonstrate the relevance of both θ-attachment (in its wide sense) as well as the Theta Reanalysis Constraint to a processing account of island violations, sharpening and extending the general principle-based processing theory in so doing.[3]

4. PROCESSING GAPS

There is now a large body of psycholinguistic evidence that given a 'filler' (*e.g.*, a *Wh*-word), syntactic 'gaps' are postulated as soon as grammatically possible (see for example McElree and Bever, 1989; Carlson and Tanenhaus, 1989; McElree and Bever, 1988; Nicol and Swinney, 1989; and references therein). In general, no explanation has been provided for this robust and interesting finding and the fact that 'gaps are filled immediately' is essentially stipulated. In fact, however, the principle of θ-attachment provides a direct explanation of these data. When a *Wh*-word is encountered during processing, grammatical knowledge determines that it heads an $\overline{\text{A}}$ chain through which it must receive both a θ-role and Case. In accord with the θ-attachment strategy, when a θ-assigner is encountered a variable argument bound by the *Wh*-word may be immediately postulated, licensing the chain and satisfying the Case- and θ-assigning properties of the head. Hence, there is an independently motivated account of the strong psycholinguistic evidence that humans postulate gaps as soon as possible given a potential filler. Given this, two crucial and related questions immediately arise: (a) are there conditions under which it is not possible to postulate gaps?; and, (b) what happens when the gap that was originally hypothesized proves not to be the globally correct gap? This latter case can be exemplified by quite straightforward examples such as the following. (The symbol $\emptyset$ indicates a gap that is temporarily posited locally and e the actual global locus of the empty category.)

(22) What$_i$ do you believe $\emptyset$ John burned e_i

(23) Who$_i$ do you believe $\emptyset$ e_i burned the toast

In both instances, though a variable is initially postulated immediately after the verb believe as its complement, it proves to be illegitimate when the actual complement clause filler is encountered. Since such sentences are perfectly acceptable, it is clear that this reanalysis cannot be problematic for the human language processor. In contrast, certain other long-distance extractions are clearly unacceptable.

(24)*What$_i$ did you eat $\emptyset$ after John burned e_i

(25)*What$_i$ did you eat toast after John burned e_i

and it is to these island constraint violations that we now turn.

4.1. Adjunct Islands

As the asterisk marking on (24) reflects, such sentences have classically been considered to be ungrammatical rather than unprocessable. Descriptively, example (24) is an adverbial or adjunct island violation. The revised extended standard theory (REST) bounding nodes definition of Subjacency (Chomsky, 1973) that prohibits movement across two syntactic nodes (S and NP for English), is incapable of dealing with the illegitimacy of such extractions. (For ease of reference I will somewhat inaccurately refer to versions of Subjacency that simply list nodes not to be crossed during a derivation as the bounding nodes definition—this as opposed to the barriers definition that is intended to introduce a derived and nonstipulative definition of bounding node.)

(26) $[_{\bar{S}}$ $[_{Comp}$ What$_i]$ $[_S$ did you $[_{VP}$ $[_{VP}$ $[_V$ eat$]]$ $[_{PP}$ $[_P$ after$]$ $[_{\bar{S}}$ $[_{Comp}$ $t_i]$
$[_S$ John cooked $[e_i]]]]]]]$

As the lower Comp should be available as an intermediate landing
site and consequently only a single S node crossed on each cycle, the fact
that extraction is unacceptable out of adverbials remained a stipulation.

Chomsky's (1986) *Barriers* approach attempts to collapse the Adjunct Condition (and more generally Huang's (1982) Constraint on Extraction Domains, that prohibits movement out of categories that are
not properly governed) with Subjacency. The adjunct PP is a Blocking
Category (BC) and hence a barrier for $[e_i]$ since it receives no θ-role
and is thus not L-marked. The higher IP thus inherits barrierhood as it
dominates a BC for $[e_i]$:

(27) $[_{CP}$ $[_{NP}$ What$_i$ $]$ $[_{\bar{C}}$ $[_C$ did$]$ $[_{IP}$ you $[_{VP}$ $[_{VP}$ $[_V$ eat$]]$ $[_{PP}$ $[_P$ after$]$
$[_{CP}$ $[_{IP}$ John cooked $[e_i]]]]]]]$

Whatever their differences, these two analyses crucially share the assumption that the global representation that results from movement out
of an island is ungrammatical. Consider now the alternative hypothesis that island violations are grammatical but unprocessable. Viewed
in these terms, examples such as (22–23) make it clear that the processor must be able to reanalyze hypothesized gaps, while sentences
like (24) reveal that the ability cannot be unconstrained. In fact, the
Theta Reanalysis Constraint provides a rather straightforward account
of many island phenomena. Since 'gaps' are instantiations of the same
constituent (a variable) by virtue of being bound by the same operator
(the *Wh*-word), they are subject to the same reanalysis constraint on
processing (the TRC) that holds of any constituent. (The reanalysis is
more precisely considered to apply to the chain rather than the variable,
but is perhaps somewhat easier to visualize as applying to the gap—that
is to the tail whose structural position is actually altered.)

For example, adjunct island violations such as (26) may be accounted
for given the principles of θ-attachment and the Theta Reanalysis Constraint. First consider how the following unacceptable sentence is processed, suppressing for the time being certain details not of direct concern here.

(28)*What$_i$ did you eat $\emptyset$ after John burned e_i

(a) *What* is encountered and identified as an NP but no attachment is locally possible.

(b) *Do* is processed and identified as a head. Grammatical principles may be maximally satisfied by projecting a CP and attaching *what* as its specifier, licensed via Spec-Head agreement, a [+Q] feature in C selecting a [+*wh*] in Spec (see Baker, 1970; Nishigauchi, 1986). The general requirement on *Wh*-words that they $\overline{\text{A}}$ bind variables (at SS in English) prevents the projection of *do* to IP and the attachment of *what* as the subject. If *do* here locally projected to IP, no attachment of *what* would be possible as no head of CP has been encountered. Globally, *what* must bind a variable in a Case and θ-position in order for the chain that it heads to be licensed.

(c) *You* is processed and an NP projected. As *do* has no features to assign to an NP complement to CP, no attachment can take place and the NP remains unlicensed. In other words, the eventual subject cannot at this point be attached into the parse tree.

(d) *Eat* is encountered and a VP projected. I would like to suggest that V also projects to IP if that projection has not been made (as it will have in a sentence with a lexically filled I, such as *John can eat beets*) even if the verb lacks inflectional features.

Although the exact mechanism involved is not entirely clear, I do not believe that this need be considered a stipulation as it arguably results from the parser's reconstruction of chains that are the result of head movement. Here, the *Wh* + *do* string has locally licensed the structure $[_{CP} [_{NP} \text{ what}] [_{\overline{C}} [_{C} \text{ do}] \ldots$ but the grammar will also require that the element in C be coindexed with an element in an as yet unseen I. Since an empty I will of course not be overtly visible to the parser, the first indicator of its occurrence will be the V that heads the VP complement of I, licensing the projection at that stage. This is consistent with the general notion that chains, almost by definition, are not constructed until both their heads and tails are licensed. In the case of argument chains the tail is licensed by an overt feature assigning head, but the evidence may be less direct in situations involving head movement.[4]

Consequently, as *do* did not in this instance project to IP given the presence of the *Wh*-word, the IP projection occurs at this point. The verb is able to assign a θ-role and Case to its subject and complement. Licensing conditions on you may be maximally satisfied at this point by attaching you as the specifier of IP, where it receives a θ-role and Case. *Additionally, an object variable gap is immediately posited in accord with*

θ-attachment. This creates a chain that can receive a θ-role and Case locally satisfying the requirements of the θ-criterion and Case theory with respect to the chain just as for overt arguments *in situ*:

$$[_{CP} [_{NP} \text{what}_i] [_{\bar{C}} [_C \text{did}] [_{IP} [_{NP} \text{you}] [_{\bar{I}} [_I] [_{VP} [_V \text{eat}] [e_i]]]\ldots$$

The alternative would involve an avoidable local θ-criterion and Case filter violation and is not pursued.

(e) *After* is recovered and a PP is projected.

(f) *John* is processed and attached as the object of the preposition.

(g) When *burn* is recovered, a VP, IP, and CP are projected.

The verb has Case and a θ-role to assign to its subject and the clause itself requires a θ-role. Rather than leaving the CP unlicensed, these conditions may be maximally satisfied by reanalyzing *John* as the subject of *burn* and the projected CP as the object of the preposition *after*. The reanalysis of *John* is not costly, however, as the clause of which it is the subject argument remains within the internal θ domain of *after* as its complement. As *burn* is obligatorily transitive, the variable bound by the *Wh*-operator must be reanalyzed as within its internal θ domain.[5]

This new locus of the gap is not within the internal domain of *eat* as it no longer receives the internal θ-role from *eat* nor, as a VP adjunct, is it dominated by any constituent that receives that role. Furthermore, it enters a θ domain internal to the adjunct itself of which it was not previously a member. (I will delay considering the important question of the attachment of the adjunct itself until section 4.4.) Treating variables parallel to overt arguments, this is a violation of the Theta Reanalysis Constraint and is correctly predicted to result in a sentence that is unacceptable. We attribute the unacceptability to a different source than typically maintained: it is unprocessable rather than ungrammatical. The parallels with the garden path in (20) are clear and surprising.

In contrast, if the reanalyzed gap remains within its initially postulated θ domain the sentence is completely acceptable as predicted by the TRC:

(29) Who do you believe Ø [e] burned the toast

(a) The analysis proceeds as above through the processing of the verb *believe* and the construal of the variable as its object.

(b) Subsequently *burn* is processed, a VP, an IP, and a CP projected. *Burn* requires a subject and the gap must be reanalyzed as within its external θ domain allowing the CP to be attached as the complement of *believe*, maximally satisfying Case and θ theory locally. However, the variable remains within the internal domain of *believe* for, though it no longer receives the internal θ-role from *believe*, the argument that dominates it, the complement clause itself, does receive that θ-role. Of course, no gap is posited after *burn* despite the fact that no overt object has as yet appeared since the *Wh*-word already binds a variable at this point in the parse. Though such a reanalysis would construct a legitimate *Wh*-chain, it would globally force the complement clause to remain subjectless, a fact determined by $\overline{X}$ theory. When the overt NP *the toast* appears, it is attached as the complement of *burn* and the parse terminates.

The parallel with the misattachment and reanalysis involved in the locally ambiguous but unproblematic example (21) is striking. Pursuing this line of analysis, the acceptability of a sentence such as:

(30) What$_i$ do you believe $\emptyset$ John burned e_i

is directly accounted for and reveals that whether a reanalyzed gap enters an external θ domain (as in 29) or an internal domain cannot be relevant:

(a) Again the sentence is processed as above through the appearance of the verb *believe*.

(b) At *burn*, a VP, IP, and CP are projected. Grammatical requirements can be maximally satisfied by construing *John* as the subject and the clause attached as object. *Burn* may license a complement and the variable must be reanalyzed as its object. Simply leaving the variable as the object of *believe* and the clause *John burned* unattached would of course involve an avoidable local θ-criterion violation and is not pursued. As in the previous example, the gap remains within the internal domain of *believe* for, though it does not receive the internal θ-role from *believe*, the complement clause that dominates it receives that internal θ-role. The Theta Reanalysis Constraint is not violated and the sentence is acceptable. This contrasts directly with (28) wherein the reanalyzed gap failed to remain a member of its initially postulated θ domain, resulting in a deviant sentence.

Examples such as the following, that contain an overt matrix object, are accounted for in precisely the same fashion as (28).

(31)*What$_i$ did you eat $\emptyset$ toast after John cooked e_i

(a) Processing occurs as in example (28) through the appearance of *eat*.

(b) When *toast* is encountered the NP is left roleless in unavoidable local violation of θ-attachment (a situation which we have seen is not highly costly) since an operator-variable chain has been constructed. Reanalysis does not occur at this point to interpret *toast* as the object of *eat* and the variable as unlicensed, as there would be no gain with respect to grammatical principles granting the reasonable assumption that any reanalysis is mildly costly and pursued only for local gain with respect to the satisfaction of grammatical principles.

(c) Processing continues as expected through the recovery of cook and the projection of VP, IP, and CP. The sentence terminates and, as *cook* necessarily licenses an object and *toast* is unattached, reanalysis must occur. The variable must be reinterpreted as the complement of *cook*, and the gap reposited within its internal θ domain. As in example (29) this violates the Theta Reanalysis Constraint, as the new locus of the gap is not within the internal domain of the original θ-assigner, *eat*. Whether *eat* itself is used transitively or intransitively is irrelevant. The interpretation of the featureless NP, *toast*, as internal argument of *eat* is not predicted to be problematic. (I delay discussion of unambiguously unergative verbs until section 4.4.)

This example serves to reemphasize the important fact mentioned above that it is operations that apply to linguistic entities themselves, not arbitrary structure *per se*, that characterize the functioning and limitations of the parser. This is expected given the view that the structure of the parser is largely derived from principles of grammar. A variable represents the same constituent throughout the parse by virtue of its being bound by the same operator. Were this not the case, we might expect sentences such as (31) to be perfectly processable. If a gap were simply an empty structural position built by the parser, we would have no reason to suspect that it might not simply be subsequently 'filled' by a subsequent overt NP, such as *toast*. Later postulation of a gap after *cook* would therefore not violate the Theta Reanalysis Constraint as the two gaps would bear no relationship to each other: no constituent would have been reanalyzed. By considering the gap to be a variable, or equivalently considering the reanalysis to apply to the chain, we predict the encountered processing effects.

Continuing to focus on extraction from adjuncts, let consider several other examples. A sentence such as:

(32)*What$_i$ did John cook $\emptyset$ before e_i burned the toast

is predicted to be deviant in a fashion parallel to (28) above, rather than acceptable similar to (29).

(a) The analysis proceeds as expected through the processing of the matrix verb and the construal of the variable as its object.

(b) Subsequently *burn* is processed, a VP, an IP, and a CP projected. *Burn* requires a subject and the gap must be reanalyzed as within its external θ domain. However, as the variable fails to remain within the internal domain of *cook* and enters a domain of which it was not previously a member, the TRC is violated and the deviance is predicted (This sentence may also be an empty category principle (ECP) or *that*-trace violation and hence unacceptable for purely grammatical reasons.)

Now consider an unproblematic example such as:

(33) What did you eat $\emptyset$ after John cooked toast

Here the initially postulated gap proves to be the correct and hence the acceptability of the sentence is predicted. As before, the tail of the chain headed by the *Wh*-word is first associated with the internal argument position of *eat*. When *cook* is encountered, no reanalysis takes place and no gap is posited since the *Wh*-chain is already licensed. When *toast* is encountered, it may be attached as the internal argument of the verb. No reanalysis of the initially postulated chain occurs and the sentence is perfectly acceptable as expected.

As long as the Theta Reanalysis Constraint is not violated, that is, if upon each reanalysis the gap remains within the same θ domain, *Wh*-movement is truly unbounded:[6]

(34) Who do you believe $\emptyset$ John suspects $\emptyset$ Steve knows $\emptyset$ Bill hates $\emptyset$ ...

Having now provided some evidence for the basic claim that island violations are amenable to a processing rather than a purely grammatical treatment, I will cease to mark such extractions as ungrammatical but instead employ the symbol used to mark garden paths (¿). As the fundamentals of the analysis being proposed should now be clear, let us move on to a consideration of a broader range of island effects.[7]

4.2. *Complex NP Islands*

Our processing account of the unacceptability of adjunct island violations extends quite naturally to the range of data descriptively characterized as violating the Complex NP Constraint:

(35) The Complex NP Constraint: No element contained in a sen-
      tence dominated by a noun phrase with a lexical head noun may
      be moved out of that noun phrase by a transformation. (Ross,
      1967, p. 70)

As formulated by Ross, this constraint was intended to account for
the unacceptability of extraction from both relative clauses as well as
from NP complements. Under Chomsky's (1973) formulation of Subjacency, both (36) and (37) are deviant as at least two bounding nodes,
NP and S, are crossed in a single movement during the derivation:

(36)¿What$_i$ do [$_S$ you believe [$_{NP}$ the claim [$_{\bar{S}}$ that [$_S$ Otto saw [e_i]]]]]

(37)¿Who$_i$ does [$_S$ Phineas know [$_{NP}$ a boy [$_{\bar{S}}$ who [$_S$ hates [e_i]]]]]

Within a barriers approach, these sentences are accounted for in
distinct fashions:

(38)¿What$_i$ do [$_{IP}$ you believe [$_{NP}$ the claim [$_{CP}$ that [$_S$ Otto saw [e_i]]]]

(39)¿Who$_i$ does [$_{IP}$ Phineas know [$_{NP}$ a boy [$_{CP}$ who [$_S$ hates [e_i]]]]

Consider first sentence (39). The lower CP is a blocking category
and hence a barrier, as it is not L-marked. The dominating NP inherits
barrierhood and thus two barriers are crossed in the movement from the
Spec of the lower CP to that of the matrix CP. This account requires
the familiar assumption that a relative clause is an adjunct and therefore not an L-marked sister of the head noun. Furthermore, adjunction
to CP must be prohibited despite its status as a non-argument maximal projection, for otherwise it would not serve as a blocking category
for the adjoined *Wh*-word, failing to dominate it, given a definition of
dominance in terms of segments.[8] The situation in (38) is more complicated. Chomsky adopts the standard assumption that the CP in this
instance is indeed L-marked as a sister to the head noun and consequently is neither a blocking category nor a barrier and does not pass

barrierhood to the higher NP. Chomsky claims that (38) is nevertheless deviant, but only weakly so, and stipulates that the embedded CP is a barrier by virtue of receiving oblique case from the head N, an otherwise unmotivated method of achieving barrierhood. Though a barrier, Chomsky stipulates that it is one that does not pass its barrierhood to NP, thus resulting in a milder violation of Subjacency since only one barrier is crossed. For a more complete discussion and criticism, see, in addition to Chomsky (1986b), Kuno and Takami (1990) and Lightfoot and Weinberg (1988).

We are now in a position to consider how this processing analysis of island violations fares in accounting for the deviance of these sentences. First consider:

(40)¿Who does Phineas know a boy who hates

(a) Processing proceeds as expected through the recovery of *know*.

(b) *A boy* is encountered. No attachment is possible since the variable occupies the internal argument position, and a harmless local violation of the θ-criterion results.

(c) *Who* is recovered but no attachment is locally licensed.

(d) *Hate* is parsed and a VP, IP, and CP are projected. A chain is formed with the embedded *Wh*-word binding the subject in the familiar fashion and the clause attached as an adjunct to the NP. Locally, grammatical principles may be maximally satisfied by reinterpreting the variable currently serving as the object of *know* as the internal argument of *hate* and attaching the complex NP as the complement to *know*, yielding $who_i \ldots [_{NP} [_{NP} a \ boy] [_{CP} [who_j] [_{IP} [e_j] [_{\bar{I}} [_{VP} hates [e_i]]]]]]$.

In this fashion all arguments are licensed and the requirements of the various heads are satisfied. The alternative would leave the complex NP unlicensed and the sentence ungrammatical involving both a θ-criterion and Case filter violation. The problematic aspect of this revision is the reanalysis of the variable and the unacceptability of such extractions is predicted. The Theta Reanalysis Constraint is violated as the variable enters a new θ domain, the internal domain of *hate*, and is also removed from its original domain. The variable ceases to be dominated by the NP that receives the role originally assigned to the variable by *know* since the gap is not dominated by all segments of that NP in the structure: $[_{NP} [_{NP} a \ boy] [_{CP} who \ hates \ e]]$. Consequently, what the definition of dominance in terms of segments is here intended to capture is the fact that although the entire complex NP does dominate the variable upon reanalysis, the actual θ-marked head of the structure does not and it is to this that the violation of the TRC is attributable.

Notice that this use of a definition of dominance in terms of segments is completely distinct from Chomsky's where it is employed to prevent a node from becoming a barrier, allowing the bounding conditions to be relaxed. Our processing theory, in contrast, forces greater locality. The *Barriers* analysis is in no way being recreated in processing terms. The interpretation of (40) in which the variable is construed as the subject of the relative clause and who as the object is subject to an analysis parallel to the one above where the variable is the object and who the subject of the relative. Since the former are violently worse than other Complex NP Constraint violations, additional factors are certainly involved; plausibly relevant are the Nested Dependency Constraint (Fodor, 1978) or some version of path theory (Pesetsky, 1982).

Now contrast a noun complement construction:

(41) (ι)What$_i$ do you believe $\emptyset$ the claim that Otto saw e_i

(a) This sentence is processed as above through the occurrence of the matrix verb *believe*.

(b) When the NP *the claim* is identified, it cannot locally be attached into the tree, as a suitable *Wh*-chain has already been formed. Though reanalysis of the variable itself as the complement of the N, *claim*, and the NP that it heads as an argument of *believe* would not violate the TRC, this is not pursued as an N may not directly license a bare NP complement, arguably for reasons attributable to Case theory, as in **John believes Bill's claim Fred.* As a result, such a reanalysis would leave the *Wh*-chain locally unlicensed (cf. **What do you believe the claim?*) and hence is not pursued.

(c) Subsequently, when the verb *see* occurs, a VP, IP, and CP are projected as in the previous example and *Otto* is attached as subject. The CP must be licensed and, as it does not need Case (cf. Stowell, 1981) and the head noun *claim* has a θ-role (but no Case) to assign, these requirements may be maximally satisfied at this point by attaching the clause as a complement to the N, attaching the NP as the complement to *believe*, and reinterpreting the variable as the object of *see*. Now, in this instance unlike the relative clause example above, the restructuring does not violate the Theta Reanalysis Constraint. Though the variable (which was most recently construed as the internal argument of *believe*) enters the internal θ domain of *see*, it is not removed from its original

θ domain since it continues to be dominated by (all segments of) the NP that receive the internal θ-role from *believe*. Evidently, we have made the wrong prediction.

However, it is quite apparent that extraction from N complements is significantly less severe than many other island violations, including extraction from relative clauses, so the fact that the TRC is not strictly violated in such examples may actually be a desirable outcome. Nevertheless, we do need to account for the noticeable deviance of noun complement extractions. Notice that there is a difference between the reanalysis involved in such examples and cases such as:

(42) What$_i$ do you believe $\emptyset$ Otto saw e_i

In a sentence of this sort, the variable is first construed as a matrix object but subsequently comes to receive its θ-role as an argument of the matrix complement, as discussed. In contrast, in noun complement constructions the variable is again initially construed as matrix object but comes to receive its role, not as an argument of the actual matrix complement, but as an argument of an argument (CP) of the matrix complement (NP). In other words there is an intervening θ assigner (the N) of which it is not possible to interpret the variable as an argument during processing. We may therefore attribute the mild deviance of these extractions to the fact that it is not possible to construct the intermediate representation, *What$_i$ do you believe the claim e_i*, before the representation, *What$_i$ do you believe the claim that Otto saw e_i*. This contrasts not only with cases of unproblematic extraction from CP complements where at each stage of reanalysis the gap may be reconstrued as an argument of the constituent that locally assumes its structural position, but also with the situation involving unacceptable extraction from adjuncts and canonical garden path sentences in which it never does so since no constituent dominating the reanalyzed argument remains within the original θ domain:

(43) (a) What$_i$ did John eat $\emptyset$ soup after Bill cooked e_i

(b) After Bill ate the child fell down

There is of course still no difficulty in accounting for long-distance dependencies:

(44) What$_i$ do you believe John suspects Doug knows Bill burned e_i

As in the previous example, the variable will initially be construed as the object of the verb *believe*, though ultimately it will prove to be the internal argument of *burn*, a position in which it neither receives the role assigned by *believe* nor is licensed in a constituent that receives that role directly, the CP of which it is an argument being the object of *know*. However we attribute 'Subjacency' effects to the relationship between each gap posited by the the parser. The variable is first taken as the object of *believe*, then subsequently construed as an argument of *suspect* and then of *know* in order each time, both to permit the attachment of the most recently parsed CP and to license the *Wh*-chain at each new stage of the parse. As a result the sentence is completely unproblematic. This recurrent gap positing and reanalysis somewhat resembles a parsing equivalent of (reverse) successive cyclicity. None of these local reanalyses violates the TRC as the variable remains within the same θ domain upon each reanalysis. This contrasts with noun complement case in which the variable is first interpreted as the object of the matrix verb and then as that of a clause which is not the argument of the higher verb but rather the complement of an intervening head noun of which it itself could not be construed as an intermediate argument.[9]

What these facts then suggest is that the definition of θ domain should be relativized to more accurately reflect the effects of intervening θ-assigners that cannot license an intermediate gap, resembling a processing version of minimality. Notice also that if it is indeed the presence of an intervening feature assigning head which cannot itself license an intermediate gap that is the source of the difficulty, this begins to suggest an explanation for the fact that pied-piping out of certain types of islands results in clear improvement.

(45) (a) About what did you hear the rumor

(b) (¿)What did you hear the rumor that Bill knew about

(c) (?)About what did you hear the rumor that Bill knew

We may attribute this to the possibility of locally construing the PP as a complement to the head noun *rumor* during the parse, thus avoiding a mild TRC violation when its ultimately reanalyzed as a complement of *know*.[10] The processing account motivated here thus directly explains the severity of CNP violations out of relative clauses: the TRC is straightforwardly violated. Extraction from noun complements on the other hand is predicted to be acceptable, perhaps accounting for their relative mildness. They too are found to be susceptible to a processing analysis given a slight revision of the approach which takes into account the role of intervening θ-assigners that cannot license intermediate variables.

4.3. *Subject Islands*

Ross's (1967) Sentential Subject Constraint was intended to account for the unacceptability of extraction from sentential subjects:

(46) Who$_i$ does that Otto saw e_i worry Stan

and was subsequently generalized (Chomsky, 1973) to account for the unacceptability of extraction from nonsentential subjects such (48) as well as (47):

(47)¿Who$_i$ does that John likes e_i bother Bill

(48)¿Who$_i$ do (John's) pictures of e_i disturb Bill

Given a bounding nodes definition of Subjacency, both are deviant as an NP and an S are crossed during movement to the matrix Comp (assuming sentential subjects to be dominated by an NP):

(49) $[_{\bar{S}}\ [_{Comp}\ \text{Who}_i]\ [_S\ \text{does}\ [_{NP}\ [_{\bar{S}}\ [_{Comp}\ \text{that}]\ [_S\ \text{John likes}\ [_{NP}\ e_i]]$
      $[_{VP}\ [_V\ \text{bother}]\ [_{NP}\ \text{Bill}]]]]]]$

(50) $[_{\bar{S}}\ [_{Comp}\ \text{Who}_i]\ [_S\ \text{do}\ [_{NP}\ \text{pictures}\ [_{PP}\ \text{of}\ [_{NP}\ e_i\ ]]\ [_{VP}\ [_V\ \text{bother}]$
      $[_{NP}\ \text{Bill}]]]]]]$

According to a *Barriers* definition, the CP dominating the sentential subject of (51) is not L-marked as it is a sister to the nonlexical category $\bar{I}$ and it is hence a blocking category whose barrierhood is inherited by the matrix IP. Movement to the matrix Spec of CP therefore crosses two barriers:

(51) $[_{CP}\ [_{NP}\ \text{Who}_i]\ [_{\bar{C}}\ [_C\ \text{does}]\ [_{IP}\ [_{CP}\ [_{\bar{C}}\ [_C\ \text{that}]\ [_{IP}\ \text{John likes}$
      $[_{NP}\ e_i\ ]]]]\ [_{\bar{I}}\ [_I\ e]\ [_{VP}\ [_{\bar{V}}\ [_V\ \text{bother}]\ [_{NP}\ \text{Bill}]]]]]$

In (52), the subject NP is again a blocking category and a barrier as it is as the sister of $\bar{I}$ and not L-marked. The matrix IP inherits this barrierhood and two barriers thus intervene between the variable and the matrix *Wh*-word.

(52) $[_{CP} [_{NP}$ Who$_i]$ $[_{\overline{C}} [_{C}$ do$]$ $[_{IP} [_{NP}$ pictures of $[_{NP}$ e_i $]]$ $[_{\overline{I}} [_{I}$ $e]$
$[_{VP} [_{\overline{V}} [_{V}$ bother$][_{NP}$ Bill$]]]]]]$

Upon initial consideration it appears that sentences such as these might constitute counterevidence to our processing account of island effects. It seems that in both cases a chain should be initially constructed with the variable in its correct position within the embedded subject, since the object of the verb like in (51) and the complement of N in (52) are θ and Case positions. Consequently, no reanalysis should be necessary when the matrix verb is encountered and the locally postulated gap will prove to be the correct gap globally. Can we attribute the deviance of these sentences to syntactic reanalysis during processing? In fact, the unacceptability of extraction from subjects is accounted for directly given the architecture of the parser we are motivating along with the Theta Reanalysis Constraint. Extraction from subjects is impossible because there is simply no local option of forming the requisite chain at the time the subject constituent is being parsed, and the subsequent reanalysis which is required to obtain such a representation violates the TRC. Consider how this is so.

(53)¿Who$_i$ do pictures of $[e_i]$ disturb Bill

(a) Processing occurs as expected through *do*, with a CP constructed.

(b) *Pictures* is recovered and an NP is projected. Since the complement position of CP does not license an NP, no attachment can be made and the NP is left locally without a θ-role or Case.

(c) *Of* is identified and a PP projected. Since the complement position of the NP *picture* does license PPs, this attachment is made. Thus the parser has at this point locally constructed two separate structures:

$[_{CP} [_{NP}$ who $[_{\overline{C}} [_{C}$ do$]$ $[_{XP}$ $]]]$ and

$[_{NP} [_{\overline{N}} [_{N}$ pictures$]$ $[_{PP} [_{P}$ of$]$ $[_{XP}$ $]]]]]$

These cannot be locally integrated at this point in the parse. Although the NP complement position is a legitimate locus for the gap by virtue of being a θ and Case position, a variable cannot be locally licensed in this position since the subject itself has not been attached into the tree, and crucially cannot be at this point since C does not possess the appropriate features to license an NP complement and certainly not the specifier position of an unprojected IP complement. In other words, no chain can be formed between the *Wh*-word in Spec-CP into the NP *pictures of* as the two phrases are not locally constituents of the same parse tree; the NP is not locally a subject at this point during the parse. Although viewed in terms of the global SS representation of the tree it would appear that the nominal complement position would be a legitimate locus for a variable, and indeed it is, this construal is locally impossible during processing. There is no subject in which to construe a gap at the time the attachment is required. (Of course, empty categories which need not be bound by material outside the subject NP could be postulated in this position, and we might expect null resumptive pronouns to be possible in similar contexts in languages allowing empty objects.)

(d) *Disturb* is recovered and a VP and IP are projected. Attachments licensed by this lexical head include integration of the unattached NP into the now existing Spec-IP position in order to satisfy Case, θ theory, and the licensing of the variable as the object of the current head *disturb*:

$$[_{CP} \; [_{NP} \; who_i \; [_{\bar{C}} \; [_C \; do] \; [_{IP} \; [_{NP} \; [_{\bar{N}} \; [_N \; pictures] \; [_{PP} \; [_P \; of] \; [_{XP}]]]]] \; [_{\bar{I}} \; [_I \; e] \;$$
$$[_{VP} \; [_V \; disturb] \; [_{NP} \; e_i]]]]]]]$$

Binding into the subject NP cannot occur at this point since the parser's attention is on *disturb* and the attachments it may license, including that of the variable.

(e) *Bill* is processed and the sentence terminates. The resulting representation is ungrammatical. *Bill* is unlicensed since the variable occupies its globally correct position, and *pictures (of)* has no complement. In an attempt to salvage the parse and locally satisfy grammatical principles, reanalysis must occur. *Bill* may be attached as a VP complement and the variable as the complement of *pictures*. However, the latter clearly violates the TRC as the variable ceases to receive its role from its original assigner or within an argument of its original assigner. Hence the reanalysis violates the TRC precisely as do the previous cases we have seen with the only difference being that what will prove to be the globally correct attachment cannot initially be considered when its licensing head is first encountered given the fundamental architecture of the parser. In the case of a matrix intransitive verb, as in:

(54)¿Who did pictures of ∅ blink

the initial attachment within subject position is impossible as in the previous example, and when the sentence terminates there is no reanalysis possible since there is no variable to reanalyze. In other words, in order to obtain the attachment of the variable as internal to the subject in either (53) or (54), reanalysis or backtracking will be required since that attachment is not one licensed by the matrix verb to which the parser has proceeded. In a situation involving a transitive main clause verb, the gap will be posited as its object and the reanalysis will violate the TRC in the familiar fashion. If the matrix verb is intransitive, no reanalysis is possible since no variable has been created to be reanalyzed. In the case of intransitives, the parser cannot simply backtrack and 'drop a gap' within the subject because no local variable was ever created and hence there is subsequently none available for reanalysis. The θ-criterion thus insures that all backtracking takes the form of reanalysis of linguistic entities (subject to the TRC), severely limiting the range of possible reanalyses.

Of course, sentences such as,

(55) Who$_i$ do pictures of John disturb $[e_i]$

are perfectly acceptable.

(a) The analysis proceeds as above through the parsing of *disturb*. No attempt is made to construe a variable within the subject NP as there is no local tree in which to do so.

(b) The verb licenses a complement and the variable is attached in this position, where it receives Case and a θ-role and the sentence is unproblematic. (Notice that upon this account, extraction from complex NPs in subject position violates the TRC in the way of extraction from subjects in general but not in the fashion that extraction from complex NP complements does. There increased severity of such extractions suggests this is correct.)

The account of sentential subjects:

(56)¿Who$_i$ does that John likes e_i bother ∅ Bill

is identical, the CP dominating the sentential subject is not licensed as a complement to C and the relevant chain formation is not possible. Reanalysis violates the TRC as the variable must be removed from the internal domain of the matrix verb and reinterpreted as a complement internal to the subject, a position outside of the main verb's θ domain.[11,12]

Consequently, subject islands, which initially appear to present a potential problem for our processing analysis of island constraints, actually are quite directly predicted given the locality condition inherent in principle-based parsers that license all attachments from local heads.

4.4. Adjunct Islands Redux

The account of the subject islands just motivated suggests a somewhat revised analysis of adjunct islands than presented in section 4.1. Recall that we have attributed the unacceptability of extraction from adjuncts, as in:

(57) What did Bill eat after John cooked e_i

to the initial misanalysis of the variable as the object of the matrix verb and its subsequent reanalysis as the internal argument of the embedded verb, violating the Theta Reanalysis Constraint since the adjunct clause is not a domain that is assigned the θ-role originally assigned to the variable. However, consider the alternative hypothesis that the construal of the variable as bound within the adjunct is impossible because adjuncts themselves are not locally licensed during parsing. Their internal structure is constructed in accord with the general principles motivated here, but their local attachment into the global parse tree is not, arguably because they are not licensed by grammatical principles such as Case or θ theory. If parsing is largely a procedure for recovering argument structure, this notion has some appeal. Since such nonarguments are not locally attached into the parse tree via standard argument licensing principles such as Case and θ theory, there is no manner in which to locally construe a variable internal to them as bound by an external operator just as in the case of binding into a subject before IP is projected. Of course, adjuncts must eventually be attached, but this may perhaps be attributed to a more global principle, such as that of Full Interpretation (FI) (Chomsky, 1986a), which conceivably requires of adverbs that they ultimately have scope over some constituent. This principle, however, is at least arguably not a local licenser in the same fashion as Case or θ theory, reflecting the fact that the syntactic locality conditions on adjuncts are far less local than for arguments. (Though we have here focused on VP adjuncts, the approach could be extended to NP adjuncts in relative clause constructions discussed previously.)

On this revised account, adjunct extraction is illicit not because of the reinterpretation of a previously misconstrued variable, but, as in the case of movement from subjects, there is no local tree in which to postulate the *Wh*-chain. Globally, when the constituent has been adjoined into the tree in accord with FI, the gap cannot be construed as internal to the adjunct without violating the Theta Reanalysis Constraint. Notice too that this account of subject and adjunct extraction is in accord with the psycholinguistic results that gaps are simply not posited within certain types of islands, for example subjects (Stowe, 1984), and furthermore that the initial unavailability of both subjects and adjuncts as loci for internal gaps may also offer an explanation as to why extraction from these elements constitute by far the most severe island violations as reflected by their additional characterization as violations of the Constraint on Extraction Domains (Huang, 1982).

This analysis additionally accounts for a body of data potentially problematic for our earlier account. Consider:

(58) (a)¿What$_i$ did you burp after John prepared e_i

(b)¿What$_i$ did you sleep after John prepared e_i

(59)¿What$_i$ do you believe ∅ John died after Bill burned e$_i$

As shown in (58), that extraction from adjuncts is also unacceptable after intransitive verbs is difficult to account for given our previous analysis, since no variable should initially be posited after the matrix verb (which presumably cannot license an internal argument). Since no variable is ever posited, reanalysis which violates the TRC should never occur. In an example such as (59), the variable remains within the internal domain of the matrix verb, but the sentence is nevertheless unacceptable. These examples are handled directly given the revised approach. Globally, after the adjunct has been attached in accord with FI, there is simply no variable available to posit internal to it. As the data discussed in this section appear to rather unambiguously favor this analysis, I will henceforth assume it rather than that discussed in section 4.1. The two analyses are quite similar; both claim that adjunct island effects are the result of irrevocable parsing decisions. They differ slightly with respect to the nature of the initial problem and of the subsequent reanalysis required. If correct, this account of subject and adjunct islands, specifically the notion that (externally) bound elements may not be posited within locally unattached constituents, seems potentially to be one of the most interesting predictions resulting from strict adherence to a principle-based model of parsing.

4.5. *Wh-Islands*

The *Wh*-island constraint (Chomsky, 1973) is intended to prevent movement out of embedded questions.

(60)¿Which movie do you wonder whether Bill saw?

(61)¿Which movie do you wonder when to see?

(62)¿Which movie do you know who saw?

Such violations are rather unusual in two respects as compared with extraction from subjects and adjuncts. First, *Wh*-island violations are subject to a great deal of cross-linguistic variation, and second, unlike subjects, adjuncts, or complex NPs, movement from within *Wh*-islands apparently involves illicit extraction directly from a verbal complement. As Sportiche (1988) notes, the correlation of these two anomalous features of extraction from *Wh*-islands is probably no accident. Such islands were accounted for quite directly by the original bounding nodes formulation of Subjacency (coupled with standard assumptions concerning doubly filled Comp and strict cyclicity) as two S nodes are crossed during the derivation:

(63) [Which movie]$_i$ do [$_S$ you wonder [$_{\bar{S}}$ [$_{Comp}$ whether
[$_S$ Bill saw [e_i]]]]]

(64) [Which movie]$_i$ do [$_S$ you wonder [$_{\bar{S}}$ [$_{Comp}$ when
[$_S$ Bill saw [e_i]]]]]

The relative acceptability of these violations is not explained by the bounding nodes approach, which incorrectly predicts severity equivalent to, for example, subject extraction, since the same number of bounding nodes are crossed.

On the other hand, within the *Barriers* framework, neither example is predicted to be problematic, precisely because the extraction is from a complement.

(65) [Which movie]$_i$ do [$_{IP}$ you wonder [$_{CP}$ [$_{\bar{C}}$ [$_C$ whether]
[$_{IP}$ Bill saw [e_i]]]]]

(66) [Which movie]$_i$ do [$_{IP}$ you wonder [$_{CP}$ [when]
                    [$_{\overline{C}}$ [$_{IP}$ Bill saw [e_i]]]]]

The lower IP is a blocking category as it is not L-marked, and barrierhood is inherited by the embedded CP which dominates it. Movement
to the matrix Spec-CP (via an intermediate adjunction to the matrix
VP) will thus cross a single barrier. As Subjacency violations require
the crossing of two barriers, the results should be perfectly acceptable.
(The Double Filled Comp Constraint will be irrelevant given that it is
CP not IP which is the barrier.) Chomsky attributes the putative weak-
ness of the effect to this fact, but it is not at all clear why either example
is worse than a sentence such as:

(67) [Which movie]$_i$ do [$_{IP}$ you believe [$_{CP}$ [that] [$_{IP}$ Bill saw [e_i]]]]

in which a single CP barrier is also crossed.

The processing account of island violations motivated here also apparently predicts such extractions to be acceptable since the reanalyzed
gap remains within its originally postulated θ domain. However, there
is some evidence that embedded question 'complements' might actually
not occupy SS argument positions. (I am indebted to John Whitman,
personal communication, for this observation and argumentation.) First,
verbs which require the CP they select to be headed by the feature [$+wh$]
also lack the ability to directly assign case to their complements:

(68)*John wondered/inquired Bill

(69) John wondered/inquired about Bill

(70) John wondered/inquired whether Bill likes him

Second, [$+wh$] complements fail to passivize unlike [$-wh$] complements:

(71)*Whether Bill was a fool was wondered/known by John

(72) That Bill was a fool was known by John

Third, the head of a [$+wh$] complement is not deletable unlike that
of a [$-wh$] complement:

(73) John knows (that) Bill likes Steve

(74)*John wonders ($\sqrt{\text{if}}$) Bill likes Steve

Since it is true that movement from a $[+wh]$ complement of any verb, not just of those which obligatorily select that feature, is degraded:

(75) ($¿$)[Which car]$_i$ doesn't John know whether Bill fixed e_i

(76) ($¿$)[Which movie]$_i$ doesn't John know when Bill saw e_i

(77) ($¿$)What$_i$ did John question whether Bill knew e_i

(78) ($¿$)What$_i$ does John wonder who knows e_i

this suggests that all $[+wh]$ complements fail to occupy SS argument positions. One possibility at least is that that the structure involved resembles:

(79) [Which movie]$_i$ do [$_{IP}$ you [$_{VP}$ [$_{VP}$ wonder
        [$_{CP}$ t]$_j$][$_{CP}$ j [$_{\overline{c}}$ [$_c$ whether] [$_{IP}$ Bill saw [e_i]]]]]]]

in which the complement has been raised to an adjoined position. Consider then how such sentences are to be processed. A variable is initially postulated as a complement to the verb. (Garden path examples such as, ¿Since Angleton wondered Philby fled the country appear to confirm that wonder licenses local NP attachments. Despite the verb's seeming inability to assign Case, Philby is apparently attached as its complement locally by virtue of the θ-criterion.) Subsequent reanalysis at fled violates the TRC leading to a GP effect. Upon reanalysis, the variable will not receive its role as the complement to wonder but within an adjunct raised from complement position.

Technically, this does constitute a violation of the TRC as the variable is not, upon final analysis, dominated by the CP which receives its θ-role from wonder as it is not dominated by all segments of that CP, failing to be dominated by the trace. However, it is also clear that adjunction structures of this sort are rather different than those considered previously. First, since it must be a lexical fact about verbs such as wonder that they license complements, albeit ones that raise to adjoined positions, adjuncts of this sort will be locally licensed in a fashion, unlike the VP adjuncts we have previously considered. In other words the difference is attributable to a distinction between being an adjunct in the sense of not being associated with an argument position and being a moved argument which occupies an adjoined position at SS. Furthermore, the CP trace and the CP are coindexed and in a sense represent same constituent quite unlike the situation involving relative clauses adjoined to NP also accounted for in terms of a failure of dominance. Consequently, this analysis apparently correctly predicts that extraction from unambiguously extraposed objects in general will present similar processing difficulty. Compare, *Who$_i$ do you doubt that Bill knew e$_i$* versus *¿Who$_i$ do you doubt it that Bill knew e$_i$*. This contrasts with this situation involving extraposed (on some analyses) subjects which do occupy argument positions at SS, *Who$_i$ is it obvious that John hates e$_i$*. I will therefore attribute the weak island status of embedded questions to the factors just discussed, obviously leaving many questions unanswered awaiting further details about the actual syntax of embedded questions.[13]

5. FURTHER PREDICTIONS AND CONCLUSIONS

Throughout this chapter I have attempted to argue for the hypothesis that island constraint violations are the result of unrecoverable parsing errors and consequently that there is no grammatical constraint, Subjacency, *per se*. The proposed account, originally motivated for traditional garden path phenomena, captures several desirable aspects and observations of previous grammar-based account of the phenomena, including: the role of L-Marking (attributable to θ-attachment); the special status of S and NP as bounding nodes (attributable to their status as potential arguments and captured in terms of the notion θ domain); the role of something resembling successive cyclic movement (expressed as a relationship between gaps recurrently posited by the parser); and the relevance of a minimality-like condition (determined by the impossibility of locally construing a variable as a complement to an intervening head). More generally, claims concerning the fundamental operation of a principle-based model of parsing have also been extended and, perhaps most significantly, it has been suggested that bound elements may not be posited within locally unattached constituents, a fact that follows automatically from Local Head Projection, in turn following from the Projection Principle.

Additionally, this processing analysis of island violations further accounts for one of the most puzzling facts about Subjacency, namely, that it holds only in the mapping from DS to SS and not from SS to LF

(Huang, 1982; Chomsky, 1986a).[14] This can be seen quite clearly from well-known English 'echo-question' data:

(80) You left after John burned what?

(81) (a) John's pictures of who worry Fred?

      (b) That fact that John likes what bothers Fred?

(82) You wonder whether Bill likes what

(83) John believes the claim that Bill likes who?

(84) John saw a boy who was eating what?

Additionally, cross-linguistic data from languages, such as Japanese, Chinese, and Korean, which lack SS *Wh*-movement support this claim.

(85) *Chinese*:
      [ni xiangxin [[Lisi mai-le   sheme de shuofa]]]
      you believe Lisi buy-Asp what   claim
      'You believe the claim that Lisi bought what?'

(86) *Korean*:
      [[etten nonmun-ul ssun] salam]-i   ceyil yumyenghapni-kka
      which paper-Acc wrote person-Nom most famous-Q
      'The person who wrote which paper is the most famous'

(87) *Japanese*:
      [[dono ronbum-o kaita] hito]-ga   itiban yuumeidesu-ka
      which paper-Acc wrote person-Nom most famous-Q
      'The person who wrote which paper is the most famous'

Quite simply, in the absence of surface syntactic movement, *i.e.*, when *Wh*-words remain *in situ* at S-structure, the island constraints do not hold, but it remains a stipulation within GB theory that LF movement is not subject to Subjacency.

We therefore conclude that the conditions of Bounding theory apply to the syntax proper, to S-structure representations or the rules forming them, not to LF representations or the rules converting S-structure to LF. (Chomsky, 1986a, p. 153)

While there seems no natural way to capture this in grammatical theory, a processing account offers a clear explanation. It is, as we have seen, the actual overt dislocation of the *Wh*-word and the necessity of locating its D-structure position online that is the source of the difficulty. LF movement involves no such ambiguity but rather simply involves the movement of an unambiguous *in situ* *Wh*-word to an unambiguous adjoined position. In other words the parser need not fill a gap and consequently, no 'Subjacency' effect results.[15]

The analysis of island constraint violations motivated in this chapter takes the notion of a principle-based parser quite seriously and clearly owes much to grammatical theory. It adopts a fundamental insight of both Chomsky's *Barriers* and of GPSG that in general extraction is permitted only from constituents which are L-marked/strictly subcategorized. The approach differs, of course, in its attempt to formulate an account of this observation in terms of processing rather than grammatical theory. I have attempted to argue for this strong thesis that all Subjacency effects are attributable to parsing concerns in the hopes that this line of investigation might lead to new insights concerning both the fundamental operation of the parser and the relationship between the parser and the grammar.

ACKNOWLEDGEMENTS

I wish to thank John Whitman and the participants at the Ottawa Psycholinguistics of Islands Constraints Conference for invaluable comments. All negative responsibility is of course my own.

NOTES

[1] The restrictions on long distance dependencies have come to be regarded by virtually all linguists as axioms of grammatical theory. Even within frameworks such as Lexical Functional Grammar (cf. Kaplan and Zaenen, 1989) and Generalized Phrase Structure Grammar which have traditionally favored a tighter integration of grammatical and processing concerns, attempts have not been made in general to derive island effects. Nevertheless, a demonstration that island violations are to be accounted for in terms of processing is potentially desirable. Chomsky (1986) attempts to reduce the stipulative and undesirable aspects of Bounding theory by eliminating the distinction between bounding node for movement and barrier for government. A similar goal is pursued here albeit via an attempt to abandon the idea of bounding node as a grammatical notion altogether. I do not attempt to argue that all deviant *Wh*-movements are attributable to a processing-based explanation but restrict my

attention to those characterized as island constraint violations and which have necessitated the introduction of some notion of bounding at surface structure within the st descended theories. Consequently, ungrammaticality attributable to the empty category principle (ECP) at LF will be assumed to be handled within the grammar as usual. Contrast:

(1) You slept after buying what? (Subjacency violation at LF)

(2)*What did you buy why (ECP violation at LF)

[2] When CP has no overt head, I know of no nonstipulative way to insure its projection other than to simply claim that the fact that IP projects up one further level to CP is part of fundamental knowledge of linguistic structure. One might explore the possibility that in embedded environments, CP is projected to allow the local attachment of the complement clause, attachment as an IP being barred for grammatical reasons relating to government of its Specifier, except in certain instances, such as ECM contexts. It is also conceivable that in certain matrix clauses, CP is not actually constructed at SS unless locally licensed by a head and that IP is otherwise the highest structure built, higher projections possibly made only at LF.

[3] The interested reader is referred to Pritchett (1987, 1988a) as well as Weinberg (1988) for a more complete explication of the approach and the discussion of a wide range of garden path data. To summarize briefly, the main types of garden path sentences are accounted for as follows. In example (15) above the reduced relative clause analysis is not initially pursued as this would create an extra NP, the complex NP itself, which requires a θ-role and Case. When the final verb is encountered and such an analysis proves necessary, the subject must be removed from its original θ domain as external argument of *race* and reinterpreted as the head of an NP subject which receives its role from *fall*, violating the TRC. In example (16), the complement clause rather than the relative clause analysis is pursued in order to maximally satisfy the θ-criterion with respect to the verb, *persuade*, which has two internal θ-roles to discharge. Reanalysis as a relative clause when the actual complement [PRO *to leave*] is encountered violates the TRC as the string *he was having trouble with* is removed from the domain of the second internal role of *persuade* and reinterpreted as within the verb's first internal domain. Sentence (17) has been discussed in detail in the text, and sentence (18) is subject to a very similar analysis. The NP, *her contributions*, is initially constructed to receive the role from the preposition. Upon reanalysis, *contributions* is removed from the θ domain of *without*, and interpreted as within the external domain of the matrix verb, violating the TRC. In (19), the entire string *her mother* is first interpreted as an internal NP argument of the verb, as *warn* cannot assign Case to two NPs. Upon reanalysis, *mother* must be reinterpreted as the subject within the second internal domain of the verb, violating the TRC. Notice that with conscious effort or exposure, many garden path sentences begin to seem quite acceptable as well as interpretable. Interestingly, this is also true of certain classes of island violations but far less so of many indisputably ungrammatical sentences. Contrast in this regard a standard Case theory violation:

(1) I am fond John

or an ECP violation:

(2) Who do you think that likes John

which are always interpretable but never increase in acceptability, with the improvement found in certain Subjacency violations (but, as will be shown, not adjunct or subject islands):

(3) What do you believe the claim that Bill read

and garden paths:

(4) After Mary ate the cake fell on the floor

[4] Therefore, in processing a question without an overt auxiliary, such as *Who saw Bill*, the attachment of the *Wh*-word will not occur until the verb is encountered as there is no earlier evidence for hypothesizing a C. The unproblematic local lexical ambiguity of a sentence such as *Who did it* is potentially revealing in this regard and reminiscent of the contrast between, *Have the boys devoured*, and, *Have the boys devoured their food*, neither of which presents processing difficulty (cf. Marcus, 1980). See Pritchett (1987) for a discussion of this type of ambiguity with respect to examples of the latter sort.

[5] I am ignoring important questions raised here concerning the processing of unaccusative verbs. Consider sentences such as:

(1) (a) John burned the house

(b) John burned

However they may differ, both the unergative and the unaccusative interpretations of the local string *John burned* will allow the discharge of a single θ-role (agent in the former instance, theme in the latter) and a single Case (nominative in both instances). Which choice the parser makes and the manner in which it chooses are not immediately obvious. If the unergative analysis is first pursued, no reanalysis will be necessary when the complement NP subsequently appears. If the unaccusative interpretation is initially preferred, reanalysis will be necessary, but not of a type predicted to violate the TRC. The chain to which the internal role was initially assigned is not reanalyzed but simply abandoned (the NP-trace ceases to exist and the antecedent NP ceases to bind anything). This contrasts with the situation involving operator-variable chains in which a variable is continually reanalyzed and the same operator continues to bind a trace. How verbs of different classes are processed in principle based parsing models is clearly an area requiring substantially more investigation but the model being proposed here does not incorrectly predict processing difficulty with respect to unaccusative/unergative ambiguities.

[6] Our analysis does not depend on the availability of Comp-to-Comp movement as we are not attempting to have the parser construct a representation consistent with the existence of a grammatical Subjacency constraint. Chomsky (1986b) suggests that Subjacency must refer not to the number of barriers between each link in a chain but rather during the formation of an entire chain (p. 38), a claim that partially undermines the original motivation for Comp-to-Comp movement. Additionally, the status of intermediate argument traces in Comp is controversial (Lasnik and Saito, 1984, 1990). Furthermore, the increasing role of adjunction, as discussed in Chomsky (1986b) makes Comp's status as an 'escape hatch' somewhat less unique. To the

extent that Comp-to-Comp movement does prove necessary, for example, to account for various ECP effects via antecedent government nothing in our approach prevents their creation at LF, but I will not explore this question in detail here.
[7] There is one set of rather fundamental data which the analysis as presented so far presented has difficulty with. The acceptability of extraction from certain double complement constructions is not accounted for:

(1) What$_i$ did you paint $\emptyset$ the house with e_i

(2) What$_i$ did you donate $\emptyset$ a book to e_i

The variable is initially posited within the first internal θ domain of the verb and subsequently as outside of that domain and within the second internal domain (as mediated through the preposition). Interestingly, a similar difficulty arose involving double object constructions in the theory of Pritchett (1987, 1988a) where processing breakdown was predicted, apparently incorrectly, in sentences such as:

(3) John gave the boys dogs to Steve

According to θ-attachment *the boys* should initially receive the first internal role and Case from *give*, *dogs* the second role and Case, and the reanalysis forced by the goal PP should violate the TRC when *dogs* is transferred into the first internal θ domain. However, such sentences do not appear to present processing difficulty. Unquestionably, the solution to both of these problems lies in the fact that although the reanalyzed argument is removed from its original θ domain, it continues as an argument of the same θ-assigning head. However, in certain other instances, rather similar reanalyses are problematic:

(4)¿The doctor persuaded the patient he was having trouble with to leave

(5)¿I warned her mother was wielding an axe

so the solution is not completely straightforward. The data may be accounted for by a perhaps somewhat stipulative revision of the definition of θ domain:

(6) θ domain: α is in the γ θ domain of β iff α receives a θ-role from β or α is dominated by a constituent which receives the γ θ-role from β.

Though this will distinguish the *give* and *paint* examples from the *persuade* and *warn* cases, I suspect the actual solution lies in the particular details of the differing predicate argument structures of distinct classes of multiple θ-role assigning verbs. Pritchett (1988b) attempted to suggest an account of this in terms of Larson's (1988) theory of double object constructions (which raises additional important questions concerning the processing of chains created by head-to-head movement). Issues related to the so-called 'inaccessibility of the inner NP' may also prove relevant. As the problem is at least rather well delimited, I will assume the more stipulative version here with the caveat that that the actual solution is likely more interesting.
[8] Dominance: α is dominated by β only if it is dominated by every segment of β. (Chomsky, 1986b, p. 7).
[9] John Whitman (personal communication) has pointed out that this predicts a contrast between:

(1) (¿) Who$_i$ do you believe the claim that Otto saw e_i

(2) ¿ Who$_i$ do you know the fact that Otto saw e_i

Though the embedded CP in (1) is arguably a complement of claim, in (2) it is an appositive relative and hence subject to an analysis more similar to that of relative clauses as previously discussed (though the syntax of such predicative relatives is less clear). This additionally raises the possibility that extraction from actual noun complements is actually acceptable and that the apparent deviance of a sentence such as (1) is attributable to the clauses ambiguity between a complement and an appositive reading, fact not having a θ-grid. Sentence (2) is unarguably unacceptable since the only possible interpretation is as an appositive. Sentence (1) is unacceptable on such a reading but possibly not on a complement interpretation. This would explain the perfect acceptability, noted by Ross, of examples such as:

(3) Who$_i$ did John make the claim that Otto saw e_i

where only a complement interpretation is possible. If this approach proves correct, then the TRC may be considered to correctly predict extraction from noun complements to be acceptable.
^{10} Similar facts may obtain in languages where Wh-words display overt morphological Case (though it is not at all clear how much attention the parser pays to such factors, especially in cases involving movement and chain-construction). Furthermore, the approach to extraction from N complements developed above suggests an account of the following contrast.

(1) (a) What$_i$ did you read a review of e_i

   (b) (¿)What$_i$ did you read Chomsky's review of e_i

Extraction from an nonsentential noun complement, though typically acceptable, is deviant if it crosses a possessor NP. We may easily account for the goodness of extraction from PP as opposed to CP complements to N as in (1a). In such examples, the preposition is arguably present only to assign Case but the complement is actually an argument of the head noun, from which it receives its θ-role. Hence, the TRC is not violated as the variable remains an argument of the constituent which comes to receive a role from the matrix verb (*i.e.*, the PP in examples of this type is not an argument).

Examples such as (1b) are ruled out by neither a bounding nodes nor a barriers definition of Subjacency and have been attributed to a so-called specificity effect which was originally collapsed with the Specified Subject Condition (cf. Chomsky, 1981; also Aoun, 1979; and Sportiche, 1988). As Chomsky notes, this is a constraint on overt movement, not representation, such effects not holding at LF:

(2) You read Chomsky's review of what?

In terms of our processing approach, if one adopts a DP analysis of such possessive constructions in which 's heads a DP of which the NP headed by *review* is the complement, we have some explanation for these facts:

(3) What$_i$ did you read Ø [$_{DP}$ [$_{NP}$ Chomsky] [$_{\overline{D}}$ [$_D$'s] [$_{NP}$ review of e_i]]]

The variable is originally interpreted as the object of *read*, but upon reanalysis becomes the complement of the N, *review*, the intermediate representation, *What did you read Chomsky's* $\emptyset$ being impossible. Just as in the case of extraction from sentential complements to nouns, the TRC is not violated, but, also as in that instance, there is an intervening feature assigning head of which the variable cannot be locally interpreted as an argument. We might attribute the very mild deviance of the sentence to the fact that the functional head, *'s*, though it selects an argument, does not θ-mark it (again see Abney, 1987), raising the possibility that the TRC is sensitive to feature reassignment rather than structure building *per se*. It is even possible that the following contrast is subject to a similar explanation:

(4) (a) (?)What$_i$ does John know that Bill wants e_i

    (b) What$_i$ does John know Bill wants e_i

These facts suggest that the Theta Reanalysis Constraint, like θ-attachment, must be made sensitive to selection of all types (which frequently coincide), not merely θ-marking, a desirable generalization but one I will not pursue further here. (The question of whether these facts are also relevant to *that*-trace effects and the generally increased acceptability of extraction from infinitival islands is also intriguing but the answer unclear.)

[11] This account of the failure of extraction from sentential subjects potentially makes an interesting typological prediction. In true V/INFL final languages, extraction from within objects as well as subjects should be impossible since such movement from within objects will be locally unsatisfiable in precisely the same way extraction from subject is in English. In certain V/INFL initial languages, extraction from both object and subject should be equally acceptable, depending on the surface structural locus of the verb and the status of INFL. There may be a correlation between the former prediction and the fact that such languages typically lack syntactic *Wh*-movement altogether.

(1) *Korean*:
    John-i   nwukwu-lul manna-ss-ni
    John-Nom who-Acc   meet-past-Q
    'Who did John meet?'

(2) *Japanese*:
    Bill-wa John-ni   nani-o   ageta-no
    Bill-Top John-Dat what-Acc give-Past-Q
    'What did Bill give to John'

It is conceivable that since the only movement possible (of, but not out of, the subject or complements) would resemble scrambling, a learnability problem might result. The latter prediction is consistent with the more controversial claim that in certain INFL initial languages, extraction from subjects is acceptable (see Chung, forthcoming, for evidence that these clauses occupy subject position).

(3) *Chamorro* (from Chung, forthcoming):
    Hayi$_i$ siguru   [na pära uginänna   i karera e_i]
    Who Infl.certain that will Infl.pass.win the race
    Who$_i$ is [the race will be won by e_i] certain
    ('Who is it certain that the race will be run by')

Our account predicts that if I, or possibly V, occupies C at S-structure, the subject constraint should hold in verb initial languages, just as in the case of *do* in C at S-structure in English. However, in languages where V arguably occupies I at S-structure, extraction should be possible as IP will be licensed. Verb medial languages, as predicted, occupy a middle ground. Clearly, the relationship between verb movement and Subjacency must be more closely investigated to support such a speculative account.
[12] We may now be in a position to account for the puzzling fact that extraction from embedded sentential subjects is much improved:

(1) (¿)Who$_i$ do you expect [$_{CP}$ [$_{IP}$ [$_{NP}$ pictures of [$_{NP}$ e_i]] [$_{\bar{I}}$ [$_I$ to]
      [$_{VP}$ [$_{\bar{V}}$ [$_V$ bother] [$_{NP}$ Bill]]]]]

(2) (¿)Who$_i$ do you believe [$_{CP}$ [$_{IP}$ [$_{NP}$ pictures of [$_{NP}$ e_i]] [$_{\bar{I}}$ [$_I$ will]
      [$_{VP}$ [$_{\bar{V}}$ [$_V$ bother] [$_{NP}$ Bill]]]]]

(3) (¿)Who did you suspect [[$_{IP}$ [$_{CP}$ [$_{\bar{C}}$ [$_C$ that] [$_{IP}$ John liked [$_{NP}$ e_i]]
      [$_{\bar{I}}$ [$_I$ e] [$_{VP}$ [$_{\bar{V}}$ [$_V$ disturbed] [$_{NP}$ Bill]]]]]]

This fact is problematic for both a bounding nodes (the same nodes are crossed as in the matrix instance) and a barrier definition of Subjacency (just as in examples (49–50), the subject constituent is a blocking category and a barrier, and this barrierhood is inherited by the dominating IP (as the CP not the IP is dominated by the matrix verb). Nevertheless, such extraction is far superior to extraction from matrix subject position. We may account for this as follows. Unlike the situation involving a main clause subject, a variable may be initially postulated within what is to become the embedded subject while it is still locally construed as a matrix object. That is, in a string such as:

(4) Who$_i$ did you expect ∅ pictures of e_i

grammatical principles are maximally satisfied in the familiar fashion by reinterpreting the gap as the complement to *pictures of* and attaching that the NP as the verbal object. Consider the effects of the subsequent reanalysis. With respect to its θ-assigning head, the variable itself is not reanalyzed as it remains a complement to that head. The constituent NP (or CP) which dominates the variable is reanalyzed, but the TRC is not violated as the NP becomes the subject of a clause which is the complement of the original θ-assigner. However, in a local structure such as (4) the variable is also within the internal θ domain of the matrix verb as the NP dominating it receives receives a role from the verb. Though the TRC is not violated with respect to the θ domain relationship between the variable and the matrix verb, additional structure is introduced similar to the situation involving extraction from noun complements discussed in section 4.2. In (1), the variable is in the internal θ domain of expect by virtue of being the argument of an argument ([$_{NP}$ *pictures of* e_i]) of the verb. Upon reanalysis as the embedded subject, it becomes the argument of an argument ([$_{NP}$ *pictures of* e]) of an argument ([$_{CP}$ [$_{NP}$ *pictures of* e] *to bother Bill*]). Once again, the milder but unmistakable deviance of such sentences suggests that the TRC be relativized to reflect the importance of the amount of intervening structure introduced even within a θ domain. See also Gibson (1988) and compare also the discussion in note 10.

[13] Whatever the precise details prove to be, a similar analysis should extend to extraction from any DS argument which occupies an adjoined position at SS. In German, for example, it appears that *Wh*-movement from within complement clauses is typically somewhat unacceptable when an overt complementizer is present but completely permissible when the complementizer is deleted.

(1) ¿Weni glaubst du daß der   Mann e_i haßt ?
   who-acc believe you that the-Nom man   hates
   'Who do you think the man hates'

(2) Weni   glaubst du haßt der   Mann e_i ?
   who-acc believe you hates the-Nom man
   'Who do you think the man hates'

Extractions of the former type appear to have roughly the same status as *Wh*-islands for some speakers. If complementizers may be deleted only when they head a constituent which is properly governed, as suggested by Stowell (1981) (compare the fact that sentential subjects do not allow complementizer deletion: *(*That*) *the world is round is obvious*), CPs lacking overt complementizers must occupy argument positions and hence extraction is predicted to be acceptable. When the complementizer is present, the CP may occupy an adjoined position at S-structure just as in the case of wonder in English and extraction should be similarly deviant, as does appear to be the case.

On the other hand, *Wh*-island violations are perfectly acceptable in a number of languages. Italian sentences comparable to the following example from Spanish:

(3) *Spanish*:
   [[A que hombre]$_i$ no crees   [por que]$_j$ odió   Juan e_i e_j
   to what man   not believe why   hate-3-s-past John
   'Which man don't you know why John hates?'

led Rizzi (1982) to posit that $\overline{S}$ rather than S was a bounding node in Italian. Alternatively, we may consider the fundamental prediction of the barriers framework as well as the present account to be correct and maintain that the Romance data reflect the expected situation when the *Wh*-complement occupies an SS argument position. To continue with this line of analysis, we will need to seek independent evidence that verbs which obligatorily select embedded questions license SS arguments in their DS positions in these languages.

[14] Nishigauchi (1986) has argued *contra* Huang (1982) and Lasnik and Saito (1984, 1990) among others for the hypothesis that Subjacency does indeed hold at LF, but its effects are obscured by pied piping, thus, in a language like Japanese, the relevant features of the LF representation of the equivalent of:

(1) Pictures of who disturb Bill

would not be as in English:

(2) who$_i$ [[$_{NP}$ pictures of e_i] disturb Bill]

but rather:

(3) [$_{NP}$ pictures of who]$_i$ [e_i disturb Bill]

Since the entire NP moves at LF, no extraction from subject position has occurred and whatever grammatical principle accounts for the Subject Constraint does not apply. There are well-known problems with this proposal. For example, certain facts concerning quantifier scope necessitate the occurrence of the *Wh*-word outside of the island at LF (Fiengo *et al.*, 1988).

(4) Who$_i$ did everybody see a picture of e_i

(5) Who$_i$ did most people like every picture of e_i

(6) *Chinese*:
meige ren dou mai-le [yiben [shei xie   de] she]
every man all bought one   who write rel book
'Everybody bought a book that who wrote?'

(7) *Chinese*:
daduoshude ren dou mai-le [[shei xie   de] meiben shu]
most   man all bought who write rel every   book
'Most people bought every book that who wrote'

The range of interpretations are identical, despite the pied-piped LF representation [*every book that who wrote*] for (7). As the LF pied-piping hypothesis is controversial, I will not further argue against it here. Fiengo *et al.* (1988) account for many of Nishigauchi's original observations via an appeal to the ECP rather than Subjacency and the reader is referred to both of those articles for further discussion. [15] Resumptive pronouns occupy something of a middle ground between *Wh in situ* and actual gaps and therefore demand investigation with respect to this parsing theory. Both in languages employing resumptives as a primary grammatical strategy and in languages like English, the parser's tail-of-chain seeking algorithm is arguably initiated by a fronted *Wh*-word.

However, in contrast to the situation involving true gaps, the tail is potentially identified by overt pronoun. As resumptives often lessen, but do not necessarily obliterate, island effects it is conceivable that the parser continues to make its initial error, positing a gap, but that the variable itself is not itself reanalyzed when the overt pronoun is encountered. Many important issues are raised, not the least of which concerns the online application of Binding theory. I postpone further consideration of this potentially revealing issue here.

REFERENCES

Abney, S.: 1987, *The English Noun Phrase in its Sentential Aspect*, Ph.D. dissertation, Department of Linguistics and Philosophy, Massachusetts Institute of Technology, Cambridge, Massachusetts.

Abney, S.: 1988, 'On the Notion GB-parser and Psychological Reality', in S. Abney (ed.), *The MIT Parsing Volume, 1987–1988*, Center for Cognitive Science, Massachusetts Institute of Technology, Cambridge, Massachusetts, pp. 1–18.

Aoun, J.: 1979, *Generalized Binding*, Foris, Dordrecht, Holland.

Baker, C.: 1970, 'Notes on the Description of the English Questions: The Role of an Abstract Question Morpheme', *Foundations of Language* **6**, 197–219.

Berwick, R.: 1988 *Principle-Based Parsing and Parsing Efficiency*, paper presented at the *University of Maryland Conference on Grammar and Language Processing*, University of Maryland and College Park, College Park, Maryland.

Berwick, R.: 1987, 1991 forthcoming, 'Principle-Based Parsing', in P. Sells, S. Shieber, and T. Wasow (eds.), *Foundational Issues in Natural Language Processing*, MIT Press, Cambridge, Massachusetts. Also MIT Artificial Intelligence Laboratory Technical Report 972, Massachusetts Institute of Technology, Cambridge, Massachusetts.

Berwick, R. and A. Weinberg: 1984, *The Grammatical Basis of Linguistic Performance*, MIT Press, Cambridge, Massachusetts.

Bever, T. and B. McElree: 1988, 'Empty Categories Access Their Antecedents During Comprehension', *Linguistic Inquiry*, **19**, 35–43.

Carlson, G. and M. Tanenhaus: 1988, 'Thematic Roles and Language Comprehension', in W. Wilkins (ed.), *Syntax and Semantics 21: Thematic Relations*, Academic Press, New York, pp. 263–288.

Chomsky, N.: 1988, 'Linguistics and Adjacent Fields: the State of the Art', unpublished manuscript, Department of Linguistics, Massachusetts Institute of Technology, Cambridge, Massachusetts.

Chomsky, N.: 1973, 'Conditions on Transformations', in S. Anderson and P. Kiparksy (eds.), *A Festschrift for Morris Halle*, Holt, Rinehart, and Winston, New York, pp. 232–286.

Chomsky, N.: 1977, 'On Wh-Movement', in P. Culicover, T. Wasow, and A. Akmajian (eds.), *Formal Syntax*, Academic Press, New York, pp. 71–132.

Chomsky, N.: 1981, *Lectures on Government and Binding: The Pisa Lectures*, Foris, Dordrecht, Holland.

Chomsky, N.: 1982, *Some Concepts and Consequences of the Theory of Government and Binding*, MIT Press, Cambridge, Massachusetts.

Chomsky, N.: 1986a, *Knowledge of Language: Its Nature, Origin, and Use*, Praeger Publishers, New York.

Chomsky, N.: 1986b, *Barriers*, MIT Press, Cambridge, Massachusetts.

Chung, S.: forthcoming, 'Sentential Subjects and Proper Government in Chamorro', in C. Georgeopolous and R. Ishihara (eds.), *Interdisciplinary Approaches to Language: Essays in Honor of S. Y. Kuroda*, Kluwer, Dordrecht, Holland.

Engdahl, E.: 1983, 'Parasitic Gaps', *Linguistics and Philosophy*, **6**, 5–34.

Fiengo, R., J. Huang, H. Lasnik, and T. Reinhart: 1988, 'The Syntax of Wh-in-situ', *Proceedings of the 7th West Coast Conference on Formal Linguistics*, Stanford Linguistics Association, Stanford, California, pp. 81–98.

Fodor, J.D.: 1978, 'Parsing Strategies and Constraints on Transformations', *Linguistic Inquiry* **8**, 427–473.

Fodor J.D.: 1983, 'Phrase Structure Parsing and the Island Constraints', *Linguistics and Philosophy* **6**, 163–223.

Fodor, J.D.: 1984, 'Constraints on Gaps: Is the Parser a Significant Influence', in B. Butterword, B. Comrie, and O. Dahl (eds.), *Explanations for Language Universals*, Mouton, Cambridge, England, pp. 9–34.

Fodor, J.D.: 1985, 'Deterministic Parsing and Subjacency', *Language and Cognitive Processes* 1, pp. 3–42.

Frazier, L. and K. Rayner: 1982, 'Making and Correcting Errors During Sentence Comprehension: Eye Movements in the Analysis of Structurally Ambiguous Sentences', *Cognitive Psychology* 14, 178–210.

Gibson T.: 1988, 'Subjacency and the Minimality Condition', *Proceedings of the New England Linguistic Society* 19, pp. 127–141.

Huang, J.: 1982, *Logical Relations in Chinese and the Theory of Grammar*, Ph.D. dissertation, Department of Linguistics and Philosophy, Massachusetts Institute of Technology, Cambridge, Massachusetts.

Johnson, M.: this volume, 'Deductive Parsing: the Use of Knowledge of Language', pp. 39–64.

Kaplan, R. and A. Zaenen: 1989, 'Long-Distance Dependencies, Constituent Structure, and Functional Uncertainty', in M. Baltin and A. Kroch (eds.), *Alternative Conceptions of Phrase Structure*, University of Chicago Press, Chicago, Illinois, pp. 17–42.

Kuno, S. and K. Takami: 1990, 'Remarks on Barriers', unpublished manuscript, Department of Linguistics, Harvard University, Cambridge, Massachusetts.

Larson, R.: 1988, 'On the Double Object Construction', *Linguistic Inquiry* 19, 335–391.

Lasnik, H. and M. Saito: 1984, 'On the Nature of Proper Government', *Linguistic Inquiry* 15, 235–289.

Lasnik, H. and M. Saito: 1990, 'Move-α', unpublished manuscript, Department of Linguistics, University of Connecticut, Storrs, Connecticut.

Lightfoot, D. and A. Weinberg: 1988, 'Review of Chomsky's *Barriers*', *Language* 64, 366–383.

Marcus, M.: 1980, *A Theory of Syntactic Recognition for Natural Language*, MIT Press, Cambridge, Massachusetts.

McElree, B. and T. Bever: 1989, 'The Psychological Reality of Linguistically Defined Gaps', *Journal of Psycholinguistic Research* 18, 21–37.

Nicol, J. and D. Swinney: 1989, 'The Role of Structure in Coreference Assignment During Comprehension', *Journal of Psycholinguistic Research* 18, 5–20.

Nishigauchi, T.: 1986, *Quantification in Syntax*, Ph.D. dissertation, Department of Linguistics, University of Massachusetts at Amherst, Amherst, Massachusetts.

Pesetsky, D.: 1982, *Paths and Categories*, Ph.D. dissertation, Department of Linguistics and Philosophy, Massachusetts Institute of Technology, Cambridge, Massachusetts.

Pesetsky, D.: 1987, 'Wh-in-Situ: Movement and Unselective Binding', in E. Reuland and A. ter Meulen (eds.), *The Representation of (In)definiteness*, MIT Press, Cambridge, Massachusetts, pp. 98–129.

Pritchett, B.: 1987, *Garden Path Phenomena and the Grammatical Basis of Language Processing*, Ph.D. dissertation, Department of Linguistics, Harvard University, Cambridge, Massachusetts (forthcoming University of Chicago Press, Chicago, Illinois).

Pritchett, B.: 1988a, 'Garden Path Phenomena and the Grammatical Basis of Language Processing', *Language* **64**, 539–576.

Pritchett, B.: 1988b, 'Processing Double Object Constructions', paper presented at the *University of Maryland Conference on Grammar and Language Processing*, University of Maryland at College Park, College Park, Maryland.

Pritchett, B.: 1989, 'Island Violations Are Garden Paths', paper presented at the *Ottawa Psycholinguistics of Island Constraints Conference*, Department of Linguistics, University of Ottawa, Ottawa, Canada.

Rizzi, L.: 1982, *Issues in Italian Syntax*, Foris, Dordrecht.

Ross, J.: 1967, *Constraints on Variables in Syntax*, Ph.D. dissertation, Department of Linguistics, Massachusetts Institute of Technology, Cambridge, Massachusetts (also published 1986 as *Infinite Syntax!*, Erlbaum, Hillsdale, New Jersey).

Sportiche, D.: 1988, 'Conditions on Silent Categories', unpublished manuscript, Department of Linguistics, University of California at Los Angeles, Los Angeles, California.

Stowe, L.: 1984, *Models of Gap-Location in the Human Language Processor*, Ph.D. dissertation, University of Wisconsin at Madison, Madison, Wisconsin.

Stowell, T.: 1981, *Origins of Phrase Structure*, Ph.D. dissertation, Department of Linguistics and Philosophy, Massachusetts Institute of Technology, Cambridge, Massachusetts.

Stowell, T.: 1989, 'Subjects, Specifiers, and $\overline{X}$ Theory', in M. Baltin and A. Kroch (eds.), *Alternative Conceptions of Phrase Structure*, University of Chicago Press, Chicago, Illinois, pp. 232–262.

Taraldsen, K.: 1981, 'The Theoretical Interpretation of a Class of Marked Extractions', in A. Beletti, L. Brandi, and L. Rizzi (eds.), *The Theory of Markedness in Generative Grammar, Proceedings of the 1979 GLOW Conference*, Scuola Normale Superiore, Pisa, Italy, pp. 475–516.

Wehrli, E.: 1988, 'Parsing with a GB-Grammar', in U. Reyle and C. Rohrer (eds.), *Natural Language Parsing and Linguistic Theories*, Reidel, Dordrecht, Holland, pp. 177–201.

Weinberg, A.: 1988, *Locality Principles in Syntax and Parsing*, Ph.D. dissertation, Department of Linguistics and Philosophy, Massachusetts Institute of Technology, Cambridge, Massachusetts.

Whitman, J.: 1987, 'Configurationality Parameters', in T. Imai and M. Saito (eds.), *Issues in Japanese Linguistics*, Foris, Dordrecht, Holland, pp. 351–374.

Department of Philosophy,
Carnegie Mellon University,
Pittsburgh, Pennsylvania 15213, U.S.A.

HOWARD S. KURTZMAN, LOREN F. CRAWFORD, AND
CAYLEE NYCHIS-FLORENCE

LOCATING WH-TRACES

1. INTRODUCTION

This chapter is an initial report of research in progress. It addresses a topic of considerable interest in recent psycholinguistics: the process by which humans locate *Wh*-traces in the course of word-by-word parsing of incoming sentences (Fodor, 1978; Stowe, 1986; Carlson and Tanenhaus, 1988; Clifton and Frazier, 1989).

Following most current work, the research reported here focuses on traces that occupy noun phrase (NP) positions within English verb phrases (VPs). It is already known that locating traces in English subject positions is easily accomplished by the human parsing mechanism (Hakes, Evans, and Brannon, 1976; Ford, 1983; Stowe, 1986). That is not surprising, because the cues to subject traces are clear: basically, if there is no overt subject preceding an auxiliary or finite verb, then that subject must be occupied by a *Wh*-trace. (It is assumed here that a *Wh*-trace is located only if a fronted *Wh*-phrase has already been identified.) By contrast, the cues to traces within VPs are not always so clear, due to the variety of possible VP structures and of NP positions within those VP structures.

Also following current work, this research examines the parsing mechanism's *initial* hypotheses concerning trace location within the VP, *i.e.*, the hypotheses that arise immediately upon recognition of the verb. We already know from intuition that the correct trace location will eventually be determined for virtually any sentence (unless it is difficult to parse for independent reasons); if the trace were not correctly located, then the sentence could not be comprehended. By identifying the parser's initial hypotheses, we can gain insight into the processing principles and the types of information which lead to its determination of the correct location of the trace.

Recent evidence suggests a role for two processing principles, both of which were first clearly formulated by Fodor (1978): the *First-Resort Principle* and the *Lexical Expectation Principle*. According to the First-

R. C. Berwick et al. (eds.),
Principle-Based Parsing: Computation and Psycholinguistics, 347–382.
© 1991 *Kluwer Academic Publishers. Printed in the Netherlands.*

Resort Principle (in pure form), a trace is hypothesized as occurring at the leftmost position that is grammatically permissible.

Thus, upon recognition of a verb that either obligatorily or optionally takes an NP immediately following it, an NP is hypothesized and it is further hypothesized that this NP is occupied by the trace. According to the Lexical Expectation Principle (pure form), the trace is hypothesized to occur at a position that is specified within the psychologically 'preferred' frame of the verb (usually taken to be the most frequently used frame). Thus, only upon recognition of a verb whose preferred frame specifies an NP is an NP hypothesized with a trace occupying it. If the verb's preferred frame does not specify an NP, then no NP is hypothesized. It is evident that these proposed principles govern not only the hypothesis concerning trace location but also the hypothesis concerning the structure of the VP.

Unfortunately, the Lexical Expectation Principle has generally been presented in an insufficiently elaborated form. The principle has usually been described as concerned only with the specification of an immediately postverbal NP; it is not clear whether a preferred frame may specify the occurrence of additional complements (such as a PP, an $\overline{S}$, or another NP). And, then, if the preferred frame did specify more than one complement, it is not clear whether the trace would be hypothesized at the immediately postverbal NP, or within another complement, or at more than one position in parallel. It might appear that Fodor's (1978) supplementary Try-the-Next-Constituent Principle deals with this issue. That principle imposes a delay on hypothesizing the trace at any position until after the parser has checked that the position is not occupied by an overt constituent. But Fodor described the effects of the principle only for the immediately post-verbal position; it is uncertain whether it is intended to apply to subsequent positions. In fact, there is little reason for it to apply at the rightmost position specified by a verb frame, for the trace must occur at that position if it has not occurred at any preceding position.[1]

Carlson, Tanenhaus and their colleagues (Carlson and Tanenhaus, 1988; Tanenhaus, Garnsey, and Boland, 1991) have offered evidence that supports the Lexical Expectation Principle as it applies to immediately post-verbal NPs. Their more recent evidence (Boland, Tanenhaus, Carlson, and Garnsey, 1989) suggests further that for verbs whose preferred frame specifies both an immediately postverbal NP and another complement, the default hypothesis is that the trace occupies the earlier

NP (at least when it is the direct object). In contrast, Clifton, Frazier, and colleagues (Clifton and Frazier, 1989; Clifton, Frazier, and Connine, 1984; Frazier, 1987; Frazier and Clifton, 1989) have argued for a role for both principles. They claim that initially a trace is hypothesized according to the First-Resort Principle (as Stowe, 1986, also claims). But if this hypothesis is inconsistent with the the preferred verb frame then it is subsequently abandoned; in this way, the Lexical Expectation Principle serves as a second-stage 'filter'.

There are, however, a number of methodological deficiencies in the experiments that have been presented in support of these claims. The most common problems lie in the stimulus sentences, especially their verbs. Verbs usually have been classified as simply transitive or intransitive (either obligatorily or preferably). But such a coarse classification is insensitive to the variety of verb frames. Of greatest concern is that distinctions have not been made between verbs that preferably take only a NP and those that preferably take both a NP and PP. Also, intransitive verbs have often included both ergative and nonergative verbs. Further, verbs have not been well controlled for their thematic and semantic properties or for their overall perceptual complexity.

There are problems with other aspects of the stimulus sentences as well. For example, in intransitive sentences, the trace frequently occurs as the object of a preposition which is uncommon or unpreferred for the verb. In fact, in Frazier and Clifton (1989), the trace is often the object of an adjunct preposition, resulting in an illegitimate or marginal form of preposition stranding (Hornstein and Weinberg, 1981). Further, Frazier and Clifton's sentences contain two PPs in succession, which in general is unpreferred and which could be providing misleading information about trace location. Another problem is seen in some of the sentences of Carlson and Tanenhaus (1988): they contain immediately postverbal manner adverbs, which are known to be infelicitous and hence possibly confusing (Heny, 1973).

Given these problems in the stimuli (as well as the sentences often being just generally awkward), it is not surprising that in several experiments overall levels of accuracy and speed were quite low. Such poor performance indicates that the experimental subjects were not engaged in entirely normal or natural processing. It is also not surprising that not all predicted effects were obtained (or reached statistical significance) and that in some experiments various details of the data were unexpected or lack a clear explanation.[2]

The series of experiments reported here attempts to test specific formulations of the First-Resort and Lexical Expectation Principles in a way that overcomes these problems. Verbs were selected according to strict criteria, and sentence structures were kept simple and constant.

The primary experimental task, speeded online grammaticality judgment, also has certain advantages over some of the tasks used in previous studies. Sentences are presented word-by-word at a rate similar to that of normal speech, and subjects are able to consistently and comfortably make rapid responses.

The results of the experiments will be described as indicating which hypotheses concerning VP structure and trace location are 'most available' or 'dominant' upon recognition of the verb. This terminology is intended to be neutral between those models of parsing which permit activation of only one hypothesis at a time and those which permit more than one hypothesis to be activated simultaneously but with varying strengths (as in the 'ranked-parallelism' of Kurtzman, 1985, and Gorrell, 1987). The issue of which type of model is most appropriate for these results will be addressed in the Discussion.

This research does not assume any particular syntactic framework. Terms such as 'transitivity', 'complement', 'thematic role', and the like are used only descriptively and according to their most common senses.

2.   EXPERIMENTAL TECHNIQUE

All experiments (except Experiment 5) utilized the *speeded online grammaticality judgment task* (Kurtzman, 1985, 1989a). In this task, sentences are visually presented, one word at a time, at the center of a computer terminal screen, such that each word replaces the one that preceded it. Each word is shown for 250 msec and is followed by a 50 msec blank mask. At some unanticipated point, either within a sentence or at the end of a sentence, presentation stops and there is a beep (*i.e.*, the beep sounds immediately after the 50 msec blank mask which follows the finally presented word). This beep signals subjects to respond whether the sentence had, up to that point, been fully grammatical according to the rules of English. Mere incompleteness does not comprise ungrammaticality. Subjects respond by pressing one of two keys on which they have their index fingers resting (the keys are marked 'Yes' for grammatical and 'No' for ungrammatical). Subjects are instructed to respond as quickly as possible based upon their first impression. Both accuracy and response time (RT), measured from the beep, are recorded.

The stimuli of experimental interest are presented among a large number of filler stimuli (the ratio of filler to experimental stimuli is approximately 3:1). These fillers are of varied lengths and structures (including question forms). Some fillers are single sentences, with some of these being complete sentences (15-20% of all fillers) and others incomplete (40-45%) at the point at which presentation stops. Other fillers are made up of two sentences, with the second sentence either complete (15-20%) or incomplete (20-25%). Among incomplete sentences, there is considerable variation in the location of the point at which presentation stops. Thus, subjects cannot ever anticipate the point at which a response will be called for, which reduces the likelihood that they will adopt special response strategies.

Further, half of each type of filler are grammatical, and half are ungrammatical. There is wide variation in the types and locations of the ungrammaticalities; however, for two-sentence stimuli, the ungrammaticality is always in the second sentence.

Subjects bring on each stimulus at their own pace, by pressing a bar with their thumb. The stimuli are in a different random order for each subject.

Each experiment had a constant number of subjects per condition, with this number ranging from eight to twelve. There were as many conditions in an experiment as stimulus versions. Stimulus versions were distributed equally across conditions.

3. EXPERIMENT 1: VERB TRANSITIVITY

The first experiment examined four classes of stimuli, which differed in the transitivity type of their verbs. The stimuli were all of the form *What did NAME VERB XXX*. (See table I, (1)–(4) for examples.)

3.1. *Verbs*

Verb type (1) (*e.g., construct*) obligatorily takes a direct object NP and also optionally takes a complement PP, although the PP is unpreferred. Verb type (2) (*e.g., steal*) preferably, but not obligatorily, takes a direct object NP; it also optionally takes a complement PP, but in the transitive form this PP is unpreferred. Verb type (3) (*e.g., escape*) optionally takes a direct object NP, but it is unpreferred; rather, the preferred form is intransitive with a complement PP.[3] Verb type (4) (*e.g., crawl*) is obligatorily intransitive and preferably takes a complement PP.

Obligatory forms were determined by consulting both dictionaries and the experimenters' intuitions. Preferred forms were determined by having naive subjects provide comparative judgments on declarative sentences containing the verbs. They made judgments on several dimensions: which verb forms seemed most frequent, which forms 'sounded' better or more natural, and how informationally complete the sentences were. Only verbs for which judgments were clear and consistent were used.

For all the verbs, the only possible complements are a direct object NP and/or a single complement PP. Thus, the verbs do not take indirect objects or sentential complements. Further, they do not occur in the ergative or middle constructions. And they do not frequently occur with particles.

For each verb the subject is an Agent and is plausibly singular and +Human. The direct object is a Theme or Patient and plausibly expresses a physical entity that is inanimate, small, and discrete.

The verbs are also perceptually simple: they are just one or two syllables long and have a high frequency of occurrence. The verbs are not ambiguous in meaning or particularly vague. The verb meanings usually concern or are associated with specific, imageable physical actions.

In this experiment (as well as in subsequent experiments), five verbs were tested within each type. No greater number of verbs could be identified for every type within the criteria followed.[4]

3.2. *Sentences*

The sentences were all direct questions in which the *Wh*-phrase was *What*, the auxiliary *did*, and the proper noun in subject position a common male human name.[5] For each stimulus sentence containing a particular verb, there were three versions, differing in the final word.

In version (a), the final word was *while*, which is a conjunction that usually marks the end of a clause. It indicated that a trace occupied the direct object and that there was no PP.

In version (b), the final word was a possessive determiner, either *my*, *our*, *their*, or *your*. It indicated that an overt NP occupied the direct object and so the required trace must occur in a subsequent PP.[6]

In version (c), the final word was a preposition with attached question mark. The preposition was one that can occur as head of a complement PP for the verb. It indicated that a trace occupied the prepositional object and that there was no direct object. The preposition chosen was the one that intuitively sounded the most frequent and natural with the verb. Prepositions that occur frequently in adjuncts, such as *by*, *for*, and *with*, were generally avoided, as was *to*. (Also, for verb type (3)— preferably intransitive—the prepositions were those that assign the same Theme or Patient role to the prepositional object as the verb assigns to the direct object in the transitive form; this will be discussed under Experiment 3.)

For the obligatorily transitive verb type in Table I (1), version (c) is ungrammatical. And for the obligatorily intransitive verb type in (4), versions (a) and (b) are ungrammatical. All other versions of sentences are grammatical (but see note 3).

The basic assumption is that if the final word is consistent with a hypothesis that was available to subjects upon their processing of the verb, then responses should be accurate and fast; if the final word is inconsistent, then responses should be less accurate and slower.

(Note that in versions (a) and (b), the sentences are incomplete and lack a question mark, while in (c) the sentence is complete with a question mark. Control experiments, described in the appendix, showed that the mere presence of the question mark does not affect subjects' accuracy or RT; hence it is legitimate to directly compare versions with and without a question mark.)

3.3. *Results*

The results are summarized in (1)–(4) of table I. Analyses of the accuracy and RT data were carried out separately for each verb type. (Only RTs for 'Yes' responses are considered here.) Planned pairwise analytical comparisons of means were performed using the modified Bonferroni correction (Keppel, 1982). All significant differences are at the corrected equivalent of the .05 level or below for both item- and subject-based comparisons. (These statistical procedures were followed for subsequent experiments as well.)

First consider the accuracy results. For the obligatorily transitive verbs and the obligatorily intransitive verbs, subjects accurately tended to respond 'No' to ungrammatical versions (see (1c), (4a), and (4b)).

Table I

EXPERIMENT 1: Example Sentences and Results

(1) Verb Obligatory Transitive, Preferably No Complement PP			'Yes' Responses	Mean RT (msec) 'Yes' Responses
What did Tom construct				
	a. while	$<NP_t >$	88[a]	707
	b. our	$<NP\ PP_t >$	35[b]	(893)
	c. from?	$<* PP_t >$	32[b]	(1045)
(2) Verb Preferably Transitive, with No Complement PP				
What did George steal				
	a. while	$<NP_t >$	93[a]	706a
	b. your	$<NP\ PP_t >$	31[c]	(750)
	c. from?	$<PP_t >$	77[b]	715[a]
(3) Verb Preferably Intransitive, with Complement PP				
What did John escape				
	a. while	$<NP_t >$	70[b]	736[b]
	b. their	$<NP\ PP_t >$	30[c]	(751)
	c. from?	$<PP_t >$	90[a]	608[a]
(4) Verb Obligatorily Intransitive, Preferably With Complement PP				
What did Tony crawl				
	a. while	$<* NP_t >$	35[b]	(811)
	b. our	$<* NP\ PP_t >$	22[b]	(588)
	c. under?	$< PP_t >$	93[a]	543

Note: Subscript t indicates phrase containing trace. Distinct superscripts indicate significant differences. Mean RTs in parentheses are computed from too few 'Yes' responses to permit meaningful statistical comparisons.

Thus, subjects did not generate hypotheses about VP structure that violated verb frame restrictions (or, if they did, they abandoned such hypotheses quickly—by the time they processed the word immediately following the verb).

For the preferably transitive verbs, subjects responded 'Yes' somewhat more frequently to the transitive version in which the trace occupied the direct object (2a) than to the intransitive version in which the trace occupied the prepositional object (2c). The reverse effect is seen for the preferably intransitive verbs (3a, 3c). Thus, whether the transitive or intransitive hypothesis was most available was determined by the particular verb. This is consistent with the Lexical Expectation Principle. (The accuracy levels for (2c) and (3a) are still fairly high, however. Thus, the hypothesis compatible with the unpreferred frame of the verb was available to some degree. The nature of this lesser availability will be taken up in section 10.)

Subjects tended to respond 'No' to all the (b) versions, in which the direct object is overt, even though for (1), (2), and (3), these versions are grammatical. This suggests that for VP structures that include a direct object, the trace is hypothesized only at the direct object position. Such a hypothesis is consistent with a version of the First-Resort Principle which states that, *within a hypothesized VP structure*, the trace is hypothesized at the leftmost possible position. Also consistent with this version of First-Resort is the moderate-to-high accuracy for versions (2c), (3c), and (4c), since, within the intransitive frame, the leftmost (and only) possible position for the trace is the prepositional object. (A pure form of First-Resort is not supported, because accuracy on (3a) is depressed.)

Turning to the RT data, comparisons were made only within the preferably transitive verb type (2) and the preferably intransitive verb type (3); comparisons could not be made for the other verb types ((1) and (4)), because in each type only one of the versions had a sufficient number of 'Yes' responses. For the preferably intransitive verbs (3), the RT data mirror the accuracy data: RT was slower for (3a) than for (3c).

However, for the preferably transitive verbs, there was no significant difference in RT between (2a) and (2c). This lack of an expected effect could be due to a complicating factor associated with the conjunction *while*, which usually indicates a clause boundary. Previous work shows that readers often delay at clause boundaries (Aaronson and Scarborough, 1976; Just and Carpenter, 1980). Such a delay may be manifested in the present experiment by a longer RT following *while* in (2a) than would be expected solely on the basis of the accuracy data. Consistent with this suggestion, the RTs for the *while* versions for all verb types are uniformly high—over 700 msec. Thus, although the RT for (2c) is also high (715 msec), consistent with its lower accuracy, it is possible that the expected RT difference between (2c) and (2a) is masked by the independent delay associated with *while*.

To summarize, Experiment 1 indicates that the parser only maintains hypotheses from among those consistent with the verb's permissible frames. Further, which hypothesis concerning VP structure is most available is determined by the verb's preferred frame. Within transitive VP structures, the trace is dominantly hypothesized at the direct object, and within intransitive VP structures that contain a PP, the trace is dominantly hypothesized at the prepositional object; this is consistent with a First-Resort Principle that applies within each VP structure.[7]

4.   EXPERIMENT 2: COMPLEMENT AND ADJUNCT PPs

The verb types tested in Experiment 1 actually do not provide a sufficient test of the First-Resort Principle. For all types, the verb preferably takes only one complement, a direct object or a PP. Thus, the results could be interpreted as showing only that the trace was dominantly hypothesized at the one NP position that occurs in the most preferred frame of the verb. In order to test the First-Resort Principle adequately, it is necessary to examine verbs which preferably take both a direct object and a complement PP. First-Resort predicts that the trace is preferably hypothesized at the direct object for these verbs as well. But if First-Resort is not valid, then the trace could be hypothesized at both the direct object and the prepositional object (in parallel) or could be dominantly hypothesized at the prepositional object (indicating a 'Last-Resort' Principle applying within the VP structure).

This approach to testing First-Resort assumes a generalized version of the Lexical Expectation Principle, such that a verb frame which specifies both a direct object and a PP can be preferred over frames which specify only a direct object (and vice versa). By contrast, most previous descriptions of Lexical Expectation have referred only to specification of the direct object.

4.1. *Stimuli*

Experiment 2 tested both this generalized Lexical Expectation Principle and the First-Resort Principle by examining two verb types, illustrated in table II, (5)–(6). Verb type (5) is the same as verb type (1): it obligatorily takes a direct object NP and preferably does not take a complement PP. Verb type (6) also obligatorily takes a direct object but preferably does take a complement PP. (The same criteria as in Experiment 1 were followed in selecting verbs for (6).)

The verbs were again inserted in a *What did NAME VERB XXX* frame. There were four versions, differing in their final word. Versions (a) and (b) were the same as in Experiment 1. In version (c), the final word was a preposition that can serve as head of a complement PP for the verb. For type (5), these were the same prepositions as in (1c); for type (6), prepositions were chosen in the same manner as Experiment 1.

In version (d), the final word was a preposition that cannot serve as head of a complement PP for the verb; it can only serve as head of an adjunct PP (outside the VP).

For both versions (c) and (d), there was no question mark attached to the preposition, and the trace was indicated to occupy the direct object.

All versions for both verb types are grammatical.

4.2. *Results*

For verb type (5), the results for versions (a) and (b) replicated those in Experiment 1: high accuracy on (a), in which the trace occurred at the direct object, and low accuracy on (b), in which the trace occurred in a subsequent PP. For verb type (6), with preferred PP, the same data pattern was obtained. This is as predicted by the First-Resort Principle.[8]

Next we turn to versions (c) and (d). For type (5), performance was slightly more accurate and was faster for (d), which indicated an adjunct PP, than for (c), which indicated a potential complement PP. (Only the RT effect was significant.) For type (6), the reverse pattern was found: better performance on (c) than (d) (with only the accuracy effect significant). These results are as predicted by the generalized Lexical Expectation Principle. Thus, hypotheses of VP structure which differ only in the occurrence of a PP can vary in their availability, depending upon the particular verb.

Table II
EXPERIMENT 2: Example Sentences and Results

(5) Verb Obligatory Transitive, Preferably No Complement PP			% 'Yes' Responses	Mean RT (msec) 'Yes' Responses
What did Tom construct				
	a. while	$<NP_t>$	93^a	707^a
	b. our	$<NP\ PP_t>$	33^b	(909)
	c. from	$<NP_t\ PP\text{-}complement>$	82^a	790^b
	d. at	$<NP_t\ PP\text{-}adjunct>$	86^a	$765^{a,b}$

(6) Verb Obligatorily Transitive, Preferably With Complement PP				
What did David remove				
	a. while	$<NP_t>$	90^a	732^a
	b. our	$<NP\ PP_t>$	35^c	(791)
	c. from	$<NP_t\ PP\text{-}complement>$	83^a	754^a
	d. at	$<NP_t\ PP\text{-}adjunct>$	70^b	761^a

Note: *PP-complement* indicates Prep can occur in either complement PP or adjunct PP. *PP-adjunct* indicates Prep can occur only in adjunct PP.

Another feature of the data is a trend toward worse performance on both the (c) and (d) versions, with prepositions, than on the (a) versions, with *while* (although not all performance decrements were significant). This can be attributed to the parser's initial uncertainty concerning where to attach the preposition—into a complement PP inside the VP or into an adjunct PP outside the VP. Most prepositions—including the ones utilized here—can occur in both complements and adjuncts. In order for the parser to determine where the preposition may be legally attached, it must consult lexical information associated with the verb. And, then, even if it is permissible to attach the preposition into a complement PP, it is not required. So, a complex series of consultation and decision processes must be undertaken in order to attach the preposition. This series of processes causes increased RTs. Also, since subjects are under time pressure, they might make errors or fail to complete some processes, causing a decrease in accuracy.[9]

To conclude, the results of Experiments 1 and 2 support a generalized Lexical Expectation Principle, such that the preferred verb frame, distinguished by its specification both of direct object and of PP, determines which VP structure hypothesis is most available. The results also indicate that the First-Resort Principle applies within each hypothesized VP structure, such that the trace is dominantly hypothesized at the leftmost possible position.

5. EXPERIMENT 3: CONTENT OF LEXICAL FRAMES

So far, lexical frames have been described as specifying only phrasal information, as in traditional subcategorization frames. However, lexical frames may also specify thematic roles, and some linguists have suggested that they specify only thematic roles, with general principles linking thematic roles to phrasal types and positions (Grimshaw, 1981; Pesetsky, 1983; Woolford, 1984). What kind of information—phrasal, thematic, or both—is specified in the lexical frames that the parser consults in determining the availability of VP structure hypotheses? (It is possible that the parser's lexical frames differ from those frames indicated by research on competence grammar.)

5.1. *Phrasal Information*

Evidence from Experiment 1 already indicates that the parser's lexical frames specify at least phrasal information. For (3)—the preferably intransitive verbs—the verb assigns the same thematic role to its direct object in the transitive version (a) as it does through the preposition in the intransitive version (c). However, performance on (c) was superior to that on (a). So, the dominant hypothesis is for a PP rather than a NP, even when the phrases express the same thematic roles. This indicates that lexical frames must be differentiated, at least in part, by the particular phrases they specify.

5.2. *Thematic Information*

To determine whether lexical frames also specify thematic information, a third experiment was performed. As shown in table III, (7)–(8), two verb types were tested. Type (7) was the same as type (3) in Experiment 1—preferably intransitive. And type (8) was the same as type (4)—obligatorily intransitive.

The same sentence frame was used as in Experiment 1. There were two versions of each sentence. Version (a) was the same as in Experiment 1: the final word was a preposition which could serve as head of a complement PP, with a question mark attached. In version (b), the final word was a different preposition with attached question mark, but again was one that could serve as head of a complement PP. Crucially, the prepositions in (a) and (b) assign different thematic roles. Although, the prepositions chosen for version (b) occurred commonly and sounded natural with the verb, independent judges rated the prepositions in (a) as somewhat more preferred than those in (b).

Performance was worse (*i.e.*, less accurate and slower) on the (b) versions than the (a) versions, for both verb types. Since the essential difference between the versions is in the thematic role that is assigned, these results indicate that the parser's lexical frames are differentiated by the particular thematic roles they specify. If lexical frames were differentiated only by their phrasal information, no difference would be expected between the two versions.[10]

Table III
EXPERIMENT 3: Example Sentences and Results

(7) Verb Preferably Intransitive, With Complement PP	% 'Yes' Responses	Mean RT (msec) 'Yes' Responses
What did John escape		
a. from?	96[a]	650[a]
b. to?	84[b]	711[b]

(8) Verb Obligatorily Intransitive, Preferably With Complement PP		
What did Tony crawl		
a. under?	96[a]	596[a]
b. from?	72[b]	690[b]

5.3. *Toward a Unified Account*

The evidence indicates that the lexical frames involved in parsing specify both phrasal and thematic information. However, rather than refer to two types of information, it would be desirable to account for the evidence in a more unified way. One possible approach would refer to a deeper, more elaborated level of the semantic representation of verbs than that of crude thematic roles (perhaps along the lines of Jackendoff, 1983). The preference for a particular frame of a verb would then be a consequence of a preference at this deeper semantic level for particular aspects or variants of the verb's meaning to be expressed. This approach could obviously be developed to account for the preposition effects in Experiment 3, because the distinct thematic roles assigned by different prepositions are associated with different aspects of a verb's meaning.

This approach can also be applied to the transitivity effects observed in Experiment 1 under (3). For, although the same thematic roles are assigned in the transitive version (a) and the intransitive version (c), there are subtle semantic differences between the transitive and intransitive forms of the verbs. For example, the transitive *John escaped prison* can mean either that John escaped the physical entity of a prison or, more abstractly, that John escaped from a prison sentence. By contrast, the intransitive *John escaped from prison* can only mean that John escaped the physical entity. Also, *John escaped punishment* is a good sentence, while *John escaped from punishment* is somewhat odd. These examples suggest that the intransitive form with preposition restricts the complement to expressing, roughly, a more physical or more specific entity. This same pattern is observed for the other verbs under (3) that were tested. Thus the transitivity preferences in Experiment 1 may be rooted in preferences at a deeper semantic level for a particular variant (or range of variants) of the verb's meaning. This approach requires much development, but it appears promising.

6. EXPERIMENT 4: *WHO*

In the preceding experiments, the *Wh*-phrase was always *what*. It is possible that the First-Resort preference for the trace to occur in the leftmost, direct object position is limited to sentences in which the *Wh*-phrase is *what* or some other −Human phrase, since such phrases canonically serve as direct objects. In order to test the generality of the First-Resort Principle, the fourth experiment investigated sentences in which the *Wh*-phrase is +Human *who*.

As (9) in table IV shows, stimuli were sentences of the form *Who did NAME VERB XXX*. The verbs obligatorily take a direct object NP and also preferably take a complement PP. Both the direct object NP and the prepositional object can plausibly (but do not necessarily) express a +Human entity. (Some of the same verbs were used as in (6) of Experiment 2.) The verbs otherwise obey the same criteria as in the previous experiments.

The three versions of each sentence differed in their final words. Version (a) ended in *while*, indicating that the trace occupied the direct object and that there was no PP. Version (b) ended in a possessive determiner, indicating that the direct object was overt and the trace must occur in a subsequent PP. And version (c) ended in a preposition that could (but did not necessarily) serve as head of a complement PP; no question mark was attached. This indicated that the trace occupied the direct object and that there was a PP. All versions are grammatical.[11]

Table IV
EXPERIMENT 4: Example Sentences and Results

		% 'Yes' Responses	Mean RT (msec) 'Yes' Responses
(9) Who did Harry conceal			
	a. while $<NP_t>$	94[a]	875[a]
	b. their $<NP\ PP_t>$	40[b]	(1289)
	c. from $<NP_t\ PP>$	84[a]	937[a]

The data in (9) show the best performance on version (a) and a trend toward somewhat lower performance on (c). Poor performance is observed in version (b). This is the same pattern of results as observed in the previous experiments in which the *Wh*-phrase was *what*. Thus, the poor performance on (b) can be attributed to the First-Resort Principle: Subjects' dominant hypothesis was that the trace occurred at the direct object. And the slightly lower performance on (c) than (a) can be attributed to the general difficulty in attaching prepositions.

We may conclude that the First-Resort Principle applies whether the *Wh*-phrase is +Human or −Human.

7. EXPERIMENT 5: FURTHER TEST OF THE FIRST-RESORT PRINCIPLE

In the preceding experiments, very poor performance was observed only for the versions whose final word was a determiner which indicated that the direct object was overt and that the trace occurred in a subsequent PP. This poor performance has been explained as due to the inconsistency of this final word with the dominant First-Resort hypothesis that the trace occupied the direct object.

However, these versions were also the only ones in which subjects were required to respond at a point in the sentence at which the actual position of the trace was not yet encountered. This suggests an alternative explanation of the poor performance: that, in this online grammaticality judgment task, subjects tend to respond 'No' if, at the response point, there is no position in the stimulus string which could be occupied by the expected trace. This suggestion is not implausible if—as Wanner and Maratsos (1978), Clifton and Frazier (1989), and others have proposed in various ways—the parser enters into an 'active' or high-load trace-expectation state upon identifying a fronted *Wh*-phrase. A failure to exit this state would then function as a cue to ungrammaticality.

The fifth experiment sought evidence for the First-Resort Principle that was not vulnerable to this alternative explanation. Each stimulus was a single complete sentence. All the words of the sentence were displayed *simultaneously* across the screen, so that the entire sentence was available to subjects before they responded. Subjects responded as quickly as possible whether or not the sentence was grammatical, by pressing a 'Yes' or 'No' button (as in the previous experiments). Once they responded, the sentence disappeared. The fifteen experimental sentences were embedded among 102 varied filler sentences, half of which were grammatical and half ungrammatical. Subjects brought on each stimulus sentence at their own pace by pressing a bar with their thumb. The sentences were presented in a different random order for each subject.

Examples of the experimental stimuli are shown in table V, (10)–(12). There were three classes of stimuli, differing in their verb type. The verbs in (10) were the same as those previously tested in both (1) of Experiment 1 and (5) of Experiment 2: they obligatorily take a direct object NP and preferably do not take a complement PP. The verbs in (11) were the same as in (6) in Experiment 2: they obligatorily take a direct object NP and also preferably take a complement PP. The verbs in (12) were the same as in Experiment 4 (and thus, some of the verbs in (11) and (12) were the same).

Two versions of each stimulus were tested. These versions were comprised of the same words, but the words following the verb occurred in different orders. In (10) and (11), the two versions were of the forms (a) *What did NAME VERB PREP the NOUN?* and (b) *What did NAME VERB the NOUN PREP?*, in which the NOUN was −Human. The NOUN was also a high-frequency word and referred to a physical object. In (12), the versions were of the forms (a) *Who did NAME VERB PREP the NOUN?* and (b) *Who did NAME VERB the NOUN PREP?*, in which the NOUN was +Human. Thus, both versions contained both a direct object and a complement PP. In (a) the trace was at the direct object, and in (b) the trace was at the prepositional object. Both ver-

Table V

EXPERIMENT 5: Example Sentences and Results

(10) Verb Obligatory Transitive, Preferably No Complement PP	% 'Yes' Responses	Mean RT (msec) 'Yes' Responses
a. What did Robert construct from the objects?	92[a]	2129[a]
b. What did Robert construct the objects from?	68b[b]	2621[a]

(11) Verb Obligatorily Transitive, Preferably With Complement PP		
a. What did David remove from the engine?	93[a]	2006[a]
b. What did David remove the engine from?	55b[b]	2478[a]

(12) Verb Obligatorily Transitive, Preferably With Complement PP–*Who*		
a. Who did James conceal from the princess?	94[a]	2172[a]
b. Who did James conceal the princess from?	42b[b]	2543b[b]

sions are grammatical, and for each stimulus both versions were rated by independent judges to have equally plausible meanings.

As (10)–(12) show, performance was worse for all classes of stimuli on version (b) than version (a). (When RT effects were not significant, there was a strong trend in the expected direction.) This is consistent with the First-Resort Principle. It cannot be due to subjects being forced to make a response to a string in which there is no possible position for the trace, because the complete sentence was available to them.

Thus, we may continue to attribute at least part of the poor performance observed previously for those versions ending with determiners to the inconsistency of the determiners with the First-Resort hypothesis of a trace at the direct object. The current experiment does not disconfirm that subjects have some tendency to respond 'No' when the string contains no possible position for the trace, but it does indicate that such a tendency is not the only source of the poor performance. That tendency could be contributing to the magnitude of the poor performance, however.[12]

The following experiments' results also bear on the validity of the First-Resort Principle and of the alternative discussed here.

8. EXPERIMENT 6: PLAUSIBILITY EFFECT (*WHAT* VS. *WHO*)

The preceding experiments indicated that, for obligatorily and preferably transitive verbs, the dominant hypothesis concerning trace location is the direct object position. But is this First-Resort hypothesis maintained even if it results in an implausible meaning? Experiments 6 and 7 examine this question.

Experiment 6 tested a new verb type. The verbs obligatorily take a direct object NP which plausibly can only be −Human, and also preferably take a complement PP which is plausibly (but not necessarily) +Human (*e.g., borrow*). The verbs obey the other criteria described for the previous verb types. As (13) shows, the sentences were all of the form *What/Who did NAME VERB DET*. Just as in the previous experiments, the version with −Human *what* was expected to show low performance because the determiner indicated that the hypothesis of a trace at the direct object is incorrect. However, if plausibility could influence whether this hypothesis is maintained, then the version with +Human *who* would be expected to show higher performance. Before

Table VI
EXPERIMENT 6: Example Sentences and Results

		% 'Yes' Responses	Mean RT (msec) 'Yes' Responses
(13) ___did Tim borrow our			
	a. What	30[b]	(923)
	b. Who	57[a]	1089

reception of the determiner, subjects would note the implausible meaning that results from the structure in which the trace occupies the direct object and would switch their dominant hypothesis to that in which the trace occurs in a subsequent position.

The data in (13) do indeed show better performance for the *who* version than the *what* version. Thus, subjects did consult information about plausibility to determine whether to maintain as dominant the First-Resort hypothesis that the trace occupied the direct object.[13]

Also, the better performance on the *who* version serves to supplement the evidence of Experiment 5 by showing that subjects in this task do not always have a strong tendency to respond 'No' to strings in which there is no possible position for the trace. However, a weak tendency of this sort can explain why the accuracy on the *who* version is still relatively low (57%) and RT relatively high compared with various versions in the earlier experiments. Another possible reason for the relatively low accuracy is that the influence of plausibility is limited—so that only sometimes does it lead subjects to override the First-Resort Principle.

9. EXPERIMENT 7: PLAUSIBILITY EFFECT
(LEXICALLY-HEADED *WH*-PHRASES)

The seventh experiment utilized the verb type of (2)—verbs preferably with a direct object and no other complement. As (14)–(15) show, the sentences were of the form *Wh-phrase did NAME VERB XXX*. The experiment was actually conducted as two separate studies (with separate subjects). In one study, illustrated by (14), the final word was a possessive determiner; in the other study, illustrated by (15), the final word was a preposition with attached question mark.

First consider (14). The final determiner indicated that the direct object was overt and that the trace must occupy a subsequent position. In versions (a) and (b), the *Wh*-phrase was of the form *Which NOUN*, with the two versions differing in the NOUN. In (a), the NOUN was selected such that the trace could plausibly occupy either the direct object or prepositional object position. In (b), the NOUN was selected such that the trace could plausibly occupy only the prepositional object position. In version (c), the *Wh*-phrase was simply *what*, as in the earlier experiments; this version was included in order to compare sentences with lexically-headed and *Wh*-headed *Wh*-phrases.

The data in (14) show somewhat better performance on (b) than (a). This shows that plausibility led the parser to increase the availability of an hypothesis in which the direct object is overt and the trace occupies a subsequent position. Thus, plausibility led to an overriding both of the verb's lexical preference (since the verb's preferred frame specifies only a direct object) and—as in Experiment 6—of the First-Resort Principle.

But—again as in Experiment 6—performance on (b) was still relatively low. This could be due to the influence of plausibility being inherently limited or to the suggested tendency to respond 'No' to stimuli which contain no possible position for the trace (or to both).

There was no significant difference in performance between (14a) and (14c). This indicates that, when all possible hypotheses are plausible, lexical preferences and the First-Resort Principle hold in the same manner for sentences with lexically- and *Wh*-headed *Wh*-phrases.

Turning to the second study, under (15), the final preposition with attached question mark indicated that there was no direct object and that the trace occupied the prepositional object position. Versions (a)–(c) varied in the same manner as in the first study.

The data show better performance on (b) than (a). Thus, plausibility led the parser to increase the availability of a VP hypothesis in which the only complement is a PP (in addition to increasing the NP-PP hypothesis, as shown by the first study). But accuracy is still a bit less and RT a bit higher than in versions in previous experiments, indicating that the influence of plausibility is limited. (The effect of plausibility in (15) does not involve an overriding of the First-Resort Principle, construed as applying within each VP structure, because the prepositional object is the leftmost—and only—position in this intransitive VP structure.)

Table VII
EXPERIMENT 7: Example Sentences and Results

		% 'Yes' Responses	Mean RT (msec) 'Yes' Responses
(14) ___did George steal your			
	a. Which basket	35[b]	(941)
	b. Which bank	58[a]	984
	c. What	28[b]	(881)
(15) ___did George steal from?			
	a. Which basket	60[b]	867[b]
	b. Which bank	85[a]	724a
	c. What	58[b]	934[b]

The data also show no significant difference between (15a) and (15c). This again indicates that verb frame preferences have the same effects in sentences with lexically- and *Wh*-headed *Wh*-phrases.

Finally, Experiments 6 and 7 showed different kinds of plausibility information influencing the availability of parsing hypotheses. In Experiment 6, plausibility was manipulated solely by varying the value of the Human feature. Thus, the locus of the effect might have been entirely at the structural-semantic level at which selectional restrictions are represented. In Experiment 7, however, plausibility was manipulated by the choice of nouns in a way that necessarily involved a level of real-world knowledge.

10. DISCUSSION

10.1. *Summary of Results*

This research provides support for particular versions of both the Lexical Expectation Principle and the First-Resort Principle. Upon recognition of the verb, the VP structure hypothesis which is consistent with the preferred verb frame attains the highest degree of availability, in accord with Lexical Expectation. A VP structure hypothesis can refer to the possibilities of both a direct object NP and a complement PP. Further, a hypothesis can specify not only phrases but also the particular thematic roles of the phrases.

For a hypothesized VP structure, the most available hypothesis concerning the location of the trace is at the leftmost possible position within the structure, in accord with First-Resort. At least for transitive structures, this hypothesis arises immediately upon recognition of the verb. There is no delay, contrary to the Try-the-Next-Constituent Principle. For intransitive structures, although there immediately arises a hypothesis for a preposition which assigns a particular thematic role, it is not clear whether the trace itself is also immediately hypothesized as object of the preposition or, instead, whether the trace is hypothesized only after the input preposition is actually received. But even if the latter holds, the data indicate that the trace can be hypothesized quite readily (see (3c) and (4c)).

The current results also indicate that these principles can be overridden if the structures they favor result in an implausible meaning for the sentence. In such cases, alternative hypotheses concerning VP structure or trace location can become more available. This shift occurs quickly, prior to reception of the word immediately following the verb.[14]

10.2. *Relation to Previous Research*

These results are largely consistent with those of Boland et al. (1989) and Tanenhaus et al. (1989). Their evidence is compatible with Lexical Expectation as it applies to direct object NPs. Their work also indicates that for verbs which can take both a direct object and another possible complement, the default dominant hypothesis is that the trace occupies the direct object. (They tested dative verbs and verbs which take infinitive complements.) Further, their evidence suggests that for cases in which a trace at the direct object results in an implausible meaning while a trace within the other complement could result in a plausible meaning, the dominant hypothesis is that the trace occurs within the other complement.[15]

The present results are inconsistent with the claims of Clifton and Frazier (1989); Frazier and Clifton (1989), who argue that for all potentially transitive verbs, including those that are preferably intransitive, the trace is dominantly hypothesized at an immediately postverbal position. Thus, they are proposing a pure version of First-Resort, rather than one that applies within particular VP structures as proposed here. They also argue that, at a subsequent point in time, the Lexical Expectation Principle applies to filter out hypotheses inconsistent with preferred verb frames.

Contrary to Clifton and Frazier's claims, the present results suggest that Lexical Expectation applies at the same time as and in interaction with First Resort. For example, in (1)-(4) under Experiment 1 there is no hint of a pure form of First Resort having a stronger effect than Lexical Expectation, as Clifton and Frazier would predict. Also, Experiment 3 suggests that the weak Lexical Expectation effects that Clifton and Frazier observed for intransitive verbs might be due to their sentence materials often containing prepositions which were thematically unpreferred for the verb.

In fact, Experiment 3's results, which indicate that verb frame preferences involve preferred thematic roles as well as preferred phrases, is consistent with work by Taraban and McClelland (1988) on the resolution of PP-attachment ambiguities in declarative sentences. The results are also consistent with Shapiro, Zurif, and Grimshaw's (1987) evidence that a verb's processing complexity is determined by its number of alternative thematic frames rather than subcategorization frames.

10.3. *Is It Really First-Resort?*

It is important to note that the available evidence for the First-Resort Principle is also consistent with an alternative principle which states that the dominant hypothesis for trace location is the highest possible position on a hierarchy of grammatical relations. On this hierarchy, Direct Object would be higher than other Complements of the verb. And Subject would be higher than Direct Object, since evidence from English, French and Dutch suggests that, when grammatically permissible, the trace is dominantly hypothesized at the Subject position (Hakes, *et al.* 1976; Ford, 1983; Stowe, 1986; Frauenfelder *et al.*, 1980; Frazier, 1987). (This hierarchy would thus provide an additional explanation for the ease of locating subject traces, aside from the suggestion, given above in the introduction, that the cues to such traces are especially clear and localized.) Boland *et al.* (1989) appear to make a similar claim for a hierarchy.

In order to tease apart First-Resort from the hierarchy view, it is necessary to examine structures in which the linear order of the constituents is not confounded with their hierarchy order, as it is in nearly all structures investigated thus far. Current work by the author is examining double-object structures and double PP structures in English. But the best tests would of course be in languages with alternative word orders.

The hierarchy view is quite reasonable; similar hierarchies have been implicated in linguistic research (*e.g.*, Keenan and Comrie, 1977). But First-Resort is also reasonable, given the common suggestion, mentioned in the introduction to Experiment 5, that the parser persists in a resource-hungry trace-expectation state from the time it identifies the fronted *Wh*-phrase until it locates the trace. A processing pressure to exit this state as soon as possible would automatically result in the parser following the First-Resort Principle. (Thus, the trace-expectation state could explain both First-Resort and the tendency, if it is real, to respond 'No' to strings which contain no possible position for the trace.)

One reason why it is important to determine which view is correct is that each carries a particular implication about the form of the parser's hypotheses about VP structure and trace location. If the hierarchy view is correct, then it is possible that the hypotheses are simply the lexical frames themselves, with annotations for which complement the trace occurs in. But if First-Resort is correct, then the hypotheses are probably not the lexical frames alone, because lexical frames, as typically conceived, do not specify the linear order of complements in surface structure. The hypotheses could take the form of the lexical frames along with a general statement that the trace occurs at the leftmost possible position in the surface structure, or they could take the form of full-fledged phrase structures with traces inserted.

10.4. *Mechanisms*

In addition to the issue concerning the form of the parser's hypotheses, other issues remain open concerning the precise mechanisms underlying the location of traces. Foremost is the issue of whether the parser can have only one hypothesis for the structure of the VP (including trace location) activated at any one time or can have more than one hypothesis activated simultaneously in ranked order. The rank of a hypothesis refers to the 'strength' or 'accessibility' of its representation.

Unfortunately, the current results do not decide this issue. Except for sentence versions which violated the First-Resort Principle, the lesser performance on various versions was not grossly poor: accuracy was generally above 70% (and always at least 60%). Thus, when a version did not comport with the verb's preferred frame, there was not a severe garden-pathing effect (cf. Kurtzman, 1985, which showed much lower accuracy levels for classic garden-path structures on this task). This result is compatible either with the view that, at the time the word following the verb was received, only one hypothesis was activated but another hypothesis could be quite readily activated as a replacement if the input required (on the basis of the alternative verb frames), or with the view that more than one hypothesis was activated but the hypotheses differed in their ranking.

The plausibility effects are compatible with either view: plausibility information either facilitates the ease of activation of alternative hypotheses (perhaps via reallocation of thematic roles, as in Carlson and Tanenhaus, 1988) or influences the ranking of alternative hypotheses.

It might appear that the grossly poor performance on the versions which violated First-Resort indicates that hypotheses incompatible with First-Resort were not activated (aside from those versions in Experiments 6 and 7 in which plausibility favored the violation). However, this may not be true, because, as suggested, it is possible that accuracy was decreased by an independent tendency to respond 'No' to strings which have no possible position for the trace. Current work is seeking to determine whether there actually is such a tendency and, if so, what its magnitude is. But for now the precise degree of availability for non-First-Resort hypotheses is unclear.

If it is the case that multiple hypotheses can be simultaneously activated in ranked order, then the question arises of what the precise ordering is. Obviously, the hypothesis which is consistent both with the preferred lexical frame and First-Resort is ranked highest. But the current data do not clearly indicate how lexical frame preferences and First-Resort would interact to determine the rank-ordering of the other hypotheses. Thus, would a hypothesis which comports with a preferred lexical frame but which disobeys First-Resort be ranked higher than, lower than, or equal to a hypothesis which comports with an unpreferred lexical frame but obeys First-Resort? (There also might be a limit on how many hypotheses can be activated at once.)

So far, we have asked about which hypotheses were activated at the time that the word following the verb was received. But even if only one hypothesis were activated at that time, it is still possible that initially more than one hypothesis was briefly activated and then all except one were deleted. This could help account for the plausibility effects. Thus, it can be suggested that immediately upon recognizing the verb, all possible hypotheses are activated along with their corresponding meaning representations. If the hypothesis that is consistent with the preferred lexical frame and with First-Resort has a sufficiently plausible meaning, then it is maintained for processing of the following word and the other hypotheses are deleted. If that hypothesis is not sufficiently plausible, then one of the other plausible hypotheses is maintained and the remaining hypotheses are deleted.

Alternatively, it could be that immediately upon receiving the verb, only the one hypothesis that is consistent with the preferred lexical frame and with First-Resort is generated. If its corresponding meaning is sufficiently plausible, the hypothesis is maintained. Only if its meaning is not sufficiently plausible is an alternative hypothesis activated. (And perhaps the alternative is not hypothesized until after the next word is received.)

So, while the current data provide evidence concerning the processing principles and types of information which guide the location of traces, their exact implementation remains to be determined.

APPENDIX: CONTROL EXPERIMENTS

Several control experiments, using the speeded online grammaticality judgment task, were performed in order to determine the influence of certain other characteristics of the stimulus sentences upon subjects' performance in the experiments above. The results of these studies support assumptions that were made in interpreting the experiments, and thereby also serve to rule out various alternative accounts of the results.

The Question Mark

One variation between sentence versions in several experiments was the presence or absence of a question mark attached to the final word. This question mark was included when it was required to completely disam-

biguate the location of the trace. But are subjects in this task actually
sensitive to this question mark? To answer this, sentences were tested
which contain the same verbs as in (1) and (5)—obligatorily transitive
with preferably no complement PP. As (16) in table VIII illustrates, the
two versions both ended in the same preposition as in (1). The only difference between the versions was that (a) had an attached question mark
and (b) did not—resulting in (a) being ungrammatical and (b) grammatical. (Although both versions were previously tested in Experiments
1 and 2, they had not been directly compared.) Subjects generally did
respond correctly that (a) was ungrammatical and (b) was grammatical.
This result indicates that subjects are indeed sensitive to the question
mark, as was assumed in the experiments above.

The next issue is whether the presence of the question mark affects
accuracy or RT when both versions are grammatical. As shown in table VIII (17), sentences were tested which contain the same verbs as
in (4)—obligatorily intransitive and preferably with a complement PP.
The two versions both ended in the same preposition as in (4). Again,
the only difference between the versions was that (a) had an attached
question mark and (b) did not. Subjects generally responded accurately
that both versions were grammatical, with no significant differences in
accuracy or RT. Thus, although subjects are sensitive to the question
mark, its mere presence does not detectably affect performance in this
task. It was legitimate in the earlier experiments, then, to make comparisons across versions which do and do not include a question mark.

The Determiner

A central aspect of the experimental results was the poor performance
on versions whose final word was a possessive determiner (although performance could be improved somewhat, as in Experiments 6 and 7).
This poor performance was attributed to a First-Resort expectation for
a trace at the direct object. It was also suggested that subjects have
a tendency to respond 'No' if the stimulus does not include a possible position for the trace. However, another potential reason for the
poor performance might be that subjects have difficulty with sentences
interrupted within a NP, i.e., prior to reception of the head noun.

To evaluate this suggestion, sentences with all the verbs of types
(1)–(6) were tested. As illustrated in (18) of table VIII, there were two

Table VIII
Control Experiments: Example Sentences and Results

(16) Verb Obligatory Transitive, Preferably No Complement PP		% 'Yes' Responses	Mean RT (msec) 'Yes' Responses
What did Tom construct			
	a. from?	23[b]	(843)
	b. from	93[a]	720
(17) Verb Obligatorily Intransitive, Preferably With Complement PP			
What did Tony crawl			
	a. under?	86[a]	630[a]
	b. under	88[a]	651[a]
(18) All Verbs			
What did George steal			
	a. your	29[a]	(630)
	b. money	25[a]	(651)
(19) Verb Obligatorily Transitive, Preferably No Complement PP			
What did Tom construct from			
	a. our	90[a]	728[a]
	b. bricks	80[a]	756[a]
(20) Verb Obligatorily Transitive, Preferably With Complement PP			
What did David remove from			
	a. our	85[a]	671[a]
	b. trees	74[a]	780[a]

versions of each sentence: in (a) the final word was the same possessive determiner as originally tested with the verb, and in (b) the final word was a noun (either plural count noun or mass noun) that was a plausible direct object for the verb and was perceptually simple (high frequency, short). Thus, version (a) was interrupted within a NP while version (b) was interrupted following a complete NP (albeit a one-word NP). (18) shows the mean percentages of 'Yes' responses and mean RTs for all verb types. For each individual verb type, there were no significant differences between the two versions. (Across verb types, mean percentage of 'Yes' responses ranged between 13% and 45%, with the obligatorily intransitive verbs showing the lowest percentages.)

These results indicate that poor performance on versions ending in a determiner are not due to difficulty arising from the interruption within a NP. The other accounts for the poor performance remain viable.

Finally, there might still be some other, more general difficulty associated with versions whose final word is a possessive determiner. To investigate this possibility, sentences of the form *What did NAME VERB PREP XXX* were tested (see (19)–(20) in table VIII). The verbs were the same as those in (1) and (5)—obligatorily transitive, preferably no complement PP—and in (6)—obligatorily transitive, preferably with complement PP. The prepositions were the same prepositions which can serve as heads of complement PPs as used before. In (a) the final word was the same possessive determiner as previously used with the verb, and in (b) the final word was a noun that was a plausible prepositional object and was perceptually simple.

The results show high accuracy on both versions. For both verb types, there are no significant differences in either accuracy or RT.[16] This study demonstrates that there is not a general difficulty associated with determiners as final words. By ruling out that possibility, we strengthen the other accounts offered for the poor performance observed in the experiments: the accounts based upon the First-Resort Principle and upon the lack of any possible trace location in the stimulus.

ACKNOWLEDGEMENTS

This work was supported by NICHD Grant 5 R01 HD20824. The authors thank John Bowers, Jacqueline Johnson, Barbara Lust, Michael Tanenhaus, and Kenneth Wexler for helpful suggestions, and Brian Armieri, Evan Forman, Martin Goldstein, Jeffrey Kishner, and Robert Kurzban for research assistance.

NOTES

[1] The First-Resort Principle also suffers from some vagueness, concerning its application to obligatorily intransitive verbs. It is unclear whether, upon recognizing a verb that can take only a single PP, there is an immediate hypothesis of a preposition with a trace as its object or, instead, the hypothesis of a trace arises only after the input preposition is actually received. (Again, the Try-the-Next-Constituent Principle might apply, but it seems unmotivated for it to apply to verbs that have just one possible position for the trace.)

[2] Here are two examples of unexpected findings: (a) Clifton, Frazier, and Connine (1984) found overall performance on transitive sentences to be superior to that on intransitive sentences; (b) Carlson and Tanenhaus (1988) found that performance on transitive sentences containing preferably intransitive verbs was worse than performance on intransitive sentences containing preferably transitive verbs. In both cases, the experimenters developed a theoretical interpretation for the finding. But such interpretations are premature because the findings might just be artifacts of the problematic stimuli tested.

[3] For type (3), it is typically marginal or highly unpreferred for the verb to take both a NP and a PP, as in *John escaped the prison to the mountains*.

[4] The norms of Connine et al. (1984) were consulted in selecting verbs, but they were of limited use. A problem of these norms is that they are purposely biased toward classifying verbs as preferably taking both a NP and PP rather than just a NP (see their page 311). Also, the norms do not include thematic role information.

[5] Male names were chosen for the subject position because they were judged to sound more 'natural' or 'plausible' with many of the action verbs. These judgments were based on the dismaying fact that sexist attitudes are still pervasive within the college student population, from which participants in this experiment were drawn. In the filler stimuli, a greater number of female names than male names were used, including female names in Agent positions for action verbs. In the entire set of stimuli, female and male names were about equally represented in various semantic roles. On this issue, see Kurtzman (1989b).

[6] The determiners a(n) and the were not used because they can initiate adjunct phrases and so do not always indicate that an overt NP occupied the direct object, as in *What did Tom construct t the other day?*

[7] Several colleagues have suggested that, for an incomplete sentence, subjects in this task primarily follow a strategy of responding 'Yes' when the sentence would be a complete grammatical sentence if there were a question mark attached to the finally presented word, and 'No' when an attached question mark would not suffice to make it a complete grammatical sentence. However, the high level of 'Yes' responses to (1a) and (2a), as well as the responses to various stimulus classes in the subsequent experiments and to filler sentences, indicates that this suggestion is incorrect.

[8] Control studies described in the appendix rule out alternative accounts which in some way attribute the poor performance on the (b) versions to specific properties of determiners.

[9] The finding of somewhat lower performance on a preposition version is replicated in Experiment 4. A more detailed account of the processes for attaching prepositions will be offered in a future report.

One puzzling aspect of the data is that accuracy on (6a), with *while*, is so high—90%. Since this verb type preferably takes a PP, it would be expected that accuracy would be lower. Apparently, both hypotheses for VP structure—with and without a PP—have a quite high degree of availability; that is, the availability of both is above a certain threshold for making generally accurate responses. (As psychologists say, performance has reached a 'ceiling'.) Nonetheless, the data for (c) and (d) show that the precise degrees of availability are different (with performance on both (c) and (d) somewhat depressed—below 'ceiling'—because of the general difficulty in processing prepositions).

[10] Following older views of subcategorization, one might suggest that lexical frames which specify phrasal information can also include specification of particular prepositions. Then Experiment 3 could be accounted for by means of phrasal lexical frames which are differentiated not by thematic information but only by their particular prepositions. But this is not a genuinely alternative account. Since each preposition canonically assigns a particular thematic role, specifying prepositions actually amounts to specifying thematic roles. The accounts differ only in how directly the thematic information is represented.

[11] *Who* rather than *Whom* was used because the former is generally preferred for these constructions by the U.S. college students who served as subjects.

[12] Following Bernstein (1977), Copperud (1980), and Hornstein and Weinberg (1981), we assume that the stranding of the complement preposition in the (b) versions is grammatical. Also, neither our independent judges nor our experimental subjects (in postexperiment interviews) reported considering it to be ungrammatical.

An inspection of the examples in usage guidebooks indicates that complement preposition stranding is stylistically acceptable when the preposition immediately follows the verb, as in *What did Tony crawl under?* But preposition stranding can be stylistically unacceptable when the preposition follows a direct object, as in the (b) versions. The stylistic unacceptability of such cases is consistent with the current results: it can be attributed to the parsing difficulty which arises from the initially dominant First-Resort hypothesis turning out to be incorrect.

We have recently obtained essentially the same results with stimuli in which indefinite a(n) is used instead of definite the, thus ruling out alternative accounts that primarily refer to dominance (Erteschik-Shir, 1979) or referentiality (Crain and Steedman, 1985).

[13] This experiment does not demonstrate that subjects switched specifically to the hypothesis that the trace occupies a prepositional object position (even though that is the only possible alternative hypothesis which is fully grammatical). Strictly, all it demonstrates is that subjects switched to hypothesizing that the trace occurs at some position other than the direct object.

[14] In the introduction it was suggested that certain aspects of previous experiments' results were unexpected in ways that indicated problems in their stimuli. We must admit that some details of the present experiments' results are also surprising, *e.g.*, the higher RT associated with final *while* and the somewhat lower performance on

versions ending in prepositions. However, it can be argued that the present experiments' results are more likely to be genuine, since the stimuli were more carefully controlled. Also, for some of the surprises, such as that concerning final *while*, there is precedent in earlier research.

[15] There are, however, at least two inconsistencies between the results of the Carlson/Tanenhaus group and those presented here. Tanenhaus *et al.*'s (1989) results indicate that, for verbs that preferably take only a direct object, plausibility factors cannot cause the dominant hypothesis to switch from one in which there is only a direct object occupied by the trace to one in which there is both an overt direct object and another complement containing the trace. (Their example verb is *call*, which can occur in *Mary called (Jane) (about the books)*.) However, the evidence in (14) in Experiment 7 indicates that such a switch can occur. The reasons for this inconsistency might have to do with the different verbs tested and/or with differing sensitivities of the experimental techniques.

Also, Carlson and Tanenhaus (1988) report that performance on transitive sentences containing intransitive verbs was markedly worse than performance on intransitive sentences containing transitive verbs. In contrast, there is little hint of such a difference in the present results (see (2)–(3) in Experiment 1). However, as mentioned in the introduction, Carlson and Tanenhaus's results should be considered with caution, because their verbs were not as well controlled as in the present experiments (*e.g.*, some of their preferably intransitive verbs were ergatives) and their sentences were somewhat awkward (in part due to their containing postverbal manner adverbs). Further research is called for to resolve these inconsistencies.

[16] In fact, the (a) versions, with determiners, show somewhat better performance than the (b) versions. However, this is primarily due to especially poor performance on the (b) versions of just two stimuli. Our retrospective judgments, as well as judgments by others, indicate that the final nouns in these versions were not as plausible as we initially thought.

REFERENCES

Aaronson, D. and H. Scarborough: 1976, 'Performance Theories for Sentence Coding: Some Quantitative Evidence', *Journal of Experimental Psychology: Human Perception and Performance* **2**, 56–70.

Bernstein, T.: 1977, *Dos, don'ts and maybes of English usage*, Times Books, New York.

Boland, J., M. Tanenhaus, G. Carlson, and S. Garnsey: 1989, 'Lexical Projection and the Interaction of Syntax and Semantics in parsing', unpublished manuscript, University of Rochester, Rochester, New York.

Carlson, G. and M. Tanenhaus: 1988, 'Thematic Roles and Language Comprehension', in W. Wilkins (ed.), *Syntax and Semantics 21: Thematic Relations*, Academic Press, New York, pp. 263–288.

Clifton, C. and L. Frazier: 1989, 'Comprehending Sentences with Long-Distance Dependencies', in G. Carlson and M. Tanenhaus (eds.), *Linguistic Structure in*

Language Processing, Kluwer, Dordrecht, Holland, pp. 273–317.

Clifton, C., L. Frazier, and C. Connine: 1984, 'Lexical Expectations in Sentence Comprehension', *Journal of Verbal Learning and Verbal Behavior* **23**, 696–708.

Connine, C., F. Ferreira, C. Jones, C. Clifton, and L. Frazier: 1984, 'Verb Frame Preferences: Descriptive Norms', *Journal of Psycholinguistic Research* **13**, 307–319.

Copperud, R.: 1980, *American Usage and Style: The Consensus*, Van Nostrand Reinhold, New York.

Crain, S. and M. Steedman: 1985, 'On Not Being Led Up the Garden Path: The Use of Context by the Psychological Parser', in D. Dowty, L. Kartunnen and A. Zwicky (eds.), *Natural Language Parsing*, Cambridge University Press, Cambridge, England, pp. 320–358.

Erteschik-Shir, N.: 1979, 'Discourse Constraints on Dative Movement', in T. Givon (ed.), *Syntax and Semantics 12*, Academic Press, New York, pp. 441–467.

Fodor, J.D.: 1978, 'Parsing Strategies and Constraints on Transformations', *Linguistic Inquiry* **9**, 427–473.

Ford, M.: 1983, 'A Method for Obtaining Measures of Local Parsing Complexity Throughout Sentences', *Journal of Verbal Learning and Verbal Behavior* **22**, 203–218.

Frauenfelder, U., J. Segui, and J. Mehler, J.: 1980, 'Monitoring Around the Relative Clause', *Journal of Verbal Learning and Verbal Behavior* **19**, 328–337.

Frazier, L.: 1987, 'Syntactic Processing: Evidence from Dutch', *Natural Language and Linguistic Theory* **5**, 515–559.

Frazier, L. and C. Clifton: 1989, 'Successive Cyclicity in the Grammar and the Parser', *Language and Cognitive Processes* **4**, 93–126.

Gorrell, P.: 1987, *Studies of Human Syntactic Processing: Ranked-Parallel Versus Serial Models*, Ph.D. dissertation, Department of Linguistics, University of Connecticut, Storrs, Connecticut.

Grimshaw, J.: 1981, 'Form, Function, and the Language Acquisition Device', in C. Baker and J. McCarthy (eds.), *The Logical Problem of Language Acquisition*, MIT Press, Cambridge, Massachusetts, pp. 165–187.

Hakes, D., J. Evans and L. Brannon: 1976, 'Understanding Sentences With Relative Clauses', *Memory and Cognition* **4**, 283–290.

Heny, F.: 1973, 'Sentence and Predicate Modifiers in English', in J. Kimball (ed.), *Syntax and Semantics 2*, Seminar Press, New York, pp. 217–246.

Hornstein, N. and A. Weinberg: 1981, 'Case Theory and Preposition Stranding', *Linguistic Inquiry* **12**, 55–91.

Jackendoff, R.: 1983, *Semantics and Cognition*, MIT Press, Cambridge, Massachusetts.

Just, M. and C. Carpenter: 1980, 'A Theory of Reading: From Eye Fixations to Comprehension', *Psychological Review* **87**, 329–354.

Keenan, E. and B. Comrie: 1977, 'Noun Phrase Accessibility and Universal Grammar', *Linguistic Inquiry* **8**, 63–99.

Keppel, G.: 1982, *Design and Analysis* (2nd edition), Prentice-Hall, Englewood Cliffs, New Jersey.

Kurtzman, H.: 1985, *Studies in Syntactic Ambiguity Resolution* Ph.D. dissertation, Department of Psychology, Massachusetts Institute of Technology, Cambridge, Massachusetts (also available from Indiana University Linguistics Club, Bloomington, Indiana).

Kurtzman, H.: 1989a, 'Extraction of Indirect Objects', In K. deJong and Y. No (eds.), *Proceedings of the Sixth East Coast Conference on Linguistics*, Ohio State University, Columbus, Ohio, pp. 173–181.

Kurtzman, H.: 1989b, 'Sex Bias in Language Stimuli', unpublished manuscript, Department of Psychology, Cornell University, Ithaca, New York.

Pesetsky, D.: 1983, *Paths and Categories*, Ph.D. dissertation, Department of Linguistics and Philosophy, Massachusetts Institute of Technology, Cambridge, Massachusetts.

Shapiro, L., E. Zurif, and J. Grimshaw: 1987, 'Sentence Processing and the Mental Representation of Verbs', *Cognition* **27**, 219–246.

Stowe, L.: 1986, 'Parsing WH-constructions: Evidence for On-Line Gap Location', *Language and Cognitive Processes* **2**, 227–245.

Tanenhaus, M., S. Garnsey, and J. Boland: 1991, 'Combinatory Lexical Information and Language Comprehension', in G. Altmann (ed.), *Computational Approaches to Speech and Language*, MIT Press, Cambridge, Massachusetts, pp. 383–408.

Taraban, R. and J. McClelland: 1988, 'Constituent Attachment and Thematic Role Assignment in Sentence Processing: Evidence For Content-Based Expectations', *Journal of Memory and Language* **27**, 597–632.

Wanner, E. and M. Maratsos: 1978, 'An ATN Approach to Comprehension', in M. Halle, J. Bresnan and G. Miller (eds.), *Linguistic Theory and Psychological Reality*, MIT Press, Cambridge, Massachusetts, pp. 119–161.

Woolford, E.: 1984, 'Dative Verbs with Unspecified Objects', *The Linguistic Review* **3**, 389–409.

(Kurtzman & Nychis-Florence)
Uris Hall,
Department of Psychology,
Cornell University,
Ithaca, New York 14853,
U.S.A.

(Crawford)
Neurosciences Training Program,
Rm. 179 Medical Sciences Building,
University of Wisconsin at Madison,
Madison, Wisconsin 53706,
U.S.A.

INDEX OF NAMES

INDEX OF SUBJECTS

Studies in Linguistics and Philosophy

1. H. Hiż (ed.): *Questions*. 1978   ISBN Hb: 90-277-0813-4; Pb: 90-277-1035-X
2. W. S. Cooper: *Foundations of Logico-Linguistics*. A Unified Theory of Information, Language, and Logic. 1978   ISBN Hb: 90-277-0864-9; Pb: 90-277-0876-2
3. A. Margalit (ed.): *Meaning and Use*. 1979   ISBN 90-277-0888-6
4. F. Guenthner and S.J. Schmidt (eds.): *Formal Semantics and Pragmatics for Natural Languages*. 1979   ISBN Hb: 90-277-0778-2; Pb: 90-277-0930-0
5. E. Saarinen (ed.): *Game-Theoretical Semantics*. Essays on Semantics by Hintikka, Carlson, Peacocke, Rantala, and Saarinen. 1979   ISBN 90-277-0918-1
6. F.J. Pelletier (ed.): *Mass Terms: Some Philosophical Problems*. 1979
       ISBN 90-277-0931-9
7. D. R. Dowty: *Word Meaning and Montague Grammar*. The Semantics of Verbs and Times in Generative Semantics and in Montague's PTQ. 1979
       ISBN Hb: 90-277-1008-2; Pb: 90-277-1009-0
8. A. F. Freed: *The Semantics of English Aspectual Complementation*. 1979
       ISBN Hb: 90-277-1010-4; Pb: 90-277-1011-2
9. J. McCloskey: *Transformational Syntax and Model Theoretic Semantics*. A Case Study in Modern Irish. 1979   ISBN Hb: 90-277-1025-2; Pb: 90-277-1026-0
10. J. R. Searle, F. Kiefer and M. Bierwisch (eds.): *Speech Act Theory and Pragmatics*. 1980   ISBN Hb: 90-277-1043-0; Pb: 90-277-1045-7
11. D. R. Dowty, R. E. Wall and S. Peters: *Introduction to Montague Semantics*. 1981; 5th printing 1987   ISBN Hb: 90-277-1141-0; Pb: 90-277-1142-9
12. F. Heny (ed.): *Ambiguities in Intensional Contexts*. 1981
        ISBN Hb: 90-277-1167-4; Pb: 90-277-1168-2
13. W. Klein and W. Levelt (eds.): *Crossing the Boundaries in Linguistics*. Studies Presented to Manfred Bierwisch. 1981   ISBN 90-277-1259-X
14. Z. S. Harris: *Papers on Syntax*. Edited by H. Hiż. 1981
        ISBN Hb: 90-277-1266-0; Pb: 90-277-1267-0
15. P. Jacobson and G. K. Pullum (eds.): *The Nature of Syntactic Representation*. 1982
        ISBN Hb: 90-277-1289-1; Pb: 90-277-1290-5
16. S. Peters and E. Saarinen (eds.): *Processes, Beliefs, and Questions*. Essays on Formal Semantics of Natural Language and Natural Language Processing. 1982
        ISBN 90-277-1314-6
17. L. Carlson: *Dialogue Games*. An Approach to Discourse Analysis. 1983; 2nd printing 1985   ISBN Hb: 90-277-1455-X; Pb: 90-277-1951-9
18. L. Vaina and J. Hintikka (eds.): *Cognitive Constraints on Communication*. Representation and Processes. 1984; 2nd printing 1985
        ISBN Hb: 90-277-1456-8; Pb: 90-277-1949-7
19. F. Heny and B. Richards (eds.): *Linguistic Categories: Auxiliaries and Related Puzzles*. Volume I: Categories. 1983   ISBN 90-277-1478-9
20. F. Heny and B. Richards (eds.): *Linguistic Categories: Auxiliaries and Related Puzzles*. Volume II: The Scope, Order, and Distribution of English Auxiliary Verbs. 1983
        ISBN 90-277-1479-7
21. R. Cooper: *Quantification and Syntactic Theory*. 1983   ISBN 90-277-1484-3

Volumes 1–26 formerly published under the Series Title: Synthese Language Library.

Studies in Linguistics and Philosophy

22. J. Hintikka (in collaboration with J. Kulas): *The Game of Language*. Studies in Game-Theoretical Semantics and Its Applications. 1983; 2nd printing 1985
ISBN Hb: 90-277-1687-0; Pb: 90-277-1950-0

23. E. L. Keenan and L. M. Faltz: *Boolean Semantics for Natural Language*. 1985
ISBN Hb: 90-277-1768-0; Pb: 90-277-1842-3

24. V. Raskin: *Semantic Mechanisms of Humor*. 1985
ISBN Hb: 90-277-1821-0; Pb: 90-277-1891-1

25. G. T. Stump: *The Semantic Variability of Absolute Constructions*. 1985
ISBN Hb: 90-277-1895-4; Pb: 90-277-1896-2

26. J. Hintikka and J. Kulas: *Anaphora and Definite Descriptions*. Two Applications of Game-Theoretical Semantics. 1985   ISBN Hb: 90-277-2055-X; Pb: 90-277-2056-8

27. E. Engdahl: *Constituent Questions*. The Syntax and Semantics of Questions with Special Reference to Swedish. 1986   ISBN Hb: 90-277-1954-3; Pb: 90-277-1955-1

28. M. J. Cresswell: *Adverbial Modification*. Interval Semantics and Its Rivals. 1985
ISBN Hb: 90-277-2059-2; Pb: 90-277-2060-6

29. J. van Benthem: *Essays in Logical Semantics* 1986
ISBN Hb: 90-277-2091-6; Pb: 90-277-2092-4

30. B. H. Partee, A. ter Meulen and R. E. Wall: *Mathematical Methods in Linguistics*. 1990
ISBN Hb: 90-277-2244-7; Pb: 90-277-2245-5

31. P. Gärdenfors (ed.): *Generalized Quantifiers*. Linguistic and Logical Approaches. 1987
ISBN 1-55608-017-4

32. R. T. Oehrle, E. Bach and D. Wheeler (eds.): *Categorial Grammars and Natural Language Structures*. 1988   ISBN Hb: 1-55608-030-1; Pb: 1-55608-031-X

33. W. J. Savitch, E. Bach, W. Marsh and G. Safran-Naveh (eds.): *The Formal Complexity of Natural Language*. 1987   ISBN Hb: 1-55608-046-8; Pb: 1-55608-047-6

34. J. E. Fenstad, P.-K. Halvorsen, T. Langholm and J. van Benthem: *Situations, Language and Logic*. 1987   ISBN Hb: 1-55608-048-4; Pb: 1-55608-049-2

35. U. Reyle and C. Rohrer (eds.): *Natural Language Parsing and Linguistic Theories*. 1988   ISBN Hb: 1-55608-055-7; Pb: 1-55608-056-5

36. M. J. Cresswell: *Semantical Essays*. Possible Worlds and Their Rivals. 1988
ISBN 1-55608-061-1

37. T. Nishigauchi: *Quantification in the Theory of Grammar*. 1990
ISBN Hb: 0-7923-0643-0; Pb: 0-7923-0644-9

38. G. Chierchia, B.H. Partee and R. Turner (eds.): *Properties, Types and Meaning*. Volume I: Foundational Issues. 1989   ISBN Hb: 1-55608-067-0; Pb: 1-55608-068-9

39. G. Chierchia, B.H. Partee and R. Turner (eds.): *Properties, Types and Meaning*. Volume II: Semantic Issues. 1989   ISBN Hb: 1-55608-069-7; Pb: 1-55608-070-0
Set ISBN (Vol. I + II) 1-55608-088-3; Pb: 1-55608-089-1

40. C.T.J. Huang and R. May (eds.): *Logical Structure and Linguistic Structure*. Cross-Linguistic Perspectives. 1990   ISBN 0-7923-0914-6

41. M.J. Cresswell: *Entities and Indices*. 1990
ISBN Hb: 0-7923-0966-9; Pb: 0-7923-0967-7

42. H. Kamp and U. Reyle: *From Discourse to Logic*. Introduction to Modeltheoretic Semantics of Natural Language, Formal Logic and Discourse Representation Theory. 1991   ISBN Hb: 0-7923-1027-6; Pb: 0-7923-1028-4

43. C. S. Smith: The Parameter of Aspects. 1991   ISBN 0-7923-1136-1

Studies in Linguistics and Philosophy

44. R. C. Berwick (ed.): *Principle-Based Parsing:* Computation and Psycholinguistics. 1991   ISBN 0-7923-1173-6

Further information about our publications on *Linguistics* are available on request.
Kluwer Academic Publishers – Dordrecht / Boston / London